Diverse Issues, Diverse Answers

Reading, Writing, and Thinking About Social Issues

Elizabeth Rodriguez Kessler, PhD
California State University, Northridge

PEARSON
Longman

New York   San Francisco   Boston
London   Toronto   Sydney   Tokyo   Singapore   Madrid
Mexico City   Munich   Paris   Cape Town   Hong Kong   Montreal

Senior Acquisitions Editor: Susan Kunchandy
Senior Marketing Manager: Melanie Craig
Production Manager: Denise Phillip
Project Coordination, Text Design, and Electronic Page Makeup:
   Stratford Publishing Services
Cover Design Manager: Wendy Ann Fredericks
Cover Designer: Joseph DePinho
Cover Photos: Clockwise from top left: Rick Gomez/CORBIS; Chung Sung-Jun/
   Getty Images News; Doug Manuez/Photodisc Green/Getty Images, Inc.; and
   Jeff Christensen/Reuters/CORBIS
Photo Researcher: Julie Tesser
Senior Manufacturing Buyer: Alfred C. Dorsey
Printer and Binder: Courier Corporation
Cover Printer: Courier Corporation

Library of Congress Cataloging-in-Publication Data

Rodriguez Kessler, Elizabeth.
    Diverse issues, diverse answers : reading, writing, and thinking about social
issues / Elizabeth Rodriguez Kessler.
        p.   cm.
    Includes index.
    ISBN 0-321-19919-7
    1. Readers—Social sciences.   2. English language—Rhetoric—Problems,
exercises, etc.   3. Critical thinking—Problems, exercises, etc.   4. Social
sciences—Problems, exercises, etc.   5. Social problems—Problems, exercises, etc.
6. Report writing—Problems, exercises, etc.   I. Title.
PE1127.S6.R628   2006
808'.0427—dc22   2005021100

Please visit us at http://www.ablongman.com

ISBN 0-321-19919-7

1 2 3 4 5 6 7 8 9 10—CRS—08   07   06   05

To Jim, David, Sherree,
and, of course, Anne

Contents

Preface

Being a lover of both reading and writing since early childhood, I had an advantage over many of my peers who did not enjoy either, who started late, or who preferred other activities. Consequently, as I grew older, my skills improved, and I realized I wanted to share my abilities with students who felt confused and/or frustrated by the blank page—and later the blank screen—before them. This text, *Diverse Issues, Diverse Answers: Reading, Writing, and Thinking About Social Issues* (DIDA), is the latest result of that desire.

I am especially excited about this composition text because the articles are timely, thought-provoking, and in many cases, humorous and fun to read. Overcoming the boredom factor is one of my primary goal for getting students to read. DIDA includes articles that consciously target the interests of both males and females. The reading selections vary in length and difficulty and address controversial topics that are of current interest: juvenile justice, health, the environment, and others. The articles in each chapter should appeal to many students, encouraging them to enjoy the reading, develop upper-level thinking skills and, ultimately, increase their desire to read more. Most important, of course, is the improvement of each student's writing, which can be done as they become more involved with their reading.

OVERVIEW

Diverse Issues, Diverse Answers is divided into two major sections: **Part One—The Reading–Writing Connection** and **Part Two—Reading About Social Issues.** Each chapter introduces the students to the basics of the mode presented and moves them into developing their skills as they acquire better understanding of the pattern they are working with. Through exposure to examples of each mode and exercises that give them an opportunity to practice it, students move gradually from paragraph to multiparagraph essays written primarily, but not exclusively, in that pattern.

In **Part Two—Reading About Social Issues,** students have an opportunity to read selections organized thematically around social issues. Within the chapters, students are presented with essays developed in different modes of writing. The selections address ideas that students are involved in or at least are aware of in their daily lives. Since there are six articles in each chapter, instructors do not have to teach each but can limit the time they spend on each issue.

PEDAGOGY

Diverse Issues, Diverse Answers is founded on several premises. The first is that good writers are good readers; therefore, the strategies for reading begin with what readers can expect when they know that they will be reading a particular kind of writing. In Chapter 1, students review different reading skills and then are required to apply them in the chapters as they read. Each chapter begins with a section on how to read that particular mode, explaining what they should be looking for in reading selections that are written in whatever mode is being featured. They then have an opportunity to analyze a paragraph or multiparagraph passage, looking for specific information. Once they have completed the reading section, they begin to read as writers, an important transition that occurs in proofreading their essays. Although it might sound as if the material is repetitive, it is not. Now the students have the opportunity to write in a particular mode, keeping their audience in mind.

The second premise is that writing is a skill; therefore, the instructional material for writing provides models, gives students opportunities to practice each element, and progresses to increasingly more complex assignments. The current philosophy concerning composition is to move away from teaching students to write in particular modes (descriptive, comparison and contrast, and so forth) because "real" writing incorporates the different modes rather than a single approach. I agree; however, this text is constructed on the premise that students must be familiar with the modes or they will not know how to write them or incorporate them into their writing. Furthermore, students might not even know that some of these modes exist. By first making students aware of the modes and their particular qualities, the instructor will help them begin to practice using a variety of patterns in their writing. With a little direction, student writers will also become cognizant of how the modes work in published writings.

A final premise this text assumes is that in learning to write, students should learn a formalized structure and should be able to write a thesis-driven essay. This is another traditional concept that some instructors reject, believing that we are imposing "artificial" restrictions upon a student's writing. This text definitely leans toward the kind of traditional construction in formal writing that is usually required in exit writing proficiency exams, administered in some institutions before a student can move from a developmental course into an academic one and before a student can graduate. To offset the feeling of being stifled by structure, students are given various opportunities for prewriting activities that encourage them to generate ideas and reader response entries, which are generally written informally, unless the instructor specifies otherwise. There are various questions and writing assignments following each selection and each chapter.

In an attempt to make the reading student-friendly, I have incorporated boxes that summarize lengthy material in a point-by-point system in Part One. This system works in conjunction with the opening section on learning styles. Although students use a variety of cognitive strategies and styles, I have described one of the easier and more popular ways to determine how students learn so that users of this book might acquire some insight into their strengths and weaknesses. Although there are not many, I have also included pictures and political cartoons at various points in the chapters when I think they will make the most impact.

Each chapter in Part 2 ends with a section on rhetorical analysis. Using one of the articles from that chapter. It begins with a paragraph introducing some of the rhetorical devices in the article, sometimes including but not limited to identification of the thesis, different modes used in the article, and an explanation of how and why the author wrote the article this way. Instructional information in the righthand margin identify reading techniques, transitions, supporting statements, modes, and other reading and/or rhetorical strategies and reference the chapter the student can refer to for further discussion of these elements. Finally, I complete the analysis by adding one or more paragraphs that explain other strategies in the essay. By doing this, I give the student an example of how to write a short rhetorical piece that pulls ideas together instead of simply identifying strategies without explaining how they work or what effect they have on the reader. The last two analyses are the most difficult as they deal with articles which have their thesis sentences at the end. By this time, students should be familiar with the various rhetorical devices and the different modes. Each of the essays is quite easy to read, but each requires some skill in being able to identify the strategies.

Acknowledgments

No book is conceived in isolation, and *Diverse Issues, Diverse Answers: Reading, Writing, and Thinking About Social Issues* is no different. In fact, because of the concerns that I address in this text, readers can tell that interaction with friends and colleagues was of primary importance. Furthermore, being aware of popular culture as well as of events going on in society at any moment was essential. But before I release this "child of my brain" to the public, I must thank many individuals who contributed to its conception and birth. And, of course, I must begin with all my former and current students who have struggled and worked hard to succeed in my composition classes. You have given me quite a bit of insight into what you want to read about and how to put ideas together to make instructional material easily understood. There are also my own professors and colleagues who taught me to strive for improvement and to revise, revise, revise.

The next individual who must be mentioned and who believed in me at the University of Houston is Dr. Terrell Dixon. Without Dr. Dixon's guidance and expertise in directing me as a student and as a future writer of textbooks, I would not have been able to produce this text.

Of course, my family comes next. My mother, Margaret Listenberger, has always been there for me, providing invaluable assistance and encouragement when I need it. My dad, Floyd Listenberger, was aware of this text, but passed away before it was completed. His presence hovers around it, and I know that he has been with me when I needed his reassurance. Jim Kessler, our son, David, and his wife, Sherree, have listened, encouraged, and offered constructive criticism, love, and patience.

To may academic circle of friends, I cannot forget Linda Daigle at Houston Community College who continues to provide photographs for me, and my other friends, Carlos Villacis, Syble Simon, Pauline Warren, and Sharon Klander, who are always there with encouragement. At California State University, Northridge, I cannot thank the following colleagues in the Department of English enough: Pat Murray, Irene Clark, Sandra Stanley, Donald Hall, Dorothy Clark, and Leilani Hall. In the Department of Chicano and Chicana Studies, I don't know how I could do without Roberta Orona-Cordova, who is always there with articles and advice and wisdom. Finally, to my new colleagues at Prairie View A&M University, I owe a big thank you, especially to Stella Thompson, John Harty III, Elline Lipkin, Melinda McBee, Dejun Liu, Ymitri Jayasundera, and most especially, Antonio Jocson.

I also want to than my editor, Susan Kunchandy, for her help and suggestions.

There are two friends without who I could never have completed this text: Maria González, my mentor. Even after I graduated she has always been there for me and will always—I hope—be there. Anne Perrin has been an invaluable friend and colleague. She saw me through a move, the death of my dad, my mother's surgery, a flood, a new job, a car accident, a concussion, and benign positional vertigo—a temporarily disabling condition—all while I was writing this book. I don't think I could ever find another friend who could put up with so much. I am especially grateful to her because she did all this in the middle of finishing her dissertation.

I would also like to thank those who reviewed the proposal and the manuscript at various stages in its development: Sandra Stefani Comerford, College of San Mateo; Maria L. Gonzalez, University of Houston; Peggy Porter, Houston Community College, Central; Linda Schuppener, Kirkwood Community College; Syble S. Simmon, Houston Community College, Central; and Joseph Ugortez, Borough of Manhattan Community College.

I hope that *Diverse Issues, Diverse Answers* exposes reading and writing for what they are: skills that can be developed, improved, and honed. I wrote it for the purpose of helping students with their instructors beside them. We are all partners in learning, and together we will move forward in improving our teaching and learning. If you have any comments or questions, please feel free to contact me at the e-mail address below.

Elizabeth R. Kessler
elizabeth.kessler@csun.edu

PART ONE

The Reading–Writing Connection

Chapter 1

Reading and Writing Successfully

READING SUCCESSFULLY

This chapter begins with the assumption that you *want* to improve your reading and writing skills. Regardless of the level at which you read and write, that level can always be improved, even when you are reading academically advanced texts and writing at advanced levels. For example, let's say your best friend is in his third year of college. That status presupposes that he has been reading and writing quite well for years. However, have you ever heard your friend complain about struggling with a philosophy class or a physics class because he simply does not understand the reading assignments? What is happening to your friend is basically what is happening to you. You have both found a weakness in a skill that each of you has been practicing since elementary school, with varying degrees of success. You have obviously been successful because you are still reading. Stop now for a moment and answer the following questions based on this paragraph:

1. To whom have you just been compared?
2. What does the author assume in this chapter?

These are simple enough questions to answer if you have been concentrating on the passage. On the other hand, if you allow your mind to wander to other pressing concerns—the bills, the test on Tuesday, the family problems—then you discover that reading is not always the issue. Concentration is. That's why it's always a good idea to stop reading occasionally and ask yourself what you have just read. An even better exercise is to write, in one or two sentences, a **summary** of the main idea expressed in the assignment after reading one or two paragraphs. If you can't answer the question or write the summary, then you should reread what your eyes may have just glanced over. Yes, it takes more time, but if you don't do it now, you probably won't be able to answer the questions your instructor asks you in class the next day either. Saying, "I really read it, but I don't remember that part," will be only partially true. Your eyes may have read the words, but you neither comprehended nor retained the message.

Many people discover that they learn best by combining learning styles: visual, auditory, oral, and kinesthetic. Thus reading (visual) in conjunction with writing (kinesthetic)—summarizing, paraphrasing, taking notes, writing questions about the passage that you did not understand—helps many students learn more easily than if they simply read the passage.

Stop here and think about how you learn best.

- Do you learn best by listening to your instructor lecture? (auditory learner)
- Do you learn best by repeating what you have read? (visual, oral and auditory learner)
- Do you learn better if you listen to the instructor and take notes while she is explaining a lesson? (auditory and kinesthetic learner)
- Do you learn better by listening and reading the points the instructor puts on the board or overhead as he is lecturing? (visual and oral learner)
- Does taking notes as you listen and read the board increase your understanding of the material? (kinesthetic, auditory, and visual learner)
- When you are studying, does underlining or highlighting specific information help you remember it better? (visual and kinesthetic learner)

Have you figured out how you learn best?

Reading and writing are skills, and as with any skill you want to become proficient in—swimming, piano playing, painting, football—you must practice. A dedicated pianist does not give up when she is faced with a difficult piece. Furthermore, she does not settle for continuing to play pieces of equal difficulty. She must challenge herself to improve. Just as a high school athlete cannot settle for high school–level training when he is competing for placement on a college team, neither can you settle for reading and writing at a level that does not advance your skills.

Therefore, just as this text is about making personal and social decisions, it is also about making decisions about academic growth.

Through practice, determination, patience, and concentration, you will steadily grow beyond the abilities you have today.

Follow-up Questions

1. What are the four different kinds of learning styles discussed in the passage? What is involved in each learning style?
2. How are the skills for reading similar to the skills for playing the piano or football?

Short Writing Assignments

1. Write a journal entry that describes your feelings about reading. What do you like and not like to read? What is it about the material you dislike that makes it difficult to read? Include a few sentences that explain the process you use to become an active reader.
2. Consider your learning style and the classes you have been successful in. Why were you successful in those classes? What learning style(s) did you use to learn what was required in your class? Write a journal entry describing the process you used to learn the material in your most successful class. Which learning styles did the process include?

VOCABULARY BUILDING FOR SUCCESSFUL READING AND WRITING

First, let's look at vocabulary learning skills that have not worked. Do you remember being in classes where you had to memorize lists of vocabulary words for a weekly test—classes like biology, foreign language, health, and so forth. How many words do you still remember today—much less use? Most of us memorized the lists, took the tests, and then promptly forgot the words. Why? Because we didn't continue to use the words, so they did not become part of our personal vocabulary. It fulfills the adage: Use it or lose it. Because we know what doesn't work, we know it will be futile to continue to repeat a process that fails.

If you look at the reading selections in Part Two of this text, you will find lists of vocabulary words before each work that will give you an idea about the piece; but some words may be unfamiliar to you. The generally recommended ways to approach vocabulary building include the following:

- Try to determine the meaning contextually.
- Look up the word in the dictionary.

- Keep a set of note cards on which you write the word, its definition(s), and the sentence the word was in when you found it in the reading selection.
- Complete an exercise that requires you to use the word in an original sentence.
- Complete matching, fill-in-the-blank, and other related exercises using the new words.
- Take a quiz that tests your grasp of the meanings of the words.
- Use the words as part of your own spoken and written language, when appropriate.

Even though each of these suggestions works, not every one works every time for every person. Looking up words can be tedious and time consuming, especially if you find many words that are difficult to understand in context. However, if you do not get an accurate definition, you will lose some of the meaning of the selection. And sometimes when you think you know the definition, the word still does not make sense in the sentence. To complicate matters further, the author may even be speaking **metaphorically,** comparing one idea to something different as in, "the child is a grumpy bear before meals." In such a case, understanding the meanings of the words may not allow you to understand the message.

Fortunately, all words and their meanings are not that complex; and you will find that working your way through the dictionary yields rewards. Now, whether you write the definition and a sentence using the word on a note card or not is your decision, but if the word is important enough to you and you think you won't remember it otherwise, you might be wise to use note cards. However, the best way to build your vocabulary is to use the words appropriately once you have learned the meanings. It might sound awkward at first, but as you continue to add new words to your spoken and written vocabulary, you will begin to see and hear a difference. You will understand more when you are reading, and your writing will sound different. A word of warning: When you incorporate new words into your writing, they must sound natural rather than like a **synonym** you found in a thesaurus. Improving your vocabulary is a cumulative process: It builds on what you have learned previously. Before you know it, your speaking and writing vocabulary will increase, and you will find yourself writing with a language that is more formal, varied, and interesting.

Follow-up Questions

1. List three ways to improve your vocabulary.
2. What are some advantages to improving your vocabulary?

Short Writing Assignments

1. To see how using big words from a thesaurus can be inappropriate, take the title of one or two of your favorite songs, look up each important word in a thesaurus, and substitute the new word for the one in the song. Write a comparison-and-contrast paragraph explaining why one title, the original or the newly created one, is better than the other.
2. Find a paragraph you wrote in your journal. Go to your thesaurus and substitute all important words (nouns, pronouns, adjectives, adverbs, and verbs) with one of the synonyms listed for each in the thesaurus. Analyze the new paragraph to determine if it means exactly what you wanted to say in the original. Write a comparison-and-contrast paragraph explaining which paragraph is better and why.

THE READING PROCESS

Because this is a writing text, you might be asking yourself why she is spending so much time talking about reading. Good reading is the key to becoming a good writer. The articles, short stories, and poems that writers read influence them in their own approach to writing. Professional writers, too, have increased their vocabulary by reading and by following steps to improve their store of words. Just as writing facilitates vocabulary building, so, too, will writing help in the reading process. Good writers aren't born knowing how to write. Like all of us, they had to develop the skills to write.

Before you read further, ask yourself this question: What does "facilitate" in the previous paragraph mean? Did you know its meaning when you read it? If not, did you stop to look it up or figure it out from context clues before you continued reading? Can you write a **paraphrase** of the sentence that has "facilitate" in it? Do you remember reading about learning styles in the preceding section? The four learning styles can be combined to "[help] many students learn more easily than if they simply read the passage." Writing is a kinesthetic learning style, one that requires movement. Therefore, from these context clues, you should be able to understand that "facilitate" means "to help" in this context. If you went through the process above, you are showing that you are not only working at building your vocabulary, but you are also becoming an effective and active reader.

To become an effective and active reader, you must follow steps that other successful readers follow. If what you have done in the past has not worked, then it's time to try a new strategy, one that that will feel comfortable and that you will continue to use in all your reading assignments.

Prereading

1. **Know what the assignment is.** Even the most earnest student sometimes goes to class unprepared because she read the wrong selection. Check your syllabus or your notes to make sure you're reading the correct work.

2. **Set aside time for your reading.** This means knowing when it is best for you to read. Some students read better early in the morning; others read better late in the evening. Snatching bits and pieces of time in between classes does not usually work for serious, sustained reading. Therefore, develop a routine that fits your needs and will help you be successful.

3. **Be prepared.** Make sure you have paper, pen, a highlighter, proper lighting, your dictionary, and any snacks you will need, to complete the reading assignment. Make sure the environment is conducive for reading and that as many distractions as possible have been eliminated. This is your time.

4. **Check the length of the reading.** If it is long, will you have to read it in more than one session? Do you have time to read it in the time you have set aside? Should you leave it for another time and complete your other assignments first?

5. **Look carefully at the title.** Does it indicate what the piece will be about? Do you have any background in the area or will you be reading about something totally new to you? Even if the assignment is short, if you are unfamiliar with the information presented, it might take a long time to read.

6. **Look at the vocabulary list** if there is one. Familiarize yourself with any term you do not know. (See the discussion on vocabulary building in the preceding pages.)

7. **Look for bold headings.** They should give you an indication of what is important in the reading. Also look for bold or italicized words. The author is trying to send a message that this is important.

8. **Check for questions at the end of the reading.** There is no rule that says you can't begin by reading the questions first. Doing so will help you get an idea of what you should be reading for. This is also a good practice to use when taking entrance exams, which ask you to answer questions after reading a passage.

9. **Determine what kind of selection you will be reading and modify your reading method for it.** Some students approach each reading assignment in the same manner; that strategy sometimes prevents them from understanding the reading. Each kind of writing has different characteristics. Is it an essay? A personal narrative? If you are

not familiar with the types of nonfiction, for example, look at the appropriate chapter in this text for an explanation about what you should be reading for.

10. **Look at the prereading sections** that precede the selection. These prereading guides should help you focus your thoughts about the selection. Some guides will give you insight into the author, and/or ask questions that provoke responses to the work.

11. **Look at pictures, charts, and diagrams.** These can give you information about the selection and the material before you begin reading.

12. **Make prereading notes, journal entries, or jot down questions.** By completing Step 10, you will be able to think about possible writing topics, questions you might want to jot down before you read, or journal entries you might want to make about the topic before you read. This last step will help you clarify in your mind how you feel about controversial issues before you expose yourself to someone else's beliefs. You should begin to see that becoming a good writer works together with becoming a good reader.

13. **Review your notes from class.** If your instructor gave you background information to supplement your reading or notes about the author, topic, or **style,** you might use them before you begin reading. If your instructor gave specific ideas to look for, questions you should answer, or a response journal assignment, you should read your class notes before you start reading the assignment.

This is how you get ready to read. It may sound as if it will take a lot of time; however, once you make it a practice to complete these thirteen steps, they will become second nature, and you will find that you can do them quickly. They can become part of your reading and writing routine, and you will be prepared to read the selection with an informed mind.

Reading

Now that you have completed the basic "warm-up exercises," it's time to read the selection. Keep in mind the purpose for reading this particular assignment. Ask yourself, is it part of a unit you are studying in class? Does your instructor want you to read it for style? Why are you reading this? If you don't know or don't remember, take a moment to review your notes and the directions your instructor gave you.

1. **Read the entire selection quickly.** This way you will get the overall idea, tone, and direction of the article.

STEPS FOR PREREADING

1. Know the correct assignment.
2. Set aside time for your reading by establishing a routine.
3. Be prepared with all the essentials you need.
4. Check the length of the reading to see if you can complete it in one session or have to break it into two or more sessions.
5. Look carefully at the title.
6. Look at the vocabulary list.
7. Look for bold headings and bold or italicized words.
8. Check the questions at the end of the reading.
9. Determine what kind of reading selection it is and modify your reading method for it.
10. Review the prereading material that precedes the selection.
11. Look at pictures, charts, and diagrams.
12. Make prereading notes, questions, and journal entries about the assignment.
13. Review your notes from class.

2. **Review the follow-up questions** again to see if you can answer any of them after your quick reading. If you can't, you will at least begin the next step with the questions fresh in your mind. If you can, answer them quickly by jotting down notes. You can come back after the second reading and expand the answers so you will be prepared for class.

3. **Begin rereading slowly and thoroughly.**

4. **Keep your pen or highlighter in hand.** You will want to mark important **details,** names of people/characters, dates, and other pertinent information you should remember. You will also want to write questions in the margins beside paragraphs you find confusing.

5. **Read each selection correctly.** If this is a **persuasive essay,** identify the **thesis** and find the points the author uses to try to persuade you. If this is an **informative essay,** look for all the **details** that describe or explain the subject. As you can see, no two selections will be read in the same way if they are different kinds of writing.

6. **If you find your mind wandering, stop immediately.** Think about the last part you remember reading and begin from there. Write a brief **summary** to help you remember what you read. List the points that the author made. If you need to take a break, do so, but return ready to concentrate.

7. **If there are breaks in the reading, places where new sections begin, stop after each and review what you have read.** Ask

---

STEPS FOR SUCCESSFUL READING

1. Read the entire selection quickly.
2. Review the questions at the end.
3. Begin rereading slowly and thoroughly.
4. Keep your pen or highlighter in hand.
5. Read each selection correctly.
6. If you find your mind wandering, stop immediately.
7. If there are breaks in the reading, stop after each and review what you have read.
8. Review the marks you have made in the reading, noticing their importance.

---

yourself questions such as: What was the main idea of the section? Were there words I did not understand that kept me from understanding the passage? Were there complex sentences that I did not understand? If you had difficulty with any of these areas, go back to the section you read and review it. Because what follows is probably dependent upon the part you did not understand, rereading the confusing passage slowly and thoroughly will help you prepare for the next section. Be sure to write questions in the margin if you still find any passage confusing.

8. **Review the marks you have made in the reading, noting their importance.**

Follow-up Strategies

Completing the reading is not the final step. To be an active reader, you must be sure you comprehend what you have read. Finish the assignment by completing the following steps:

1. **Answer the questions at the end** when you finish the second reading. Sometimes they are based on a literal reading, which means that they are asking if you remember the details of the selection. Some questions, however, will be more thought-provoking. These in-depth questions will not have answers you can find in the reading. Instead, they will require that you look at the ideas presented from different perspectives or apply your previous knowledge and experience to the reading. They may even ask you to evaluate the reading selection based on a given criterion. These questions are important for developing higher-level thinking skills. Now is the time to practice writing the full answers. This will help you practice paragraph development and fluency in your

writing skills. Instead of answering questions with a simple *yes* or *no*, set up a **topic sentence** that states your position and write a paragraph of four or five additional sentences that support that position. This will not only help you prepare for your class, it will also help you in responding to short-answer questions that your instructor might ask you in a quiz about the reading. You will also be able to use these responses as you participate in class discussion.

2. **Take notes for class discussion.** Do this first by reviewing the parts of the reading you have marked. You might want to use them for class discussion. If you have questions, jot them down in the margin of the selection next to the paragraph that caused you difficulty. This way you will be prepared to ask specific questions in class about what you read. You will be able to direct the instructor and the class to the exact page and paragraph without having to thumb through the pages and look unprepared.

3. **Write a reader response journal entry about this selection.** Be sure to follow your instructor's directions. Your instructor might ask you to write a summary of the reading passage, or to respond. Remember that responding is different from summarizing. When you respond, explain one or more of the following points:

- If you agreed or disagreed with the article and why
- If you liked or disliked the article and why
- If you can associate with the events in the article and how
- If you can identify with any of the characters/people in the article and how
- If you learned anything from the article
- If you would recommend this article to a friend and why
- What your response might be if you had a chance to talk to the author.

There are, of course, other ways you might respond, but these are a few of the most frequently used responses.

4. **Mentally review how you felt about the reading.** Go back to the points mentioned above and review them in your mind. You might answer some of the following questions: Do you agree or disagree with the author? Why? Does the selection answer the questions you have about the topic, or do you have more questions for the author? Does the story end the way you want it to end? How do you feel about the characters? Even though you are not required to do so, you might want to make notes for class discussion.

Successful reading and writing take time and dedication. If you have had difficulties in the past, don't be discouraged. You are beginning a new self-improvement plan, and as with any other, it will be slow at

---

FOLLOW-UP STRATEGIES

1. Answer the questions at the end.
2. Take notes for class discussion.
3. Write a reader response journal entry or a summary.
4. Mentally review how you felt about the reading.

---

first, but the rewards will come if you are consistent in your practices. When you encounter problems, your instructor will be there, ready to help you move forward. And as with all improvement plans, you must want to change because you see a need. If you follow a routine that fits your needs, not only will you begin to improve your reading and writing skills, you may also find that reading gives you a new way to relax and enjoy yourself and that writing provides an outlet for your ideas, feelings, and creativity that you had not recorded before.

Follow-up Questions

1. List the three major steps in approaching a reading assignment.
2. Each major step has smaller steps or directions for successful reading. List two small directions from each major step and explain why you think each is important.
3. Explain what it means to "Read each selection correctly." Give an example of at least two different kinds of writing and how each should be read.

Short Writing Assignments

1. Write a **reader response journal entry** about this section, "The Reading Process," discussing the following points.
   - What did you think about the directions?
   - Will you try to use any of the suggestions? Why?
   - Which directions do you already use that are successful?
   - Which new directions do you think could help you most?

   Do not just answer the questions. Create a well-developed paragraph that addresses these and any other issues you can think of.
2. Find a younger person, possibly a sibling, a friend, or your child, who is learning how to read or who is having trouble reading. Practice these directions with the young reader for several days in short time periods. Watch the reader's progress. Talk to the reader after she comes home from school and practices the method on an assignment. Did the reader express satisfaction with her work in class that

day? Write a short paper **describing** the reader, the reading assignment, the **process** you used to help the reader, and the feelings expressed by the reader after the assignment was due. **Evaluate** the results of the process after using it several times with the same reader.

WRITING SUCCESSFULLY

While the main purpose of the preceding section was to help you improve your reading skills, it also emphasized the role that being a good reader plays in becoming a good writer. Steps to improve your reading skills that also incorporate writing to help you remember are **listing, summarizing,** and **paraphrasing.** To help you analyze and understand, you should write questions about the material in the margins and answer the questions at the end of the selections—first in brief form and then in fully elaborated paragraphs. Finally, you might keep a journal to express your feelings, jot down questions, respond to the reading, or write creative pieces. At the end of the section, as well as at the end of the preceding sections, you were asked to begin practicing your writing skills. This chapter will build on these skills, with the guidance of your instructor, help you polish your skills in writing various assignments, and teach you how to write some types of assignments you may never have written before.

Purpose of Writing

Before you begin writing, it's important to know the purpose of writing. Why do you write? Some students respond by saying that the only reason they write is because they have to complete assignments that their instructors have given them. Other students acknowledge that they write **letters,** e-mail messages, notes to friends, or private poems and short stories. And employers say they write memos to their employees, business letters, and letters of reference or recommendation. Even though the reasons for writing any particular piece varies, the purpose remains the same: to communicate with someone who is not able to speak with you directly. If a student turns in a paper, the student is trying to communicate to his instructor, the extent to which he has understood the assignment or acquired the knowledge or information the instructor assigned. Whether it is through a paper, a memo, or a letter, the writer always has the responsibility of being clear and precise so that the message will be delivered accurately. For example, read the following response to a birthday party invitation. The writer is responding for herself and for her friends:

```
Dear Shamika,

Thanks for the birthday party invitation. I talked
to Mary Jane Peggy Sue and Alicia. We will all be
there.

Sincerely,

Cindy
```

Unless Shamika knows everyone who has been invited, she will have difficulty knowing if four (Mary Jane, Peggy Sue, Alicia, and Cindy), five (Mary, Jane, Peggy Sue, Alicia, and Cindy) or six (Mary, Jane, Peggy, Sue, Alicia, and Cindy) people are attending. If Shamika were speaking to Cindy, the inflection in Cindy's voice would clarify the number; however, verbal as well as nonverbal communication is missing when we write. Facial expressions, hand gestures, nods, winks, and other physical indications we make to punctuate what we say and indicate if we're serious, teasing, or being ironic or sarcastic are missing from the written page.

Some writers, however, feel free to insert :-) (for smile) or :-((for frown) in e-mail or informal correspondence to help the reader get a clearer sense of the message. Those signs, however, do not replace correct punctuation or precise word choice. For example, **synonyms** do not always convey the same connotations even though they may be close in meaning. Charles Dickens would not have made the following potential mistake:

Choose the correct word:

(Petit or Tiny) Tim had no Christmas presents because of his family's poverty.

Although *petit* and *tiny* have the same denotative meaning, *small*, petite is usually an adjective that refers to women; therefore, the two cannot always be substituted for each other. Furthermore, structure sometimes creates confusion. In the following example, which statement is correct?

Running across the street, the car hit the dog.
or
Running across the street, the dog was hit by the car.

The key is, who or what was running? The dog or the car? The phrase that opens the sentence describes the subject. Therefore, the first

Accurate communication requires the writer to

- be clear.
- be precise.
- use correct punctuation.
- use correct structure.

sentence is wrong because the car could not have been "running across the street."

Audience

Because the purpose of writing is communication, you must also remember your audience. You do not speak to everyone using the same language, so naturally you will not write to everyone using the same language, either. Imagine that you need to apply for a job. You've had several jobs while you were in high school, and you've worked as a trainer of new sales staff after working in a retail clothing store for a year. You also started as a stocker and moved up to sales staff. Christmas is coming, and a new clothing store is opening, selling clothes that appeal specifically to teens, similar to the one you worked at previously. This store is hiring all positions: stockers, sales staff, trainers, and managers. Because of your work experience and your age, you want to apply for the position of manager, but you are afraid that you won't be hired. You decide to apply for trainer *and* for manager, but the letter for the managerial position goes to a person different from the one for trainer.

Brainstorm for a few moments about the changes you will have to make in your writing style and approach to communicate with the person who hires managers as opposed to the person who hires stockers, sales staff, and trainers. As you can see by the **list** you have made while brainstorming, there are differences you will have to take into account because of your audience. There are different issues that must be addressed and different levels of vocabulary that must be used. Of course, these kinds of problems will not arise in your classes because you know what kind of writing your instructors expect. Consequently, you are relatively comfortable writing for your instructors. The problem comes when you forget that not everyone reads at the same level or for the same purpose.

Applying for a job creates some of these same problems. Should you use a certain kind of style when you type your résumé? What work-related experience do you highlight in each cover letter? Therefore, not only what you write but to whom you are writing makes a big difference.

You will continue to have new experiences and interact with others who may have more or less experience than you in certain writing situations. You might find yourself as the leader in group work that involves writing in a particular mode or about a particular topic with which you are familiar. At other times, you might be a participant who follows, receiving help and instruction rather than providing guidance. If you are in a peer-editing situation with another student, you will have to depend on what you have learned to help your peer prepare to revise a paper. Regardless of your role, you play an important part in your own success as well as in the success of your group and your class. By working independently as well as collaboratively with others, you will find yourself growing in ways you never imagined—and your writing will also improve.

Follow-up Questions

1. What four qualities does accurate writing require?
2. Why should writers consider their audience before they begin writing?

Short Writing Assignments

1. Pretend you want to take a one-week vacation from work and you have vacation time coming. Your company requires a letter notifying your employer of any time off you will take that extends beyond two business days. Write a letter to your employer explaining what and when you will take your vacation.
2. In addition, you have to let your child's school know you will be taking her out of school for a week for a family vacation. However, you know that this violates the attendance policy at your daughter's school. Will the letter you write to your employer be copied and sent to your daughter's school or will you have to change the content? Write a letter to each audience and be ready to discuss each in class.

THE PARAGRAPH

The fundamental stepping stone to good writing begins with the word. A writer then places it in combination with others to make sense and create thoughts by writing phrases and sentences. The diagram below gives an example:

The Word	*The Phrase*	*The Sentence*
storm	the stationary storm	The stationary storm in Houston caused extensive flooding and several deaths.

As a thought grows and expands, sentences multiply, creating a paragraph, a group of sentences that develop one idea. If you take the above example to the next stage, you will discover that you can write a variety of paragraphs that are identified by their pattern: descriptive, personal narrative, comparison-and-contrast. Although there are more patterns, we will explore each in the appropriate chapter.

Prewriting

Let's say your writing instructor assigned the class a topic: Write a paragraph about weather. Rather than give directions immediately, your instructor lets you and the class determine the kind of approach you want to take. Dave, a student in the class, was recently in a bad storm in Houston, and he knows that he has a lot to say about it. His first step is to narrow down the topic not only from weather to the Houston storm but also in how he wants to approach the topic. To do so, he must first complete a prewriting step. This may be done in one or more of the following ways: free writing, focused free writing, brainstorming, collaborative brainstorming, clustering, or answering journalistic questions.

In **free writing** you are completing an activity that is comparable to a warm-up exercise that you might do before you go jogging or running. Let your mind wander and then begin writing about whatever comes to mind. Because you are trying to discover a topic for your essay, you will move from total freedom to the topic that you have in mind—something dealing with your assignment. Write quickly for a time that you have set, say five minutes, and do not worry about spelling, punctuation, grammar, or anything else. The goal of free writing and focused free writing is to get your mind actively engaged in discovering a topic for this paper. When you are finished, review what you have written, highlighting any idea that is relevant to your assignment. You can add the details later.

Because Dave was in the dangerous storm and he knows that he wants to write about it, he can complete a focused free writing instead of allowing himself to write whatever comes into his mind about the weather. He will probably find that he has anecdotes that tell about the death and destruction Houstonians suffered. He might write about one of those experiences, or he might want to write about the total loss of the Law Library at the University of Houston. As you see in the boxed word–phrase–sentence example above, the general topic needs to be developed into a more specific and detailed one. In focused free writing, you allow your mind to move from one idea to the next without censoring yourself about what should or should not come next. This exercise is meant to generate ideas that can later be developed.

Another prewriting strategy is **brainstorming** (or **collaborative brainstorming**). To brainstorm, determine the topic that you have to write about and then quickly jot down ideas, questions, phrases, words, or comments that might be related to the topic. For example, if you were writing about the weather, you might have a piece of paper with the following brainstorming notes.

Focused Brainstorming

Weather—the 2001 Summer Flood in Houston

How much damage in $ amounts?

30 inches of water

Worse than some hurricanes

People left homeless

UH closed

Cars flooded on the freeways

People stranded on top of cars and in trees

Weather-related deaths

The Theatre District and hospitals under water

Costumes, props, medical equipment destroyed

Experiments in Medical Center destroyed

Underground shopping and parking completely flooded

Bayous, rivers, and creeks overflowed their banks

As you can see from the previous example, **focused brainstorming** moves in different directions, questioning and associating freely based on the narrowed topic that is given. When you participate in collaborative brainstorming, you have the opportunity to brainstorm with a small group in class or with the class as a whole. In that kind of exercise, even more ideas can be raised because of the number people participating.

Since Dave already knows he will write about the Houston flood, he does not necessarily need to participate in collaborative brainstorming unless he thinks other students' suggestions or questions might help him add to his own ideas. Others might have had experiences similar to his, and he might want to jot them down. Or he might want to talk to someone who had different kinds of experiences. This will give him material for writing a compare-and-contrast paper.

Clustering

If you decide to use the **prewriting strategy** called **clustering,** you will make free associations with the topic of your choice, allowing yourself to add more to each point that you associate. (See the following example.)

You will sometimes find that as you complete the clustering (or **webbing** or **mapping,** as this strategy is sometimes called), you will have a disproportionate diagram as well as extensive information you will have to narrow down for a single-paragraph assignment. You will also find that some associations will be unequal in number. Look at Dave's clustering exercise.

When you use **journalistic questions,** you ask the following:

Who?	When?	How?
What?	Where?	Why?

These questions allow you to explore the **plot** of your **narrative** or other mode of writing to get ideas to develop your topic. Dave had sufficient

information that is already beginning to develop; therefore, he did not feel a need to use the questions.

Prewriting Exercise 1

Now that you have read the section on prewriting, you are prepared to practice prewriting exercises on your own. Below is a list of general topics that can be used with any of the prewriting strategies discussed above. If your instructor does not assign this, you might take a little time on your own to **free write, brainstorm, cluster,** or answer **journalistic questions** to help you feel at ease with these techniques.

holidays	vacation spots	languages
cars	sports	cultures
summer jobs	music	traditions

Prewriting Exercise 2

Now complete a prewriting exercise on the topic that your instructor has given you for your paragraph. Remember that you do not have to use all four strategies. Choose the one that feels most comfortable for you and the one that will give you the most supportive information to choose from.

PREWRITING STRATEGIES

1. **Free writing** and **focused free writing**—exercises that depend on free association in writing as quickly as possible about as many ideas as you can generate in a set time, either about the topic or without restrictions.

2. **Brainstorming** and **collaborative brainstorming**—exercises that list as many points as possible in single words, phrases, sentences, questions, and so forth that are associated with your topic. Collaborative brainstorming is completed with a group.

3. **Clustering, webbing,** or **mapping**—exercises similar to brainstorming but with the added component of associating not only with the key topic but with the topics that are spinning off the main idea.

4. **Journalistic questions**—exercises in which you answer the questions who? what? when? where? why? and how? on the topic you are writing about.

Taking Control

If you look back at the brainstorming and clustering strategies one student completed, you will see that, because there are so many ideas present, he has to take control of the direction his paragraph will follow. This means narrowing his topic. Looking at the numerous ideas in the clustering example, you can see that the writer has a couple of options: He can write a descriptive paragraph about the 2001 Houston flood, or he can write a personal narrative. If he talked to others who lived through the flood, he can also write a comparison-and-contrast paper. He might choose, however, to focus on only one of the modes: comparison-and-contrast.

SUMMARY

The following chapters are organized rhetorically, that is, according to the patterns of development or modes people use to develop their ideas. You will find instruction for reading and writing in each mode, selections that are written predominantly in a given mode, and suggested topics for you to use as you write in that mode. Because most of the writing you will do in your classes will be multi-paragraph, the chapters also give instructions about writing the essay and how to incorporate more than one mode into your essays.

Chapter 2

Reading and Writing Description

HOW TO READ DESCRIPTION

Good descriptive writing paints pictures or **images** that readers can see in their mind's eye. Whether a reader is reading about a car accident reported in a newspaper article or a beautiful beach setting described in a travel brochure, the audience wants relevant details to stand out and grab their attention. Graphic details of a fatal accident are normally omitted to respect the sensibilities of the readers as well as the privacy and feelings of the victims' friends and families. On the other hand, vacationers want as much descriptive information as possible about prospective sites so they can make informed decisions about where to spend their time. Thanks to the Internet, many travelers have access to pictures and descriptive information that attempt to lure interested parties to various tourist areas.

Exercise 1: Reading Analysis

1. Choose one of the following vacation sites you might like to visit: Disney World, Alaska, Lake Tahoe, New York City, New Orleans, Paris, or the Canadian Rockies.
2. As a class or individually, brainstorm a list of questions you might want answered about the site before you decide to go there. For example: What is the price range of hotels surrounding the site? What is the weather like in July?
3. Go to the Web site for the vacation spot you chose:
   - http://disneyworld.disney.go.com/waltdisneyworld/index
   - http://www.alaskatravel.com/

- http://www.virtualtahoe.com/
- http://www.nycvisit.com/home/index.cfm
- http://www.paris.org
- http://neworleanscvb.com
- http://canadianrockies.net

4. Answer the following questions: Did the Web site
   - answer all your questions?
   - provide links to other information you didn't think to ask about?
   - give detailed information?
   - provide enough pictures?
   - persuade you to go to the vacation spot? Why or why not?
5. Look at one of the other Web sites and write a descriptive paragraph explaining which Web site you prefer. Use descriptive language. You might also use **comparison and contrast.**

Using Physical Senses

The Internet sites you visited provided pictures of lakes, snow, museums, mountains, and other features travelers might want to explore. Sometimes, however, individuals must rely on brochures, pamphlets, or other descriptive passages that might have only one picture or none at all. Thus, images must be created with words. Readers have certain expectations that should be met when they find a piece of descriptive writing. Description must rely not only on the reader's ability to visualize but also on the writer's ability to appeal to the reader's other physical senses: smell, touch, hearing, and taste. Writers also want to involve the reader's feelings, for example exciting the potential traveler to go to a location for a particular activity: What it feels like to ski in the mountains surrounding Lake Tahoe, snorkel in the Pacific surrounding Hawaii, hike around the lakes in the Canadian Rockies, or eat freshly baked pastries at a sidewalk café in Paris.

Exercise 2: Reading Analysis

1. Look at the description of the beaches surrounding Hilo in an essay (below) that a student wrote about her recent trip. Before you begin reading,
   - jot down some questions you might want answered, knowing that this is a beach in Hawaii.
   - be prepared with a marker or pen.
   - check the length of the passage.

- look carefully at the title to see if you know anything about the setting.
- determine the kind of selection you'll be reading (descriptive, causal analysis, exemplification, argumentation, etc.).

My Trip to Hilo

Although I have been to the beaches in Florida, Texas, and Southern California, none of them compare to those in Hilo, Hawaii. One of the first differences I found was the beautiful black lava that met the crystal clear water on almost every beach. The lava was not simply there as individual rocks, but as it flowed to the water and cooled, it created wavy patterns that look like rope in the molten rock as it hardened, capturing many seashells in its folds. Tourists can also go to Volcanoes National Park and safely watch lava flowing into the Pacific while steam rises as it meets the cooler water. Signs warn visitors not to stand in the plume of the steam as it is composed of gases with an acrid smell and contains microscopic bits of glass that can damage lungs if it is inhaled. Another contrasting image not found on the mainland beaches is the black lava against the blue water and the sand, created by bits of sharp, broken shells. Whereas the sand at some of the beaches on the mainland packs down firmly, the sands around Hilo are loose and difficult to walk on. But one aspect I noticed in Hawaii more so than at any other beach was the presence of two magnificent wonders: whales and rainbows—each of which contributed to feelings of awe and inspiration. The whales came in pods off shore and blew streams of water as they swam by slowly and gracefully. If the whales were close enough to shore, swimmers could hear the hissing of the water as it sprayed into the air. Otherwise, they glided by noiselessly. On the other hand, the rainbows began forming on one end, and observers could sit still and watch them complete their arches miles away. Then the rainbows slowly faded into the mist, leaving visitors to watch another typical Hawaiian sight: surfboard shops. Because the water around Hilo was not very rough while I was there in January, the surfboard rentals were slow, but the grass huts where the boards were kept made interesting sights. I highly recommend the beaches surrounding Hilo for their beauty, warmth, and quiet serenity contrasted with the power of the nearby volcanoes and for the sense of awe visitors feel watching the natural environment.

2. Did the author answer the questions you had about the beaches of Hilo? If she did not, why do you think she didn't?
3. Write a one-sentence summary of this paragraph.

4. Did the writer appeal to the physical senses as well as the emotions of the reader in her description? List each sense she used by quoting the sentence where each sense can be found. List each time she referred to personal feelings by quoting the sentence where they were mentioned.
5. Did the topic sentence suggest you would read a descriptive passage? Explain.
6. If you are a person who enjoys the beach, would you enjoy going to Hilo based on this description? Explain your answer.

Now, look at the paragraph as it was marked by another reader. The underlined sentence is the <u>topic sentence</u>, and the gray shaded words are details.

MY TRIP TO HILO

<u>Although I have been to the beaches in Florida, Texas, and Southern California, none of them compare to those in Hilo, Hawaii.</u> One of the first differences I found was the beautiful black lava that met the crystal clear water on almost every beach. The lava was not simply there as individual rocks, but as it flowed to the water and cooled, it created wavy patterns that look like rope in the molten rock as it hardened, capturing many seashells in its folds. Tourists can also go to Volcanoes National Park and safely watch lava flowing into the Pacific while steam rises as it meets the cooler water. Signs warn visitors not to stand in the plume of the steam as it is composed of gases with an acrid smell and contains microscopic bits of glass that can damage lungs if it is inhaled. Another contrasting image not found on the mainland beaches is the black lava against the blue water and the sand, created by bits of sharp, broken shells. Whereas the sand at some of the beaches on the mainland packs down firmly, the sands around Hilo are loose and difficult to walk on. But one aspect I noticed in Hawaii more so than at any other beach was the presence of two magnificent wonders: whales and rainbows—each of which contributed to feelings of awe and inspiration. The whales came in schools off shore and blew streams of water as they swam by slowly and gracefully. If the whales were close enough to shore, swimmers could hear the hissing of the water as it sprayed into the air from the whales' blowholes. Otherwise, they glided by noiselessly. On the other hand, the rainbows began forming on one end, and observers could sit still and watch then complete their arches miles away. Then the rain-

bows slowly faded into the mist, leaving visitors to watch another typical Hawaiian sight: surfboard shops. Because the water around Hilo was not very rough while I was there in January, the surfboard rentals were slow, but the grass huts where the boards were kept made interesting sights. I highly recommend the beaches surrounding Hilo for their beauty, warmth, and quiet serenity contrasted with the power of the nearby volcanoes and for the sense of awe visitors feel watching the natural environment.

While descriptive writing often uses adjectives (**beautiful black lava**) and adverbs (glided by **noiselessly**), authors also use other ways to describe. The writer of this paragraph described the lava, comparing it to rope, "wavy patterns that look like rope." This is an example of a **simile,** a comparison of two unlike objects (lava and rope) using the word *like* or *as.* Contrasting images also create description: "Quiet serenity contrasted with the power of the nearby volcanoes." An activity can also be used as description: "fade into the mist" describes the disappearance of the rainbow. Finally, the use of examples, or **exemplification,** of concrete objects is especially useful to help readers visualize the point the author is attempting to make. Reread the above paragraph, looking for specific examples that support the author's topic sentence.

Chronological and Spatial Description

Two other elements readers consciously or unconsciously expect to find in descriptive writing is a form of organization. This can be done in two ways: **spatially** or **chronologically. Spatial description** involves how a scene is organized—from top to bottom, side to side, front to back, and so forth. If you look at the above paragraph, you will see that the organization is spatial. The author begins with what is happening on the beach, and after she has described everything about it, she moves to the water, and she finally adds the rainbows that are found above it.

Chronological description involves how a written piece is organized in relation to time. When we move to Chapter 4, Reading and Writing Narrative, chronological organization will be discussed further.

Purpose

An important point to remember about descriptive writing is that description is used for a purpose rather than just as an exercise to describe something. In the above paragraph, the author describes the beaches in

Hilo to persuade readers to consider them as a future vacation spot. Description can also be used to give information. For example, the more a patient can describe how symptoms feel to a doctor, the better the chances are that the doctor will be able to diagnose the condition. Description can also be used to give directions. Sometimes, instead of using geographical terms (north, south, etc.), the person will give prominent landmarks: Go right at the giant oak tree just past the cornfield. Description for entertainment can make people laugh or cry, or it can compliment. There are multiple reasons to use description, but it generally serves a purpose beyond simple description.

Reflection

1. After reading the material about description, think about what you have learned. Write a reflective journal entry summarizing and listing the information you now know. Don't look at the reading before you do this. Just sit down and let this be a quick check on how much you have retained.
2. Think about any descriptive material you might have read before you learned about description in this chapter. For example, think about class descriptions in college/university catalogues, billboard ads, television commercials, spam on the Internet, as well as other examples. What is especially striking about any one of them? Explain. If you could write an ad for something you use, how would it look? What audience would it be directed to? What elements would you include that you think readers would expect to see?

Before you read the selections that include descriptive passages, review the expectations most readers have about reading description. Now that you are more aware about descriptions, you, too, will probably be looking for the elements consciously or unconsciously.

HOW TO WRITE DESCRIPTION: DESCRIBING OBJECTS

Because description is usually, but not always, part of a larger work, short assignments follow. An informative description could be a paragraph that offers your opinion about a particular object. You've been in this position frequently when someone asks you for your opinion about which car, dress, sofa, restaurant, or other object you prefer. Rather than just choose, you've probably had to answer why you like the one you selected better

AUDIENCE EXPECTATIONS
FOR DESCRIPTIVE PASSAGES

1. Use of words that appeal to the physical senses:
   - Vision
   - Hearing
   - Touch
   - Taste
   - Smell
2. Use of words that appeal to emotions and feelings
3. Use of words other than adjectives and adverbs
4. Use of exemplification
5. Organization
   - Spatial
   - Chronological
6. Purpose

than another one, no doubt using your physical senses and sometimes your feelings to describe your preference. Look at the two pictures on the next page and choose one that especially appeals to you.

Before you describe the picture, complete a prewriting exercise to help you generate your ideas. You might want to answer the following questions.

Step One—Prewriting: Generating Ideas

1. What first caught your attention about the picture you selected?
2. What is the title of the selection? Does it add to or detract from your response to the work?
3. Does the image arouse emotions? How does the image make you feel? Why?
4. What is the subject/action of the picture?
5. Why do you like the picture?
6. What would you want someone who has never seen this picture to know about it?

Obviously, you will not be able to refer to all of the physical senses when you describe the picture; however, you might recall a time when you were at a wedding or at a street fair to help you add personal details to the description.

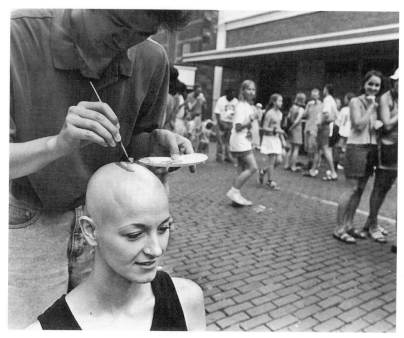

"Lost Identity, II"   *Photographer Franka Bruns*

"Traditions?"   *Photographer Elizabeth Kessler*

Before you write your first **draft,** review your answers and decide if you will use all the information you wrote to create your paragraph. Remember to keep your readers' expectations in mind as you write. The list of expectations can be found on page 29.

Step Two—Write the First Draft

1. Select one of the above pictures and write a descriptive paragraph about it, using ideas you generated in your prewriting exercise.
2. After you have completed the paragraph, use the following Evaluation Rubric to see how well you described the picture and how well you developed your paragraph. You may complete this as a self-evaluation or as a peer evaluation.

EVALUATION RUBRIC

The author	Yes	No	Almost
Description			
1. explained the action in the picture. ____			
2. explained who was present. ____			
3. discussed what caught his or her attention. ____			
4. described and explained the feelings he or she felt. ____			
5. related the picture to his or her own experiences. ____			
6. explained why the audience of this paragraph should see the picture. ____			
Structure			
7. began with a topic sentence. ____			
8. organized the paragraph logically. ____			
9. developed the ideas fully. ____			
10. ended with a concluding sentence. ____			

11. What is the strength of this paragraph?

12. What suggestions would you make to the author to improve this paragraph?

13. After reading this paragraph, would you like to see the picture? Explain.

Although you have written a paragraph, you might discover that this draft is not ready to be submitted to your instructor. If this is the case, do not start over. Everything you wrote has potential elements that can be saved and used in the next draft. Look at the Evaluation Rubric for checks under the "Yes" category. As you begin to revise, you should discover that part of your paragraph can be worked into the new version. Before you begin rewriting, however, look at point #7 on the rubric. Did you have a topic sentence? This is important because you will control not only the flow of your paragraph with a topic sentence, but you will also direct your readers by introducing them to the topic and beginning to meet their expectations. Look at the following topic sentences and determine which one—like the picture—captures your attention.

Topic Sentences

Street fairs provide various activities individuals can observe or become involved in.

Pictures of street fairs often capture observers being entertained, not only by the activities but also by the participants.

Because this assignment is not about street fairs as such, the first topic sentence will allow both the reader and the writer to move easily off topic. The second topic sentence controls the flow of the paragraph by limiting readers' expectations to what the *picture*, rather than the *street fair*, reveals. Look at the next pair of topic sentences.

Topic Sentences

Wedding pictures bring back happy memories both for those who attended the wedding and those who got married.

The candid shot of a young bride tossing her bouquet revealed a very interesting twist to the tradition.

Choosing between these two sentences may be a little harder as both refer to the picture and indicate it is a wedding photo. However, while the first sentence can be seen as a valid assertion, it remains too general. If the assignment were about various wedding pictures or about other aspects of weddings and friends, the first sentence would be a good, general sentence for an introduction. The second example, however, captures the interesting element of the picture: a twist in the tradition. If the readers have not seen the picture, the opening sentence should raise their curiosity about how the activity is different from the traditional bouquet toss.

If you did not write a topic sentence or if your topic sentence needs revision, now is the time to do it. When you complete your new topic sentence, share it with a friend for feedback. If no one is available, switch to your reader persona and determine if it is a sentence that would make you curious about the picture.

Step Three—Revision

Using your Evaluation Rubric and the comments your evaluator gave you, begin making changes to your paragraph. When you finish, you will be ready to edit your paper for errors in mechanics, spelling, and wording. Read the following revised paragraph. The text in bold is new, and strike-throughs indicate what has been deleted.

Traditions?

The candid shot of a young bride tossing her bouquet reveals a very interesting twist to the tradition. As usual, unmarried females line up behind the bride as she stands with her back to them. ~~All~~ **Four young women** are standing ~~in a row~~ **close to each other with their feet firmly planted on the ground. At the end of the row, slightly apart from the others, is an older woman, with her right foot stretched forward and her right arm rising in anticipation. All are** waiting **in different degrees of excitement—from almost none to obvious participation.** The picture captures the bride with her arms up and the bouquet barely visible. She has turned her head to watch what is normally a frenzied rush of young women fighting for the flowers. Instead, viewers see three ~~young women~~ **participants** standing with their hands at their sides and one holding her hands with no apparent desire to capture the prize. On the other hand, the older woman is pictured moving toward the flying flowers. **I found it curious that the young women lined up unenthusiastically, betraying, perhaps, a desire not to be the next bride but that the older participant was not only a part of the tradition but the only one who wanted the bouquet and what it symbolized.** This is quite an interesting picture that reveals at least one ~~group's~~ generation's changing attitude about marriage.

Readers should discover that the first draft, the part *not* in bold type, left out many details. Look at the difference between the following sentences: "All are standing in a row" and "Four young women are close to each other with their feet firmly planted on the ground." Although each provides information, the second adds visual details. The same is true of the other three sentences the author added. Finally, readers see four sets of strike-throughs. The first two are replaced by the above sentence. The third strike-through was replaced by a different word, "participants," to avoid repetition; and the fourth was replaced by a more specific term, "generation," which gives a different meaning not only to the sentence but to the implication of the scene; it also helps to explain the question mark in the title.

Exercise 3: Reading Analysis

1. Does the paragraph meet your expectations when reading for description? Explain.
2. What is the relationship of the title to the paragraph?

Exercise 4: Writing Practice

Follow the directions and then use the rubric on the next page to see how well you met the reader's expectations of descriptive writing.

1. Write a descriptive paragraph about *one* of the following objects:
   - A Hershey's Kiss
   - The desk/chair you are sitting in
   - The shoes you are wearing
   - Your favorite piece of jewelry
2. Write a descriptive paragraph about one of the following locations:
   - Your bedroom
   - The classroom you are in for this class
   - The landscape surrounding the building for one of your classes
   - Your favorite hair salon or barber shop

Use the following rubric when reading descriptive writing. Respond to the writing prompts at the end of the rubric. NA stands for *Not Applicable* and NI means *Not Included*.

READER EXPECTATIONS FOR DESCRIPTIVE WRITING

	Excellent	Good	Fair	NA/ NI
1. Words that appeal to the physical senses				
Vision				
Hearing				
Touch				
Taste				
Smell				
2. Words that appeal to				
Emotions				
Feelings				
3. Use of words other than adjectives and adverbs				
Metaphors				
Similes				
Activities				
4. Use of Examples				
5. Organization				
Spatial				
Chronological				
6. Purpose of description				
7. Use of author's/narrator's				
Feelings				
Emotions				
8. Explanation of				
Object being described				
People being described				
Activity being described				
Location being described				
Concept being described				
9. Other expectation				
10. Other expectation				

Answer the following questions about the paper.

1. Did you find the thesis/topic sentence of this essay/paragraph? What is it?
2. Does the writer support the thesis/topic sentence? Give examples.
3. What are the strengths of this paper?
4. What one weakness do you think should be corrected in this paper?
5. What other comments would you like to make about this descriptive writing?

Chapter 3

Reading and Writing Exemplification

HOW TO READ EXEMPLIFICATION: SINGLE EXAMPLE

Exemplification, the use of examples or illustrations to support and/or develop assertions, is a pattern of development that can be used to write a complete article or can be incorporated into a larger work. In Chapter 2, Reading and Writing Description, readers learned that exemplification can be used as a method to describe, thus developing the idea the writer is discussing. Exemplification is frequently, but not always, signaled by terms such as *for example, the following*, and *such as*. Concrete examples and illustrations frequently help readers understand complex or **abstract** information. Many speakers and teachers use this technique to clarify their message. If you watched the presidential debates and speeches when Al Gore and George W. Bush were running against each other in 2000, you might have heard Gore discuss HMOs as a general concept but then create a concrete context by referring to specific families with specific medical problems. To help the general listening public understand a complex issue, Gore used exemplification, incorporating everyday illustrations everyone could identify with.

Multiple Examples

The above discussion about the Bush–Gore debates was an illustration of exemplification. Its success, however, depends on readers being familiar with that event. If readers did not see the debates, the example could be meaningless. On the other hand, if you were reading about the major you chose or the majors you are interested in, you might find examples of careers you could possibly enter with a degree in that major. You would be *reading* a kind of exemplification. By using various examples to clarify a point, the writer meets readers' expectations that the material will clarify dense or difficult ideas.

In "The Same Old Same Old" paragraph below, the author clearly wants her students to write in their own voices by avoiding the use of clichés. The paragraph will work only if students understand that a **cliché** is "a trite phrase or expression; something that has become overly familiar or commonplace." Read the paragraph and see if you can find examples of clichés.

Reading Process

By now you have probably been using the Reading Process repeatedly and have been quite successful in your skills. However, before you read this passage, be sure you have completed the essential prereading steps for this particular assignment:

- **Be prepared.** Make sure you have highlighter or pen/pencil.
- **Look carefully at the title.** This title is particularly important for the content.
- **Determine what kind of selection you will be reading. And modify your reading method for it.** Because it is an exemplification paragraph, you should be looking for as many examples of the topic as you can find.
- **Review your notes from class.** This is particularly important so you can remember the definition of cliché.

Now read the selection, following the steps for reading:

- **Read the entire selection quickly.** See if you can pick out the clichés you are familiar with.
- **Begin rereading slowly and thoroughly.** Now you will be able to spot clichés you might have missed in the first quick reading.
- **Keep your pen or highlighter in hand.** Be sure to mark each cliché as you find it.
- **Read each selection correctly.** Because this is a paragraph, you should be looking for the main idea by identifying the topic sentence.
- **Review the marks you have made in the reading, noting their importance.** After reading the paragraph, you should have found that the entire paragraph is composed of clichés.

The Same Old Same Old

Teaching students to recognize and rid their writing of clichés has been an uphill battle. Teachers fight tooth and nail to convince their writers to reduce the number of clichés because readers can spot them a mile away. Therefore, instead of producing original writing, students use "trite, stereotype expressions" that they think will work well for them but that only leave them sadder but wiser when they get their grade back. However, regardless of the many times teachers get on their soapbox, students dig their heels in and refuse to toe the mark. Sometimes teachers think they have put the cart before the horse by telling students what not to do before teaching them vocabulary skills. In fact, some teachers are afraid of throwing the baby out with the bath water by stifling the students' creativity. Needless to say, it's a never-ending battle that almost requires the heart of a lion to jump into the fray and try to succeed despite all odds, knowing it's in their students' best interest that they give it the All-American try and help them win one, if not for themselves then, for the Gipper.

When you finish reading the passage, you should be ready to discuss clichés. Although there are no questions at the end of the paragraph, the assignment was to read this paragraph for exemplification. Did you find the topic sentence that gave you the main idea of the paragraph? If so, you discovered that the writer begins immediately with the idea of clichés. How many did you find?

Compare the markings you made when you read the paragraph with the markings another reader made. The underlined sentence is the topic sentence. The highlighted words are examples of clichés.

The Same Old Same Old

<u>Teaching students to recognize and rid their writing of clichés has been an uphill battle</u>. Teachers fight tooth and nail to convince their writers to reduce the number of cliches because readers can spot them a mile away. Therefore, instead of producing original writing, students use "trite, stereotyped expressions" that they think will work well for them

but that only leave them sadder but wiser when they
get their grade back. However, regardless of the
many times teachers get on their soapbox, students
dig their heels in and refuse to toe the mark. Sometimes teachers think they have put the cart before
the horse by telling students what not to do before
teaching them vocabulary skills. In fact, some
teachers are afraid of throwing the baby out with
the bath water by stifling the students' creativity.
Needless to say, it's a never-ending battle that almost requires the heart of a lion to jump into the
fray and try to succeed despite all odds, knowing
it's in their students' best interest that they give
it the All-American try and help them win one, if not
for themselves then, for the Gipper.

Hopefully, you not only recognized the number of examples the
writer used to make her point, you also saw the humor in the piece. By
using **exaggeration** and **repetition**, teachers convey their ideas to their
students without necessarily boring them or antagonizing them. The use
of examples and illustrations provides an excellent way to clarify information.

The Extended Exemplification

The second kind of writing that exhibits exemplification is the extended
form, which usually results in a longer piece. For example, if someone
were to ask you to write a letter of recommendation, you would be writing an extended form of exemplification. This letter would not only be
indicating examples of the individual's worthiness for the position he or
she is applying for, but it would also be indicating that this person is an
example of the kind of employee the company is looking for. There are
different kinds of letters of recommendation. The example below is one
that recommends a student for a course that is highly competitive. The
letter provides examples both of why the student is an excellent choice
for acceptance as well as what she does that describes her as an excellent
student.

25 March 2003

Columbia Publishing Course
Graduate School of Journalism
Columbia University
New York, NY 10027-6902

Dear Members of the Admissions Committee:

It is my pleasure to recommend Ms. Victoria
Matt for admission into the Columbia Publishing
Course. I have taught Ms. Matt in two of my
classes, once each in a lower and an upper
division American literature course. In each
class, I have found Ms. Matt to be quite
interested in the material and mature in her
approach to it and to her research and writing.
She is a quiet, thoughtful student whose ideas
are presented in cogent, unified, and thorough
papers.

I am aware that Ms. Matt is interested in the
publishing industry for her career choice. As
such, she works at LAgraphico twenty to thirty
hours per week. This semester she is working as
a staff member on The Northridge Review
Literary Magazine, the English Department's
creative writing journal. She is also taking a
class that is specifically designed for
students who are working on the journal.

Last semester, when she took my Survey of
American Literature I class, Ms. Matt was
required to complete a Service Learning
component which involved interviewing survivors
of World War II, transcribing their oral
histories, and creating a cohesive and unified
personal narrative from their stories. Ms. Matt
not only did the required work, she worked
tirelessly for several weeks, including
Thanksgiving break, to set up the manuscript in
Quark so that it could go to the printer in
final format ready to be printed and bound. She
and three other students edited the manuscript,
completed the layout, including pictures of
most of those interviewed, and created a cover
with a picture and with the title on the spine.
Ms. Matt did this on her own time, knowing that
she would not be receiving any special credit

for her work and knowing that this would be good experience for her in her future endeavors.

Even though Ms. Matt is busy working in her field, she is also able to keep a 3.89 grade point average and will graduate magna cum laude in May.

She has also been placed on the Dean's list every semester from 2001 through 2003. Thus she is able to maintain her academic as well as her career-oriented activities. I have watched her manage her schedule so that nothing is slighted.

I know that Ms. Matt will be a contributing and valuable student in the Columbia Publishing Course and that she will learn a great deal in preparing for her graduate work in publishing. If you have any questions, please feel free to call or e-mail me.

Sincerely,

Lynn Baker, Ph.D.

Lynn Baker, Ph.D.
Assistant Professor

Finally, another kind of extended example is the **analogy**. Similar to the metaphor, the analogy takes a comparison of two unlike objects and extends it to make a specific point. For example, read the following letter of complaint that makes a comparison between the job the person has and another job.

Dear Mr. Green:

I am responding to your letter that denies me early promotion and that suggests that the duties I am performing in my capacity are illegal.

Regarding my position, I believe that as the Director of Operations for this company, I should have a promotion to full member of the administrative team, as I was hired for the job, and I am completing the duties as described in the job description manual. I was hired at the same time as the president of our company. Does Mr. Baumgarten have to wait three years before he can become a full administrative member of the company?

Furthermore, by denying me the right to full administrative power, you are saying that I am conducting parts of the job that I was hired to do illegally. Let me ask you the following question: If I were a real estate lawyer and you hired me as such, would I have to wait three years before I could complete the duties I was hired to do? Would you assign my specialized legal duties to someone who is working in corporate fraud or in criminal law for three years until I reached the three-year requirement? I think not. My job, like that of any other specialist, requires that I have certain status and access and clearance to certain information allowed only to those of administrative positions. I cannot complete my job fully without this promotion.

I request that you reconsider my request for early promotion to administrative level based on the job description, my consistent and excellent work, and the letters that support the quality of work I have performed for the company.

Respectfully,

Lourdes Delgado

Lourdes Delgado

Thus, you can see that writers incorporate exemplification in various ways to develop and clarify their material. Writers do not have to limit the use of exemplification to persuasion or report writing; they may add it to letters, description, or any other mode of writing to help readers increase their understanding

HOW TO WRITE EXEMPLIFICATION

If your assignment is to write a persuasive essay, you will want to use exemplification within the argument. For example, to write a paper similar in style to "The Same Old Same Old," you will need enough information to describe, support, and clarify your position as you write.

AUDIENCE EXPECTATIONS FOR EXEMPLIFICATION PASSAGES

Readers expect exemplification to

- provide examples and/or illustrations that clarify dense or difficult subjects.
- provide examples they can relate to.
- move from generalities to specific examples.
- support **assertions** that writers make.
- be signaled by transition words such as *for example, the following, for instance*, and *such as*.

Step One—Prewriting

Because writing exemplification requires the use of clear examples that are relevant to the material being discussed, clustering is an excellent prewriting strategy to use to generate specific ideas and organize them logically. Look at the following cluster set up to generate ideas on the topic "The need for a stop light at University and Broadway."

The Need for a Stop Light at University and Broadway

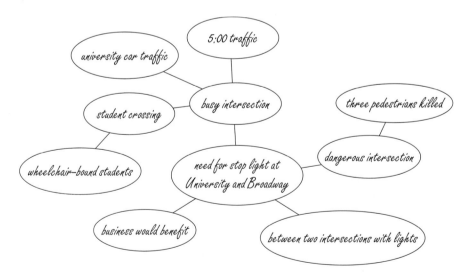

The clustering exercise reveals that the writer has generated a variety of ideas to support the need for a traffic light at University and Broadway; however, he has mixed general ideas with specific ones. This results in some clusters being left undivided and incorporated into larger, more general topics. For example (signal for exemplification), look at "busy intersection." It is a general idea that has generated multiple ideas that support the writer's position. On the other hand, the cluster "student crossing" is a specific example and was easily moved over to the "busy intersection" cluster. By beginning with a cluster exercise, a student can jot down ideas, move them around, or eliminate them entirely before writing begins.

Exercise 1: Clustering

1. Choose one of the following topics for a persuasive essay:
   • Reducing the time to get a visa into the United States
   • Using mass transit instead of private cars
   • Being eligible for an organ transplant more than once
   • Requiring the use of helmets for bicycle and motorcycle riders
2. Create a cluster for the topic, going from general to specific supports.

If we refer to the traffic light cluster again, we can see that the writer chose one cluster and developed it into the following paragraph:

Traffic Light Necessity

After a month of attempting to cross the street at the intersection of University and Broadway, I believe the city planners need to install a traffic signal. This intersection is one of the busiest intersections at all hours of the day and is hazardous to pedestrians. Regardless of when I try to cross, the cars from a fast-food business, a bank, and a small grocery store also compete with traffic traveling on Broadway. When 5:00 traffic or even traffic from the university all day competes with pedestrians, the pedestrians must wait for law-abiding drivers to observe individuals in the crosswalks, or walkers must go two or more blocks out of their way to cross safely. This becomes especially difficult for the number of wheelchair-bound individuals crossing Broadway to go to campus or to the store. In their need to move into the flow of traffic, fast food customers frequently speed up into the lane, crossing the intersection,

almost hitting the hard-to-see wheelchair crossers or
swerving to miss them and almost creating car accidents. Thus, for these reasons, I believe that the
City Council should vote to spend the funds to install
a light at University and Broadway.

Step Two—Thesis and First Draft

The writer also used the prompt, "the need for a stop light at University
and Broadway," as the foundation for his thesis. Rather than just make
an assertion about the need for a traffic signal, the author personalized
the topic sentence to indicate firsthand experience with the situation that
needs correction.

Look at another paragraph that stopped the cluster exercise without expanding it to include specific examples.

The Need for a Signal

The intersection at University and Broadway is
definitely in need of a traffic signal. It is a very
busy intersection. It has become a dangerous intersection for pedestrians. The businesses on both sides of
the street would benefit from a light. Since the intersection is also between two already working signals,
the speed of the traffic increases as the drivers try
to avoid stopping at the next light. Thus, the Traffic
Department needs to observe the problems at University
and Broadway and install a traffic signal.

The main difference between the two first drafts is that the first
student writing uses specific examples to make the argument, and the
second relies on generalizations. "The Need for a Signal" is clearly a
draft that needs development and elaboration. Although the author provides assertions that support his topic sentence—"It is a very busy intersection"—he is vague. "Traffic Light," on the other hand, uses a
variation of the same assertion but also follows it up with concrete details that support the topic sentence. Both paragraphs are first drafts;
however, "Traffic Light" appears to be closer to completion than does
"The Need for a Signal." Another difference between the two paragraphs is the personalized approach the author of "Traffic Light" takes
to the problem. While the second author is attempting to complete the
assignment by giving general reasons, the reader feels that the first author is not only aware of the problem but has experienced and witnessed

it on many occasions. As the audience of these persuasive paragraphs, which one would you be more inclined to listen to? Why?

Step Three—Revision

Because "Traffic Light" is closer to completion and because you can see it as a model for "The Need for a Signal," we will use it to show revision. Although the writer has presented well-developed content, he needs to add "exemplification signals" or transitions into the examples that he will present. He also needs to work on more precise and less repetitive word choice. Take a moment to review the first draft of "Traffic Light."

Exercise 2

1. In the margins or between the lines, make what you think are appropriate revisions to "Traffic Light."
2. Let the writer know what you think the strength of the paragraph is.
3. Make a suggestion for improving a weakness of the paragraph.
4. Share your ideas with your classmates.

Below is the revised version of "Traffic Light." Compare his revisions with the ones you suggested. The strike-throughs represent the original wording, and the bold print indicates the words he added.

Traffic Light

After a month of attempting to cross the street at the intersection of University and Broadway, I believe the ~~city planners~~ **City Council** needs to install a traffic signal. This ~~intersection~~ **corner** is one of the busiest intersections at all hours of the day and is hazardous to pedestrians. **For example**, regardless of when I try to cross, the cars from a fast-food business, a bank, and a small grocery store also compete with traffic traveling on Broadway. When 5:00 traffic or even traffic **caused by students entering or leaving** ~~from~~ the university all day competes with pedestrians, the pedestrians must wait for law-abiding drivers to ~~observe~~ **stop for** individuals in the crosswalks, or walkers must go two or more blocks out of their way to cross safely. This becomes especially difficult for the number of wheelchair-bound individuals who must cross Broadway to go to campus **or even to go to the store**. In their need to move into the flow of traffic, fast food customers

```
frequently accelerate into the lane, crossing the
intersection, almost hitting the hard-to-see wheel-
chair crossers, or swerving to miss them, and almost
creating car accidents. Thus, for these reasons, I
believe that the City Council should vote to spend
the funds to install a light at University and
Broadway.
```

How did you feel about your suggestions in comparison to the revisions the writer chose to make? Which version of the essay seems better to you? Let's look at two changes: *For example* and *corner* versus *intersection*. Although the writing clearly indicates that the writer will begin presenting details that support and develop the preceding assertion—that University and Broadway is a busy intersection—using the transition words that signal exemplification guides the readers into the example. As a writer, you want to control the readers' direction in the material, so giving them as much information as possible prevents them from losing the ideas you are trying to develop. As for *corner* versus *intersection*, the writer has used *intersection* twice in the sentence, so to avoid repetition, he changed the word to *corner*. The rest of the revisions are self-explanatory.

HOW TO WRITE EXEMPLIFICATION— SINGLE EXAMPLE

All forms of exemplification development do not have to be as thoroughly detailed as the one you just read. In fact, some assignments may include a single detail or example with some explanation about it rather than multiple examples. In this case, the single detail is used to clarify the material being presented rather than develop the material. Read the following example:

Romanticism

```
    Romanticism is a style of writing that came into
prominence in the United States in the nineteenth
century, 1830-1865. In America it replaced the seri-
ous writing that led to the American Revolution, as
well as the religious writing of the Puritans. Ro-
mantic writers were varied so that someone such as
William Cullen Bryant, who wrote about nature in a
light and beautiful way, could be classified as a
romantic along with Edgar Allan Poe, who wrote about
```

death and lost love in a dark, heavy, and imaginative way. Thus, the emotion displayed by a poet who
enjoys nature could be equally romantic as the emotion displayed by a lover who has lost his love. Romanticism, generally, changed the purpose of reading
so that now enjoying literature for its own sake instead of for what it had to teach became important.
But Romanticism did not die in 1865; it lived on in
the writing of numerous authors who wrote well into
the twentieth century (Holman 392-93).

Instead of being filled with example after example, this brief paragraph mentions only two examples of distinctly different romantic writers: William Cullen Bryant and Edgar Allan Poe. Even though you
might not know Bryant, most students who have taken an American literature class have read works by Poe and understand that he is not a
nature writer.

Using a single example embedded within the paragraph is probably more popular than writing an essay that is completely filled with
examples, details, and/or illustrations. In the example, the author used
two contrasting examples to clarify the differences in Romanticism;
even though she could have used many more. However, once writers become aware of exemplification, they find that it is easy to write, and they
want to use it frequently. When you use exemplification, however, be
sure that your examples are precise, relevant, and timely. The details are
there to help your audience understand the material, and anything that is
strange or unusual might not help them.

Exercise 3: Reading Analysis

1. Does the paragraph about Romanticism meet your expectations
   about reading exemplification? Explain.
2. Do the two examples with their explanations help you understand that
   Romanticism is a style with many variations? Explain.

Exercise 4: Writing Practice

1. Write an informative paragraph with numerous examples about one of
   the following topics:
   • Pets
   • Computers
   • Careers in education
   • Cars

2. Write a descriptive paragraph with only one or two examples about one of the following topics:
   - Redecorating one room in your home
   - Doing the laundry
   - Friends
   - Cooking your favorite meal

Chapter 4

Reading and Writing Narrative

HOW TO READ NARRATIVE

Most of us have been reading narrative since childhood. Any good story is a narrative; however, there are differences in the approach in that some are fiction while others are autobiographical or nonfiction. The narratives that follow are nonfiction. They are incidents related by individuals about an event that happened to them or to someone they know. One form of narrative, memoirs, can be personal—about the writer—or it can be biographical—about someone else.

Chronological Organization

Readers of narratives have certain expectations, and if those expectations are not met, readers can be confused, disappointed, and unfulfilled. Primary expectations assume that the story will be organized, and that events will follow a logical sequence, moving from point to point in an orderly manner. One of the most common organizing patterns is chronological: telling a story as it happens in time so that it has a beginning, a middle, and an end. The following short narrative is organized chronologically. Although it does not have the traditional transitional words (first, next, then, etc.) that move the reader from one moment to the next, readers can tell that time is passing. Another expectation is that readers will know who the individuals are in the narrative. If a writer includes individuals in the narrative, he or she should identify them clearly so as not to confuse the audience. Finally, there should be a clearly defined setting that has descriptive and vivid details. In other words, a nonfiction narrative has many of the same characteristics as a short story.

As you read, look for the words the author uses to show the sequence of events, determine who is present in the story and what their function is, and find the details.

When my dad fell on the driveway while he was going to check for the mail, he broke his hip and suffered a mild case of sunburn. Unable to move, Dad found himself at a loss. Not only was he alone on a hot Tuesday afternoon, he was aware that everyone in the neighborhood was at work or at school. His quiet yard was not even punctuated by the regular blue jay squabbles so noisy in the morning hours. The monotony of silence left Dad with nothing to do but wait. As he lay there, the pain in his hip filled his mind and body, making the minutes feel like hours. Unsure of whether he dozed off or became unaware of his surroundings, Dad said he missed several opportunities for help as he heard a car or two pass by, but neither driver noticed him. Eventually, he tried to lift himself by putting his weight on his uninjured hip, but the pain immediately stopped him. His scraped elbows wouldn't let him use them for leverage either. By now sweat from the pain as well as from the slowly moving sun drenched his shirt, and he could feel his lips chapping in the heat. All he could think of was how long it would be before a neighbor got home. As he closed his eyes and shaded his face from the sun with one hand, he dozed off. Suddenly he woke with a start, moaning as his sudden movement sent a sharp pain down his leg and up his back. He heard someone calling his name, but it sounded far away. Opening his eyes, all he could see was a dark figure framed against the light. The mailman had arrived, and Dad knew he would be delivered.

If you followed the steps of the Reading Process (including pre-reading) you probably found yourself reading more successfully. Because the assignment is short, you did not have to linger over all the steps, but some steps are especially important, for example, in the Pre-reading stage:

1. **Know what the assignment is.** The sentence preceding the passage indicates that you should read for three things:
   - Words the author uses to show the sequence of events
   - Who is present in the story and their function
   - Details

Traditional clues like *first, next,* and *then* are not present, so you have to be aware of other ways to see time pass. What indicators give you clues about time passing?

2. **Be prepared.** By having your highlighter or pen in your hand and ready to use, you can take notes and mark important passages immediately.

3. **Check the length of the reading.** It's one short paragraph.

4. **Look carefully at the title.** No title is provided; therefore, you had no hint what this paragraph was about before you started.

5. **Look at the vocabulary list if there is one.** No list is provided, but you were prepared to look up anything you didn't understand.

6. **Look for bold headings.** None.

7. **Check for questions at the end.** No questions are given at the end, but you knew what to look for from the sentence that preceded the paragraph.

8. **Determine what kind of selection you will be reading.** The instructional material indicated a narrative with chronological organization; therefore, you were expecting a story related sequentially.

The Reading stage should have taken more time.

1. **Read the entire selection quickly.** This allows you to understand the overall idea, tone, and direction of the narrative. Without rereading,
   • write a one-sentence summary of the paragraph.
   • include the individuals in the narrative, the setting, and vivid details.

2. **Keep your pen or highlighter in hand.** Did you mark the words that indicate time passing?

3. **Read each selection correctly.** This paragraph reveals a chronological pattern of development. Write the words or idea the author used to indicate time passing. If you completed Step 2, you don't have to reread the story again; just list the words or phrases you highlighted.

Now that you have finished reading, the Follow-up exercise will be easy, especially since there were no questions or assignments made. You might, however, write a journal entry and think about how you felt about the paragraph. Practicing reading skills should also include recognizing the topic sentence of this passage. If you have not already marked it, go back and underline it now.

Your paragraph should look similar to the one below. The gray shaded areas indicate time, and the **bold** words indicate details. The topic sentence is underlined.

When my dad fell on the driveway while he was going to check for mail, he broke his hip and suffered a mild case of sunburn. Unable to move, Dad found himself at a loss. Not only was he alone on a hot Tuesday afternoon, he was aware that everyone in the neighborhood was at work or at school. **His quiet yard was not even punctuated by the regular blue jay squabbles so noisy in the morning hours.** The **monotony of silence** left Dad with nothing to do but wait. As he lay there, the pain in his hip filled his mind and body, making the minutes feel like hours. Unsure of whether he dozed off or became unaware of his surroundings, Dad said he missed several opportunities for help as he heard a car or two pass by, but neither driver noticed him. Eventually, he tried to lift himself by putting his weight on his uninjured hip, but **the pain immediately stopped him.** His **scraped elbows** wouldn't let him use them for leverage either. By now sweat from the pain as well as from the slowly moving sun drenched his shirt, and he could feel his lips chapping in the heat. All he could think of was how long it would be before a neighbor got home. As he closed his eyes and shaded his face from the sun with one hand, he dozed off. Suddenly he woke with a start, moaning as his sudden movement sent a **sharp pain down his leg** and **up his back. He heard** someone calling his name, but **it sounded far away.** Opening his eyes, all he could see was a **dark figure framed against the light.** The mailman had arrived, and Dad knew he would be delivered.

One thing you might have noticed is that the preceding paragraph was written from a third-person perspective. It was a story about the narrator's father, not about the narrator. This kind of narrative is called a **memoir.** Usually written autobiographically, memoirs can also be biographically written by someone close to the subject of the story.

Spatial Organization

Chronological organization is not the only way to organize. Another method involves spatial organization: from top to bottom, side to side, inside to outside, and so forth. Read the following paragraphs and watch as the narrator uses chronological and then spatial organization as she searches for lost items. Trace the pattern of her search.

The Lost Bills

After finishing the morning paper, I realized that the inevitable time of the month had arrived: bill-paying time. Unable to procrastinate any longer, I found my checkbook and methodically wrote check after check: mortgage, phone, cell phone, electricity, and gas. Knowing I would be going grocery shopping later, I left them on the breakfast table, waiting for their stamps, and I went about my Saturday routine. Unfortunately, as the day progressed, I found I could not go to the store, so I decided to mail the bills on Sunday. That was not my favorite choice of days, considering there would be no mail pick-up until Monday morning. So when I finally went to the store late Sunday morning, I left the bills at home. Once I returned home, I was able to concentrate on paperwork that had to be completed by Monday. By the time midnight struck, I was not only tired, but I was also pleased at my accomplishments. Papers were strewn everywhere, and there were so many books in front of me that I feared for my glass-top table. About to turn out the lights, I grabbed my purse and spied my checkbook peeking out from beneath the messy pages. The bills! I suddenly remembered that I hadn't mailed them.

I looked on the counter where I usually place the keys and envelopes to be mailed. Keys, yes, bills, no. Then I went to the living room to look on the coffee table—my second favorite spot to leave mail. Nothing. My other favorite spot to leave things that must be mailed is on the entry hall table downstairs, an obvious place to see things as I walk in and out. I rushed downstairs, but I found nothing. Well, I thought, maybe I placed them by the computer. I had stopped to check my e-mail before I left this morning, knowing I could load some things into the car while the computer "booted up." Now I moved papers around, but I couldn't find the bills.

Paranoia began to spread as I thought of all that money floating around somewhere. Could I have dropped them in the store? Check the car! Stepping into the garage from the entry hall was easy, even though my bare feet tingled against the cold cement floor. Peering in through the windows, I found no lost envelopes hiding in corners or stuck between seat and console.

I gathered my thoughts and banished panic from my mind. Let's go back to the computer and then upstairs to the kitchen, I told myself rationally. When both of those searches proved fruitless, I went upstairs to see if I'd left them on the bathroom counter while I was getting ready. Of course not—that's too simple.

Tired and frustrated, I slowly descended to the kitchen and sat once more at my cluttered table. I glanced over the books, three-ring binder, papers scattered across the table like leaves across a lawn, and sighed. The bills were nowhere in sight. In a tired and hopeless moment of renewed energy, I slowly began closing books and binder, organizing them against the wall. I could almost hear the table whisper "thank you." As I lifted sheets of typing paper to throw away, familiar corners poked out from beneath the ruined pages. Still waiting for stamps, the bills were on the corner of the table. I hadn't moved them to the counter, to the hall table or to the computer desk. They hadn't leapt out of my purse to play in the car. No, they were, as my mother is always fond of saying, right where I had left them: on the breakfast room table.

Exercise 1: Reading Analysis

Reading for Chronological Organization

1. The author uses chronological as well as spatial organization. How much time passes in these paragraphs?
2. What phrases indicate how much time passes?

Reading for Spatial Organization

1. How many floors does the narrator have in her home?
2. What floor does the narrator begin on? What words indicate that?
3. What floor is the computer on? How do you know that?
4. What rooms did she search on the second floor?
5. Draw your concept of her house. Obviously you don't know every room she has, but you have enough information to complete a rough sketch of each floor.
6. Now trace the narrator's journey to find the keys in numbered steps. For example:
   1. She began in the _____.
   2. She moved to the _____.

Reflection

1. After reading the material about narratives, think about what you have learned. Write a reflective journal entry summarizing and listing the information you now know. Don't look at the reading before you do this. Just sit down and let this be a quick check on how much you have retained.

2. Think about any narratives you might have read before you learned about them in this chapter. Can you list their titles? Do you remember anything especially striking about any one of them? If you do, what made that narrative so memorable. Is there anything about any narrative you've read that you would like to incorporate into your own writing? Reread the one that you remember and see if you can identify any stylistic points that you would like to use.

Before you read the narrative selections, review the expectations most readers have about narratives. Now that you are more aware of narrative structure, you, too, will probably be looking for the elements consciously or unconsciously.

HOW TO WRITE NARRATIVE

In the preceding section, you learned that nonfiction narrative can be written from a first- or third-person point of view. Aside from the point of view, another difference is tone. While a personal narrative is normally **subjective**—using emotional language as in "Lost Keys"—a memoir may be subjective or **objective**—describing the subject without using an emotional tone. In the first example above, the narrator dis-

---

READER EXPECTATIONS FOR NARRATIVE WORKS

- It is a story with a beginning, middle, and end.
- The events are organized chronologically or spatially.
- A topic/thesis sentence that usually indicates what the narrative will be about will be given early in the narrative.
- The individuals in the narrative are clearly identified and defined.
- The narrative has specific and vivid details.
- The author provides a realistic closing, sometimes providing a lesson that was learned or a solution to a problem.

tances herself from her father's story. She does not become emotionally involved in telling his story. However, if you look at Cherríe Moraga's narrative, the first selection in the reading, you will find a different approach. Although she relates her father's emotional release, she is also part of the story, and her tone is subjective.

Knowing what readers expect from a narrative is not all there is to writing one. To give readers what they expect, writers must work diligently to make the story interesting and seamless. The narrative must let the reader know at some early point what the story will be about. Then it must flow smoothly from one point to the next. It must show **unity**—a controlling idea, which draws the parts of the writing to a whole—and **coherence**—connection between ideas through transitions.

Step One—Prewriting: Choosing the Topic

Your instructor might give you a list of general topics from which to choose or you might choose an important event you want to discuss. Whether it is general or specific, you should begin with prewriting. Use one of the prewriting strategies—free writing and focused free writing; brainstorming; clustering, webbing, or mapping; or journalistic questions—to begin your personal narrative. Jonathan chose to write about an incident he was involved in during a vacation with his father. To get ideas about the trip to London, Jonathan began with clustering, jotting down memories about the trip.

From this strategy, Jonathan narrowed his topic to his experience of going to the theatre. For this he moved to journalistic questions:

Who?	A stranger and I
What?	A trip to the theatre to see <u>Phantom</u>
When?	One afternoon in London
Where?	On the subway and in the Theatre District
Why?	To make money
How?	Drug deal

Step Two—Writing the Topic/Thesis Sentence

As with the descriptive paragraph, you must take control of the direction of the paragraph by constructing a topic sentence that indicates that this will be a narrative. In this case, since the incident happened to Jonathan, the topic sentence needs to indicate that he is the main participant. Because the paragraph is also going to tell a story, the topic sentence should also briefly announce the event.

Trip to London

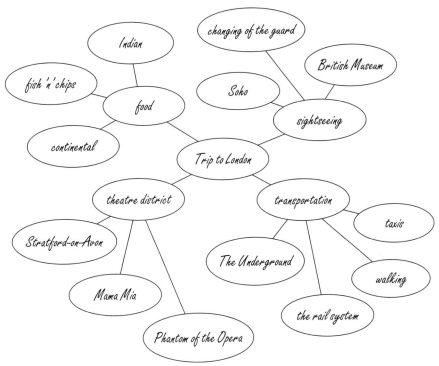

Topic/Thesis Sentence for the Personal Narrative

I decided to go to the theatre without my dad.

As you can see, Jonathan mentions both himself and the incident. However, this is somewhat boring in light of the event that he is about to discuss. Even he realizes that it does not convey the impression he wants, so he rewrites it.

Topic/Thesis Sentence for the Personal Narrative

I was excited about going to see *The Phantom of the Opera* alone.

Even though this is closer to the truth and more interesting, Jonathan knows something is still missing.

Topic/Thesis Sentence for the Personal Narrative

Little did I know I would have a dangerous experience when I was going to see *The Phantom of the Opera*.

Now Jonathan has arrived at the point he wants to make. He has created a sentence that piques the reader's curiosity and makes the event sound interesting.

Step Three—Writing the First Draft

Jonathan has decided what he wants to focus on in his account of his trip to the theatre without his father. By looking at the journalistic questions, we discover that he had some sort of experience with a drug dealer. Since his topic sentence indicates that he was involved in a dangerous experience, he must meet some of the expectations of the readers:

- It is a story with a beginning, middle, and end.
- The events are organized chronologically or spatially.
- A topic/thesis sentence that usually indicates what the narrative will be about, will be given early in the narrative.
- The individuals in the narrative are clearly identified and defined.
- The narrative has specific and vivid details.
- The author provides a realistic closing, sometimes providing a lesson that was learned or a solution to a problem.

Because this is a personal narrative, he should also provide the following elements to keep his readers interested:

- A subjective rather than objective tone
- Emotional tension
- A first-person point of view
- Dialogue, although not necessary
- Use of past tense
- Description

Because this is a personal narrative, Jonathan decided to organize the story chronologically. Consequently, he had to use transitions that show time passing. He also included spatial organization as he moved from the hotel to the Theatre District. Since the reader is more interested in what is happening than in details about getting to his destination, Jonathan focused on the most important parts of the trip. Look at the topic sentence, where he indicates that he would have a "dangerous experience." Now he must explain *how* it was dangerous.

The First Draft

Even though I have a good time with my dad, I was looking forward to exploring London alone while he was at work. Little did I know that I would have a dangerous experience when I was going to see <u>Phantom of the Opera</u>.

Because our hotel was far from the Theatre District, I had to take the subway and transfer twice. I didn't think anything was wrong until I noticed someone getting on and off the cars at the same stops I made. There weren't many people riding at that time because I was going to a matinee. As I got off in the Theatre District, the stranger approached me, walking very close to my side and mumbled something under his breath. I couldn't understand him because he had a British accent and his tone was low. I walked faster, trying to get away from him. The stranger came up behind me and told me he had a "dime bag" in his pocket. All I could think was that streetlights in London were much slower than those at home. I saw a bobby across the street in front of the theatre. When the light changed I walked up to the police officer. I looked behind me, and the stranger seemed to have disappeared. The bobby strolled away. I walked to the theatre, handed the ticket taker my ticket, and sat down to watch the play.

Although Jonathan relates the facts of the event, he does not build the tension that he felt when he was approached by the stranger. He might have been scared, which he indicated by explaining that he "walked faster, trying to get away from him"; but he left out too much detail. He needs to rethink the tone and the words that will create the tension he felt. The following in his next draft. The **bold** words indicate his additions.

Even though I have a good time with my dad, I was looking forward to exploring London alone while he was at work. Little did I know that I would have a dangerous experience when I was going to see <u>Phantom of the Opera</u>.

Because our hotel was far from the Theatre District, I had to take the subway and transfer twice. I didn't think anything was wrong until I noticed someone getting on and off the cars at the same stops I made. There weren't many people riding at that time because I was going to a matinee. As I got off in the Theatre District, the stranger approached me, walking very close to my side and mumbled something under his breath. I couldn't understand him because he had a British accent and his tone was low. I walked faster, trying to get away from him. **As I approached the theatre, I saw a crowd. I hoped I could mingle with the people and lose the stranger. When I got to the corner, the light changed, and I had to stop.** The stranger came up behind me and told me he had a "dime bag" in his pocket. **He was so close, I could feel his breath against my ear.** All I could think was that streetlights in London were much slower than those at home. I saw a bobby across the street in front of the theatre. When the light changed, I walked up to the police officer. I looked behind me, and the stranger seemed to have disappeared. **He was gone!** The bobby strolled away **not even noticing that I had stopped beside him.** I walked to the theatre, handed the ticket taker my ticket, and sat down to watch the play.

The addition of the five sentences and a dependent clause definitely heighten the sense of fear Jonathan was feeling. However, the ending seems to drop the reader. To have just experienced the "dangerous" situation, it is anticlimactic to just sit down "to watch the play." In the next revision, he changed his last sentence in the following way, indicated in bold:

I walked to the theatre, handed the ticket taker my ticket, and **faded into the safe twilight darkness of the theatre.**

This is much better, as the reader now gets the sense that Jonathan feels safer and not as visible and vulnerable as he was outside on the street. One more part needs improvement: the introduction. Jonathan jumped right into the topic without giving his audience much background. To correct this, he added the following sentences:

When I was sixteen, my dad had to go to London on a business trip and he asked me to go with him. Was I excited!

By indicating his excitement at the beginning of the narrative, Jonathan is able to capture the reader's attention quickly. The contrast between excitement and danger pulls the reader into the narrator's story. Since this is now a two-paragraph paper, Jonathan's controlling sentence is a thesis rather than a topic sentence.

Now look at the narrative in its completed form. Revisions are in bold.

London Drama

When I was sixteen, my dad had to go to London on a business trip, and he asked me to go with him. Was I excited! Even though I always have a good time with my dad, I was looking forward to exploring London alone while he was at work. Little did I know that I would have a dangerous experience when I was going to see <u>Phantom of the Opera</u>.

Because our hotel was far from the Theatre District, I had to take the subway and transfer twice. I didn't think anything was wrong until I noticed someone getting on and off the cars at the same stops I made. There weren't many people riding at that time because I was going to a matinee. As I got off in the Theatre District, the stranger approached me, walking very close to my side and mumbled something under his breath. I couldn't understand him because he had a British accent and his tone was low. I walked faster, trying to get away from him. **As I approached the theatre, I saw a crowd. I hoped I could mingle with the people and lose the stranger. When I got to the corner, the light changed, and I had to stop.** The stranger came up behind me and told me he had a "dime bag" in his pocket. **He was so close, I could feel his breath against my ear.** All I could think was that streetlights in London were much slower than those at home. I saw a bobby across the street in front of the theatre. When the light changed, I walked up to the police officer. I looked behind me, and the stranger seemed to have disappeared. The bobby strolled **away not even noticing that I had stopped beside him.** I walked to the theatre, handed the ticket taker my ticket, **and faded into the safe twilight darkness of the theatre.**

Not only does Jonathan have a much better narrative, he also adds an interesting title that adds a twist to his story.

Exercise 1: Reading Analysis

1. Read Jonathan's narrative from the point of view of a reader rather than a writer. Does the narrative meet your reader expectations? Explain.
2. Read Jonathan's narrative from the point of view of a writer. Do you see all the elements of narrative he should include? Explain.

NARRATIVE MEMOIR

1. Tells a story about an event that happened to the author or someone the author knows
2. Includes descriptive details
3. Is usually subjective, but in the case of a memoir, it can be objective
4. Can be organized chronologically or spatially
5. Uses transitions to move the action smoothly from one point to the next
6. Has a defined beginning, middle and end
7. Sometimes builds emotional tension
8. May be written from first- or third-person point of view
9. Usually includes other individuals
10. May, but does not have to, include dialogue
11. Provides a **conclusion** that indicates that the experience is over and any problems have been resolved or no longer exist
12. Is usually written in past tense
13. May or may not include a lesson that was learned from the experience

Chapter 5

Reading and Writing Definition

HOW TO READ DEFINITION

Reading definition goes beyond looking up a word in a dictionary, also known as finding the **denotative** definition. Although that is usually the first form of definition that people rely on, longer, more subjective definitions—or **connotative** definitions—also provide more descriptive explanations of a term. Connotative definitions frequently incorporate **exemplification, description,** and even **personal narrative** to give the reader a definition with more depth than a standard dictionary can normally provide.

Denotative Definitions

Denotative definitions provide explanations of words in simple, direct, and objective language. In addition to the meanings, dictionaries provide information about the word: its pronunciation, part of speech, and etymology or origin. The most well-known dictionary that provides the best background and the fullest denotative definition is the *Oxford English Dictionary,* informally known as the OED. In the OED, researchers can find out when the word they are looking for first came into use with a particular meaning. Other specialized dictionaries, such as those that provide meanings for slang, medical terms, real-estate terms, literary terms, legal terms, and so forth, are also especially helpful when students do research.

Look at the following definition from a *Webster's Students Dictionary*:

Like (lik), *adj.* [AS. *Gelic*, fr. *ge-* + *lic* body, and orig. meaning, having the same body or shape, and hence, like] 1. Resembling; similar; as, a face *like* an angel's; specif.: a. Characteristic of; as, such conduct was *like* him. b. Indicative of; as, it looks *like* good fishing. c. Inclined toward; as, I feel *like* taking a walk. 2. Colloquial. Likely: as, they are *like* to meet again. *–adv.* 1. In a manner characteristic of; so as to equal in speed, skill, etc.; as, no one can recite *like* her. 2. In the manner of one that is; as, he ran *like* mad. 3. Likely; probably; as, *like* enough he will come. *–conj.* In the same manner or to the same extent or degree as. *–n.* that which is like another; counterpart.

As a person who needs the definition of a term such as *like*, you might become confused with so lengthy an entry. However, this dictionary breaks down the explanation in several ways:

- (lik)—pronunciation
- adj., adv., conj., and n.—the different parts of speech in which *like* can be used
- []—origin of the word in brackets
- 1., 2.—definitions of the word broken down by part of speech
- a., b., c.—further ways the word can be broken down
- "as,"—an example in a phrase or sentence
- "Colloquial"—special meaning in regional speech

Because *like* has various meanings, you will need to know the context of *like* in the material you are reading to determine the correct definition. For example, "resembling" and "indicative of" are clearly two different definitions, which depend on their context for meaning.

Exercise 1

1. Look up several of the following words in a standard dictionary, copy the definitions, and write a brief descriptive paragraph explaining what you found.

light	nature
mark	point
play	root
snap	mother
high	toast

2. Go to the library and find the OED. Copy the definitions of two of the words that you already looked up. Write a paragraph comparing and contrasting the standard dictionary entry with the OED.

READERS' EXPECTATIONS FOR
DENOTATIVE DEFINITIONS

1. Pronunciation
2. Part of speech
3. Origin of the word in brackets
4. Definitions broken down by part of speech
5. An example in a phrase or sentence for clarity
6. Any regional meanings

---

3. Find a recently published dictionary of slang and copy the definitions of the words from the above list. Write a paragraph explaining how the meanings differ from a standard dictionary and the OED.

Connotative Definition

The second kind of definition, connotative, attaches emotional or personal meaning to certain terms. For example, while a *home* is normally considered a residence, to think of *home* in terms of family, love, and warmth is to attach a connotative or secondary meaning to the word. When you read paragraphs that define a term, you can expect the writer to use patterns or modes of development such as **narration, exemplification, description,** or **process analysis.** Read the following **exemplification** paragraph and you will find that the author incorporated a **denotative definition** and numerous examples to define the term *mother* even further. Analyze the paragraph using your reading activities and highlight the denotative definition and underline the connotative definition.

Mothers

Mother's Day is the one day set aside to honor the woman who gave birth to a child/children or who raised the child/children as her own. When we think of our mothers, we frequently recall incidents such as the time she left work early to be present at a recital or when we were sick, and she stayed up all night at our bedside. The qualities of love, dedication, sacrifice, concern, and nurturing appear instantly in those incidents, and we have an image in our minds of a woman who is forever young and always there when we need her. Today's mom, however, has changed somewhat from Hallmark's saccharine depiction. The contemporary mom, in many cases, has replaced the apron (she probably doesn't even own one) with a briefcase and her time embroidering with chauffeuring children to different activities. Homemade cookies are now baked from the rolls of dough found in the refrigerated section in the grocery store, and pizza delivery is now a routine way to provide dinner. Mothers may have changed in their activities, but we know that their love and care haven't.

Look at how the paragraph has been analyzed according to the reading activities that you have been practicing. The gray shaded words indicate the denotative definition, and the underlined words the connotative definitions.

Mothers

Mother's Day is the one day set aside to honor the woman who gave birth to a child/children or who raised the child/children as her own. When we think of our mothers, we frequently recall incidents such as the time she left work early to be present at a recital or when we were sick, and she stayed up all night at our bedside. The qualities of love, dedication, sacrifice, concern, and nurturing appear instantly in those incidents, and we have an image in our minds of a woman who is forever young and always there when we need her. Today's mom, however, has changed somewhat from Hallmark's saccharine depiction. The contemporary mom, in many cases, has replaced the apron (she probably doesn't even own one) with a briefcase and her time embroidering with chauffeuring children to different activities. Homemade cookies are now baked from the rolls of dough found in the refrigerated section in the grocery store, and pizza delivery is now a routine way to provide dinner. Mothers may have changed in their activities, but we know that their love and care haven't.

In comparing your highlighted paragraph with the one above, you should have discovered several interesting points. First, according to the

Merriam-Webster's Collegiate Dictionary online, the definition of *mother* is the following: "**1 a**: a female parent **b** (1): a woman in authority; *specifically*: the superior of a religious community of women (2): an old or elderly woman." None of those words appear in the paragraph; however, a paraphrasing of the first definition, "a female parent," is given when the author writes, "the woman who gave birth to us or who raised us as her children." The fact that the terminology is not quoted exactly from the dictionary but is paraphrased does not change the fact that this is still a denotative definition. At this point the author has not added anything personal or subjective.

Second, because you read the material that preceded the unmarked paragraph, you were probably expecting examples. The author provided them throughout the paragraph. However, you were only prepared for two kinds of writing: **definition** and **exemplification.** The author used a third, **comparison-and-contrast.** By using this pattern of development, the author appeals to readers who might know a mother who wears aprons and enjoys embroidering; but the author also shows how mothers have evolved. The author changes her style to emphasize the changes in mothers' activities instead of mothers themselves by indicating that they have not stopped providing for their families. Instead, they have simply found more convenient ways to perform the same loving duties while still completing other tasks that mothers who lived decades ago might not have had to do.

Another way writers incorporate definition is through the use of **extended definition.** By recognizing that people, as well as dictionaries, have multiple meanings of a word, an author can write about what one word means to himself or herself. The previous reading was written as nonfiction prose, but many writers incorporate extended definition in their creative pieces. Read the following excerpt from Sandra Cisneros's chapter, "My Name," taken from the novel *The House on Mango Street.*

My Name

    In English my name means hope. In Spanish it
means too many letters. It means sadness, it means
waiting. It is like the number nine. A muddy color.
It is the Mexican records my father plays on Sunday
mornings when he is shaving, songs like sobbing.
    It was my great-grandmother's name and now it is
mine. She was a horse woman too, born like me in the
Chinese year of the horse—which is supposed to be
bad luck if you're born female—but I think this is a

```
Chinese lie because the Chinese, like the Mexicans,
don't like their women strong.
```

Unless you have read the novel or know what the word for hope is in Spanish, you won't know the actual word the **narrator** is describing. The word, however, is not really the issue. Rather the narrator's feelings about her *name* are key to the messages in this chapter. Here, the narrator is using various devices to define her name connotatively. Reread the two paragraphs and find characteristics from other patterns of development you have read about. Highlight the word to be defined and determine how the words defining the term are used.

My Name

```
    In English my name means hope. In Spanish it means
too many letters. It means sadness, it means wait-
ing. It is like the number nine. A muddy color. It is
the Mexican records my father plays on Sunday morn-
ings when he is shaving, songs like sobbing.
    It was my great-grandmother's name and now it is
mine. She was a horse woman too, born like me in the
Chinese year of the horse—which is supposed to be
bad luck if you're born female—but I think this is a
Chinese lie because the Chinese, like the Mexicans,
don't like their women strong.
```

Compare your findings with the one above. Although the two paragraphs are written as a connotative definition of the narrator's name, she also uses other modes to explain her feelings. The underlined words indicate connotative definitions. The words with a curved line indicate **figurative language** using metaphor and simile. The sentences in brackets give personal narrative. The paragraph about the narrator's great-grandmother gives a contrasting perspective about the name. Instead of asserting that the name suggests weakness or unpleasant images, the name, when associated with the narrator's great-grandmother, indicates strength. Thus, this excerpt of creative writing incorporates definition to inform while entertaining the reader.

Exercise 2: Reading Analysis

1. Using the two paragraphs from "My Name," explain how the first sentence could be considered a denotative definition.

READER EXPECTATIONS FOR
CONNOTATIVE DEFINITIONS

1. Some form of denotative definition for initial clarification
2. Subjective or emotional explanation
3. Use of different patterns of development
4. In extended definitions, multiple examples

2. How do metaphor and simile advance your understanding of the narrator's name?
3. What is the narrator's name? What kind of dictionary did you use to find it?

HOW TO WRITE DEFINITION

Unless you are asked to write an extended definition, you will usually incorporate denotative and connotative definitions to develop a longer work. Many instructors like to see definitions used in the introduction of an essay to establish background information for the body of the paper. An added benefit for using definition in the introduction is that it gives your audience an immediate understanding of how you will be using a specific term, especially if that word has multiple meanings. You can narrow your topic from the outset and ensure that your readers are limited to your choice of development.

Step One—Know Your Term

To begin, you must have a term that will be central to the development of your assignment. If it is a specialized term, you might have to use resources beyond your standard dictionary. For example, if you are writing a literary paper, a literary handbook like C. Hugh Holman's *A Handbook to Literature* (1980) or M.H. Abram's *A Glossary of Literature Terms* (2005) will help you define examples of **figurative language,** styles, theories, and so forth. (Refer to "Romanticism" in Chapter 3 for an example of definition.) Sometimes you can look in your textbooks for definitions of key terms. If you need to include characteristics, be sure to copy them also. You might need to provide dates, causes, examples, and so forth.

Step Two—Decisions: To Quote or to Paraphrase?

Once you have located your definition, you must decide whether to quote it or paraphrase it. (Refer to "Mothers" in this chapter for an example of a paraphrased definition.) If you want to use the author's definition word-for-word, you will have to use quotation marks and will need to cite your source in parenthesis at the end of the quotation or at the end of the sentence. If you prefer to paraphrase the definition, you must change the wording significantly, and you will have to cite the source of the paraphrased definition if it is not common knowledge. In the paragraph "Mothers," the author did not use documentation for her paraphrased definition because most people know the common meaning of *mother*.

Step Three—Prewriting

If you are giving the definition for background information, you should give several examples of the term to familiarize your reader with your understanding of the term. However, if you will be writing an extended definition, you might begin with a prewriting exercise, such as clustering, to generate examples, characteristics, qualities, emotions, and so forth.

Step Four—The First Draft

1. Select one of the following terms and write a single paragraph definition, incorporating both connotative and denotative definitions. Remember to keep your readers' expectations in mind as you write.

woman or man	teacher
car	brother
doll	kitchen

2. After you have completed the paragraph, use the Evaluation Rubric at the end of the chapter to see how well you developed your paragraph. You may complete this as a self-evaluation or as a peer evaluation.

   In the following introductory paragraph, Sarah writes a definition paragraph about the term *doll*.

Society's Blindness

In the traditional language of most people, the term *doll* refers to a small, life-like image that a child plays with. This toy can be in the form of a female figure, like a Barbie Doll; an infant, like a Cabbage Patch doll; or anything in-between. Most people would not refer to a GI Joe as a doll. Instead, most call him an *action figure*, distancing the image of a male from the toy females traditionally play with. However, in keeping with the sexist approach, the term *doll* has also been used to refer to a female, usually in a slang way. In fact, a doll, like its toy counterpart, is usually referring to a "pretty but often empty-headed young woman" (*Merriam-Webster's Collegiate Dictionary* online). No male would want to be referred to as a *doll* nor would he want his *action figure* to be considered empty-headed either. Yet there is another definition that was popularized in the 1960s but has lost its wide circulation: a doll was used to mean drugs. In Jacqueline Susann's novel <u>Valley of the Dolls</u>, she was not talking about a toy nor about a slang meaning for a woman. While the title can be seen as one that has a double meaning, it became popularized as an addiction to prescription drugs. At the time of Susann's novel, society could not see the pervasive problem that many women were suffering from, and even though it has been brought out into public awareness today, addiction to prescription drugs continues to be a silent addiction that women suffer from and that many people in society, even doctors, are blind to.

Use the Evaluation Rubric that follows to evaluate the above paragraph. Remember that Sarah is writing an introductory paragraph rather than a full essay, so she might not have all the elements on the rubric. You will find, however, that she incorporated many of the criteria in her introduction into a topic that is not simply a definition of the term *doll*.

Step Five—The Final Draft

After you have revised and edited the paper based on the Evaluation Rubric, prepare the paper for submission. Be sure to reread it once more before you turn it in. Sometimes you might find an error that you missed in your last proofreading. If you can catch it and correct it before you submit it, then it will be one less error your instructor will find.

EVALUATION RUBRIC

The author	Yes	No	Almost	NA
Definition				
1. incorporated a denotative definition.				
2. used a quotation.				
3. paraphrased the definition.				
4. expanded the definition with				
• characteristics				
• qualities				
• personal feelings				
• personal experiences				
• emotions				
• examples				
5. developed the paragraph using different patterns of development:				
• description				
• comparison				
• contrast				
• figurative language				
• personal narrative				
• exemplification				
Structure				
6. began with a topic sentence.				
7. organized the paragraph logically.				
8. developed the ideas fully.				
9. ended with a concluding sentence.				

10. What is the strength of this paragraph?

11. What suggestions would you make to the author to improve this paragraph?

12. Did you understand the denotative definition the author provided?

13. Did the connotative definitions expand your understanding of the topic? Explain.

14. Which definition do you find unnecessary? Why?

Exercise 3: Writing Practice

Follow the directions and then use the rubric below to see how well you met the readers' expectations of writing definition.

1. Write a definition paragraph about one of the following topics.

my house	my best friend
my child	my job
my sister	my favorite pair of shoes

2. Write an expanded definition using one of the choices above.

Use the following rubric when reading definition writing. Respond to the writing prompts at the end of the rubric. NA stands for *Not Applicable* and NI means *Not Included*.

READER EXPECTATIONS FOR DEFINITION WRITING

Definition Writing	Excellent	Good	Fair	NA NI
1. The definition appeared early in the selection.				
2. The denotative definition was clearly written.				
3. The connotative definition(s) expanded my understanding of the term.				
4. The connotative definition(s) included				
characteristics				
qualities				
emotions				
feelings				
personal experiences				
metaphors				
similes				
examples				

Definition Writing	Excellent	Good	Fair	NA NI
5. The development was expanded through the use of				
appropriate organization				
description				
comparison				
contrast				
personal narrative				
exemplification				

1. Did you find the thesis/topic sentence of this essay/paragraph? What is it?
2. Does the writer support the thesis/topic sentence? Give examples.
3. What are the strengths of this paper?
4. What one weakness do you think should be corrected in this paper?
5. What other comments would you like to make about this descriptive writing?

Chapter 6

Reading and Writing
Division and Classification

HOW TO READ DIVISION

Division and **classification** are related modes of development that are usually discussed together; however, the modes are different from one another. A division paragraph breaks a single item into many of the components that form a whole. For example, if you look at the Table of Contents in this text, you will see that each chapter is divided into various parts or smaller units, creating an orderly approach to instruction. Another example of division is a house. A house does not normally consist of one large room, and even when it does, for example a loft in a converted building, the residents use dividers to create spaces with certain purposes—living room, kitchen, bedroom, and so forth—and separate them from the other spaces.

Consider the following scenario.

> You have an aging parent who is still in good health but who needs more attention and activity than you are able to provide. You are not familiar with the services that facilities provide for elder care. One day you decide to drive by the various homes near your residence and gather pamphlets that advertise the services each provides.

The material you are about to read describes four different facilities and their services, which are divided into smaller, more specific units that are part of the entire package. Examine the services described inside the brochures provided by the four different homes. Use your reading skills. Answer the questions that follow the brochures.

Ads

FIRESIDE MANOR
A CONVALESCENT COMMUNITY
WE PROVIDE ATTENTIVE
CARE FOR OUR CLIENTS.

- ACUTE CARE
- POST OPERATIVE
- ACTIVITIES DIRECTOR
- DIETARY NEEDS
  - NUTRITIONIST ON DUTY DAILY
- CHRONICALLY ILL CARE
  - AMBULATORY
  - 24-HOUR MEDICAL STAFF SERVICES
- DINING ROOM OR TRAY SERVICES
- BEAUTY SALON
- LIBRARY

Hospice of the Hills
Serenity for your Loved one
LOVING CARE FOR OUR RESIDENTS

☞ 24-HOUR CARE

☞ 24-HOUR NURSING STAFF

☞ DOCTORS ON CALL

☞ PRIVATE ROOMS

☞ 24-HOUR RELIGIOUS CONSULTANT

☞ GUESTROOMS

☞ FINAL PREPARATION AND TRANSPORTATION

Exercise 1: Reading Division

1. Which services are not needed for the parent in the scenario?
2. Which services are best for the parent, based on the description in the scenario?
3. If money were not a concern, which facility would you choose for the parent in the scenario? Why?

Consider the following paragraph about the choice of an elder care facility for the writer's mother. Remember that when you read division as a pattern of development, you are looking for parts that create a whole. In this case, the whole is the set of services offered by a care provider. Use your reading skills to look for the parts that satisfy the writer.

Choices

Because my mother is still an active, vital woman who needs the companionship, activities, and care I cannot provide, she moved into an assisted living facility, The Towers of Cliff Manor Estates. This was a perfect choice for her because her apartment is quite large, accommodating much of her furniture and giving her a sense of living at "home."

Many of the other facilities we visited offered a
large single room that was frequently shared by a
roommate. The Towers has several floors on which individuals with different needs live. My mother has
the companionship of others who are in similar
health condition, active, and relatively independent. The friends she has made in the building are
mainly her neighbors who enjoy many of the same activities offered by the staff: gardening, bridge,
and weekly trips to the mall and grocery store. Another component of The Towers is the care they provide. My mother is on a floor that has a registered
nurse to dispense medication three times a day for
residents who need it. The nurse also offers daily
blood pressure screening, nutrition advice for residents with special dietary needs, exercise classes,
and office hours for personal consultation. The living conditions, residents, and care are components
that answer the needs of many looking for an assisted living facility.

As you read the paragraph, you probably noted that the author,
Mark, breaks down the services offered at his mother's facility into individual elements. He also uses **contrast** to describe how his mother's living quarters are different from those offered by other senior citizen
homes.

Exercise 2: Reading Division

1. How many of the services offered in the brochure did Mark mention
   as he described his mother's new home?
2. Did Mark's mother choose the same facility you chose?
3. Why do you think Mark's mother chose The Towers of Cliff Manor
   Estates?

HOW TO READ CLASSIFICATION

A classification paragraph differs from a division paragraph through
presentation of the material. Instead of taking a single piece of information and breaking it down into various parts, the writer categorizes many
items on the basis of shared characteristics. In "Choices," we can discover how classification works. The facts about the mother are that she
is a healthy, older woman who needs companionship and activity. Her

son has no extra time to provide for his mother's needs and knows nothing about the different kinds of elder care facilities. If he had known, he would not have visited inappropriate care facilities near his own home. Look at the description of each facility. If you create a cluster for the large concept, elder care facilities, you will come up with **divisions** that can be categorized/classified later. Here the division mode of development will help you begin the prewriting for **classification.**

Apparently, there were more than four options for Mark, but for personal reasons, he limited his search to facilities near him, and from reading his paragraph, we can conclude that his mother is satisfied with The Tower. From the cluster, we can see that even though the kinds of care facilities are numerous, they can be classified, as in the table following the cluster by the kind of accommodations they offer, the clientele they accept, the specialized services they give, and the activities they provide. By classifying the categories, it's possible to see that not all facilities are appropriate for the author's mother.

Cluster for Elder Care Facilities

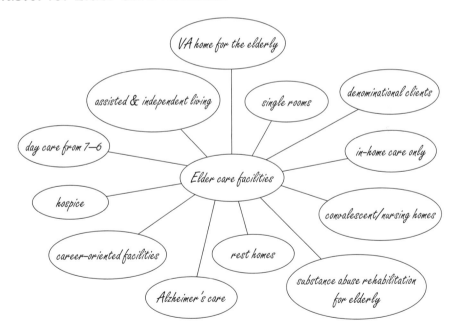

CLASSIFICATION OF ELDER CARE FACILITIES

Specialized Services	Accommodations	Clientele	Activities
Alzheimer's care	day-care drop off	specific denominations	trips
Substance abuse rehab	single room living	career-oriented	group activities
Nursing care	apartment	veterans	physical therapy
Hospice	cottages	terminal	educational activities
Rest homes	in-home care	chronically ill	religious services

The key to clear **classification** is selecting categories that are as limited as possible to prevent overlapping. If you look at Specialized Services and Clientele, you might think that they could be combined; however, some facilities recruit clientele with specific kinds of interests while others attract those with special needs. A retired teacher might prefer a facility that is a community of retired teachers, but if he or she has Alzheimer's disease or needs specific and constant medical care, the client might choose a facility that offers specialized services. Or, the teacher could ignore "Accommodations" in favor of living among other retired teachers, regardless of the accommodations and activities. To categorize the facilities Mark visited, we have to look at the brochures. Fireside Manor and Hospice of the Hills provide specialized services that the mother does not need. The Towers and Valley View, on the other hand, provide a variety of accommodations and activities that might appeal to a relatively independent client. In the case of Mark's mother, varied activities and accommodations were her preferences, and fortunately, the facility that offered her her preferred accommodations also provided the kind of activities she enjoyed. Therefore, to categorize the four facilities that Mark found, he would simply have to match the facility with the categories that are listed.

Exercise 3: Reading Classification

1. Find a copy of the *Yellow Pages* and look up one of the following topics:

restaurants	doctors	schools	churches

How did the compilers categorize your topic? Were the categories overlapping or distinct? Did the categories help you find information easily? Explain.

2. Visit several of the following locations:

    a zoo   your campus   a shopping mall   a hospital

Find a map of the place you visit. Examine the map for its organizational layout. Are certain areas/activities grouped together or is everything jumbled together without apparent logic? How are things categorized? Explain how the maps are examples of both division and classification modes.

Analyze the following introduction written by another student, Sue-Li, who has done research in the subject and used the above prewriting strategies. Rely on the reading techniques you have used earlier to help you discover the different elements she incorporated.

Senior Citizen Facilities

In recent years, the need for senior citizen care has grown enormously. In the past, elders moved in with one of their children or a daughter gave up marriage in favor of staying home and caring for her aging parent, especially if the parent was a widowed mother. Today, however, many young women choose marriage or independent living over staying home. Today, two incomes are needed in family households, or the requirement to relocate for one's career prevents adult children from providing personal care for their parents. Time, income, and patience seem to be in short supply in today's households when an additional person comes in with special needs and the desire for normal attention. Thus, the care industry filled the need. Companies expanded the traditional nursing or convalescent homes that were created primarily for individuals who are sick and in need of medical attention but not sick enough for hospitalization. New facilities include homes for healthy or moderately healthy senior citizens who might need some assistance in their daily routine or who want a community of relatively same-age individuals who can share common memories and participate in common interests. Now consumers have a variety of facilities to choose from: those that offer specialized services, varieties of accommodations, communities for specific groups, or a wide variety of activities.

This paragraph introduces a classification essay that will be divided into four paragraphs, one for each of the kinds of elder care facilities mentioned in the thesis. Let's look at how to read this paragraph. The following points should have been marked: the topic or introductory sentence, the first mention of senior citizen facilities, any definitions of the topic, the **division of the topic** into classes, and the *thesis sentence*. Your paragraph should be marked like the one that follows.

Senior Citizen Facilities

In recent years, the need for senior citizen care has grown enormously. In the past, elders moved in with one of their children or a daughter gave up marriage in favor of staying home and caring for her aging parent, especially if the parent was a widowed mother. Today, however, many young women choose marriage or independent living over staying home. Today, two incomes are needed in family households, or the requirement to relocate for one's career prevents adult children from providing personal care for their parents. Time, income, and patience seem to be in short supply in today's households when an additional person comes in with special needs and the desire for normal attention. Thus, the care industry filled the need. Companies expanded the traditional nursing or convalescent homes that were created primarily for individuals who are sick and in need of medical attention but not sick enough for hospitalization. New facilities include homes for healthy or moderately healthy senior citizens who might need some assistance in their daily routine or who want a community of relatively same-age individuals who can share common memories and participate in common interests. *Now consumers have a variety of facilities to choose from:* **those that offer specialized services, varieties of accommodations, communities for specific groups, or a wide variety of activities.**

Notice also that Sue-Li included background history about how the elderly used to be cared for and contrasted it with contemporary

---

READER EXPECTATIONS FOR DIVISION AND CLASSIFICATION

Division

1. Large concept is introduced.
2. Concept is broken into smaller parts.
3. Smaller parts are the sum of the whole.

Classification

1. Multiple objects, ideas, concepts, locations, and so forth, are introduced.
2. Distinct categories are created.
3. Each category is defined either denotatively or connotatively.
4. Individual items are classified under each category.
5. The division pattern of development can be incorporated into writing a classification paper.

---

care. She has also contrasted the feelings of the young women of the past with those of young women of today. Now she must explain what examples in each classification do and, using the variety of facilities available, classify them into the correct categories.

HOW TO WRITE DIVISION AND CLASSIFICATION

To write division and classification papers, we are going to begin with the material discussed above and then use Annette's work as a model for your assignment. What is especially important is the use of clustering. Instead of using this prewriting technique to generate ideas that Annette is already familiar with, she used it as a way to present information she had found as she researched her topic. She began with the larger topic, senior citizen care facilities, and broke down the facilities in twelve different ways, reflecting different aspects. What she did not do was move directly into naming the specific care facilities. That's a step that will come as Annette moves into classification.

Step One—Prewriting

Let's begin the process with subjects most people are familiar with so you will have to do little or no research. Without naming specific examples you will work with, create a cluster for one of the following topics:

- Movies
- Pets

- Restaurants
- Religions

Use the senior citizen care facility cluster as your model. Below is the cluster Annette created to find ways to divide movies into their various kinds.

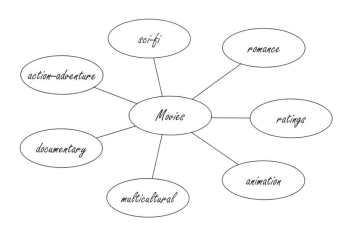

Step Two—Determining Categories

The above cluster clearly works as a way to define many of the movies that are made today and as such can lead to a good introduction to a classification paper. However, because most ways to divide the movies listed are not distinct categories, Annette will have difficulty classifying specific movies. For example, *Shrek* is a movie that can fit into animation, action–adventure, and romance. But what about an older movie like *Driving Miss Daisy*? Annette left out the drama category into which many movies might be classified. There is, however, one category mentioned that can be used as a way to classify movies without danger of overlapping: ratings. Ratings provide distinct characteristics for defining a movie.

Step Three—Develop Your Thesis

Now that you have a subject, categories that you will use to classify, and examples you can use, what is the point? Why are you writing this paper? When writers examine a subject using division and classification, they could be doing so to write an informative paper (government spending, the family court system, education in the United States), a persuasive paper (government spending should be limited; the family court system has grown too large to be effective; the system for teacher training should be a standardized method used in all states), or an entertaining paper (government spending ruined my wedding; the joys of a family court reporter; ways to survive graduate school without going broke). Looking at the thesis for Senior Citizen Facilities, we see that Sue-Li wrote an informative paper: "Now consumers have a variety of facilities to choose from: those that offer specialized services, varieties of accommodations, communities for specific groups, or a wide variety of activities."

Before you write your **thesis,** determine the purpose of your paper and the audience to whom it is directed. Remember the following important points.

Points about the Thesis

The thesis

- is the controlling idea of the essay.
- should be an assertion rather than a question.
- should reflect the purpose of the essay—to inform, persuade, or entertain.
- should be as concise as possible—one or two sentences.
- may list the points that you will make in your paper, but it does not have to.

Now take some time to think about your purpose, audience, and the point or points that you want to make. When you finish, write several sentences that could be your thesis and share them with your classmates. If they have questions or feel that the examples do not express the topic completely or clearly, you know that revision is in order.

Here is the first draft of the thesis written by Annette, who is working on the movie topic:

> Today's parents have enough worries to concern them without having to worry about the movies their children go see; therefore, many parents limit their children's viewing by relying on the rating systems used to classify each film.

It definitely needs revising, as it is somewhat repetitive and unnecessarily lengthy. Here is her revision.

> Today, parents use a standard rating system that has many more classifications than it did in the past to limit their children's movie selections.

The author has chosen to write an informative paper, classifying the movies according to standard ratings. In her introduction, however, she has also incorporated the points she used in her cluster, thus developing her paper through the division pattern. Read her paragraph and notice how she moves from general to specific.

The Movie Dilemma

Choosing the appropriate movie to spend your evening viewing whether it is alone, with a special person, or with your family has become a challenge. I remember when I was growing up, I could walk into almost any romantic, comedy, action-adventure, or science fiction movie, knowing that I would be entertained tastefully. My mother might have raised an eyebrow if I wanted to see a romantic movie starring Elvis Presley and Ann Margret instead of one with Doris Day and Rock Hudson or Audrey Hepburn and any leading man. But she knew that a few "racy" scenes would not damage my "innocence." Today, however, "racy" has become erotic, and regardless of whether the movie is a drama, animation, or multicultural, there is always the fear that children will be exposed to violence, explicit sexuality, inappropriate language, or nudity that they are not prepared to watch or sufficiently mature to understand. Today's parents have enough concerns without having to worry about the movies their children see. Today, parents use a standard rating system that has many more classifications than it did in the past to limit their children's movie selections.

Notice that Annette did not include the ratings nor did she include titles of any movies. Those will come within the body of the essay.

Because she has a firm understanding of the categories she will use in her paper, she can now move forward to develop her ideas. Like her, you must have your purpose in mind. She has chosen to write an informative paper, and her thesis is structured as such. Now she—and you—must not only know the classifications but also what they mean. In case the audience is unclear, writers should always provide a brief definition—either denotative or connotative—to help the reader understand their categories. Take a moment before you begin the body paragraphs and jot down a brief definition, explanation, or background about the categories. Below are the explanations about the movie ratings that Annette wrote.

G – for a general audience of any age

PG – recommends parental guidance—language, some crude humor, and material unsuitable for children.

PG13 – recommends parental guidance especially for children younger than thirteen—objectionable thematic references, language, adventure action, violence, or sensuality

R – restricted for viewers eighteen or older or for individuals seventeen or younger with a parent or adult companion—nudity, strong language, intense violence, and mature themes

NC17 – refuses admission to anyone seventeen or younger

When you are doing prewriting of this sort, you don't have to write in complete sentences any more than you did when you did clustering. This is informal and will be worked into the body of the essay in a formal way.

Share your definitions with a friend and ask her to see if she understands what you are saying about the categories. Regardless of her reply, find another friend, and ask him if the categories are clear. It is usually best to try to find more than one reader to look over your paper.

Now, make sure you have specific examples that you will insert into the discussion of each category.

Step Four—Writing the First Draft

You should now be ready to write your first draft.

Points for Writing First Draft

- Let your thesis be your guide: Always return to it to make sure you are supporting it and developing it.
- Remain focused: If you are writing an informative paper, don't slip into persuasion.
- Be sure to include the examples to support your categories.
- Give a little explanation about the examples because your audience might not be familiar with the examples you chose.
- If you notice that your examples do not fit the requirements of your category as you are writing, change the category or find appropriate examples.
- When you write your conclusion, begin with your thesis and either draw conclusions based on your information or state your personal opinions.

- Don't worry about mechanics or construction too much right now; you'll be able to revise your paper after you've written the first draft.

Gather your prewriting notes and your materials, and find the right spot to write your paper. Remember that even though this is your first draft, you want to do the best job you can so that you won't have too many revisions to make.

Step Five—Peer Editing

Before you begin editing your own draft, take a moment to **evaluate** Annette's first draft. Use the Peer Evaluation Guide to determine what areas need revision.

The Movie Dilemma

Choosing the appropriate movie to spend your evening viewing whether it is alone, with a special person, or with your family has become a challenge. I remember that when I was growing up, I could walk into almost any romantic, comedy, action-adventure, or science fiction movie, knowing that I would be entertained tastefully. My mother might have raised an eyebrow if I wanted to see a romantic movie starring Elvis Presley and Ann Margret instead of one with Doris Day and Rock Hudson or Audrey Hepburn and any leading man. But she knew that a few "racy" scenes would not damage my "innocence." Today, however, "racy" has become erotic, and regardless of whether the movie is a drama, animation, or multicultural, there is always the fear that children will be exposed to violence, explicit sexuality, inappropriate language, or nudity that they are not prepared to watch or sufficiently mature to understand. Today's parents have enough concerns without having to worry about the movies their children see. Today, parents use a standard movie rating system that has many more classifications than it did in the past to limit their children's movie selections.

If their children are eighteen years old or younger, parents may allow them to choose from movies labeled G for a general audience of any age or PG, a category that recommends parental guidance because of language, some crude humor, and material unsuitable for children. PG13 is another category that recommends parental guidance with parents being strongly cautioned to give guidance to children younger than thirteen because the movie may contain some objectionable thematic references, language, adventure action, violence, or sensuality that some children are not ready for. On the other hand, movies rated R are restricted for viewers eighteen or older or for individuals seventeen or younger with a parent or adult companion because of scenes of nudity, strong language, intense violence, and mature themes; and NC17 admits no one seventeen or younger. This system, while only as good as the ticket salespeople, is better than no system at all for concerned parents.

Thus, parents now have a better system with more categories for guidance than they did years ago.

By completing a peer evaluation with an anonymous student's paper, you might be inclined to make comments and mark criteria that you might not otherwise.

PEER EVALUATION GUIDE FOR DIVISION AND CLASSIFICATION ESSAY

The student	Yes	No	Almost	NA
Division				
1. chose a broad subject.				
2. divided the topic into parts.				
3. divided the topic adequately.				
4. provided a brief definition/ explanation of the topic.				
Classification				
5. provided at least three categories.				
6. provided relatively distinct categories.				
7. provided enough examples to develop the categories.				
8. showed no or little evidence of examples overlapping into more than one category.				

The student	Yes	No	Almost	NA
9. explained how overlapping could exist if needed. _____				

Structure

	Yes	No	Almost	NA
10. constructed an introduction in the following ways:				
• General to specific _____				
• Background information provided, if applicable _____				
• Definition(s) provided, if applicable _____				
• Thesis was the last sentence _____				
11. developed each category in a separate paragraph, or if necessary, combined two categories into a single paragraph. _____				
12. provided transitions between paragraphs. _____				
13. provided transitions between ideas within paragraphs. _____				
14. maintained focus _____				
15. provided a well-stated thesis in the conclusion. _____				
16. provided a conclusion developed with either opinions or conclusions. _____				
17. ended with a good concluding sentence. _____				

Short Answer Responses

1. Do you have a better understanding of the topic than before you began reading? Explain.
2. What is the strength of this paper?
3. What suggestion can you make to strengthen the paper?

Hopefully, you saw the following problems discussed after the Peer Evaluation.

Points 7 and 8 are in serious need of revision, as Annette did not provide any examples to put into the categories.

Points 11 and 12 are also in need of revision, as Annette wrote only one paragraph, putting all the categories into the paragraph without full discussion and development.

Points 15–17 also need work, as Annette wrote only a one-sentence conclusion and her thesis is not restated well. She left out the main topic of the essay—movie ratings.

Now that you have had an opportunity to practice, it's your turn to complete an evaluation. Look at your own paper and read it from a reader's perspective instead of a writer's perspective. Be as honest as possible and try to find the problem areas. When you finish, share your paper and your evaluation profile with a fellow student or a volunteer reader so he or she can complete an evaluation also. Discuss the reader's responses. If you have time, find a second reader and go through the process again.

Step Six—Revision

Yes, most students hate revision; however, all writers recognize its importance and understand that even their best attempts do not always convey the message they want to send to their readers. The best way to determine that is by getting complete and honest feedback from someone not familiar with your writing. If the reader does not understand your paper, you must revise, as communication is the goal of writing.

Revision is *not* looking for the misspelled words or missing commas. That is editing, which comes after you have successfully revised your content. Below are steps you should follow to revise your paper successfully.

1. Look at your evaluation profile and find all the checkmarks under "No" and "Almost." Those are the points in your paper that need work. According to your reader(s), everything else is fine. Be sure to reread your material anyway, just to make sure that your reader(s) did not miss something.

2. If you do not understand what the reader had problems with, ask for clarification and guidance.

3. Begin making revisions. You might want to arrange a conference with your instructor at this point to make sure you are progressing correctly. Scheduling a second appointment when you finish revising might also help you catch something you did not see or help you smooth out wrinkles created by newly added or deleted information.

4. Look at the revisions Annette made in her movie paper. New material is in **bold.** Notice that she added a sentence in her introduction that was not required but that helps expand the ideas. She also moved the last sentence of her body paragraph to the last sentence of her conclusion.

The Movie Dilemma

Choosing the appropriate movie to spend your evening viewing whether alone, with a special person, or with your family has become a challenge. I remember that when I was growing up, I could walk into almost any romantic, comedy, action-adventure, or science fiction movie, knowing that I would be entertained tastefully. **I could even sit with my parents through romantic scenes without being embarrassed.** My mother might have raised an eyebrow if I wanted to see a romantic movie starring Elvis Presley and Ann Margret instead of one with Doris Day and Rock Hudson or Audrey Hepburn and any leading man. But she knew that a few "racy" scenes would not damage my "innocence." Today, however, "racy" has become erotic, and regardless of whether the movie is a drama, animation, or multicultural, there is always the fear that children will be exposed to violence, explicit sexuality, inappropriate language, or nudity that they are not prepared to watch or sufficiently mature to understand. Today's parents have enough concerns without having to worry about the movies their children see. Today, parents use a standard movie rating system that has many more classifications than it did in the past to limit their children's movie selections.

If their children are eighteen years old or younger, parents may allow them to choose from movies labeled G for a general audience of any age. **Shrek or Monsters, Inc. are great examples of movies for viewers of any age. They are funny, have elements of romance, and send messages viewers can learn from. Children will enjoy the animation, and adults should be able to recognize the satire in Shrek and the moral of the story in Monsters, Inc.**

The difference between G and PG is quite apparent. PG **is** a category that recommends parental guidance because of language, some crude humor, and material unsuitable for children. **Movies like Agent Cody Banks, What a Girl Wants, and Spirited Away are labeled PG. The comedies could be difficult for younger children to understand, and the language** definitely includes vocabulary that might be objectionable to parents but used with some restraint. **PG movies are difficult to find because producers seem**

to be making more PG13 films. These productions appeal to a wider audience. PG13 is another category that recommends parental guidance with parents being strongly cautioned to give guidance to children younger than thirteen because the movie may contain some objectionable thematic references, language, adventure action, violence, or sensuality that some children are not ready for. Movies like <u>Chicago</u>, <u>Anger Management</u>, and <u>Phone Booth</u> are categorized under PG13. These definitely are unsuitable for youngsters, and many adults may also object to the violence and overt sexuality. Even though <u>Chicago</u> won many Academy Awards, it was not intended for young or sensitive viewers.

Finally, movies rated R or NC17 or even X are made specifically for an adult audience. R-rated movies are restricted for viewers eighteen or older or for individuals seventeen or younger with a parent or adult companion because of scenes of nudity, strong language, intense violence, and mature themes. Because so many adults have spendable income, R-rated movies abound in the theaters. For example, seven R-rated movies, <u>House of 1000 Corpses</u>, <u>Dysfunctional Families</u>, <u>A Man Apart</u>, <u>Basic</u>, <u>Dreamcatcher</u>, <u>The Hunted</u>, and <u>Old School</u> are advertised in one theater with one movie rated G, four rated PG, and four rated PG13. On the other hand, NC17 movies are hard to find, and the only explanation of this category is that it admits no one seventeen or younger. One movie <u>Spun</u> is in that category. Finally, the X-rated movies are pornography and usually shown at "art" theaters that do not show other movies, especially those rated G or PG. <u>XX/XY</u> is one showing at a theater with other R-rated movies but with no other categories.

Thus, parents now have a better **movie rating** system with more categories for guidance than they did years ago. Unfortunately, the theaters appear to have different ratings for a single title. At some theaters, <u>Anger Management</u> was rated PG13 while at others it was rated R. At one theater <u>Phone Booth</u> was rated PG, and at another it was rated R—quite a difference. *This **updated** system, while only as good as the ticket salespeople, is better than no system at all for concerned parents.*

The revision that occurred in this sample paper came from a step Annette omitted in her prewriting: research. She did not take the time to go to the movie section of her newspaper to see which movies were playing and how they were rated. Taking that step then would have prevented the extra work that she had to do for revision. Now that the examples are added, readers who have seen the movies or who have heard about them will have a better understanding about their content.

Another point to note in the revision is that Annette did not have to begin from scratch. Many students believe that if they are required to revise, they have to start over. In fact, the opposite is true. Unless you are writing about the wrong topic, do not throw away what you have written. You can always add to what you have or salvage parts that can be inserted into new material.

Step Seven—Editing

Editing involves the correction of errors in grammar, mechanics, wording, and format. If you have a grammar handbook, you can discover how to correct errors such as sentence fragments, run-on sentences, subject–verb agreement, comma splices, pronoun–antecedent agreement, and so forth. If your instructor has given you directions for formatting, you can check those to make sure your margins, headings, and pagination are correct. You should also run your spell-checker one more time, especially if you added material or changed wording.

Once you have completed all your corrections, you can submit your paper.

EMERGENCY EDITING STEPS

- If you have to make last minute changes with a liquid correction fluid, make sure they are done neatly.
- If you have to cross out a word, do so with one line and preferably in black ink.
- If you have to insert or change a word, write it in black ink in the space above the line and in the spot where the word should go. Print it as neatly as possible.
- If you have to insert punctuation, write it in black ink in the space where it is needed.

Exercise 4: Writing Practice

Follow the directions and then use the Reader Expectations rubric below to see how well you met the readers' expectations of writing division and classification.

1. Look at one multipurpose room in your house and divide it into components. Write a **division** paragraph that describes each component using at least one other **pattern** for writing in this section.
2. Go to your local grocery store and **analyze** the method of classification. Remember, you need more than two classes, so refrigerated and non-refrigerated foods are categories that are still too broad. Write a paper that **classifies** the food in your grocery store and use several **patterns** of writing discussed in this section. Be sure to give examples of the foods in each category.

Use the following rubric when reading division and classification writing. Respond to the writing prompts at the end of the rubric. NA stands for *Not Applicable* and NI means *Not Included*.

READER EXPECTATIONS FOR DIVISION AND CLASSIFICATION

Division	Excellent	Good	Fair	NA NI
1. Large concept is introduced.				
2. Concept is broken into smaller parts.				
3. Smaller parts equal the sum of the whole.				
4. Some background information or definitions are given.				
Classification				
5. Multiple objects, ideas, concepts, locations, or so forth, are introduced.				
6. Distinct categories are created.				

Classification	Excellent	Good	Fair	NA NI
7. Each category is defined either denotatively or connotatively.				
8. Individual examples are classified under each category.				
9. Examples are explained.				
10. Division has been incorporated into writing the classification paper as necessary.				
11. The development was expanded through the use of examples.				

Short Answer Responses

1. Did you find the thesis/topic sentence of this essay/paragraph? What is it?
2. Does the writer support the thesis/topic sentence? Give examples and explanations.
3. What are the strengths of this paper?
4. What one weakness do you think should be corrected in this paper?
5. What other comments would you like to make about this division and classification writing?

Chapter 7

Reading and Writing Comparison and Contrast

HOW TO READ COMPARISON AND CONTRAST: DEFINITIONS

Many students confuse the terms **compare** and **contrast**, thinking they mean the same thing. To **compare** means to take two objects—people, animals, concepts, and so forth—and point out their similarities. You want to find as many characteristics as possible that they have in common. For example, if you have siblings who have gone to the same school you attended, you might have heard former teachers tell you, "You are just like your sister." They are making a comparison between two people. Sometimes history instructors want you to find comparable points between the causes of two wars or two strategies used to fight a war. A biology teacher might want you to **compare** an ant colony and a bee hive. An English instructor might want you to **compare** two poems or two characters in a novel. An art instructor might want you to **compare** two styles of painting. What they are asking you to do is to look at objects, concepts, writings, fictional characters, and behaviors to find their similarities. These assignments require higher level thinking skills because you have to **analyze** the objects and so forth for particular qualities and look at them individually to see which characteristics they share.

The same is true of **contrast**; however, when you complete a **contrast** exercise, you are finding the differences between two given elements. For example, your former teachers may have told you, "You are so different from your brother." Or the instructors cited in the above paragraph may change the assignment from "**compare**" or "find their similarities" to "**contrast**" and "find their differences."

Purposes

One purpose of comparison-and-contrast analysis is to present information. However, if you look at the previously mentioned assignments by instructors in different classes, you can see that there might be another purpose for writing in a comparison-and-contrast mode. The history instructor might want the students to compare and contrast battle strategies to determine which one is better, thus using this mode as a form of **argumentation.** The art instructor might ask a student to compare and contrast styles of paintings to encourage the student to make an **evaluation** of the styles from his or her own point of view. This kind of comparison-and-contrast exercise is frequently done when shoppers are trying to determine which brand to buy, which sofa would look better in their living room, which bank account will yield better interest, and so forth. Although you may be writing one of your first compare-and-contrast papers, you will find that you perform this kind of analysis in your daily life. You are simply formalizing a process that you have been working with for years.

Expectations for Reading Contrast

According to the definition of contrast, readers will be looking for differences between the topics to be discussed. These differences and details should be significant to the readers so that they can make an informed decision or evaluation. Thus, your skills in looking for details as you read will become important. You perform this kind of analysis in your daily life. For example, if you are looking for a watch, you might be very concerned about the color of the face. If you find two watches you like very much but one has a white face with black hands and the other has a gold face with gold hands, you might choose the former because it is easier for you to see. Some people who might not have trouble seeing would find background color irrelevant; however, details, such as the kinds of numbers (Arabic, Roman, or none at all), presence of a second hand, color of the face, or brand name might make a big difference to someone else in deciding which watch to buy.

Organization

There are generally two ways to present contrasting information. One pattern is known as **point-to-point,** where each point is countered immediately within the same paragraph. Very little development is made in point-to-point. The other method that can be used is **subject-to-subject.** In this pattern, an idea is more fully developed and can be countered within the same paragraph, moving into the opposite or a similar idea with the help of a transition, or it can be developed in the next paragraph with an equal amount of development.

If you have a topic that has very specific points to contrast, like the watch topic, you might consider the point-to-point, as each point needs little elaboration and can sometimes be contrasted within a single sentence. If, on the other hand, you have a broader topic that requires more description, exemplification, and so forth, you might consider subject-to-subject. When reading subject-to-subject organization, you might find that a writer develops the ideas in two separate, contrasting paragraphs.

Because comparison and contrast is simply a mode or pattern of development, the information is not normally written as an end in itself. It could be used in a complete article that ends with a conclusion that evaluates or attempts to persuade. For example, an editorial could be written to persuade readers to vote for a particular mayoral, presidential, or school board candidate by contrasting two competing individuals. It might end with the writer drawing conclusions and attempting to persuade readers why X candidate is the best. Therefore as a reader, you should not only expect relevant details to be contrasted, but you should also see a purpose for the use of the mode. Sometimes it might just be informative so as to provide details about a topic, and the material is used to support and develop a larger issue. At other times, it might be used to convey humor about a topic. As a reader, you should have some expectations about why the author chose to use comparison and contrast.

HOW TO READ CONTRAST

The following two paragraphs were written in response to an assignment requiring students to write about pets. In the first paragraph, the student writer, Julian, has two female cats, bought at approximately the same time and at the same place. They are almost the same age, and except for a few days, they have grown up together. Therefore, he will rely on observed behavior rather than on gathering information from others about their cats. Each sentence is numbered for easy reference later. In the second example, Shaunté's essay develops the same patterns as Julian's; however, her use of comparison and contrast differs somewhat from her classmate's. Using the points discussed above, read each paragraph looking for the expectations readers have of comparison and contrast.

- Highlight each time a contrast is made.
- Look for the specific details that are being contrasted.
- Identify the kind of organization that is used in each paragraph.
- Determine if development is used appropriately in each paragraph.
- Find the topic sentence and determine if it prepares you for a contrast paragraph.
- Determine the purpose of the use of compare and contrast in each paragraph.

Kitty Companions

[1]My cat, La Llorona, is quite different from my other cat, Gabby, in the areas of size, personality, and health. [2]Both cats were purchased at the same time; however, Gabby is much bigger even though Llorona is the "senior" cat. [3]This comes from their heritage. [4]Gabby is a tabby that has bigger bones and puts on weight more easily. [5]Llorona, on the other hand, is part Siamese even though she does not display the color typical of a Siamese. [6]Siamese cats are more nervous and active than tabbies, which accounts for their difference in size. [7]Llorona is quite slender even though she eats almost as much as Gabby. [8]Being from different cat families could also explain the difference in their personalities. [9]While Gabby likes to find a quiet spot or a comfortable lap for a nap after she eats, Llorona races around the house, chasing real or imaginary flying bugs. [10]As a kitten, Llorona always chased her tail, but Gabby couldn't be bothered with such activity. [11]Today Llorona continues to tail chase while all Gabby catches are dreams. [12]When they go outside, their personalities become more apparent in different directions. [13]Llorona crouches in tall grass, attempting to catch birds, squirrels, or other trespassers in her yard. [14]Her nervous impatience, however, warns her prey when they see the grass shaking. [15]Gabby, on the other hand, finds activity tiresome and prefers to sit in the sun and preen in preparation for another long nap. [16]Although they are both in generally good health from eating and sleeping, if one is going to get sick, it will be Llorona. [17]Her Siamese nervousness frequently affects

her stomach, making her have diarrhea. Gabby, on the other hand, goes through life comfortable and without Llorona's misery. [18]Even though they are different, they are good companions and provide quite a bit of entertainment to me and my family.

Now compare Shaunté's descriptive comparison and contrast paragraph with Julian's. Use the same expectation points you used to analyze Julian's.

My Puppies

Hercules is certainly different from the first dog I found when I was still living at home with my parents. Hercules was a gift from a dear friend. She had wrapped him up in a warm towel and brought him to me. He was the tiniest dog I had ever seen, and since he was almost hairless, he was shivering inside his makeshift nest. Since it was Christmas, the weather was freezing, and no amount of warmth seemed to be enough for him. I took him to my fireplace and put him snuggly inside one of my warm house slippers. After a short time, he stopped shivering and looked at us, too tired to lap the warm milk my friend had heated while I watched him carefully. While we tried to warm him some more, I told Edie about my other dog, Reindeer, whom I found on a different Christmas morning sniffing through the discarded wrapping. Reindeer was a beautiful, large golden retriever. He had obviously been taken care of, but his owners were no where to be found. Friendly and eager to please, Reindeer came up to me, tongue hanging out and eyes bright. I brought him into the house, and he seemed to be respectful of the tree and furniture. My mother was not pleased, but my brothers and father fell in love with him almost as quickly as I did. We decided to keep him until we could find his owners, but no one ever answered the ads. After three weeks of trying, Reindeer became my dog, but I gladly shared him with my family.

Now that you have read both examples of contrast, discuss your findings with your class. Did each paragraph meet your expectations in its attempt to describe differences between the owners' pets?

1. List the sentence numbers in Kitty Companions in which contrasts were made.
2. Which points did Julian develop? Was the development effective? Explain.
3. How are the two cats alike?
4. Did the paragraph support the topic sentence?
5. How did you label each paragraph? Explain.
6. Which paragraph organization did you prefer? Explain.

HOW TO READ COMPARISON

Some textbooks give the definition of comparison as using both similarities and differences. Here the discussion will focus on the similarities, and the use of comparison and contrast will come later. The focus of this section is on identifying and discussing the similarities between two subjects.

Expectations for Reading Comparison

In reading comparison, the audience expects to find similarities between objects, ideas, locations, and other subjects being discussed. The topic sentence for a comparison paragraph, however, differs from that of a contrast sentence. For example, Julian's topic sentence for his contrast paragraph is the following:

Topic Sentence

My cat, La Llorona, is quite different from my other cat, Gabby, in the areas of personality, size, and health.

The following sentence indicates that he has switched his approach to similarities:

Topic Sentence

My cat, La Llorona, shares many qualities with my other cat, Gabby, in the areas of predatory behavior, finicky eating habits, and age.

Surprisingly, Julian has picked up on some of the same ideas he used in the first paragraph; however, he is using a different approach with them. The topic sentence, much like his first, clearly responds to the readers' expectations by using a phrase that indicates comparison: "shares many qualities." Furthermore, readers do not have to wait to discover which qualities are shared; Julian reveals the three he will discuss. Although this technique is not required, it helps both readers and writer to remain focused.

Just as writers must choose significant details for contrast, so, too, must authors select significant details in comparing two subjects. The general areas of predatory behavior, finicky eating habits, and age are important to animal owners; thus, the details will help readers understand how two cats from different families and species can be sufficiently similar to be companions.

When writing comparison, poets use various techniques. For example, they might include a simile: "Between my finger and my thumb / The squat pen rests; snug as a gun"; or they might use a metaphor: "Love is a woman's moon and sun." These comparisons are used to make something unfamiliar more familiar to a reader or to show a particular characteristic that distinguishes the strength or uniqueness of the initial object being described. For example, the pen, for the first poet, has the strength and power of a gun, an obviously powerful weapon. In the second comparison, a metaphor that does not use the word *like* or *as* to show the similarity, the poet shows love's importance to a woman by comparing it to the moon and the sun. In both cases, the object in question can never literally be the object it is being compared to. For example, in the following description "My husband is a bear in the morning until after he drinks his first cup of coffee," we know that this is not a literal description. The husband cannot ever be a bear but can take on the *qualities* of an unhappy one. However, if a writer describes a child as "a pretty, little girl dressed in yellow," this is not a comparison but a description. Read the following short essay and find the various kinds of comparative examples the student writer, Jill, provides.

The Perils of Similarity

During my last years of high school, I met Nancy, and we became the closest and most similar best friends two people could be. Our friends even called us Thelma and Louise. Imagine having a friend who enjoys the same music, clothes, classes, boys, and food! Nancy and I could have been twins in those respects. However, our similarities, unfortunately, created more problems than we expected. Our favorite activity, shopping, led to our first major fight.

Nancy and I were always ready to go to the mall or boutiques, and because we really enjoyed dressing up for dates, we helped each other choose the right outfits, complete with accessories and shoes. But even when we weren't doing "serious" shopping, we enjoyed going into stores and trying on outrageous hats, sampling really weird colognes, and even combining men's ties in different ways. One day we walked into a really expensive hat shop and headed for our favorite: fur hats. When we tried them on, giggling and pretending to be glamorous movie stars, a stuffy saleslady, more like Godzilla than anything else, asked us to leave.

Our first fight—much like World War III without the guns—came over a prom dress. We were seniors and excited about the most important event of our high school experiences. Until then clothes had been just for fun, but now they were important. We had dates with two guys whom we had dated all year. We double-dated every weekend, so we were looking forward to our big prom night. Unfortunately, when we went shopping, we both picked the same dress: a black chiffon dress with a layered skirt and uneven hems. Because we are both tall, it looked good on both of us, but because I have a larger bust than Nancy, I thought the V-neckline looked better on me. I couldn't believe she couldn't see that. We argued over the dress for days, being two people who also had hot tempers and loud voices. Finally, we grudgingly reached an agreement: we would take our moms with us and agree on whatever decision they made. We took them to the store and left them in the sitting area waiting for us to appear. Then we came out together, elegant models, with the hems floating around our calves and the bodices revealing just enough but not too much. We could see that our moms were as impressed as we had been. They told us to change and come back. When we came out, barely speaking to each other, they were gone. When we found them, they each were holding silk shawls with long fringe, but one was pink and one was red. They also had identical pins to fasten the shawls at our shoulders. The effect was great. We bought the dresses and the accessories, and we immediately made up. Our friends at the prom thought it was really "cool" that two best friends could agree to wear the same dress to the prom and still be friends.

We still go shopping when Nancy is in town from her university, and we still have fun trying on the same clothes. I think that as we grow older, our tastes will begin to change, especially since Nancy now lives in New York and is majoring in fashion design. However, our experience with the prom dress taught us a very important lesson: our friendship is more important than a clash over clothes.

Exercise 2: Reading Analysis

1. List the metaphors and similes and identify each.
2. Jill uses point-by-point to reveal the similarities she shares with her friend, Nancy. What are they?
3. Jill uses one subject, shopping, to develop fully. What other similarities do you discover about her and Nancy embedded in the shopping section? Are the details she provides trivial or important? Explain.
4. Jill reveals that there is at least one area of difference between herself and Nancy. What is it? Does including contrast in this essay detract from or add to your understanding? Explain.
5. This essay is a personal narrative primarily using a compare and contrast pattern of development. Jill also uses other modes. Identify the other modes she uses and give examples of each.
6. Did the title prepare you for certain expectations? Explain.

The Extended Comparison: The Analogy

In Chapter 3, Reading and Writing Exemplification, part of the discussion involves the extended example or the analogy. An **analogy** is a comparison made between two subjects that moves beyond a simple comparison. Instead, it develops the discussion by giving examples and multiple points to clarify the similarities. In the above essay, Jill provided metaphors and similes to clarify a specific point. In the extended analogy, the entire work revolves on the description of two people, objects, locations, and so forth, to show the similarities. Read the following paragraph written by Yolanda about being an elementary teacher.

The Mommy-Side of Teaching

The profession of teaching children in the early years is one of the most challenging and important aspects of education in the entire field, for if students do not get a good grounding in their reading, writing, and math skills, they might have serious difficulty catching up to grade-level expectations later. However, being an elementary teacher involves more than just teaching, and I find myself frequently assuming the role of mother to my students. For example, moms often have to comfort their children after they suffer real or imagined injuries. As a first grade teacher, I sometimes have to put Band-Aids on "boo-boos," and dry tears after someone has been called a "bad" name. Moms also have to be a disciplinarian when siblings fight or when a son or daughter breaks "house rules." In the classroom, children sometimes fail to understand the necessity of quiet time for reading and must be disciplined to different degrees for breaking classroom rules. They often argue over crayons or scissors they have to share, thus demanding my attention. When children become tired and cranky after lunch, I, much like a mother, must be sensitive to their condition and provide activities that are not too academically challenging nor especially rigorous. Sometimes children come to school sick or become sick at school. At those times, I, like a mom, must be nurturing, ministering to their sniffles and coughs, as well as teach them appropriate hygiene habits. Finally, like Mom, I should always be encouraging and loving, knowing that regardless of their academic needs, they cannot learn if their emotional, psychological, and physical needs are not also being met. Thus, those individuals who look at teaching from a distance and believe that all there is to teaching is teaching need to spend a day with twenty-five children and discover the joy of the mommy-side of teaching.

Exercise 3: Reading Analysis

1. Look at the above paragraph. Is its organizational development similar to or different from the previous essay? Explain.

READER EXPECTATIONS FOR COMPARISON AND CONTRAST

- Comparison primarily presents similarities.
- Contrast presents differences.
- Methods of organization are point-by-point or subject-by-subject.
- Ways to compare include the following techniques:
    similes
    metaphors
    analogies
- Comparison and contrast can be included in the same work.
- Significant details are presented.
- Comparison and contrast can be used to develop different kinds of essays.
- Comparison and contrast usually has a purpose:
    informative
    evaluative
    persuasive
    humorous

---

2. What makes this paragraph an example of an analogy? Explain with specific examples.
3. How does this paragraph compare with Julian's paragraph about his two cats? Explain.

HOW TO WRITE COMPARISON AND CONTRAST

In the preceding section, comparison and contrast development was explained as a pattern that can be used to elaborate information in various kinds of essays to express similarities and/or differences between topics. When you decide to write your assignment, you must choose which approach you want to use:

- Primarily comparison
- Primarily contrast
- A relatively equal development of both comparison and contrast

To determine this, you must also decide on your purpose for writing the piece:

- To inform
- To persuade

- To evaluate
- To entertain

Finally, you need to consider your method of organization: point-to-point or subject-to-subject.

Step One—Choosing a Topic

Whatever topic you choose, it should be significant to you and provide details that are also relatively significant. For example, the cliché about comparing apples and oranges conveys a speaker's feelings about working with two different and possibly insignificant things. Below is a list of topics. Choose one that you will use to write your practice paper. Use either comparison or contrast for your approach. You can fill in the blanks with "compared to" or "contrasted with" in each pair.

Topics

My senior year of high school _____ my freshman year of college

My first job _____ the job/profession I am planning for

My parents' home _____ my own home

My car _____ my best friend's/significant other's car

The best party I've been to _____ the worst party I've been to

My best friend _____ my worst enemy

Step Two—Prewriting

After you choose one of the topics, brainstorm aspects about each half, listing them in two columns. Find the points you want to compare or contrast and organize them side by side. Look at the chart Yolanda made for her extended comparison paragraph, The Mommy-Side of Teaching.

Being a Mom	Being a Teacher
Nurturing	Same
Comforting	Same
Disciplinarian	Same
Sensitive	Same
Encouraging	Same
Loving	Same
Teaching informally	Teaching professionally

Return to the paragraph and see if she included all the points she listed. Did she elaborate each of them? Notice that on the teacher side of her chart she did not rewrite each quality because she saw teachers having the same qualities. However, she added qualities to teaching, informally and professionally, because they are different. How does she incorporate teaching into the paragraph? For a contrast chart, look at the points Julian put on his.

	La Llorona	Gabby
Size	Small	Heavy Big
Personality	Nervous Playful	Calm Sleeps a lot
Health	Stomach problems	Healthy
Age	Five years old	Five years old
Species	Siamese	Tabby
Color	Black and white	Gray and white

Julian created a chart much like that used in division and classification writing. He found two subjects, his cats, and divided his description into six exclusive categories. Then he classified their characteristics beside each category, making the writing of the contrast easy because he could look at the chart and develop his paragraph point-by-point as Yolanda did for her analogy paragraph.

Take some time to create your chart using comparable or contrasting points. Notice that Julian included one category, age, that provided a comparison rather than a contrast. Why do you think this was important? If you are writing primarily comparison or primarily contrast, you might want to consider including one or two of the opposite points if they are important to the understanding of your subjects.

Step Three—Topic Sentence

Now that you have established the points that are possible candidates for the paragraph, you must determine what the main point of your writing will be. Look at the topic sentences used by Shaunté and Jill.

Topic Sentences

Hercules is certainly different from the first dog I found when I was still living at home with my parents.

Our favorite activity, shopping, led to our first major fight.

Although the first topic sentence clearly indicates that the paragraph will be developed in a contrast mode, Jill's thesis subtly suggests comparison (our favorite activity) but indicates a personal narrative. What we discover as we read is that she uses comparison in the form of details, similes, and metaphors to develop her narrative. Take some time to write your topic sentence and share it with your classmates, a friend or your instructor to determine if you are starting out correctly.

Step Four—The First Draft

At this point, putting the draft together should be relatively easy. You have your topic sentence and your points. Now you need to organize the approach. Will you use point-by-point as Julian and Yolanda did? Will you use subject-to-subject as Shaunté did? Or will you use analogy as Yolanda also did in her point-to-point organization? Once you decide, you should begin writing. Before you begin, however, look at the following first draft paragraph Julian wrote.

> My cat, La Llorona, is quite different from my other cat, Gabby, in the areas of personality, size, and health. Both cats were purchased at the same time; however, Llorona is a few weeks older than Gabby. Despite the fact that Llorona is the "senior" cat, Gabby is much bigger. This comes from their heritage. Gabby is bigger because she is a tabby that has bigger bones and puts on weight more easily. Llorona, on the other hand, is part Siamese even though she does not display the color typical of a Siamese. Siamese cats are more nervous and active than tabbies which accounts for their difference is size. Llorona is quite slender even though she eats almost as much as Gabby. Being from different cat families could also explain the difference in their personalities. While Gabby likes to find a quiet spot or a comfortable lap for a nap after she eats, Llorona races around the house, chasing real or imaginary flying bugs. As a kitten, Llorona always chased her tail, but Gabby couldn't be bothered with such activity. Today Llorona continues to tail chase while all Gabby catches are dreams. When they go outside, their personalities become more apparent in different directions. Although they are both in generally good health from eating and sleeping, if one is going to get sick, it will be Llorona. Her Siamese

```
nervousness frequently affects her stomach, making her
have diarrhea. Gabby, on the other hand, goes through
life comfortable and without Llorona's misery.
```

A comparison and contrast exercise of your own with this draft and the one you write will reveal that there are definite differences in the two works. Discuss the differences with the class or with your instructor.

Step Five—Peer Evaluation

Now that the class has had time to complete the writing assignment, you can share your paper with someone in the class or with a friend who will give you honest feedback. Use the following Grading Profile for Comparison and Contrast to determine how well you wrote your first draft and to discover what changes might be necessary to improve it as you write your final draft.

GRADING PROFILE FOR COMPARISON AND CONTRAST

First, read the paragraph completely without marking it. Second, answer each question by making a check or an X beneath the word Yes, No, or Almost.

Criteria	Yes	No	Almost
1. Does the writer provide a topic sentence?			
2. Does the topic sentence indicate a comparison-and-contrast mode or one of the two?			
3. Do you know the subjects the writer will compare and/or contrast?			
4. Do you know the qualities the author will use to compare and/or contrast?			
5. Is each point sufficiently explained in the paragraph?			
6. Is each point discussed in the order given in the topic sentence?			
7. Did the writer focus only on the qualities announced in his topic sentence?			
8. Does the writer provide a good concluding sentence?			

Short Answer Questions

9. What questions do you want to ask the writer about his first draft? _____

10. What suggestions would you give the writer to correct any criterion that was not marked Yes? Address each individually. _____

11. What kind of organization did the writer use? Was it appropriate? Explain. _____

Step Six—Final Draft

Now you are ready to revise and complete your final draft. Be sure to edit any errors in mechanics that you might have made and to format it according to your instructor's directions. Be sure that all points on the Grading Profile marked "No" have been changed to "Yes."

Exercise 4: Writing Comparison and Contrast

1. Write an analogy paragraph over one of the following topics:
   - My sofa is like _____.
   - My senior _____ teacher is like _____.
   - My neighborhood is like _____.
   - My house looks like _____.
2. Write a contrast paragraph over one of the following topics:
   - My pet and my friend's pet
   - Football and soccer
   - A fast food restaurant and a fancy restaurant
   - Living at home and living in a dorm/apartment
   - Mexican food and Chinese food
3. Write a metaphor for each of the following topics:
   - Romance
   - The beach
   - The moon
   - My feet
   - My own singing
4. Write a simile for each of the following topics
   - My breath
   - Last week's leftovers
   - The laundry
   - My desk
   - My cooking skills

THE COMPARISON-AND-CONTRAST PATTERN OF DEVELOPMENT

- The pattern of development can be one of the following:
  primarily comparison
  primarily contrast
  relatively equal attention to both comparison and contrast
- Comparison and contrast can be used to do one of the following:
  inform
  persuade
  evaluate
  entertain
- Organization can be point-to-point or subject-to-subject.
- Comparisons can be developed through
  details
  similes
  metaphors
  analogies
- Comparison and contrast can be used to develop other forms of writing.
- Significant details must be present.
- The topic should be significant.

Use the following rubric when reading division and classification writing. Respond to the writing prompts at the end of the rubric. NA stands for *Not Applicable* and NI means *Not Included*.

READER EXPECTATIONS FOR COMPARISON AND CONTRAST

Comparison	Excellent	Good	Fair	NA NI
1. Two significant subjects have been chosen.				
2. Subjects have significant details in common.				
3. The appropriate organizational pattern was used.				

Comparison	Excellent	Good	Fair	NA NI
4. Development of the idea was sufficient.				
5. The author used the following appropriately:				
• Details				
• Similes				
• Metaphors				
• Analogies				
6. The author included contrasting elements appropriately.				
Contrast				
7. Two significant subjects have been chosen.				
8. Subjects differ in significant details.				
9. The appropriate organizational pattern was used.				
10. Development of the idea was sufficient.				
11. The author used the following appropriately:				
• Details				
• Similes				
• Metaphors				
• Analogies				
12. The author included comparing elements appropriately.				

Short Answer Questions

1. Did you find the thesis/topic sentence of this essay/paragraph? What is it?

2. Does the writer support the thesis/topic sentence? Give examples and explanations.
3. What are the strengths of this paper?
4. What one weakness do you think should be corrected in this paper?
5. What other comments would you like to make about this comparison-and-contrast writing?

Chapter 8

Reading and Writing Process Analysis

HOW TO READ PROCESS ANALYSIS: PROCESS

Sometimes known as **how-to** writing, a **process analysis** can be written for either of two reasons: (1) to show how something works (process)—the digestive system, a jet motor, an ant colony, a factory—or (2) to give step-by-step instructions for how to do something (analysis)—a recipe for German chocolate cake, directions for building a model airplane, how to program a VCR, how to install software on your computer. With the number of self-help books on the market that instructs readers how to lose weight, gain self-esteem, reduce the risk of heart attack, become a millionaire before they are thirty, and so on, this must be a relatively easy pattern to follow. Describing a **process** takes knowledge of the system being explained, whereas giving instructions involves being able to give clear, sequential steps so that someone can follow the directions. Try teaching a child how to tie his shoelaces or remember the last time you had to follow written directions to hook up your printer to your computer or assemble a child's toy, and you can appreciate the necessity for clear writing.

Reader Expectations: Process

Readers generally look at process writing for information. Consider the number of articles you have read in your experience with research. For example, if you had to give an oral presentation about the heart in a biology class, you might have had to consult texts that describe not only where the heart is located and its function, but also how it works. In some texts, the author might use scientific terminology that medical students or doctors understand but that you as an undergraduate might not.

Thus, you might have had to find other texts that address the topic in less technical language that is written for readers who are not experts in the field. These articles or books are written in an objective, usually third person narrative style.

On the other hand, you might have knowledge of the field you are investigating, but you need an explanation about procedure. For example, suppose you have just been hired as a nurse's aide to work in a doctor's office. You understand the specialized equipment you have to use, but you are uncertain about the routine, even though you have worked for other doctors and you know the extended hours you are often required to work. Read the following **informative** process paragraph that **describes** the procedures used to run a doctor's office.

Most people who have had to wait to be seen in a doctor's office think that it is run inefficiently and is insensitive to those who are sick; however, there is usually a system that attempts to ensure that all patients are seen in a timely manner. Dr. Zepeda's office was no different. At nine o'clock, Ms. Morales and her assistant receptionist open the office, check the office systems, and begin answering the phones, making last minute appointments. By 9:30, the first appointments begin arriving, well aware that the doctor will not be there until 10:00 because he is completing rounds at the hospital or performing surgery. At 9:30, the nurse's aide arrives and begins preparing rooms, and restocking empty jars with tongue depressors, cotton balls, and other required items. She also begins the pre-examination phase at 9:45, just as the nurse arrives. The nurse's aide takes the patient's weight, height, temperature, and blood pressure, listens to and records their symptoms, and tells them how to undress in preparation for the doctor. When the nurse arrives, she socializes with others, ensures that all is ready, reviews the patients' charts, and makes sure all the rooms are filled so Dr. Zepeda can begin seeing patients after he reviews the charts at 10:00. By 10:10, Dr. Z has spoken to the staff, put on his white coat, and begun seeing patients. Although patients have been scheduled every ten minutes, some obviously take longer than others. After they are seen, patients pay their bill, make another appointment if necessary, and leave. By 11:30 everyone is

ready for a fifteen-minute break followed by a continuation of the assembly-line process that continues
until 3:00 when everyone breaks for a thirty-minute
lunch. In between patients, the nurse's aide also
cleans rooms and instruments, refills jars, and puts
new patients into rooms. Meanwhile, the office staff
makes appointments, checks insurance forms, keeps
track of billing and payments, and refiles charts.
At 5:00, the office doors close, but Dr. Zepeda and
his nurse continue to see late or waiting patients.
The assistant receptionist and nurse's aide leave at
that time. At 5:45, Dr. Z stops seeing patients to
reconcile the day's activities and fee collection
with Ms. Morales. By 6:00, she leaves and his nurse
assumes office staff and nurse's aide's duties until
they finish seeing patients. By 7:00, Dr. Zepeda and
his nurse leave the office. Although some patients
have to wait to see Dr. Z after their appointed time,
he sees everyone and gives each patient his undivided attention and concerned care that is always
reflected in a well-run office.

The above passage was definitely written by someone who knows firsthand the workings of that doctor's office. Notice that the tone is **objective,** not allowing for personal feelings to slip in. The purpose of this kind of paper, written in the third person, is to convey information so that the reader will understand the **process.** While there are only a few specialized terms used (tongue depressors, blood pressure), the writer does not define or explain the terms, assuming that the reader will know what they are. Furthermore, the writer describes the office procedures in chronological order thus helping you, as a new employee, understand the rhythm of the day. A more detailed description of each phase of the day is not needed.

Exercise 1: Reading Analysis

1. Find and underline the topic sentence. Use a ⌒⌒⌒ to underline the part of the topic sentence that indicates this paragraph will be about a procedure.
2. List terms you do not understand and define them.
3. In describing this routine, the author names specific duties to be performed at certain times. Highlight the duties and who performs them.

4. Since this paragraph describes a routine, highlight, in a different shade, the times events occur.
5. How does the **concluding sentence** bring closure to the paragraph? Does it satisfy your sense of closure? Explain.

Most people who have had to wait to be seen in a doctor's office think that it is run inefficiently and is insensitive to those who are sick; however, there is usually a system that attempts to ensure that all patients are seen in a timely manner. Dr. Zepeda's office was no different. At nine o'clock, Ms. Morales and her assistant receptionist open the office, check the office systems, and begin answering the phones, making last minute appointments. By 9:30, the first appointments begin arriving, knowing that the doctor will not be there until 10:00 because he was completing rounds at the hospital or performing surgery. At 9:30, the nurse's aide arrives and begins preparing rooms, and restocking empty jars with tongue depressors, cotton balls, and other required items. She also begins the pre-examination phase at 9:45, just as the nurse arrives. The nurse's aide takes the patient's weight, height, temperature, and blood pressure, listens to and records their symptoms, and tells them how to undress in preparation for the doctor. When the nurse arrives, she socializes with others, ensures that all is ready, reviews the patients' charts, and makes sure all the rooms are filled so Dr. Zepeda can begin seeing patients after he reviewed the charts at 10:00. By 10:10, Dr. Zepeda has spoken to the staff, put on his white coat, and begun seeing patients. Although patients have been scheduled every ten minutes, some obviously take longer than others. After they are seen, patients pay their bill, make another appointment if necessary, and leave. By 11:30 everyone is ready for a fifteen-minute break followed by a continuation of the assembly line process that continues until 3:00 when everyone breaks for a thirty-minute lunch. In between patients, the nurse's aide also cleans rooms and instruments, refills jars, and puts new patients into rooms. Meanwhile, the office staff makes appointments, checks insurance forms, keeps track of billing and payments, and refiles charts. At 5:00, the office doors close, but Dr. Zepeda and his nurse continue to see late or waiting patients. The assistant receptionist and nurse's aide leave at that time. At 5:45, Dr. Z stops seeing patients to reconcile the day's activities and fee collection with Ms. Morales. By 6:00, she leaves and his nurse assumes office staff and nurse's aide's duties until they finish seeing patients. By 7:00, Dr. Zepeda and his nurse leave the office. Although some patients have to wait to see Dr. Z after their appointed time, he sees everyone and gives each patient his undivided attention and concerned care that is always reflected in a well-run office.

How well does the analysis of your paragraph match with the one above?

HOW TO READ PROCESS ANALYSIS: ANALYSIS

The difference between process and analysis papers lies in their function. A process paper gives readers information about how an activity is performed. It is written *for* the reader and is normally written in the third person. An analysis, on the other hand, is written *to* the reader, primarily using second person, and breaks down a process into individual steps that the reader can follow to complete the activity. In some cases, a paragraph or two might precede the steps to give the reader information about the equipment or tools he or she will need to complete the activity. For example, explaining the steps to bake a cake or change the oil in a car involves having specialized items to work with that should be gathered before proceeding with the activity. In some cases the author will include explanatory information with the individual steps, but in other directions, the author might list only a series of steps. In all cases, however, readers expect clear directions written in a logical sequence and a list of special tools or equipment and terms specifically associated with the activity, such as sauté, sand, file, needed to complete the activity. Because readers frequently like to know why they must complete particular steps, explanatory information is often added.

Additional help can be given in various ways. The old cliché "A picture is worth a thousand words," applies here. For example, if specialized equipment is needed, readers might appreciate a picture of a Bundt cake pan or a Phillips-head screwdriver. If you are giving instructions about how to track progress of a hurricane in the Atlantic as it moves into the Caribbean and the Gulf of Mexico, you might want to include a tracking chart that has the latitude and longitude lines as well as a map of the affected area. The chart provides visual clues as the reader follows the directions. Another aid for the reader is the use of anecdotal information, incidents the writer has experienced. Readers often appreciate reading about the frustrations or ease the writer had attempting to complete the same activity they will soon try. The following paragraph provides an example of annotated directions.

```
        I have completed many pieces of embroidery and
    crewelwork, but no one can imagine my shock when I
    opened the package of a beautiful picture entitled
    "Lady Mime" and discovered that there was no pattern
```

printed on the fabric. Where do I begin? If you have ever considered completing a counted cross-stitch piece, let me offer some directions the package does not give. First, separate the threads into colors using the guide on the package as your number guide. Many people who work with numerous colors of thread use a piece of plastic or cardboard with several small, numbered slits along one edge. Each thread is matched with the number and inserted into the appropriate slit to separate it from the others. If you have only five or six colors of thread, that's fine; but if you have ten, fifteen, or twenty, you run the risk of tangling the thread as each color intertwines with its neighbors. Buy ziplock bags instead, which can be held together with a key ring. You can use as many as the ring will hold; the thread stays clean, and it doesn't tangle with others. If you have beads, get holders that seal tightly and are easy to dip a needle into. Divide the beads into their properly marked containers and put them aside because they won't be used until the stitching is complete. Next, unfold and iron the fabric. You must find the center point on the fabric, but because it's been folded for packaging, it hasn't been done with precision. Iron out the wrinkles. Then before you fold, either baste the raw edges or use masking tape folded around the edges of the fabric to prevent raveling. Now fold the fabric in half and then in half again. The corner that does not open (three corners open and one does not) is the center of your fabric. Mark it by creasing the fabric lightly there or by marking it with a straight pin. Open the fabric, keeping the center marked. That is where you will begin stitching. The rest of the directions should be clearly explained on the enclosed directions sheet. Regardless of whether you are a novice counted cross-stitcher or an old hand, read the directions completely to avoid surprises. With concentration and perseverance, you should produce an heirloom.

This paragraph was written by someone who has experience with the **process** of doing a cross-stitch project. The importance of her directions is that she provides "trade secrets" newcomers don't know and have no way of knowing without trial and error. When the author gets readers to the point where the directions provided by the manufacturers give adequate instruction, she stops and sends readers on their way.

Exercise 2: Reading Analysis

1. Underline the topic sentence. Use a ⌣⌣⌣ to underline the part of the topic sentence that indicates this paragraph will be an analysis.
2. What transitions does the author use to indicate another step in the process? Find each transition and highlight it.
3. The first step appears to have multiple activities. Do you think each activity should be divided into separate steps or put together as it is? Explain your reasoning.
4. Is this paragraph written *to* or *for* the audience? How can you tell?
5. If you had to follow the directions, do you think you would be able to? Explain.

Look at the following marked paragraph and see if yours matches.

I have completed many pieces of embroidery and crewelwork, but no one can imagine my shock when I opened the package of a beautiful picture entitled "Lady Mime" and discovered that there was no pattern printed on the fabric. Where do I begin? <u>If you have ever considered completing a counted cross-stitch piece, let me offer some directions the package does not give.</u> First, separate the threads into colors using the guide on the package as your number guide. Many people who work with numerous colors of thread use a piece of plastic or cardboard with several small, numbered slits along one edge. Each thread is matched with the number and inserted into the appropriate slit to separate it from the others. If you have only five or six colors of thread, that's fine; but if you have ten, fifteen, or twenty, you run the risk of tangling the thread as each color intertwines with its neighbors. Buy ziplock bags instead, which can be held together with a round key ring. You can use as many as the ring will hold; the thread stays clean, and it doesn't tangle with others. If you have beads, get holders that seal tightly and are easy to dip a needle into. Divide the beads into their properly marked containers and put them aside because they won't be used until the stitching is complete. Next, unfold and iron the fabric. You must find the center point on the fabric, but because it's been folded for packaging, it hasn't been done with precision. Iron out the wrinkles. Then before you fold, either baste the raw edges or use masking tape folded around the edges of the fabric to prevent raveling. Now fold the fabric in half and then in half again. The corner that does not open (three corners open and one does not) is the center of your fabric. Mark it by creasing the fabric lightly there or by marking it with a straight pin. Open the fabric, keeping the center marked. That is where you will begin stitching. The rest of the directions should be clearly explained on the enclosed directions

---

READER EXPECTATIONS FOR PROCESS ANALYSIS PASSAGES

Process

1. The thesis or topic sentence reflects the mode.
2. Narration is usually third-person point of view and written *for* an audience.
3. The level of explanation can vary in approach, depending on whether the audience is familiar with or has expert understanding of the topic or has little or no understanding.
4. Discussion is organized in a logical sequence.
5. Each step is explained and linked to the next to show a complete picture of how a process works.
6. Specialized terms are explained.

Analysis

1. The thesis or topic sentence reflects the mode.
2. Narration is usually second-person point of view and written *to* an audience.
3. Equipment and/or tools needed to complete the activity are listed.
4. Multiple steps, some in combination, are listed with or without anecdotal or explanatory information.
5. Steps are arranged in a progressive series that start at the beginning and end with the completion of the activity.
6. Pictures, charts, diagrams, or other visual aids are often provided.
7. Advice and/or warnings are added if necessary.

sheet. Regardless of whether you are a novice counted
cross-stitcher or an old hand, read the directions
completely to avoid surprises. With concentration
and perseverance, you should produce an heirloom.

Exercise 3: Reading Analysis

1. Get a cake mix and read the back panel of the box. Evaluate the degree
   to which you would be able to follow the directions and use the equipment required.
2. Find the section in a user's manual for hooking up a VCR or DVD player
   to a television set. Evaluate the directions according to the following
   questions:
   - Did the writer adequately explain the wires on the VCR or DVD and
     where the connections are on the television?
   - Were all the wires appropriately color coded or identified?
   - Did you need tools that were/were not included in the directions?
   - How long did the hookup take you to complete? Was this indicated
     in the directions?
   - Did you have to have help from someone else?
3. Find a set of complex directions, such as for assembling a bicycle or a
   crib, building a model (airplane, ship, car, etc.), changing a tire, or
   completing income tax forms. Follow the directions exactly as they
   are written. Evaluate.
4. Find two or three descriptions that provide process information about
   one of the following topics:
   - An infant's first year of life
   - Raising a specific breed of animal
   - How cholesterol builds up to produce heart problems
   - A successful relationship
   - A battle in a major war

   Identify the audience for whom they were written; the use of unexplained, specialized terminology; the sequence of activities in the
   event; and the conclusion. Evaluate each description, select the one
   you favor, and explain why you chose it.

HOW TO WRITE PROCESS ANALYSIS: PROCESS

A process paper is a form of "how-to" analysis; however, rather than
give directions to a reader so she can complete the activity, process describes how an activity proceeds. You have read several process pieces

so far, and now you will write your own. You can do this in either of two ways: (1) You may choose an activity you are familiar with and describe it from a detached, third-person point of view, or (2) you may research a process you are interested in and write a **summary** of the activity. The remainder of this section will be a discussion of how to write an original process paper.

PROCESS VERSUS ANALYSIS WRITING

Process	Analysis
Usually **expository**	Usually directional
Written *for* the reader	Written *to* the reader
Uses third-person point of view, primarily	Uses second-person point of view, primarily
Results in understanding	Brings about a desired outcome

The subject of an original process paper can come from an experience you had in which you changed or from an activity you completed or learned how to do. The following example is about how Jeffrey moved from being a high school student to being a college student. Although the difference is subtle because he is still a student, Jeffrey's reflection about his transition to college and his first semester on campus describes a process he experienced. He began writing his paragraph by prewriting, making a list of characteristics and activities for his senior year in high school and his freshman year in college.

Step One—Prewriting

Senior in high school	Freshman in college
1. Popular, everyone knew me	Stranger
2. Had several teachers I'd had before	New teachers—professors
3. Structured, regimented routine	Freedom
4. Parents	No parental guidance
5. Girlfriend was in most classes	Girlfriend not here
6. Varsity football player	Freshman player
7. Home life	Dorm life
8. Home cooked meals	Dorm or fast food
9. Car	No transportation
10. City	Small town
11. Easy classes	Difficult classes
12. Little studying needed	Hours of study needed

| 13. Many grades taken in each class | Few grades taken in each class |
| 14. Little responsibility | Responsible for everything |

Looking at Jeffrey's prewriting list reveals a young man who has taken the reflection assignment quite seriously. His move from high school to the university created a complete upheaval in his life, and he is able to list specific points that affected him; however, he must narrow his focus to create a process paper rather than just a paper that compares and contrasts the two years. Thus, Jeffrey will probably use multiple patterns of development as he writes the process of moving from high school to university student. Although comparison and contrast usually develops a paper, it also serves a greater purpose. In this case, its purpose is to show a process.

Rather than write an essay, Jeffrey decided to write a paragraph describing his process. He did, however, recognize the possibility that it could expand to a longer work.

Step Two—Topic Sentence

Jeffrey looked over the list and attempted to write an appropriate topic sentence. The **bold** comments reflect his teacher's criticism about each attempt.

Although each sentence gets a little more specific, Jeffrey is trying to include too much information in a single paragraph. The third attempt would make a good thesis sentence if he removed the repetition, but he wants to write a paragraph. He finally writes the following sentence: *Going away to school after I graduated helped me learn to be a more responsible and better student.* Jeffrey recognized that he had several good points in his last attempt, so he decided to focus on them rather than all three points.

TOPIC SENTENCES

- When I went to college, I changed. **Too abrupt**
- Going to college helped me improve. **Leaves a lot for the reader to guess about**
- Leaving home, making new friends and being responsible for my own academic progress made me more responsible. **Repetitive and too complex for a single paragraph**

Step Three—The First Draft

Jeffrey decided to focus on his academic life, even though he listed a variety of areas that were affected by his transition to college. Since he has so much information, he can use this paragraph later as a component of an essay, incorporating other elements from his list. Jeffrey's topic sentence reveals he will use personal narrative and cause and effect, and he suggests a process paper. It also suggests that he might incorporate comparison and contrast. The superscripts number each sentence and will be referred to after the paragraph.

Growing Up Academically

[1]Although some students recognize the importance of their education while they are in high school, I simply had a good time, becoming the traditional "late bloomer." [2]Going away to school after I graduated helped me learn to be a more responsible and better student. [3]High school years passed quickly as I became a popular person on campus, both with students and teachers. [4]I learned quickly to smile, be polite, and appear to be attentive and prepared resulted in good participation grades and being a favorite among my teachers. [5]All I had to do was nod in agreement and rephrase what the "A" students without adding anything new, and I became a star. [6]Most of the time, my classmates didn't even realize my strategy. [7]Those who did weren't part of my crowd anyway. [8]As a result, I didn't have to study much. [9]Things, however, changed drastically and quickly in my university courses. [10]All my smile got me was a nod of acknowledgment. [11]And my trademark answers were met with, "Can you expand that answer?" or "Elaborate a little more, please." [12]Obviously, since I had neither read the assignment nor heard further explanations, I was caught. [13]Additionally, the "pop quizzes" in courses like American History and biology, where I was simply a number among 150 faces, were intended to weed out students like me immediately. [14]By week four, I knew I had to change my ways or face probation and be kicked off the football team at the end of my first semester. [15]I began going back to the dorm after my classes since most residents were in class. [16]In the evenings after practice, I'd clean up and go to the library. [17]My

football buddies immediately noticed my absence at
our evening gatherings. [18]I quickly learned to save
my "party time" for Saturday nights after the games.
[19]I also began taking advantage of my professors' and
teaching assistants' office hours. [20]Finally, I met
with study groups instead of secretly sneering at
them. [21]Mid-semester grades were lower than I would
have liked, but I'll end the semester with A's and
B's that I earned through hard work and study rather
than through smiles and a good personality.

Fortunately, Jeffrey had good composition teachers whom he paid attention to in high school. Once he mastered his topic sentence, he got the rhythm of the paper, fully understood the subject, and wrote the draft in one sitting. His self-reflection and prewriting sparked his creativity, and he wrote a draft that needs only a little revision.

Step Four—Revision

Sentence 4 was rewritten: I learned quickly **that** to smile, **to** be polite, and **to** *appear* to be attentive. . . .

In Sentence 5, Jeffrey added **said** after "students."

Finally, between sentences 15 and 16, Jeffrey added one more sentence: [16]**The silence allowed me to read or complete my math assignments.**

Step Five—Editing and Formatting

The last steps, editing and formatting, are completed before you submit your paper. Be sure to use your spell-checker and/or dictionary for correct spellings. Even more important, however, is good proofreading. Check for frequently confused words, such as *two, to,* and *too* or *their* and *there.*

Also be sure to use MLA format or the format that your instructor requires. Before you begin your own writing assignment, use the Peer Editing Analysis rubric below to analyze Jeffrey's paragraph.

Peer Editing Analysis for Process Analysis Paper: Process

Answer each of the following questions completely:
1. Did the introduction provide sufficient background explanation about the procedure? Were there any terms that the author left unexplained or that needed more explanation? If so explain below.

2. Identify the topic sentence and write it below. Does it introduce an informative essay that suggests a process or procedure? Explain.

3. Is the essay written in the third person? Is it written *for* the reader?

4. Summarize briefly the steps in the procedure, eliminating the descriptive information.

5. Did the writer explain the procedure in such a way that you could easily follow it? Did the writer present the steps of the process in sequential order, using appropriate transitions? Explain.

6. Describe the strength of the paper.

7. Identify one weakness and offer suggestions to change it.

HOW TO WRITE PROCESS ANALYSIS: ANALYSIS

To complete an analysis is to break a large concept into smaller components. The sample process article you read in the preceding section provides information that is broken into smaller elements that create a whole. Remember, the difference between process and analysis is that process shows a reader how something works and analysis gives a reader step-by-step directions about how to complete a project or an activity. In the former, the reader is given the steps or points that create a procedure building toward a complete operation. For example, if you read a description of a battle, you see how it was fought, but you do not get a manual that provides step-by-step instructions about how to wage a battle.

In this section you will write an analysis that gives readers directions about how to complete a process that you are familiar with. You might choose to list the steps involved in how to care for and insert contact lenses, how to mow a lawn, how to plan a party, how to make an omelet, how to do a particular procedure at your job (clean teeth, file paperwork, open a checking account for a customer), and so forth. Use the following steps.

Step One—Prewriting

Brainstorming is probably the best strategy to use because it allows you to consider all the activities you know how to do for which you might well give directions. If you babysit for siblings or other children, you might complete a set of directions for beginning babysitters. You might consider telling someone how to wash a car, use a spreadsheet on a computer, create a haiku, or tie a fly for fly-fishing.

You might want to extend your prewriting to clustering or listing. At this point, you should jot down all the steps you take to complete the activity. You don't have to put them in sequential order yet; just get the steps down as you remember them and the organization can come in the draft. Read Lisa's prewriting list of steps to mow her yard. Notice that she uses bullets instead of numbers.

- Get the lawn mower out of the garage.
- Be sure the spark plug wire is connected to the spark plug.
- Pull the starter string or push the button if it's a self-start mower.
- Mow the lawn.
- Pick up fallen branches and pinecones.
- Find your goggles and gloves.
- Be sure you have oil and gas in your mower.
- Buy gasoline if you don't have any.
- Wear appropriate clothing.
- Use sun block.

Notice that each step in the list begins with an action verb. Because this list is being written *to* the audience, the sentence structure is imperative (do this, do that), and the subject is understood to be *you*. Before she begins her first draft, Lisa will add to and reorganize her preliminary list.

Step Two—Thesis Sentence

Next, Lisa considers a thesis sentence. Because she will be giving directions, she has to keep this in mind and write a thesis that lets the reader know that the predominant mode of development is **process analysis.**

Thesis Sentence

To mow the lawn, I follow a routine that helps me organize the job and complete it as quickly as possible.

Although this is a good thesis sentence, it prepares the reader for a process paper that suggests an overview of a procedure, similar to the doctor's office procedure, rather than directions given to the audience. Here's Lisa's second attempt.

Thesis Sentence

If you are someone who does not like to mow your yard, here are several steps I take to organize the job and help me complete it as quickly as possible.

This thesis sentence is much better as it addresses the reader directly, indicates that Lisa will give directions, and as the one above it, suggests that it is an efficient and fast process.

Step Three—The First Draft

Before Lisa begins her draft, she will reorganize and complete her list. Since she has her thesis sentence ready, she can begin writing.

Summer Day Duty

When I was growing up, I had various chores to complete around the house. Although I didn't mind fixing dinner or cleaning the kitchen, I wasn't excited about having to cut the grass twice a month for my grandmother. My dad, a believer in the feminist theory that women can do any job, introduced me at the age of thirteen to the lawn mower and gave me the job of taking care of my grandmother's grass. Since I wasn't fond of this chore, I learned early to have a routine that would help me complete the job quickly. If you are someone who does not like to mow your yard, here are several steps I take to organize the job and help me complete it as quickly as possible.

Step 1 comes from the old Boy Scout Manual: be prepared. Trust me, if you skip this step, you'll have to stop when your machine stops, probably have to clean up if you don't have gasoline in reserve, go to the gas station, come back, and start over.

Step 2. Once you are ready to begin mowing, you should be dressed appropriately. If you don't like dirt and grass between your toes, tennis shoes are a better choice than sandals. You might also prefer jeans or long pants to prevent nicks on your legs from flying branches or other missiles. Gloves will also help prevent blisters on your hands, and goggles will help prevent foreign objects like specks of dust or grass from flying into your eyes. Since you'll probably be outside while the sun is shining, sun block is an important aid in preventing sunburn.

Step 3. Before you begin, a tour of your yard is helpful. Picking up pinecones and fallen limbs before you begin mowing helps the activity proceed smoothly so that you don't have to stop and restart your mower several times. More importantly it helps prevent injury and dulling your blades. Another obstacle you should look out for is anthills. There's almost nothing worse than mowing over an undetected anthill and having dirt and ants flying into your face and clothes. A close second is stepping into an anthill and not realizing it until you feel the ant bites around your ankles. If this happens, keep some anti-itch medication close by.

Step 4. Now that the lawn is ready, you're dressed appropriately, and the mower is filled with gas and oil, make sure that all parts of the mower are ready so it can be started. For example, if it is not electric, you need to check the spark plug to make sure the wire is connected. On some mowers there is a gas level switch you must turn. If the mower is self-propelled, you must engage its clutch. Finally, before pulling the start mechanism or pushing the button, you must hold down the bar that allows the machine to start and remain in continuous operation. Once this safety device is released, the mower's engine stops to prevent accidents if you walk away from the machine. If it is self-propelled, you must also engage another lever on some machines to set it in motion. Now you may begin.

Step 5. As you cut the grass, you have several options. You can collect the clippings, bag them, and discard them. You can collect the clippings and put them on a mulch pile. Or you can let the clippings remain on the lawn either to stay or to be raked up later. I usually let the clippings fall back into the lawn to act as a natural fertilizer.

To make the process faster, I usually cut around trees and curved areas, such as circular flower beds and walks to make straight rows. The few seconds it saves for each pass adds up to help me finish sooner. As I cut, I overlap each row a little to make sure I get all the grass that might have been rolled over by the wheels.

Step 6. When I finish mowing, I take out my Weed-Eater and trim hard-to-reach places to give the yard a smooth look. For a finishing touch, I edge around the driveway and sidewalks.

Step 7. While I'm trimming and edging, I'm allowing the mower to cool down before I clean it up and put it and other items—gloves, goggles, gasoline, oil, trimmer, edger—away. The final step is to clean off the driveway, patio, and sidewalk, removing dirt and grass. If you have a blower, the job is easier and faster. Once this is completed and everything is put away, your job is done.

Cutting grass is definitely more complicated than simply getting out the mower and pushing it around the yard; however, by being organized and systematic, you can complete the job in about an hour if you have a medium-sized yard. Once you finish, you'll be proud of your effort, and eager to clean up. The only other suggestion I might make to get an equally well-manicured lawn is to find a volunteer or pay someone who is even faster than you. It's worth the expense!

Looking over Lisa's first draft reveals a relatively good beginning. She does, however, have several spots that need revision. Important and interesting aspects of her paper to note are her incorporation of several modes of development: personal narrative, cause and effect, division, exemplification, and contrast. She also uses second person almost exclusively in the body of the essay because she is talking directly to her audience. Finally, she ends on a humorous note in her conclusion.

Step Four—Revision

Lisa wrote an excellent introduction and conclusion; neither needs revision. However, because she is so close to the process she writes about, each step needs a little revision.

In Step 1, Lisa added an explanation of her topic sentence. She also added a sentence at the end to explain the need for oil and a new paragraph.

Step 2 needed only one minor reference to contact lenses, and Lisa makes it by adding a phrase.

Prior to Step 3, Lisa had been ambivalent about where to discuss mosquito repellant. Originally, she wanted it in both Steps 1 and 2, but since it flowed better after the discussion of ant bites, she decided to add it there.

In Step 4, Lisa realized that her audience might not have a self-propelled mower; therefore, she added directions for members of that audience also.

Steps 5 and 6 were appropriately written; however, Step 7 needed a better transition. Lisa also needed to provide the completion of a contrast she began. Below is the final copy with the revisions in bold type.

Summer Day Duty

When I was growing up, I had various chores to complete around the house. Although I didn't mind fixing dinner or cleaning the kitchen, I wasn't excited about having to cut the grass twice a month for my grandmother. My dad, a believer in the feminist theory that women can do any job, introduced me at the age of thirteen to the lawn mower and gave me the job of taking care of my grandmother's grass. Since I wasn't fond of this chore, I learned early to have a routine that would help me complete the job quickly. If you are someone who does not like to mow your yard, here are several steps I take to organize the job and help me complete it as quickly as possible.

Step 1 comes from the old Boy Scout Manual: be prepared. **This means that you should check your gas and oil levels before you begin.** Trust me, if you skip this step, you'll have to stop when your machine stops, probably have to clean up if you don't have gasoline in reserve, go to the gas station, come back, and start over. **If, on the other hand, your mower runs out of oil, you could burn up your** motor, and if the damage is serious enough, you'll have to buy a new machine.

Another important aspect of being prepared involves knowing the temperature. If you plan to cut the grass on a hot day, do so in the early morning or early evening when the sun is not as hot. And also be sure to have plenty of water available because dehydration occurs very easily and can be accompanied by heatstroke. Taking precautions early can prevent mild to serious illness.

Step 2. Once you are ready to begin mowing, you should be dressed appropriately. If you don't like dirt and grass between your toes, tennis shoes are a better choice than sandals. You might also prefer jeans or long pants to prevent nicks on your legs from flying branches or other missiles. Gloves will help prevent blisters on your hands, and goggles will help prevent foreign objects like specks of dust or grass from flying into your eyes, **especially if you wear contact lenses.** Since you'll probably be outside while the sun is shining, sun block is an important aid in preventing sunburn.

Step 3. Before you begin, a tour of your yard is helpful. Picking up pinecones and fallen limbs before you begin mowing helps the activity proceed smoothly so that you don't have to stop and restart your mower several times. More importantly, it helps prevent injury and dulling your blades. Another obstacle you should look out for is anthills. There's almost nothing worse than mowing over an undetected anthill and having dirt and ants flying into your face and clothes. A close second is stepping into an ant pile and not realizing it until you feel the ant bites around your ankles. If this happens, keep some anti-itch medication close by. **Another aid you might consider is mosquito repellent, especially if you live in an area where mosquitoes breed or where Culex mosquitoes live or where the West Nile virus has been detected.**

Step 4. Now that the lawn is ready, you're dressed appropriately, and the mower is filled with gas and oil, make sure that all parts of the mower are ready so it can be started. For example, if it is not electric, you need to check the spark plug to make sure the wire is connected. On some mowers there is a gas level switch you must turn. If the mower is self-propelled, you must engage its clutch. Finally, before pulling the start mechanism or pushing the button, you must hold down the bar that allows the machine to start and remain in continuous operation. Once this safety device is released, the mower's engine stops to prevent accidents if you walk away from the machine. If it is self-propelled, you must also engage another lever on some machines to set it in motion. **If you own a less complicated machine, such as one that you must push, there are fewer gadgets to operate. Furthermore, if you own a push-mower, that does not take gasoline, oil, or sparkplugs, you can begin your chore almost immediately after removing it from its storage area.** Now you may begin.

Step 5. As you cut the grass, you have several options. You can collect the clippings, bag them, and discard them. You can collect the clippings and put them on a mulch pile. Or you can let the clippings remain on the lawn either to stay or to be raked up later. I usually let the clippings fall back into the lawn to act as a natural fertilizer.

To make the process faster, I usually cut around trees and curved areas, such as circular flower beds and walks to make straight rows. The few seconds it saves for each pass adds up to help me finish sooner. As I cut, I overlap each row a little to make sure I get all the grass that might have been rolled over by the wheels.

Step 6. When I finish mowing, I take out my Weed-Eater and trim hard-to-reach places to give the yard a smooth look. For a finishing touch, I edge around the driveway and sidewalks.

Step 7. **Even though everything appears finished, it's not.** While I'm trimming and edging, I'm allowing the mower to cool down before I clean it up and put it and other items—gloves, goggles, gasoline, oil, trimmer, edger—away. The final step is to clean off the driveway, patio, and sidewalk, removing dirt and grass. If you have a blower, the job is easier and faster **than sweeping.** Once this is completed and everything is put away, your job is done.

Cutting grass is definitely more complicated than simply getting out the mower and pushing it around the yard; however, by being organized and systematic, you can complete the job in about an hour if you have a medium-sized yard. Once you finish, you'll be proud of your effort, and eager to clean up. The only other suggestion I might make to get an equally well-manicured lawn is to find a volunteer or pay someone who is even faster than you. It's worth the expense!

A final step process analysis writers should take as they revise their essay is to follow their own directions as they are written. Any changes should be made at that time.

Step Five—Editing and Formatting

After you finish working with the content of your paper, you need to check for spelling, mechanics, and grammatical errors. Running your spell-checker is a good idea, but proofreading your paper is essential to catch words that are used incorrectly rather than spelled incorrectly. Make sure the sentences flow together well and that the paper reads smoothly.

Finally, remember to format the paper according to MLA format or according to your instructor's directions. When you have finished, it will be ready to submit.

Short Writing Assignments

1. Go back to the opening sections of Chapter 1 and reread the explanations of learning styles. Write a **process** paragraph that tells your readers what steps they will need to take to determine what kind of learner they are. You might need to complete a little research that explains the characteristics of each learning style more fully.

2. Everyone is good at doing something. Some people are good at putting on their contact lenses, others are good at baking cookies, while others are good at training dogs. Determine what skill you have that

you are very good at. Write a step-by-step set of directions for completing the activity. When you finish writing, follow the directions precisely as they were written, making revisions when needed. Once they say what you want them to say, give them to a friend to follow. Listen to your friend's suggestions, complaints, or compliments, and revise accordingly. Finally, prepare a copy of the directions for your instructor and present the directions orally to the class, bringing all equipment needed to complete the activity.

3. Complete the following Peer Editing Analysis.

PEER EDITING ANALYSIS FOR PROCESS ANALYSIS—ANALYSIS

The student provided	Yes	No	Almost
1. A strong introduction that creates interest.			
2. A thesis that clearly indicates an analysis essay.			
3. Steps that are arranged in sequential order.			
4. Steps that are easy to understand and follow.			
5. Steps that might include smaller, related directions within a larger direction.			
6. Steps that provide explanations as necessary.			
7. Second person narration primarily.			
8. Two to three additional patterns of development.			
9. Transitions between steps.			
10. Warnings about any problems that might occur.			
11. A conclusion that brings closure to the directions.			

Respond to the following:

12. Do you believe you could complete the activity with these directions? Explain.

13. Are there any steps that need clarification?
    List the steps and explain your confusion.

14. Identify the strengths of the essay.

15. Identify one weakness.

Chapter 9

Reading and Writing Causal Analysis

HOW TO READ CAUSAL ANALYSIS

To read causal analysis is to read for causes, effects, or both. Most actions usually cause something to happen. The well-known adage, "If we do not learn from the past, we are destined to relive it," is an excellent example of cause and effect.

Single Cause and Effect

The following is an example of a single cause and effect:

> My alarm failed to ring this morning, so I was late to work.

The first action (alarm failed to ring) caused the second action (the writer's late arrival at work): Another way to state this cause-and-effect scenario is the following:

> I was late to work this morning because my alarm failed to ring.

Cause and effect sentences are frequently written this way.

Multiple Causes and Effects

There are, however, sometimes multiple causes for an event. The above scenario can become even more complex by showing other actions that led to the narrator's late arrival to work. The following paragraph fills in the details.

Excuses, Excuses

This morning started off badly, and it only got worse. First, my alarm failed to ring, so I overslept. Then I had to hurry and got a speeding ticket, slowing me down even more. When I finally got to work, all the nearby parking spaces were taken, and I had to park several blocks away. By the time I walked in, I was an hour late. Even though I had to work hard to catch up, I finally got back on schedule, and the rest of my day went well.

The complexity of this scenario arises from multiple causes as well as multiple effects arising from the multiple causes. We can **analyze** the events in the following ways:

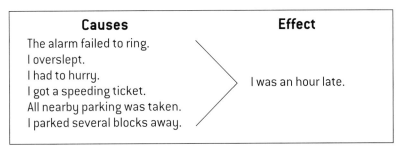

Looking at the same scenario, we can also see multiple effects or events caused by the initial action:

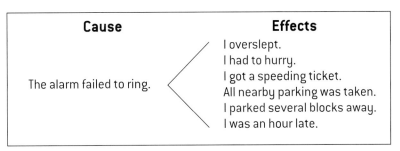

Finally, we can look at each action both as a cause and as an effect:

cause	cause	cause	cause
The alarm failed to ring →	I overslept →	I had to hurry →	I got a speeding ticket →
	effect	effect	effect

cause		cause	
Nearby parking was taken →	I had to park several blocks away →		I was an hour late.
effect		effect	effect

The above blocks analyze the paragraph by listing the causes and effects individually. In a paragraph, however, writers must use transitions that indicate either chronology or sequence to make the ideas flow smoothly from one to the next. Look at the paragraph and mark the transitional words that move the reader along from one event to the next. You should have marked *first, so, then, when, and, by the time.* Other examples of chronological or sequential transitional words include *once, ago, formerly, finally, first, second, and last.*

Causal analysis is important in many areas of our daily life. Doctors usually want to know the symptoms leading up to an illness so they can find the cause(s). Since there can be numerous causes that result in similar conditions, the doctor must discover as much as possible to make an accurate diagnosis. Other areas of our life are frequently affected by events that we can prepare for. For example, from June 1 to November 30, weather conditions create hurricanes in the Atlantic Ocean, the Caribbean, and the Gulf of Mexico. An important question that is asked at this time is, "What would happen if a hurricane hit X city?" When a hurricane or tropical depression threatens, emergency preparedness centers become active, putting into effect the plans made for the possible storm effects.

Psychologists are concerned about the causes of human behavior. For example, faced with a young person who is clearly underweight or overweight, the doctor will want to explore the causes for what appears to be anorexia or obesity. Similarly, professors ask students to investigate causes or effects of wars, pollution of lakes or air, economic depression, gentrification, mass transit, the passage of certain bills in Congress, and so forth. Although immediate effects might not be readily discernable, professors might want students to consider possible long-term effects.

Slippery Slope Fallacy

When an author decides to write a causal analysis, either as part of a longer essay or as the entire essay, he must be careful to use logical thinking and to be sure that each effect is connected to the cause. Sometimes overzealous individuals predict that numerous unrelated effects can occur from a single event. This is known formally as the **Slippery Slope Fallacy** or informally as the **Domino Theory.** For example, in June 2003, the Supreme Court overturned the *Lawrence and Garner v. Texas* case, ruling that the Texas sodomy law was unconstitutional when applied to a private act performed between consenting adults. Various political and religious individuals argued that legalizing sodomy in that case would open the door to gay marriage, threaten traditional marriage, and lead to the legalization of incest, bestiality, polygamy, and so forth. This is clearly an example of an argument relying on the **Slippery Slope Fallacy.**

Critical Thinking Exercise 1: Causes

Read the following short passages that describe causes. List the possible effects that result from the causes. Be sure to avoid using the Slippery Slope Fallacy.

1. During the early settlement of the United States, a competition, called a "side hunt," was held, usually on Christmas Day or on the day after Christmas. Those who ran the event, held as a competition, awarded prizes to men, who, in teams or individually, could kill the most number of birds, squirrels, or other designated game. After the competition was over, the animals were discarded rather than used.
2. In 2003, President Bush severely weakened the Clean Air Act.
3. Several states reduced their speed limit from 70 to 55 miles per hour.
4. In 2003, the Texas legislature declared that a fetus has rights.
5. The baby boom generation has participated in more exercising and life-extending activities than any generation before them.

In the following exercise, you will have to think backward instead of forward. Ask yourself questions like Why? or What caused x to happen? Imagine *because* at the end of the sentence.

Critical Thinking Exercise 2: Effects

Read the following effects and list possible causes for each.

1. A senior in high school has been diagnosed as anorexic.
2. The wolf population has decreased significantly in the last ten years.
3. Universities are providing self-defense classes for their coeds.
4. New buildings in California are being built on rubber and other flexible foundations.
5. Immigration laws have become stricter.

Now, take the above effects and consider them causes (imagine *because* at the beginning of the sentence). What possible conditions could occur from these actions? Be sure to avoid the Slippery Slope Fallacy.

Now that you have thought about and created your own causes and effects, you will have an opportunity to read a personal narrative that

---

READER EXPECTATIONS FOR CAUSAL ANALYSIS

Readers expect to find the following elements:

- Action that creates one or more consequences
- Consequences or effects arising directly from the actions
- Short- and/or long-term effects that occur from the actions
- Transitional words that indicate chronological or sequential effects
- A lesson that can be learned from the cause and effect actions

---

was written primarily in the causal analysis pattern of development. But first, read the following Reader Expectations for Causal Analysis.

Read the following personal narrative Anne wrote about her experience visiting the Grand Canyon. Her primary pattern of development is causal analysis. Use the above list of Reader Expectations, marking the points as you find them.

The Grand Canyon Mis-Adventure

Ever since I was in elementary school, I have wanted to see the Grand Canyon, and after taking a geology class, I knew that one of my vacations had to include a trip to see it. I talked with my traveling companion and convinced her that we should include it on our next trip, and when she agreed, I was delighted. Even before summer was near, I began preparing for our vacation, especially visiting the Canyon on our way home. However, I never expected something as simple as a cold to affect my Grand Canyon visit as well as the rest of my life.

Two days before arriving at the Grand Canyon, I got sick in Las Vegas. Even though I only had a cold, it was bad enough to keep me in bed for another one of our anticipated stops. On the second morning, I felt so sick, I had to find a doctor for a prescription for cough medicine and an antibiotic. My traveling companion and I spent the rest of the day in Las Vegas: she explored the new hotels, and I stayed in bed with a fever and a cough. By the next morning, I began to feel the effects of both medications, and I was ready for my long-awaited visit. We arrived at the Grand Canyon late in the afternoon and were able to see a little before we checked into our hotel.

The next morning, I woke up, still coughing but

feeling much better. We drove around the south rim, stopping at many of the observation points and walking the trails. By noon, I began to get red bumps on my legs and abdomen—215 red, itchy bumps. Since I was wearing shorts, I thought I had brushed against shrubs that caused an allergic reaction. We went back to the hotel, and I bought Calamine lotion to ease the irritation. Unfortunately, it didn't help very much.

The next morning, we had planned to do more sightseeing, but when I woke up, I was covered with twice as many red, itchy bumps as I had had the day before. We decided to begin the drive home instead of continuing our adventure. I called my doctor from the car and made an appointment, knowing we would be home in three days, cutting the Grand Canyon part short and omitting our extended visits to Santa Fe, Albuquerque, and San Antonio. The trip back was awful. I coughed and scratched while my friend drove as fast and as long as possible. I continued to hope that what now looked like a full-body rash would stop itching since I was away from vegetation, but I was wrong. Not even the Calamine lotion helped. Not having much else to do in the car, I examined the bumps more carefully, and I changed my diagnosis from an allergy to chigger bites.

When I finally got home, I went to the clinic at the appointed time. My doctor concurred with my latter diagnosis and prescribed Benadryl. It began to work immediately. However, by this time, I was also getting over my cold. Not only were the "chigger bites" going away, but so were all the other cold symptoms. When I returned to my doctor ten days later, I was cured. As we chatted, she asked about the rest of the trip, and I told her about the Las Vegas cold, cough and doctor's visit. At that point, she realized that both of us had given the incorrect diagnosis: I didn't have chigger bites at all. I had had a severe reaction to the antibiotic caused by exposure to the sun. When I stopped taking the pills, the rash began to disappear. She advised me never to take that particular antibiotic again, and I decided that I would also rather not visit the Grand Canyon again either.

Although I had wanted to visit this Wonder of the World for more years than I can count, I came away from it miserable and disappointed. Although the Canyon itself did not contribute to my misery, I found that I do not want to return. If I had paid attention to the warning labels on the prescription bottle, maybe I would not have had the allergic reaction; maybe I would have enjoyed the sight that I had wanted to see since I was a child; or maybe I would not have the feeling that the Grand Canyon is not so grand.

Reading Exercise 1

1. Does the thesis prepare you for a causal analysis essay? How?
2. What was the first event in the series that created the effects?
3. List the individual events in a timeline that shows what led to the final, long-term effect.
4. What lessons did Anne learn from her experience?

HOW TO WRITE CAUSAL ANALYSIS

If you have been given an assignment by a professor to write about the effects of high ozone levels in the atmosphere or about the causes of deformed frogs in certain ponds, you will be writing causal analysis. In some cases, you might be focusing on only one aspect of this pattern of development: causes *or* effects. In other assignments, you might be writing about both. For example, a different professor might ask you to write about the causes and effects of Puritanism in Colonial America.

When you receive a causal analysis assignment, you must (1) decide which aspect you will develop, (2) choose an appropriate prewriting strategy to help you generate ideas, (3) organize your thoughts, and (4) write your draft. For some assignments, you might have to conduct research—either primary, gathering facts yourself, or secondary, reading what others have discovered. From your findings, you will be able to arrive at conclusions about short-term or long-term effects. For other papers, like the one Anne wrote earlier in this chapter, you might be able to use a personal experience that had an impact on you.

Step One—Prewriting

If you cannot readily decide on a topic, you might begin with brainstorming: listing all possible ideas that come to mind. You might also consider whether you want to write about the event primarily as a cause of subsequent effects—like the alarm not ringing and creating a series of events—or primarily as an effect, and look at all the events that led up to it.

Jonathan's class was asked to write a paper beginning with a cause and to discuss the effects. The class was also reminded to avoid the Slippery Slope Fallacy. Not knowing what to write and not being given a set of topics, Jonathan made the following list of events from which many effects arose in his life:

Causes

1. I failed my driving test.
2. I enrolled in a creative writing class as an elective.
3. I asked my girlfriend to marry me before I left for college.
4. I got lost on campus my first day of classes.
5. I got a job while going to school full time.

Jonathan wrote for approximately five to seven minutes and generated a list of topics, any of which might be developed into a full essay. However, rather than begin writing, Jonathan created a cluster to expand his ideas about the topic that he chose. Since his assignment was to write a paragraph rather than an essay, he did not have to develop an elaborate cluster.

Jonathan took some time to reflect about his experience, and he was able to recall numerous details about the class and the effects it had on him.

Jonathan's Cluster

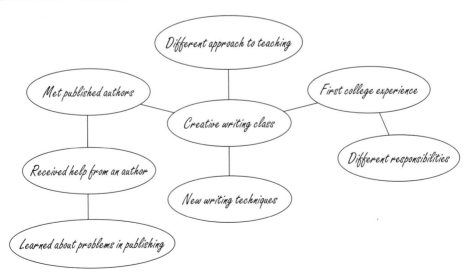

Step Two—The Topic Sentence/Thesis

Next, Jonathan sat down to create a topic sentence for the single-paragraph assignment. Had he chosen to write an essay, he would work on possible thesis sentences. Below are his attempts, with his professor's comments in **bold.**

Topic Sentences

Taking a creative writing class during the summer was the best decision I've ever made. **Your sentence shows enthusiasm but does not introduce a causal analysis paragraph. Why was it the "best" decision?**

Taking a creative writing class helped me improve my writing skills. **Better sentence but there are so many details included in the cluster that you might want to elaborate a little more. Try one more time.**

During the summer between my junior and senior year, I had an opportunity to enroll in a creative writing class at one of the local universities, and it has made a difference in my writing. **This is much better and definitely the one you should use.**

Now Jonathan is ready to write his first draft.

Step Three—First Draft

Read the following paragraph and use the Grading Profile that follows it to evaluate Jonathan's causal analysis.

```
Doing What I Like Best—and Being Rewarded for It

     During the summer between my junior and senior
year, I had an opportunity to enroll in a creative
writing class at one of the local universities, and
it has made a difference in my writing. I have always
enjoyed writing short stories, and I have always
wanted to be published. When I heard about the class
for high school students, I immediately asked my
parents if I could spend the first six weeks of summer
in the class and they approved. The class was fun and
exciting. I was able to write short stories and have
them edited by my peers, who understood the ideas
```

that I was writing about better than any of my high school teachers did. The best part of the experience was when our professor, a published author herself, brought in several writers to talk to us about their experiences, how they began, and the problems they ran into. At the end of the semester, our professor asked another author to read our papers and critique them privately with us individually. The last assignment we had to complete was to send one of the stories we wrote in class to any magazine or journal for possible publication. Our professor wanted us to understand the feeling of getting back either an acceptance or rejection letter. Several months later, I received my first acceptance, and now I'm a published author! I believe that that class introduced me to many aspects of writing and publishing that I was unaware of. My writing has improved, and I understand the importance of revision and editing even more than I did before. That summer experience changed my assumptions of what writing is about and made me a better writer I am looking forward to majoring in creative writing.

GRADING PROFILE FOR CAUSAL ANALYSIS

The student provided	Yes	No	Almost
1. A thesis / topic sentence that indicates causal analysis.			
2. A paragraph / essay that discusses a cause or an effect.			
3. A chronological or sequential series of causes or effects.			
4. Transitional words.			
5. A sense of conclusion or closure of the activity.			
6. A lesson learned from the experience.			

Respond to the following:

1. Identify the strength of the paper.

2. Identify one weakness and make a suggestion to the author for fixing it.

Although Jonathan has a good draft, he needs to revise it somewhat. Before he begins his final copy, he must also complete the editing process, following directions from his professor.

Step Four—Revision and Editing

Jonathan has a good control of the topic and language, but he has spots that can be improved for a better paper. He also has committed some errors in his use of grammar and mechanics. Can you find the following weaknesses in the paper?

1. Areas for elaborating on causes and effects (revision)
2. Missing comma between independent clauses (editing) and a missing period between independent clauses
3. Wrong word (editing)
4. Run-on sentence (editing)
5. Number agreement (editing)

Go back into the paragraph and elaborate on causes and effects and correct the errors. When you finish that, reread the paragraph and decide if Jonathan needs to reword any of his sentences to make them flow better or to help them make better sense. Below is Jonathan's final copy.

Step Five—Final Draft

Jonathan took his instructor's advice, and he revised and edited his paragraph. Below are the results, his final draft with the corrections made and revisions in **bold.**

Doing What I Like Best—and Being Rewarded for It

The summer between my junior and senior years, I had an opportunity to enroll in a creative writing class at one of the local universities, and it has made a difference in my writing. I have always enjoyed writing short stories, and I have always wanted to be published. When I heard about the class for high school students, I immediately asked my parents if I could spend the first six weeks of summer in the class and they approved. The class was fun and exciting. I was **finally** able to write short stories and have them edited by my peers, who understood the ideas that I was writing about better than any of my teachers did. **Being in this class let me meet other students who enjoyed writing and were interested in improving their own and helping others improve also.** The best part of the experience was when our professor, a published author herself, brought in several writers to talk to us about their experiences, how they began, and the problems they ran into. **I had never met professional writers before, and their stories let me know that my experiences were not unique.** At the end of the semester, our professor asked another author to read our **stories** and critique them privately with us individually. **If I had not taken this class, I probably would not have had this kind of experience.** The last assignment we had to complete was to send one of the stories we wrote in class to any magazine or journal for possible publication. Our professor wanted us to understand the feeling of getting back either an acceptance or rejection letter. Several months later, I received my first acceptance, and now I'm a published author! I believe that that class introduced me to many aspects of writing and publishing that I was unaware of. My writing has improved, and I understand the importance of revision and editing even more than I did before. That summer experience changed my assumptions of what writing is about and made me a better writer. **Now** I am looking forward to majoring in creative writing.

Jonathan has corrected his errors and expanded his ideas, and he has produced a better paper.

Writing Causal Analysis

1. Select one the following topics below to use as the *cause of multiple effects*. Be sure to avoid the Slippery Slope Fallacy. Write a multiparagraph essay.

Graduation from high school	The birth of my youngest sibling
My new job	Talking on a cell phone while driving
Being a teenage mother	Serving in the armed forces
Volunteering in a women's shelter	Having a computer virus

2. Select one of the following topics below to use as the *effect of multiple causes*. Write a multiparagraph essay.

CAUSAL ANALYSIS CHARACTERISTICS

- A thesis or topic sentence introducing cause and/or effects
- An action/cause that produces specific results/effects
- An event/effect that occurred because of one or more actions/causes
- Chronological or sequential development
- Transitional words
- Part of a larger essay or an essay unto itself
- A lesson or understanding that arises from the causes and/or effects

Bankruptcy	Academic probation
A wedding	A visit to the zoo
A special dinner at a nice restaurant	Beginning college at the age of 40
A dentist appointment	A vacation

Chapter 10

Reading and Writing Persuasion and Argument

HOW TO READ ARGUMENT

Most individuals consider the term *argument* to mean a heated conversation between two or more individuals who are attempting to prove that they are right about a particular topic. This is one definition; however, when considering rhetoric and composition, there is another. In writing, an argument is the presentation of material in a way that presents a point and defends it. According to Andrea Lunsford, a leading composition theorist, "Everything is argument." And if you consider that statement carefully, you can see that she has a point. Think about any of the essays or paragraphs that you have written up to this point. If you wrote a paper that has a thesis, for an essay assignment, or a topic sentence, for a paragraph assignment, you stated a position and proceeded to defend and develop it. You have written an argument. When someone is defending her position against one or more persons, she is within the realm of argument. It can be about one's rights within a household or one's rights in society. Regardless of the complexity of the issue, the argument is usually developed with logic and emotion. Furthermore, it must have evidence to support the **claims** that are being made. In writing, an argument need not be heated; however, it must have certain elements: a *purpose,* an *issue* that is in contention, a *claim,* sometimes referred to as the *thesis,* that states the position of the party, *evidence* that supports the position, and *refutation* or evidence that supports the opposition's point of view. Most arguments are developed in this way.

Purpose

Although some people will argue for the sake of arguing, most arguments have a purpose. The most common purpose in an argument is to *convince*. The next most common purpose is to *persuade*. Students frequently confuse the two, thinking that they are the same; however, they are not. In attempting to convince the opposition, you are merely attempting to get him to agree with your position, that is, to think the way you think or believe what you believe. Persuasion, on the other hand, encourages readers to act, to do something. Read the following examples:

Convincing Claim

Elvis is a better singer than either Johnny Cash or Mick Jagger.

Persuasive Claim

You should buy an Elvis CD instead of a Rolling Stones CD.

In the first example, the Elvis fan is attempting to convince the audience that the quality of Elvis's singing is better than that of Cash or Jagger. In the second, she is trying to persuade the audience to do something: buy an Elvis CD. In the first, the audience does not have to do anything but agree or disagree with the fan; in the second, the audience is encouraged to act.

Another purpose of argument is to *negotiate*. In this method, the writer acknowledges the value of multiple sides of an argument to arrive at a compromise or consensus. Look at the following scenario and determine how you would compromise.

Lake-view Property vs. Wooded Acreage

Issue: A couple wants to buy property for a weekend retreat. One party wants a lake-view lot while the other wants wooded and pasture acreage.

Lake-view	Wooded
1. The view	1. Privacy
2. Access to fishing	2. The view
3. Less maintenance	3. Quiet—no neighbors
4. Utilities are already in	4. More land for the money

Compromise #1 Buy acreage within a short driving distance to a lake.

Compromise #2 Buy what is affordable and available.

Reading Exercise 1

1. Look in a magazine or newspaper to find an ad that argues to persuade or to convince. Take it to class and be ready to analyze and discuss it.
2. Many billboard ads are created to persuade readers to buy a particular product. Find one that does so without words but relies on images instead. How is this a form of reading? Be prepared to describe the billboard, its product, and its method of persuasion.
3. Find a brochure for a hotel or resort. Analyze the ways the creators persuade the reader to visit and/or stay at the particular place.

The Issue

The issue that a writer develops and supports in an argumentative piece must be one that is debatable. Because facts are not debatable, the assertion or thesis should be created from an opinion that can be supported with facts. A belief that is purely subjective in nature, a personal opinion, cannot be argued on the basis of facts. The Elvis versus Cash or Jagger argument mentioned previously will be quite difficult to support because this is a matter of opinion based on taste and style. Elvis sang rock and roll, country and western, gospel, and blues, but he had a style that was unique, even though many attempt to imitate him. Cash sang not only country and western and gospel, but he also sang songs about drug reform. Jagger is the lead singer for the Rolling Stones. They sing primarily hard rock songs. This argument will probably be reduced to a matter of opinion. Therefore, writers should avoid writing papers that attempt to argue quality or beauty or the advantages of one thing over another unless there are concrete aspects to be debated, like the advantages of a brick house over a log house. Abstract issues are the hardest to defend and to develop.

As noted earlier, another point that cannot be argued is a fact. For example, readers of the following sentence cannot argue about it because it is composed of facts: "Our local grocery store manager recently hired a sushi chef for the deli department, and he provides sushi for customers daily." Customers might argue the freshness, the quality, or the variety available, but they cannot argue the points listed in the original assertion.

Finally, an issue should be worth arguing about. Most of us have read arguments about issues and come away wondering what the point of the argument is. For example, writing an argument about the benefits of asparagus over broccoli is not a substantial issue. The issue needs to be something that others care about and want to see resolved or settled in some way, for example, preserving wetlands or clearing the land for a new airport.

Reading Exercise 2

Read the following assertions and determine if they are fact or opinion.

1. Cell phones cause brain tumors.
2. The Houston Rockets won the NBA championship when Robert Horry was on the team.
3. Losing Robert Horry to the Los Angeles Lakers cost the Houston Rockets the NBA championship.
4. Consistent exercise prevents heart attacks.
5. The death penalty prevents criminals from committing serious crimes.

The Claim or Thesis

In **exposition,** the controlling idea of the essay is known as the *thesis;* however, in argumentation, it is known as a *claim.* The claim must follow the purpose of the essay and take its form from that pattern of development. Look at the following examples:

Convincing Claim

Elvis is a better singer than either Johnny Cash or Mick Jagger.

Persuading Claim

Music lovers should buy more Elvis CDs than CDs by Johnny Cash or Mick Jagger.

Claims for negotiating arguments, on the other hand, are more difficult to discern because the point or position the author takes appears at the end of the article after the various sides to the issue have been stated. In the conclusion, the writer will arrive at a compromise after listing the points from each side as objectively as possible. Similarly, a claim for an argument of inquiry will come at the end after the writer has thought through all possible evidence about the issue. At that point, the writer will arrive at a conclusion based on all the facts.

Evidence

Evidence for a claim should be *compelling, reliable, timely,* and *relevant* to the issue the writer is presenting. Readers will frequently find that the author has completed research to support the position he is arguing for. To ensure that the information is reliable, the reader should recognize the author or the journal that the information is taken from. If a reader is concerned about the effects of a heart transplant after her father leaves the hospital, she would look for information supplied by a heart specialist like Dr. Michael DeBakey or other well-known doctors who has made a career in cardiology. Other people the researcher might consult could be individuals who have had transplants. She should consult more than one, because different people have different reactions.

Another element that is important in evidence is the *timeliness* of the information. Although there will be articles that are still classics in their field, even if they were written years ago, new technology is regularly producing new methods, treatments, statistics, tools, and so forth about living in today's world. For example, if a reader wants to know about the latest developments in computer technology, she should look at current computer journals, magazines, or online information. Material published six months ago might already be outdated.

The *relevance of the information* that one reads is also important. When a woman is having a child, she might want to know about nutrition and health concerns while she is pregnant. Reading magazines written especially for pregnant women or articles written specifically about food and how to stay fit during pregnancy are relevant to the mother's as well as the child's condition. Finding information about reading to the child or playing particular music while the child is still in utero is not relevant.

Compelling evidence is also information that readers need to see to be able to make a decision about a certain topic. Statistics, personal testimonies, changes in the environment over the last few months, or other quantifiable or definitive studies can produce compelling evidence about issues. If you saw the movie *Erin Brockovitch*, you watched the main character prove that the pollution that was seeping into the ground water from a particular industry was causing cancer in individuals who drank the water. To make her case, she had to gather medical evidence about, and from, everyone who had cancer or who had died from cancer and lived in the area as well as collect water samples to take to laboratories for analysis. She produced compelling evidence for a cancer cluster in that community, which was caused by the pollution of the ground water released by the industry.

Refutations

In most arguments, readers will find that the authors include information that supports the opposition. This is done sometimes to challenge the points the opposition presents with equally compelling evidence. Another reason is to present a balanced view and prove that the author is aware of the opposition's arguments so that the reader will not believe the author is biased or ignorant of the facts. Another reason to present the opposition's side is to be able to dismiss it before the audience has time to think about it seriously and become convinced or persuaded by points the author wishes to control.

Reading Process for Argumentation

Read the two paragraphs below and use the following steps to analyze the passage for the elements of argument. The sentences have been numbered for easy reference after the paragraph.

1. Determine the purpose—to convince, to persuade, or to negotiate.
2. What is the issue/topic?
3. What is the claim/thesis? Write the assertion, without the supporting points, in your own words.
4. List the points the author uses to support the claim.
5. What evidence is used?
6. Is the evidence
   - reliable?
   - compelling?

ELEMENTS OF AN ARGUMENT

Arguments should have the following elements:

- A purpose—to convince, to persuade, or to negotiate
- An issue—a topic that is **concrete,** worth arguing about, and of interest
- A claim—also known as a **thesis,** the point of the essay
- Evidence—information that supports the issue and should be compelling, reliable, timely, and relevant
- Refutation—information that argues the opposing view

- timely?
- relevant?

7. Does the author include refutation/points from the opposition?
8. Does the paragraph support the claim?

Cleaning Up Air Pollution

[1]Tightening the federal regulations on industrial air emissions should be delayed because of insufficient data to determine effects on health, the financial burden of such added regulations, and limited number of personnel qualified to regulate such controls.

[2]One of the main concerns proponents of air pollution clean-up use to foster their argument for stronger regulation of industrial air is the issue of health. [3]Problems related to circulation, such as heart and lung diseases, and to skin irritation are among the pro-regulators' main arsenal of weapons aimed at the industrial sector's perceived abuse of the country's air quality. [4]However, what such proponents fail to provide is a direct one-to-one correlation between a particular factory's emissions and the health issues of the community. [5]Nor do such groups possess any community-wide data or study which shows any type of chemical interaction between the various types of waste air generated by the community's industrial companies. [6]Instead of adding more regulations to the industrial sector, including more devices to monitor the size of pollutants expelled into the air, the proponents of industrial clean-up should consider not only the fumes created by the automobiles they drive but also the household chemicals used directly within their own home, chemicals which often carry poison warnings on them and which are in constant and close proximity to the individual family members.

In this paper, the author, Steve, separated the claim from the body of the paragraph to give it more importance and so that the reader could easily identify the position he is taking. He also states his position in a relatively positive way. Rather than saying that the federal government *should not* tighten federal regulations on industrial air emissions, his assertion is that the regulations *should be delayed*, indicating that he is not opposed to tightening regulations but sees problems in doing it now. The proponents, those who support tightening federal regulations, are now

---

READER EXPECTATIONS FOR ARGUMENT AND PERSUASION

For argumentation and persuasive essays, readers expect the following:

- A purpose for the essay—to convince, to persuade, or to negotiate
- A clearly stated issue
- A claim that might come at the end as well as at the beginning of the piece
- Evidence that is compelling, reliable, timely, and relevant
- Refutation or rebuttal
- Transitions that signal a change in position
- An essay that supports the writer's claim

Steve's *opponents* because they oppose *his* position. An important writing technique that Steve uses, and that has been mentioned in previous chapters, is the use of transition words. Notice that Steve begins with his opponents' position and switches to his position in the fourth sentence. To signal that he is moving to his own position, he uses the transitional word, *however.*

HOW TO WRITE ARGUMENT AND PERSUASION

Just as in writing an informative paper, writing an **argumentative** or **persuasive** paper requires preparation. Knowing the stumbling blocks discussed in the preceding pages should alert writers to possible problems. The next step is to consider the audience.

Audience

The question of whom the writer is trying to convince is crucial. If a writer were attempting to justify the actions of Vietnam War "draft dodgers" to a Veterans of Foreign Wars group or to members of the American Legion, that writer would likely be unsuccessful. If a writer were attempting to convince a group of environmentalists to stop President George W. Bush from drilling for oil in the Arctic National Wildlife Refuge in Alaska, that writer would also be wasting time. Look at the diagram below, which indicates a continuum of opinion on an issue.

Opponents	*Undecided*	*Proponents*

Student writers should target members of the undecided group in the middle rather than staunch proponents or opponents of a proposition. Those individuals in the middle who are wavering need well-developed, thoughtful arguments that provide fresh, new evidence or a fresh approach that raises their interest. The writer should always assume that the audience will be skeptical and possibly hostile if the issue is highly controversial. In these cases, the writer must build sound, strong arguments.

Step One—Prewriting

Prewriting is crucial to writing a successful **argumentative essay.** Let's consider the "Cleaning Up Air Pollution" piece in which Steve attempts to *convince* readers to agree with him that "Congress should delay sending forth any bill that would tighten federal regulations on air emissions." First, in considering his audience you will see that he is not writing to members of Congress; instead, he is writing to readers of newspapers or magazines, like *Newsweek* or *Time*, expressing his opinion about the issue.

Second, readers want to know exactly what the issue is. Since this article is titled, "Cleaning Up Air Pollution," readers have an idea what they will be reading about. It is an important issue that should interest individuals living in communities where air pollution is a problem or where industries that release pollution into the air are located.

Third, readers usually want to know immediately where an author stands on an issue. If the author is unsure, this is the time when he can begin to do research about the activities that are required to tighten federal regulations and what the effects of tightening them might be. During prewriting, Steve can make two lists: one that states reasons supporting the tightening of controls and one that states reasons opposing it. This does not mean that Steve has chosen a position yet; it only means that he has found points that support and oppose the topic. Many students have difficulty understanding why they need to know the opposition's point of view. Keep in mind that if you do not know what the opposition thinks, you are at a disadvantage. Knowing the opposition's point of view provides the writer with the opportunity to present the rebuttal or refutation. To **refute** a point is to prove how it is in error or wrong; to **rebut** is basically the same process, to oppose with proof to the contrary. Thus, not to know the opposition's stance is to leave yourself open to a surprise attack for which you have no defense or rebuttal. If you are aware only of the points that will support your position you reduce your credibility, and appear narrow-minded. Such a narrow point of view means that you cannot concede or acknowledge any constructive aspects of the opposition's argument and that you have made no provisions to accommodate or compromise. Below are the lists Steve made while investigating his topic.

CLEANING UP AIR POLLUTION

Points in Favor	Points in Opposition
1. It decreases health problems such as lung cancer, heart attacks, and emphysema.	1. It requires trained inspectors to test the amount of pollution in the air.
2. It cuts down on the problem of global warming.	2. It requires people to identify companies that are violating the law.
3. It provides visually pleasing views.	3. It requires regular and costly monitoring systems to be implemented to measure pollution being released into the environment.
4. It prevents damage to seals around windows.	4. It is too costly to install air pollution filtering devices in equipment already in place.
5. It helps preserve the older architecture and statues.	5. It would require a change in driving laws, reducing the speed limits from 70 miles per hour to 55 miles per hour.
6. It reduces buildup in air filters in cars and air conditioners.	

Now that Steve can see the points made by opposing sides, he is prepared to determine his position, select the points that will defend his position, eliminate irrelevant or weak points, select the counterarguments, and write his claim.

Writing Exercise 1

From the list below, select one topic, and write points that support the issue and points that oppose it. You might have to do some research to supply points. Be sure that your sources are current and reliable.
- The use of HMOs
- Government-subsidized child care for working women
- Affirmative action

- Free college education for any student in the top 10 percent of his or her high school graduating class
- Reducing the highway speeds from 70 miles per hour to 55 miles per hour

Step Two—Writing the Claim

Now that Steve has found points that support and oppose the issue of cleaning up air pollution, he must determine what his position is. After reviewing the information, he has decided that it is important to support the issue, but he does not believe that this is the time to do it. Thus, he begins writing tentative claims. Below are the four attempts he made, with teacher comments in **bold**.

The Convincing Claim

It is not time for Congress to tighten regulations on industries for clean air. **You need to think about your position more and add reasons that will support it.**

Congress has not taken the time to consider the problems in tightening regulations for industries, and therefore, should wait, consider the problems, and vote later. **Your claim sounds like you're criticizing Congress, and you have not given specific points. Try again.**

Tightening the federal regulations on industrial air emissions should be delayed until Congress can gather data to determine how pollution affects health, how much money industries will have to pay and the consumer will have to be charged, and how many personnel will have to be trained and hired to regulate the controls. **Much better but it needs to be tightened up. It's too wordy, and you are beginning your argument within the claim.**

Tightening the federal regulations on industrial air emissions should be delayed because of insufficient data to determine effects on health, the financial burden of such added regulations, and limited number of personnel qualified to regulate such controls. **Good.**

Step Three—Writing the First Draft

Because this assignment is to write a short argumentative paper, Steve is not going to write an essay. Instead, he will write two paragraphs—one for his claim and the other to develop the points in his claim briefly.

Readers will see that he has eliminated many of the points from his lists and selected only those that are relevant and compelling to the topic.

The following is Steve's first draft of the paper.

Cleaning Up Air Pollution

Tightening the federal regulations on industrial air emissions should be delayed because of insufficient data to determine effects on health, the financial burden of such added regulations, and limited number of personnel qualified to regulate such controls.

One of the main concerns proponents of air pollution clean-up use to foster their argument for stronger regulation of industrial air is the issue of health. Problems related to circulation, such as heart and lung diseases, and to skin irritation are among the pro-regulators' main arsenal of weapons aimed at the industrial sector's perceived abuse of the country's air quality. However, what such proponents fail to provide is a direct one-to-one correlation between a particular factory's emissions and the health issues of the community. Nor do such groups possess any community-wide data or study which shows any type of chemical interaction between the various types of waste air generated by the community's industrial companies. Instead of looking to the industrial sector, which is already heavily regulated and monitored by state and federal agencies, the proponents of industrial clean-up should consider not only the fumes created by the automobiles they drive but also the household chemicals used directly within their own home, chemicals which often carry poison warnings on them and which are in constant and close proximity to individual family members.

Even though Steve has a good beginning here, he does not support his claim fully. He has begun to discuss the points he listed, but he stops short. He needs to revise.

Step Four—Peer Editing for Revision

Using the following Peer Editing Profile for Argumentation and Persuasion, analyze Steve's essay and determine where it needs to be revised. Be honest in your assessment.

Writing Exercise 2

1. Using the topic you chose from **Writing Exercise 1,** look at the points you listed. Determine the position you will take in your paper and write your claim, incorporating three points you will use to support your position.
2. Write the first draft of your paper, stating the claim first and developing your material by following the points you have listed.
3. Before you complete a peer editing exercise, use the Peer Editing Profile and complete a self-evaluation of your paper. If you do not have everything that is listed on the Profile, make revisions. Remember to read this as a reader rather than as the writer of the paper. Be honest in your assessment of your own paper.
4. Complete a peer editing exercise, using the Peer Editing Profile.

PEER EDITING PROFILE FOR ARGUMENTATION AND PERSUASION

The student provides	Yes	No	Almost	NA*
1. A claim.				
2. Points to be used to support the claim.				
3. Evidence that is compelling.				
4. Evidence that is reliable.				
5. Evidence that is timely.				
6. Evidence that is relevant.				
7. Refutation or rebuttal.				
8. Sufficient development of the points.				
9. A strong conclusion (position or compromise).				
10. Only the writer's position in the conclusion.				
11. A paper that supports the claim.				

*NA—*Not Applicable*

Respond to the following:

1. Discuss the strength of the paper.

2. Point out one weakness in the paper and suggest how the writer might fix it.

3. Explain why you agree or disagree with the writer. If this is a persuasive paper, explain why you would or would not do what he wants his readers to do.

4. If this is a negotiation paper, do you agree with the concluding compromise(s)? Can you offer any other suggestions? What are they?

Step Five—Revision

In considering what he must do for his revision, Steve recognizes that he should first return to his claim and determine which supporting points he used and which he did not use. If he wants to eliminate any of the points, he is free to do so because the claim is not final until the paper is complete. However, as you will see below, he chose to incorporate the remaining points rather than weaken the paper. He also added a concluding sentence.

Although he does not provide specific evidence in the form of statistics or examples, he does make suggestions about what should be offered by the proponents of tightening the regulations. He is asking for the other side to provide the evidence to convince him that time has come to tighten the regulations. He indicates that it is their responsibility to provide these data rather than make opponents of the action do so. Finally, looking at sentence 10 reveals that Steve ends the paragraph with his original assertion but omitting the points.

Cleaning Up Air Pollution

[1]Tightening the federal regulations on industrial air emissions should be delayed because of insufficient data to determine effects on health, the financial burden of such added regulations, and

limited number of personnel qualified to regulate
such controls.

[2]One of the main concerns proponents of air pollution clean-up use to foster their argument for
stronger regulation of industrial air is the issue
of health. [3]Problems related to circulation, such as
heart and lung diseases, and to skin irritation are
among the pro-regulators' main arsenal of weapons
aimed at the industrial sector's perceived abuse of
the country's air quality. [4]However, what such proponents fail to provide is a direct one-to-one correlation between a particular factory's emissions
and the health issues of the community. [5]Nor do such
groups possess any community-wide data or study
which shows any type of chemical interaction between
the various types of waste air generated by the community's industrial companies. [6]Instead of adding
more regulations to the industrial sector, including
more devices to monitor the size of pollutants expelled into the air, the proponents of industrial
clean-up should consider not only the fumes created
by the automobiles they drive but also the household
chemicals used directly within their own home, chemicals which often carry poison warnings on them and
which are in constant and close proximity to individual family members. [7]**Furthermore, these devices
will add a financial burden to industries, which, in
turn, will be passed on to the consumer.** [8]**Finally,
employing and training more personnel to regulate
such controls will be prohibitive on the federal
budget as well on the industry's part.** [9]**If the current number of qualified personnel are required to
regulate the new controls in addition to their other
duties, the quality of their work could diminish and
there could be a slowdown in the amount of time they
take to complete their inspections, thereby slowing
down the monitoring of the emissions.** [10]**Therefore,
Congress should delay sending forth any bill that
would tighten federal regulations on air emissions.**

This draft is definitely stronger and better developed. If he had
time or if the assignment were for a longer paper, he could add an introduction that might give background or history of the air pollution problem he writes about, and he could also add a concluding paragraph
restating only the points that support his position. Doing so reminds the

readers why they should agree with Steve without being reminded that the opposition has their points also. Beginning and ending the paper on the strongest points is in keeping with reading theory that asserts that most readers remember what they read at the beginning and end of an article. If writers remember that and keep that theory in mind, then a strong conclusion that focuses on the writer's position and eliminates the opposition's points should leave the writer's argument firmly embedded in the reader's mind. Look at Steve's concluding sentence. It has done in one sentence what reading theory recommends: He ends the paragraph restating his position.

Step Six—Editing and Formatting

The content of Steve's paper is no longer an issue. However, there are points that might be improved in his syntax. When you are editing your papers, you will need to follow your instructor's directions for smoothing it out, correcting punctuation, and adding the appropriate formatting, as well as responding or not responding to your peer editor's comments.

Step Seven—Final Draft

After Steve finishes editing and formatting in response to his instructor's directions, he will be ready to submit it for a grade and possibly as a brief letter to the editor in his local newspaper. He can also put this in his portfolio and use it later for an extended essay about air pollution.

Writing Exercise 3

1. Revise the paper that you wrote based on the comments that your editor made on the Peer Editing Profile. If you think a comment is not correct or if you think you do not need to make the correction, you should rely on your writer's instinct. However, consider that your reader had a problem seeing what you thought you had written clearly. If you haven't talked with your editor, you might want to do so before you begin your editing and revision.
2. Editing means that you need to work on grammar, mechanics, or other areas of your paper not directly related to the content. Be sure to follow your instructor's directions about what you need to change.
3. After you have edited and formatted your paper according to the appropriate style, read it one more time to proof for errors before you submit it. If you find errors, ask your instructor how he wants you to

CHARACTERISTICS OF ARGUMENTATION

When writing argumentation, writers must include the appropriate elements:

- **The issue,** which should be important and of interest to the audience
- **The claim,** which states the position of the writer either at the beginning or the end of the article
- **The purpose,** which should become apparent from the claim—to convince, to persuade, or to negotiate
- **The points** to support the claim, which can be included but do not have to be
- **Evidence,** which should be compelling, reliable, timely, and relevant
- **Refutation or rebuttal**, which argues the opposing view
- **The conclusion,** which should reiterate only the supporting points or should include the compromise if it is a negotiating paper

make corrections on the copy you are to submit. Then, submit your paper.

PART TWO

Reading About
Social Issues

Chapter 11

Courtesy and Customs: How We Present Ourselves in Society

For many individuals in contemporary society, courtesy has outlived its usefulness. It is a dying relic of the days of chivalry and King Arthur. After all, who has the time in today's rapidly moving world for the niceties that the slower-paced civilizations had? On the other hand, is today's lack of civility, kindness, and respect to others a sign of an ego-centric attitude? Because society demands so much more of us today, many people excuse their lack of awareness of others' needs, or even others' presence, with an "I'm in a hurry" or "I'm too busy." We have come to accept this attitude without thinking of what it means.

As with many other problems in society, we frequently fail to notice our own contributions to the deterioration of manners, but we usually notice others' rudeness—or what we assume to be rudeness, actions that do not conform to our Euro-American expectations. For example, how do you feel when the person a few steps ahead of you—and obviously in a hurry—walks through a door and lets it close on you rather than taking a few seconds to hold it open until you can reach for it? Or did you notice the person who, in a fit of "road rage," screeched past you on the shoulder to get ahead of you before the road narrowed to two lanes, while waving a gesture that was not intended as a thank-you? Or have you ever been in a situation like Kathy Bates in *Fried Green Tomatoes*? You've circled the parking lot repeatedly, finally found someone leaving, waited patiently as the driver pulled out, and lost the space at the last second as someone cut in ahead of you and "stole" the space?

The *Oxford English Dictionary* (OED) defines courteous behavior with a reference to a fourteenth-century understanding: "having such manners as befit the court of a prince." Obviously, America has no royal courts, and few of us are expecting dinner invitations from the White

House or the governor's mansion; but that does not mean that courteous behavior did not exist prior to courtly settings. The Golden Rule, "Do unto others as you would have them do unto you," has been around much longer. Thus, many of us have been taught to treat others the way we wish to be treated—with respect and kindness. There are individuals, however, who seemingly do not have an investment in being treated kindly. Does that give us license to treat them rudely?

The OED, however, continues, explaining that courteous also means "graciously polite and respectful of the position and feelings of others; kind and complaisant in conduct to others." In other words, courteous means displaying an attitude that can be synonymous with words such as *polite, respectful, deferential,* or *mannerly.* Its opposite could include words such as *rude, arrogant, disrespectful,* or *unmannerly.* In Spanish a person who is rude is said to be *mal criada* or badly raised or ill bred, thus reflecting negatively on one's parents or family. Today's society reflects a divergent population composed of various ethnicities and cultures, many of which construct their own rules of etiquette or proper conduct different from mainstream society. Consequently, many of us are sometimes ignorant of someone else's socially acceptable and unacceptable behavior. For example, I had to learn that at my Japanese friend's home, visitors—regardless of ethnicity—remove their shoes at the door. Once I became aware of this practice, I, too, removed my shoes when I visited him, even though I am not Japanese. I see this as an act of respect for his beliefs. Obviously, there are many other instances of "proper behavior" that are socially constructed, and to follow those rules means many things: We know the rules and accept them; we don't want to be seen as rude, even if we disagree with them; we believe we don't have a choice; we want to be accepted; we want to be treated well by others; we want to be a good example for younger people to follow; we'll get "in trouble" if we behave otherwise.

Being polite or rude, civil or uncivil, or courteous or discourteous is a choice, and a complex one that all of us have to make. But first, we need to heighten our own awareness of others' feelings and expectations. In the movie *My Fair Lady,* Professor Higgins, after failing to take Eliza Doolittle's feelings into consideration, tells her, "It's not whether I treat a duchess like a flower girl or a flower girl like a duchess but that I treat everyone the same." Unfortunately, today's pluralistic society no longer allows for that kind of all-inclusive behavior. The articles in this chapter discuss the benefits and disadvantages of manners and what they mean to society. They begin with a critique of American society and how it has slipped in its observance of everyday manners and moves discussion to the roles of customer and salesperson to a reconsideration of the necessity of manners. The chapter concludes with a look at the customs and manners of individuals whose cultural expectations are clearly different from those of mainstream America but are just as important to those who practice them. Thus, it's good to keep in mind that while some individuals might call the way they speak to others just their style, others may find what and/or how they say it offensive. Being aware of and respecting ethnic differences is important.

Take a few minutes to brainstorm some everyday situations that call for courtesy and civility in society but that are sometimes taken for granted; for example, returning phone calls, making introductions, or simply saying good morning to a building custodian or a lawn maintenance person. Compare this list with your classmates and discuss your attitudes and reactions. Finally, make some decisions about the question, "Should I be courteous in today's society?"

MANNERS IN AUSTRIA: A CROSS-CULTURAL VIEW

Margaret H. McFadden

Margaret McFadden, professor of Interdisciplinary Studies at Appalachian State University, was granted a Fulbright Fellowship to teach at the University of Klagenfurt in Klagenfurt, Austria, a small provincial city, the capital of Carinthia, near the Slovenian and Italian borders. In addition to teaching in the United States and Austria, McFadden has also taught in Finland and has traveled extensively throughout Europe. She also cofounded and directed the Women's Studies Department at Appalachian State University and was the editor of the National Women's Studies Association Journal. *Professor McFadden describes in the article below, the adventures and learning experiences she had in her new living environment and with her new colleagues. Her article raises some questions about what individuals who have lived in the United States believe to be customs and norms of other Western countries. How similar are our ways of life to those of different countries of Europe?*

Prereading: The issue of cultural expectations is not only different between countries, it is also different among individuals living in the United States but who have different backgrounds. Even if you haven't traveled abroad or out of your home state, consider the friends and acquaintances you have. How are some of their cultural expectations different from yours?

Prewriting: Create a list of friendly pointers that you might give to a new friend coming to the United States and that reflects the way most of your friends act and expect those around them to act.

Vocabulary: Looking up and understanding the following words prior to reading should prepare you for the author's message. Other words will be defined in the margin.

Fulbright professor

After having recently spent nearly six months in southern Austria as a Fulbright Professor at the University of Klagenfurt for a semester, I have some thoughts on the cross-cultural differences in manners there and in the U.S.A. These were subtle differences that nevertheless combined to make my stay often frustrating. I'm sure I was often misunderstood, and many times I misinterpreted people's actions. I should say at the outset that I know quite a bit of German; can read signs, menus, and easy newspapers; and managed markets and transportation systems. I never heard English on the street, and people in shops, banks, and post offices were patient with my halting German. Still, I communicated with colleagues and students most often in English and taught three courses in Gender Studies in English. What I want to do here is to delineate* some of the areas of manners in which I had the most problems—meeting people and introductions, being a guest, and classroom manners.

delineate: to describe in detail

MEETING PEOPLE AND INTRODUCTIONS

Austria is much more formal than the U.S.A., and being properly introduced is essential to finding one's place in this culture, even in the more informal university society. If one has not been introduced, then it is impolite to speak directly to a colleague. For me, this caused problems, since I was not introduced to other professors, and I could not make the first move to find a colleague in, say, history or English (my specialties). Because I was not introduced, I did not meet like-minded colleagues until the very end of my stay.

Everyone shakes hands when meeting and greeting, even if the two people are good friends already. When one person, either male or female, greets a whole group (at a pub, for example, or restaurant), shaking hands all around, both to greet and to say goodbye, is *de rigueur*.

de rigueur: required by fashion, etiquette, or custom

Women (and occasionally men) who know each other well will often greet and say farewell with the Italian/Mediterranean greeting of air kisses on both cheeks. There are no hugs in the American style, as that is considered too intimate.

imbedded:
made an
important
part of

The most important part of manners in Austria, however, is imbedded* in the German language. The formal "you" form (*Sie*) is still used in all beginning introductions and personal relations (and always in a more traditional area like Carinthia), even though most young people will use the informal you (*Du*). Since I was used to using only *Du* forms (this includes separate verb and adjectival forms) from my classroom work in German conversation, I had to quickly shift to *Sie*. I therefore made several impolite gaffes, such as using *Du* with the student assistants whom I wanted to treat as colleagues. The use of *Du* suggested that I felt I was better than they and was treating them as children or underlings. I, of course, apologized when I realized what I had done.

BEING A GUEST

Being a guest and inviting others to your house are important parts of getting to know any culture and what makes up a particular culture's manners. In this region of Austria, if one is invited for a particular time, one is expected to be no more than 5 minutes late. In Finland, where I lived for a year and have returned several times, one must be exactly on time: when I invited students to my apartment there, they all arrived exactly on the appointed hour. In Austria, I found that occasionally people would arrive very early, perhaps even 45 minutes in advance. Since the norm in the USA is to arrive fashionably late for an invitation to a get-together (not a dinner party), an hour early does create some consterna-

consternation:
amazement that
throws one into
confusion

tion* in the hostess, still struggling to finish the hors d'oeuvres or set the table after just getting home from work. This happened to me twice in Austria, although one of the times there was a mix-up in the time of the invitation.

Telling the time of an invitation can cause many cross-cultural difficulties. If the appointed time of the gathering is 6:30 in the evening, in German one says *"halb sieben"* (half seven), not *"halb sechs"* (half six). But if the invitation is for 6:45 in the evening, one says *"Viertal vor sieben"* (quarter before seven) or *"dreiviertal sechs"* (three-quarters six). Then there is the twenty-four hour clock, the way that all formal and written times are noted, including all transportation schedules. Thus, 6:30 in the evening would be written 18:30, and even in conversation, one must be prepared for *"Achtzehn Uhr dreisig"* when invited somewhere for 6:30 in the evening. On arrival, always remove your shoes. This will be obvious, since an entryway will be full of shoes.

If, on accepting an invitation, you ask what you can bring, you will be told "nothing." Nevertheless, you are expected to take flowers, a bottle of wine, or chocolates. Flowers are the gift that is most often given, and the hostess always arranges them immediately and puts them in the room with the guests. The American-style potluck supper, where everyone brings some of the food, is not a part of Austrian culture. Since I was teaching a course on "Women and Food," I invited all my students to my apartment at the end of the semester and asked them, as a course requirement, to bring some food to share that was representative of either themselves or course material and to talk about what they had brought. I have used this assignment successfully in the U.S. and it is a good way to get to know each other. My Austrian students were not used to potlucks, but they rose to the challenge and brought "Reindling," a traditional Carinthian sweet bread with cinnamon, raisins, and hazel nuts; espresso coffee (because her fellow students needed it for exams!); salad with home-grown greens and Carinthian pumpkin seed oil; special Austrian chocolate bars with jalapeño peppers; buckwheat muffins. I had made 22-ingredient chicken mole (with bitter chocolate, almonds, walnuts, and Hungarian chiles) for everyone (although it was quite difficult to find the peppers and the corn tortillas in Austria), since we had studied the history of chocolate.

CLASSROOM MANNERS

degenerated: declined in quality

laissez-faire: practice of individual freedom of choice and action without restrictions or interference

Although it may in fact be the case that classroom manners in U.S. college classrooms have degenerated*, that we have students who chew tobacco, wear baseball caps, come late, and talk with each other instead of paying attention in class, nothing prepared me for the laissez-faire* attitude of the Austrian university student. Students come in late (very late, even 40 minutes late), and leave early, interrupting the class and the lecture or whatever activity or student report is going on. Sometimes the students would tell me in advance that they would be late, but usually they did not. Since none of my courses in Gender Studies was required, students came and went as they wished. I would never know who would be in the class from week to week. It was nearly impossible to have a class discussion, since no one had read anything and was not prepared to participate, even though I had handed out the readings the week before (but those students might not show up the next week).

Even in the seminar, where two students agreed each week to begin the discussion the following week with reading points and questions on one of the short readings assigned, often those students did not show up, or came in an hour late to their own presentation. Part of the difference in manners has to do with the difference in the European university system, where comprehensive exams are given and students can attend class or not as they wish. Part of it comes from the fact that Gender Studies and Women's Studies are not real fields (*"Fach"*) in Austria, and both students and faculty view these courses as only extras, not important. But a substantial part of the difference is a difference in the manners acceptable in the university culture. University students see themselves as a breed apart, and their actions at the university are nothing like their manners in their very traditional families. Thus, the use of the familiar *Du* form of conversation, smoking in non-smoking areas, and interrupting classes by coming late and leaving early, talking to each other in the classroom, and not showing up for their own presentations.

I have come to see that a great part of the disconnect that I felt during my stay in Austria was due at least as much to cross-cultural differences in manners as to my own lack of facility in the German language. My best advice to those in similar situations would be to learn as much in advance as possible about the culture one is visiting, especially from others who had already been there. Previous Fulbrighters gave me much information on the university system, but there were many circumstances I had to learn from experience.

Reading for Meaning

1. To whom does McFadden attribute the difficulties she encountered in her stay in Austria? Explain.
2. List two things you learned from each of the three sections of this article about how the manners in Austria differed from those in the United States. Add your personal feelings about each.

Reading Deeper

1. Explain the difference between *Sie* and *Du* that McFadden had to learn to use. Do you know of any other languages that make this distinction? Which one(s)?
2. Explain the differences found in Finland, Austria, and the United States with regard to time of arrival for a gathering or party. How do you feel about this?

3. How are the attitudes and actions of the university students at odds with the formality of the general attitudes and customs of Austria? Explain and give examples.

Reading for Writing

1. McFadden writes a description of the way things are run in an Austrian university and university classrooms. From your university experiences, write a **comparison-and-contrast description** of how things are run in your university and your classrooms.

2. Even though McFadden was surprised about the formality of the handshake when entering a group as well as when leaving, this is a practice that occurs in some cultural groups in the United States. Do you or members of your cultural group have ritualistic practices that are not part of mainstream expectations? Write a **descriptive** paper about these rituals, identifying the culture that requires them and the rationale that supports the practices.

IS THE CUSTOMER ALWAYS RIGHT?

Roberta Orona-Cordova

Once upon a time, in a land far away—sounds like a fairy tale doesn't it? Well, once upon a time, probably in California or in places across the United States, salespeople were taught that "The customer is always right." When was it that that custom slipped away? Was it when department stores stopped providing salespeople to fit you for shoes and instead placed the racks out that have all the available shoes in all the available sizes and colors for customers to find themselves? Or was it when salespeople stopped coming to the dressing room to check to see if clothing fit or if you needed a different size? Maybe it was when department stores stopped providing salespersons in each department and put one person in charge of several. Whenever it happened, Roberta Orona-Cordova, writer and assistant professor at California State University, Northridge, noticed that neither she nor many other customers were getting the courtesy they received once upon a time.

Prereading: Are there times when the customer is wrong? What should happen when a salesperson discovers that he or she must disagree with a customer? Have you ever been wrong about a transaction? How did you handle it?

Prewriting: Write a descriptive paragraph relating a time when a salesperson was particularly nice to you.

Every time I shop at a retail store I find that the young employees working behind the counter are more interested in talking about their Saturday night dates than they are in assisting customers. I have had numerous experiences whereby I stood and listened to "workers" chatting or gossiping to each other while I stood and waited for them to offer their assistance. More often than not, I have to ask, "Can you help me, please?" I can shop in any store in a large mall and come out with a new story relating how discourteous or how inattentive a retail clerk was. I usually have to say "thank you" when a salesperson hands me a receipt, instead of the other way around; for example, "Thank you. We hope you come back soon."

Is this a problem represented by a generation of young people who are oblivious to "the other," and thus they are only concerned about themselves? Can we place blame on management for not providing top-notch customer service training? Or is the problem reflective of liberal, casual, informal California?

It is easy to point a finger at the so-called "MTV generation." The young media junkies are influenced by hip-hop, sex, and drugs, which TV displays instantaneously, and without people having to leave their living rooms. When do our young receive messages from our media culture that politeness matters, that caring about others is as important as caring about family? Can we ask parents to teach their children how to be polite, how to say "please" and "thank you"? Society generally gives the responsibility to parents, and they want the schools to instruct their children in all areas. How about asking our local and national governments to initiate advertising campaigns that drill into our young people that "Courtesy Counts"?

Management often fails to train their employees to welcome a customer, to greet a customer with sincere courtesy, to assist the customer without making the man or woman feel as if he or she is under suspicion of stealing. Maybe it is management's fault and not the salesperson's. Often, I have said "thank you" with emphasis, an effort to remind a salesclerk that it is her or his role to offer the "thanks." But, no, a salesperson will turn around and continue a personal conversation that was started before I approached the counter.

Department store salespeople are worse than employees at small boutiques. Or is it California—Los Angeles in particular—especially because of the proximity to Hollywood and Beverly Hills, where *dress* and appearance determine what kind of service a customer receives? I can walk into a department store in Century City (adjacent to Beverly Hills), wearing a sweat outfit from Big-5 ($15.00 a set), seek help from a salesperson, who will either ignore me or keep an eye on me, instead of asking to be helpful. In contrast, if I wear the latest "Juicy" outfit ($85 to $150), a salesclerk will be quite attentive.

I am reminded that at 19 years old I had the good fortune of working in a Piggly Wiggly grocery story as a "checker." Everyday, before we went "on the floor," we were given "reminders" in the form of handouts: "Always greet the customer with a warm, friendly smile." "Never hesitate to say 'thank you.'" "Be particularly helpful to 'a new face.' We want each and every person to come back." "Treat the customer the way you want to be treated when you shop." "Remember, the customer is always right."

How do we instruct our young people about manners and courtesy? Do we tell them, on the spot, "You are supposed to say 'thank you,' after I've completed my purchase"? Or should I hand the salesperson a note that says, "Courtesy Counts" or "How about a 'thank-you?'" Or even, "How about a smile?" One sure way is to ask a salesperson a question to get the employee interested in you. For example, "How was your day today?" "How are you doing these days?" "What's the best feature about your job?" You might even compliment the salesclerk: "What a nice hairdo." "Gosh, your tattoo is cool" (they like that one). "I like the way you apply your make-up." For the men: "Great tie." "You have great taste in clothes." If you are at Costco, Wal-Mart, or K-Mart, you can always offer cashiers the welcome comment: "You sure are an efficient cashier."

It's too bad we have to instruct our young people today on courtesy and manners. Of course, you have an option of writing a letter to the company, but how many letters would you have to write?

Reading for Meaning

1. What reasons does Orona-Cordova give for the rudeness of salespersons?
2. Who has the responsibility of teaching children manners? To whom has it been shifted, according to Orona-Cordova?
3. What recommendations does Orona-Cordova offer to help salespeople learn their manners? List three.

Reading Deeper

1. What does Orona-Cordova suggest about class and wealth in her essay?
2. What responses do you think customers will give when they are greeted with courtesy instead of with the distracted attitude many salespeople show? Explain.
3. Do you think Orona-Cordova offers hope for customers in the future or do you think she predicts that salespersons will continue to be rude? Defend your answer.

Reading for Writing

1. Closely related to salespeople is the job of waitstaff. It is expected that customers give the waitstaff 15 to 20 percent of the price of the meal for particularly good service. If the service is not good, 10 percent is normal. Have you ever received particularly good service or particularly bad service? What did you do about it? Write a paper explaining what a good customer should do when he or she receives either good or bad service from waitstaff. This should include **process analysis** and **description.**
2. Write a formal business letter to the management of a business, store, or restaurant for particularly good service you received from one of the company's employees. Remember to include the name of the person and the date of the service. This should include **description** and **exemplification.**

THE MATTER OF MANNERS

by the Editors of U.S. News and World Report

As with most things that begin as good or have a good motive, manners have a side that some people identify as negative. In this article, the editors of U.S. News and World Report *argue the negative side of manners and courtesy. They place the blame squarely on the rules themselves, which means that they blame manners for suppressing the voice of those who hold views that differ from the majority. On the other hand, we see numerous examples of "educated" individuals protesting, marching, and causing disruptions at formally organized events. Recently, at the graduation ceremonies of a large state university, a group of students protesting for their cause began parading in an area behind and above the speaker's podium. Although they protested quietly, it was clearly a distraction. As they began, the president of the university graciously stopped her address to the graduates, smiled, introduced the marchers, explained their cause and allowed them to complete their parade. When they had moved to the area behind the audience, she finished her address. Ironically, educated young people had their moment, granted by the individual they were protesting against after they had had several meetings with her. Thus, the question of manners rages on.*

Prereading: The title of this essay does not provide readers with a sense of which direction the authors are leaning. However, if you have read the other articles on manners in the order they are organized, you should have a basic idea about the tone of this article. Look quickly at the preceding articles and try to determine what this article will be about.

Prewriting: When the movie *Gone with the Wind* debuted, the same year as *The Wizard of Oz,* it created quite a scandal because of Rhett Butler's last spoken line to Scarlett: "Frankly, my dear, I don't give a damn." The use of such language was unheard of and never used in "polite" society or with ladies present. Today's movies, music, radio and television shows use language that is much more explicit. Write a paragraph explaining your feelings about the use of explicit language in today's society and if you feel there is a connection between language and manners.

Vocabulary: Looking up and understanding the following words prior to reading should prepare you for the author's message. Other words will be defined in the margin.

Clarence Thomas   Alexis de Tocqueville

---

civility:
courtesy

starkly:
strongly

contrarian:
opposite; not
being in
conformity with

discourse:
conversation

M any Americans seek a restoration of civility,* but is it overrated? "America at its best matches a commitment to principle with a concern for civility." With those words, George W. Bush hit one of the high notes of his elegant inaugural address, recapturing a theme he had trumpeted throughout his campaign.

Just last week, however, Supreme Court Justice Clarence Thomas jarred Washington with a starkly* contrarian* view of civility in American discourse.* "Today, there is much talk about moderation," Thomas told the American Enterprise Institute, but there is an "overemphasis on civility." The justice went on to argue that, as the country is embroiled in a cultural war, "civility cannot be the governing principle of citizenship or leadership."

All of which raises the question: Is civility overrated?

restoration: return to

percolating: spreading gradually through

stifle: prevent, stop

For much of the last decade, Americans have cried out for a restoration* of civility—in our politics, in our schools, in our pop culture. But for all the talk about restoring manners and morals, there seems to be some civic resentment percolating*. For some, "civility" appears to do little to improve our daily public lives and perhaps more to stifle* our public debate.

ubiquitous: seeming to be everywhere

ideological: based on a particular set of ideas, especially political

Of course, much hinges on how one defines civility; it is one of those slippery terms in our cultural discourse. Just as "morality" has been slapped on every debate from "explicit lyrics" music labels to missile defense, "civility" has become equally ubiquitous.* For most, civility involves fundamental democratic values—respect for the dignity of the individual and an embrace of religious, cultural, and ideological* distinctions. For others, it is simply checking your impulse to raise a middle finger toward the driver who just took your parking space. Etiquette, in other words. The two often go hand in hand; without etiquette, many argue, it is nearly impossible to achieve more fundamental respect. But today, people have also come to see civility as a synonym for compromise and an excuse to cool passionate arguments.

disintegrating: breaking apart to be destroyed

caustic: extremely unkind and full of criticism

trite: often used to the point of being boring or insincere

contrived: false, not natural

chasms: big differences in opinions, beliefs, and so forth

partisans: strongly supporting a particular party, plan, or leader

Etiquette. According to legal scholar and social critic Stephen Carter, when we ignore what Alexis de Tocqueville called the "etiquette of democracy," our social fabric unravels. In his book *Civility: Manners, Morals, and the Etiquette of Democracy,* Carter argues eloquently that civility is disintegrating* because Americans have forgotten the obligations they owe one another and are consumed with self-indulgence.

Carter is just one voice in a chorus of leaders claiming that our civic culture is crumbling. Yet even with the spotlight on morals and etiquette, we haven't changed our manners at all. Last summer, 78 percent of respondents to a CNN/*USA Today*/Gallup Poll said that in recent years, rude behavior has increased in stores, on highways, and in airports. And how are people responding to rude behavior? Nearly 4 out of 5 say more people are getting angry about it than just a few years ago. Road rage and airport rage, along with caustic* lawyers and foul-mouthed teens, now seem trite*.

And what's worse, the many calls for civility may be chilling our political debate. Instead of the fundamental respect Carter and others advocate, politicians substitute contrived* politeness, papering over ideological chasms* with political niceties. And as soon as their views are aggressively challenged, partisans* cry foul, regardless of the merit and honesty of the criticism.

In the same vein, critics worry that calls for manners will send us back to the "golden age of civility"—the 1950s—where etiquette reigned, civic organizations were strong, and you didn't hear vulgarities on the radio. But it wasn't a golden age for African-Americans, gays, and women—all of whom had to dispense with "please" and "thank you" to advance their causes. So the question becomes: Can we restore civility without returning to the constrictive* social order that so often accompanies it? Is "civility" just a way to muzzle those who hold controversial views and feel they need to shout to be heard?

During the Florida recount, the nation took a magnifying glass to the political process and saw perpetual* manipulation,* clawing and scraping for every advantage, knocking down opponents, and claiming moral high ground. While we may eliminate the low blows, politics will remain a contest of body blows. The same can be said of life in the new economy, where freer trade, fiercer competition, and greater efficiency have unleashed capitalism, creating a world where, in the words of Intel Chairman Andrew Grove, "only the paranoid survive." If only the paranoid* survive, how can we expect the self-restraint that Carter says is necessary to restore civility? And if we can't expect it at work, where we spend most of our days, how can we expect it at home and in the community?

constrictive: limiting of one's freedom

perpetual: continuing all the time without change

manipulation: making someone do something by deception or influence

paranoid: those who believe others want to harm them

Reading for Meaning

1. The authors pose a question for readers to consider as they read: "Is civility overrated?" What is the answer they want you to arrive at, based on their discussion? Do you agree with their feelings? Why or why not?
2. List three examples of civility that the authors provide.
3. How are morality and civility similar according to the authors?

Reading Deeper

1. What does Stephen Carter mean when he says that Americans "are consumed with self-indulgence"?
2. Capitalism is again referred to but this time as a reason for our lack of civility. Explain.
3. Look at the last sentence of the article. The authors list work as the first place to expect self-restraint and civility, with home and community coming in second and third. Do you agree or disagree with the authors' ranking of these places?

Reading for Writing

1. A question is posed in this essay: "Can we restore civility without returning to the constrictive social order that so often accompanies it?" Within this question, the writers make the assumption that they think the readers believe: The social order that promotes civility is, indeed, constrictive. Write an essay that addresses one of the following assertions:

   - The social order was constrictive, but we can restore civility without being constricted.
   - The social order was not constrictive, and we can still be civil.
   - Today's society has allowed individuals so much freedom that restoring civility will be difficult.
   - Today's society has allowed individuals so much freedom that restoring civility might be achieved on a limited basis.
   - Based on the current social needs and activities, the civility that currently exists is sufficient and need not be changed.

   This assignment should include **definition, exemplification,** and **argumentation.**

2. Various protests go on daily around the world. For example, people protest war, U.S. involvement in other nations' affairs, abortion, the selling of fur coats, the use of pesticides, and many other issues. Frequently, these protests interfere with traffic, block pedestrians, interrupt formal proceedings, and disrupt speeches and lectures. Assuming that you believe in the First Amendment and people's right to free speech, write a "courtesy book" giving directions on how to conduct an orderly and effective protest. This should include **process analysis, definition,** and **exemplification.** It might also include **comparison and contrast.**

FROM *HONOR AND SHAME*

Lila Abu-Lughod

Lila Abu-Lughod is a professor of anthropology and Middle Eastern Studies at New York University. Professor Abu-Lughod is interested in feminist studies and gender politics in the Muslim world. Her research involves how women acquire power in a patriarchal society and what they lose as they adopt modern values and standards. She has published Veiled Sentiments: Honor and

Poetry in a Bedouin Society *(1986) and* Writing Women's Worlds: Bedouin Stories *(1993).*

Education and marriage are two important issues that have impacted the lives of women for centuries. Both Eastern and Western civilizations have minimized women's worth by assigning them tasks inside the home and denying them the opportunity to learn or to develop their talents. The following essay from a young Bedouin woman reveals both the historical and the contemporary attitudes she and her peers were subjected to. The description in this essay resembles a snapshot in that readers see the activities Bedouin women engage in.

Prereading: Consider your beliefs about marriage before college and college before marriage.

Prewriting: What is the relationship between marriage and education in your culture? Write a brief descriptive paragraph about it.

Vocabulary: Looking up and understanding the following words prior to reading should prepare you for the author's message. Other words will be defined in the margin.

Bedouin   lineage   Qur'an

Because [my sister] complained so much, I had asked her in the summer after she graduated to write me an essay on how young Bedouin women's lives were changing and what of the past she hoped the Awlad'Ali would retain and what she wished they would aban-

candid: marked by honest, sincere expression; blunt

don. . . . You can trace, in the stilted words of her essay and the candid* comments (in parentheses) she made as she read it aloud to me, the outlines of the new world she hoped to gain by marrying. . . .

The Education of Girls
An Essay on the Young Bedouin Woman of Egypt
And the Changes in Her Life over 40 Years

If we are to speak of the Bedouin girl in Egypt, we find that her life differs from one era to another. The circumstance of the home and family relations change from one age to another. If we go back to discuss the way she was around forty years ago, we find that the Bedouin girl was living a life in which she was of no value. When she came of age, or maturity (as the Egyptians say—I mean the years when she is ready for marriage), she had to do housework at her family's home—for example, cooking, washing clothes, and preparing firewood. (Her only value was in the housework she did—the sweeping and washing—and if she didn't do it they'd laugh at her and gossip about her laziness. She was forced to do it, even if she weren't capable. No matter what her health was like. I'm talking about those who were my age, from around the age of twelve on.)

Also, she used to spin and weave, even though it is very difficult, painful, and strenuous. (When she was around fifteen, her mother or any woman in the household, an aunt for instance, would teach her. It's supposed to be the mother, though. Her goal was to teach her daughter to spin and to make something, anything. The important thing was for her to weave something, if only a border for the tent.) She had to learn this skill. (This is what is important for the Bedouins, housework, weaving, and such things. Forty years ago [1960s] this was what a girl had to put up with.)

Education for the Bedouin girl used not to exist. It was impossible for her to study. (Forty years ago she lived a life, as I said earlier, that had no value at all.) She was governed by the customs and traditions that the Bedouin families followed. These customs and traditions forbade* a girl to leave the house under any circumstances. So going to school (this is an example) would be the greatest shame. She couldn't say that she wished to study, no matter what. Even if, as they say, she was the daughter of a tribal leader. (So for example, a girl's father would be a tribal leader and she'd want to study, but her relatives would say no you can't. She'd say, but I'm the daughter of the head of a lineage. I must learn. They'd forbid her.)

forbade: to command against; not allow

ARRANGED MARRIAGE

She had no right to an opinion in any matter, however much the matter might concern her personally. She had no say even in the choice of a husband. She had absolutely no say in this matter. (And to this day, no matter how educated she's become, very seldom does she have any opinion. . . .) In this matter what she had to do was carry out her family's orders even if she didn't want to. It was not right for her to refuse. (Even if she didn't want him, she had to agree to it against her will. Even if he was older than she was, for example, or very different from her, she had to agree to what the family wanted. . . .)

THE DANGERS OF SCHOOLING

Life began to change for the Bedouins, a change of conditions and location. Those Bedouins who began living in town started sending their sons and also their daughters to school to learn right from wrong, prayer, and writing. (That was my father's single goal in educating us. He wanted us to know this. They don't put us in school to learn—who cared if I got educated? My own reason for being there was to learn right from wrong and the Qur'an. That's all.) After that they would pull them out of school. (Even if a girl was clever and came out first in her class, once she had learned right from wrong and had come to understand, they would say to her, "Come on, that's enough.") Some might let her stay through secondary school. (Like me. After I finished secondary school, that was it.) The Bedouin girl could even gain such a mastery of learning and knowledge . . . that she could enter the university. (In Alexandria you'll find Bedouin girls who've gone to the university.)

What happened was that people began competing over the schooling of girls. (For example, my father sees Aisha's father, who has educated all his daughters; so my father looks at him and says, "Why should he educate his daughters and not me? I have to educate my daughters." One looked at the next until all of them started educating their daughters. . . . But around here, they see that others' daughters aren't in school. No one here has daughters in university. In Marsa Matruh they all sent their girls to school, each imitating the other. My father looks over at Aisha's father and his daughters. If one of them did anything wrong—may God protect us!—*anything* wrong, my father and all of them would decide not to follow. But when I look, I see the Bedouin girl does not give up her Bedouin values. The girls went to school and nothing bad happened.) The Bedouin girl made them see clearly that their daughter was as good as any girl from the biggest city—in intelligence and level of learning. She would get the highest grades in all fields of learning. . . .

EGYPTIANS

The Bedouin girl preserves the traditions and customs she was raised by. (. . . Me, for example, I grew up knowing this was shameful and that was not right, there are customs, there's respect and modesty. Even when I'm old and my hair is grey, I'll have to follow these.) She has a sense and preserves her family's reputation. . . . The Bedouin girl tries to overcome the special obstacles she must confront. . . . She attempts to live a life enlightened by learning, happiness, and contributions to her country and family.

She doesn't forget her origins or her customs and traditions. She raises her children as well as the people of the city do.

Reading for Expectations

1. This informative essay describes the life of Bedouin women from the perspective of one young woman. What feelings and attitudes does she incorporate into the article? Give three specific examples.
2. The title of the essay embedded within the larger work suggests that her article will be written using a chronological organization. Does the article fulfill your expectations? Explain your answer.

Reading for Meaning

1. What did members of the culture fear would happen if a young Bedouin woman left home to pursue an education?
2. Describe three differences between the young Bedouin woman of forty years ago and a young Bedouin woman of today.

Reading to Write

1. The sister presents the life of young Bedouin women in general, and the author of the larger work inserted the sister's opinion in parenthesis. Select one example of this and explain your feelings as a reader. Does the parenthetical style help your understanding? Confuse you? Further develop the information?
2. Think about the different requirements your cultural heritage has for males and females. Choose one requirement and, using **exemplification** and personal opinion write a one-page description, using the sister's first section, "Arranged Marriage," as a model.
3. Select a cultural event that you are familiar with and have participated in. For example, you might have attended a Bar Mitzvah, Christmas mass, a posada, Chinese New Year's celebration, and so forth. Write a **descriptive, informative** "snapshot." Use descriptive words, **similes** and **metaphors,** and **exemplification.** Sometimes guests at such events are expected to participate in certain rituals; otherwise, they will be considered disrespectful. For example, male guests at the Bar Mitzvah in the temple are expected to wear a yarmulke and women are also expected to cover their hair. Discuss any such ritual you were expected to observe.

What's in a Name?

Henry Louis Gates, Jr.

How important is it to you that people know your name? Have you ever felt insulted if someone called you by the wrong name acci- dentally? In the following personal narrative, Henry Louis Gates, Jr., as a child, learns the ugliness of racial prejudice when he dis- covers that an older white man in his community refuses to take the time to learn the difference between one African American and another, preferring to call them all by the same name.

Prereading: Individual differences are first acknowledged when people can distinguish you from those around you. Consider your identity, how it is part of your self-esteem and your self-confidence. Most people take great care in constructing their own characteristics by which they can be recognized. To be placed in a group of people who are considered indistinguishable from one another is to become invisible, anonymous, and insignificant.

Prewriting: Visibility is an important part of life for many people. How do you ensure that you are known to your professors, friends, coworkers, and others around you? Write a paragraph that describes the outstanding physical and personal characteristics that distin- guish you from others.

Vocabulary: Looking up and understanding the following words prior to reading should prepare you for the author's message. Other words will be defined in the margin.

affluent   Riley   Sugar Ray   Jackie Robinson

I had forgotten the incident completely, until I read Trey Ellis's essay, "Remember My Name," in a recent issue of the *Village Voice* (June 13, 1989). But there, in the middle of an extended italicized list of the by-names of "the race" ("the race" or "our people" being the terms my par- ents used in polite or reverential* discourse, "jigaboo" or "nigger" more commonly used in anger, jest or pure disgust) it was: "George." Now the events of that very brief exchange return to mind so vividly that I won- der why I had forgotten it.

reverential: deep respect

My father and I were walking home at dusk from his second job. He "moonlighted"* as a janitor in the evenings for the telephone com- pany. Every day but Saturday, he would come home at 3:30 from his reg- ular job at the paper mill, wash up, eat supper, then at 4:30 head down

moonlighted: to work at an additional job after one's regular job

town to his second job. He used to make jokes frequently about the union official who moonlighted. I never got the joke, but he and his friends thought it was hilarious. All I knew was that my family always ate well, that my brother and I had new clothes to wear, and that all of the white people in Piedmont, West Virginia, treated my parents with an odd mixture of resentment and respect that even we understood at the time had something directly to do with a small but certain measure of financial security.

He had left a little early that evening because I was with him, and I had to be in bed early. I could not have been more than five or six, and we had stopped off at the Cut-Rate Drug Store (where no black person in town but my father could sit down to eat, and eat off real plates with real silverware) so that I could buy some caramel ice cream, two scoops in a wafer cone, please, which I was busy licking when Mr. Wilson walked by.

overture: offer

Mr. Wilson was a very quiet man, whose stony, brooding, silent manner seemed designed to scare off any overtures* of friendship, even from white people. He was Irish, as was one-third of our village (another third being Italian), the more affluent among whom sent their children to "Catholic School" across the bridge in Maryland. He had white straight hair, like my Uncle Joe, whom he uncannily* resembled, and he carried a black worn metal lunch pail, the kind that Riley carried on the television show. My father always spoke to him, and for reasons that we never did understand, he always spoke to my father.

uncannily: extraordinarily

"Hello, Mr. Wilson," I heard my father say.

"Hello, George."

I stopped licking my ice cream cone, and asked my Dad in a loud voice why Mr. Wilson had called him "George."

"Dosen't he know your name, Daddy? Why don't you tell him your name? Your name isn't George."

For a moment I tried to think of who Mr. Wilson was mixing Pop up with. But we didn't have any Georges among the colored people in Piedmont; nor were there colored Georges living in the neighboring towns and working at the mill.

"Tell him your name, Daddy."

"He knows my name, boy," my father said after a long pause. "He calls all colored people George."

ensued: followed

A long silence ensued*. It was "one of those things," as my Mom would put it. Even then, that early, I knew when I was in the presence of "one of those things," one of those things that provided a glimpse, through a rent* curtain, at another world that we could not affect but that affected us. There would be a painful moment of silence, and you would

rent: a tear in the fabric

wait for it to give way to a discussion of a black superstar such as Sugar Ray or Jackie Robinson.

"Nobody hits better in a clutch than Jackie Robinson."

"That's right. Nobody."

I never again looked Mr. Wilson in the eye.

Reading for Expectations

1. How would you describe Gates's father?
2. If you had been Gates's father, what would you have said to your son about Mr. Wilson's comment?
3. Who are Sugar Ray and Jackie Robinson, and why are they so important to Gates's community?

Reading for Meaning

1. Gates mentions that his family was treated with an "odd mixture of resentment and respect" because of their financial security. Why would it be odd, and why is there resentment added to the respect?
2. Why does Gates never look Mr. Wilson in the eye again?

Reading to Write

1. Gates asks a simple but very powerful question in his title, "What's in a Name"? Write an essay explaining how you would respond to this question, taking into account the multiple ways a name identifies who a person is, whether positively, negatively, or simply as a way to conduct one's life, such as "doctor."
2. When two cultures come together, there is frequently conflict that shows itself in different ways. Here it is relatively subtle. However, there are other ways that prejudice is practiced. Write a **descriptive exemplification** essay discussing an incident in which you have received treatment that was clearly prejudiced or an incident that you've observed that was prejudiced. Draw conclusions from what you experienced or observed.
3. Gates points out in his essay how humor was a way to cope in a world often devoid of anything humorous at all. Watch several programs that feature comedians who employ comedy as a way to cope with life's problems and also as a way to break through social barriers so that cultures have a common ground on which to come together. If you feel that the comedian was ridiculing a culture, make note of how the comment could be taken negatively. Then write an essay explaining the various subjects that the comedians made fun of and how

such humor acted as a way to join a community or cultures, rather than separate them.

4. According to Gates, his narrative was a response to a specific word—"George"—that held great emotional meaning to him. Think about your own lifetime and consider a specific word, whether positive or negative, which holds great personal significance for you. Then write a paragraph identifying the word and explaining how it is significant to you. If you can not think of a specific word, possibly a short phrase is important, such as "It's a girl!"

5. Gates's mother had a phrase that she applied to certain situations: "one of those things." Gates applies this phrase to Mr. Wilson's failure to call his father by his correct name. Consider the times in your life when you have had to move beyond a situation that was difficult and do nothing about it. You probably had to think like Gates's mother: It was "one of those things." Write a brief **narrative** describing the situation and how you handled it.

MAMA SARAH

Fortuna Benudiz Ippoliti

The traditions surrounding aging and death vary among cultures. Here a young Moroccan Jewish woman describes the mourning rituals she was exposed to as a young girl, rituals quite different from those practiced by members of contemporary Anglo-American society. Mother of two daughters whom she and her husband are raising in traditional Jewish custom, Fortuna Ippoliti has recently begun writing as a way to find her voice and to express her deepest feelings. She has passed on this love of writing to her daughters who are also prolific. An immigrant who fled to the United States with her family from Morocco as a child, Ippoliti has lived in Los Angeles for most of her life. The closeness her family felt for her grandmother and other family members that Ippoliti reveals in her essay is a reflection of that closeness which she shares with her family today and the customs she is also passing on to her daughters.

Prereading: Regardless of how cultures display their respect for the deceased, the surviving friends and loved ones experience the loss and express their grief in their own personal way. While some traditions have changed, Ippoliti believes that those she experienced taught her a great deal about herself and her community. Consider your family's method of grieving before you read this article.

Prewriting: Consider the traditions/rituals surrounding death and burial. Do you think that they are "essential traditions"? Write a brief paragraph explaining your views.

———

The year was 1962, and I was an energetic, wiry young 10-year-old girl living in Los Angeles. Everything in my little universe was exciting and new. We were living in a new land, new city, and a new house. My parents, my sister Sarah and myself had arrived from Morocco just six years earlier and everything in life for me was an adventure. Though my parents were struggling to acculturate themselves to this new land and new language, I just went about my life thinking everything was grand.

My maternal grandmother, Mama Sarah, was living with us as well. She had come from Morocco to the United States in 1957 to help my mother with the birth of my brother Solomon. Even though his arrival meant extra work for my sister and me, we somehow managed to escape the drudgery of washing and folding all his diapers thanks to Mama Sarah. She always came to our aid as my sister and I sat there starting at this mound of diapers waiting to be folded. And then Mama Sarah got sick, very sick, and had to go to the hospital.

My mother would take 3–4 buses every day to visit her at the hospital. In those days, children were rarely, if ever, allowed to enter adult wards. I was mildly curious but somewhat relieved that I couldn't go to visit her. After ten days, my mother told us that Mama Sarah was coming home from the hospital. My sister and I were so excited as we missed her terribly (not to mention the fact that our diaper duty was wearing thin!). My mother and father came home to collect some clean clothes for Mama Sarah's homecoming when the telephone rang. It was the hospital. My mother's expression went from joy to confusion to anger. She kept repeating, "No, there must be some mistake, you must have her confused for someone else . . . No, no, she is being discharged today . . . we're just on our way to pick her up, no, no, no." She then dropped the phone and fell to her knees and let out a wail.

Her death was so unexpected. How could this have happened? My mother blamed herself for not being with Mama Sarah when she died. My mother and father's agonizing screams of disbelief were too much for me. I remember running to the closet and holding my ears to block the terrible sounds coming from my parents. What was happening? Why couldn't someone explain to me what was happening? Of course, my parents were in too much shock and pain to know we even existed. Though I was unclear as to what was happening or how could it have possibly happened, I knew enough to know that my carefree existence was shattered.

In the Jewish faith, the deceased gets buried within 24–48 hours. During the period right after my grandmother's death, I remember my mother going through the motions of life trance-like, as if she were sleepwalking. The Moroccan Jews are unlike the American Jews, who are primarily of Ashkenazi descent. As Moroccans, we are Sephardic, originating from Spain centuries ago. Consequently, we view life and death very differently from American Jews. Among Jews in general, grief and sorrow are powerfully expressed. Among the Moroccans, in particular, the belief in outward grieving is so vital that in Morocco, there were professional "wailers" or "grievers" who, through their loud shrieks, pulling their hair, and other displays of frenzy, were instrumental in assisting mourners who were so unable or in shock to begin the mourning process. This process creates an almost palpable rawness in the reality of death. The belief behind this overflow of pure unadulterated emotion is that the more quickly the wound of death is opened, the more quickly the healing can begin for the mourners.

On the day of her funeral, my sister Sarah, my brother Solomon and I stayed home with an adult friend of my mother's. Once again, we were kept apart from the rituals of death and burial. Though now as an adult I can understand my mother's attempt at shielding her children from the sorrow expressed at my grandmother's funeral, I still wish I could have attended, if for no other reason than to say goodbye. We couldn't see her at the hospital nor be a part of the mourners. After the funeral, everyone came to our house to eat and reminisce about Mama Sarah. When I saw my mother entering our house, hunched over like the elderly, I noticed that her black blouse was torn. In the Jewish religion, relatives of the deceased tear a piece of their garments, a custom completed at the beginning of the funeral service. I was once again frightened and hid in my favorite closet to gather my thoughts. After gathering up my nerve, I ventured out and sought out my mother. I so desperately wanted to console her, to stroke her, to tell her everything would be okay, but she was inconsolable.

For seven days, the rabbi, friends and family, and quorum of ten men (Minyan) came to our house to pray and give comfort to my family. All the mirrors in our house were covered up completely with cloth and the cushions on our sofas were removed so my mother and her sisters could sit at a lower level than the guests. This period of time and mourning is called *Shivah*. My poor mother was in a complete fog the entire week. To this day, I have never felt so completely and totally helpless as I did then. There was nothing my sister nor I could do to "cheer" my mother up. In my child's way of thinking, I couldn't understand why my mother couldn't snap out of it. How long would this blanket of gloom continue? If Mama Sarah was with G-d now, why wasn't everyone happy for her instead of crying all the time?

I never did get answers to any of my questions, but it was then that I learned that the exciting and exhilarating adventure was over. As is customary among the more religious Jews, my mother was in mourning for one year. That meant no parties, no listening to music, or dancing. For one year, there was a dark pall that hung over our lives. Mama Sarah was such an integral part of each and everyone's lives, that no one was ever the same without her. Even after the year of official mourning ended, it took us many, many months to reenter the world of festivities and happiness.

For me, that year marked a turning point in my life. I learned at a tender age to appreciate the carefree times. On some level, I learned that life is indeed an adventure, but one with many twists and turns. The year of mourning also taught me about a sense of Jewish community. According to Jewish custom, the year of mourning is designed for the bereaved to gradually adjust to life. It was through the aid of my family's friends that gave us all great comfort and support during the more difficult times. Through their visits, I learned even more about Mama Sarah, my family and Judaism.

My Mama Sarah probably taught me much more after she died than while she was still alive. I learned to cherish the joyful times in life and to let those you care for know now, while still alive, how much you love them. And for all that, I will always cherish you, Mama Sarah.

Reading for Meaning

1. Why does Ippoliti appreciate her grandmother's presence in her home?
2. How are the Moroccan Jews culturally different from the American Jews?
3. What are some of the particular customs of *Shivah* which the Sephardic Jews associate with death in the narrative?

Reading Deeper

1. Write a paragraph or short essay that explains what you would consider the causes for mourning the loss of a loved one for one year.
2. Ippoliti describes the Moroccan view of "outward grieving," which includes "professional" mourners as a way to help the mourning process for the deceased's family. Explain your understanding of the

mourning process and why it might be necessary to have others help relatives of the deceased mourn.

Reading to Write

1. Children often hide from the harsh realities of life. In Ippoliti's narrative, she hides in a closet. However, children have other ways to cover up or hide from a harsh truth. Research a major form of denial that children use to cover up their feelings. You may want to **interview** a person knowledgeable in psychology. Then write an essay that explains your findings.
2. Ippoliti mentions the Sephardic Jews in her essay. Research the various forms of Judaism that exist today and explain your findings in an **informative** essay format using various **patterns of development.**

RHETORICAL ANALYSIS

This section will give you one more opportunity to reread one of the articles and analyze it from a rhetorical perspective. In the left-hand margin there are notes that direct you to appropriate chapters in this textbook for discussion about the techniques the author used to write the essay or that comment directly about the underlined techniques the author used.

In the following article, "Is the Customer Always Right?," Orona-Cordova begins by asking a question that she will answer at the end of the essay in an implied way. Rather than begin the essay with a stated thesis that asserts her position about the role of salesperson and customer, she provides scenarios that she has been involved in and that give the reader an idea of where she is going with her essay. Another reason for not providing a stated thesis is that she does not want to lose her audience if readers disagree with her point. Read the essay and identify each of the techniques Orona-Cordova uses as you read. Some are explained beside the essay.

Ch. 4, Reading and Writing Narrative gives guidelines for writing a personal narrative.

Is the Customer Always Right?

Every time I shop at a retail store I find that the young employees working behind the counter are more interested in talking about their Saturday night dates than they are in assisting customers. I have had numerous experiences whereby I stood and

In Ch. 2, Description and Ch. 3, Exemplification. She tells about the clerk and then shows through an example.

listened to "workers" chatting or gossiping to each other while I stood and waited for them to offer their assistance. More often than not, I have to ask, "Can you help me please?" I can shop in any store in a large mall and come out with a new story relating how discourteous or how inattentive a retail clerk was. I usually have to say "thank you" when a salesperson hands me a receipt, instead of the other way around; for example, "Thank you. We hope you come back soon."

Ch. 10, issue of the essay

Is this a problem represented by a generation of young people who are oblivious to "the other," and thus they are only concerned about themselves? Can we place blame on management for not providing top-notch customer service training? Or is the problem reflective of liberal, casual, informal California?

Ch. 3, Exemplification

It is easy to point a finger at the so-called "MTV generation." The young media junkies are influenced by hip-hop, sex, and drugs which TV provides instantaneously, and without people having to leave their living rooms. When do our young receive messages from our media culture that politeness matters, that caring about others is as important as caring about family? Can we ask parents to teach their children how to be polite, how to say "please" and "thank you"? Society generally gives the responsibility to parents, and they want the schools to instruct their children in all areas. How about asking our local and national governments to initiate advertising campaigns that drill into our young people that "Courtesy Counts"?

See Ch. 10, evidence to support claim.

Management often fails to train their employees to welcome a customer, to greet a customer with sincere courtesy, to assist the customer without making the man or woman feel as if he or she is under suspicion of stealing. Maybe it is management's fault and not the salesperson's. Often, I have said "thank you" with emphasis, an effort to remind a salesclerk that it is her or his role to offer the "thanks." But no, a salesperson will turn around and continue a personal conversation that was started before I approached the counter.

See Ch. 10, evidence to support claim.

Department store salespeople are worse than employees at small boutiques. Or is it California—Los Angeles in particular—especially because of the proximity to Hollywood and Beverly Hills where dress and

Calls attention to a special word through the use of italics. See Ch. 1 for pre-reading steps.

Ch. 1 for reading and Ch. 2 Description.

Ch. 4, Narrative—she uses her own experiences to develop the essay.

Ch. 3, Exemplification: gives specific examples of handouts. Suggestions to improve the situation.

Suggests that modeling courtesy might help salespeople improve.

Ch. 1, author addresses the audience directly. Who do you think it is?

appearance determine what kind of service a customer receives? I can walk into a department store in Century City (adjacent to Beverly Hills), wearing a sweat outfit from Big-5 ($15.00 a set), seek help from a salesperson, who will either ignore me or keep an eye on me, instead of asking to be helpful. In contrast, if I wear the latest "Juicy" outfit ($85 to $150), a salesclerk will be quite attentive.

I am reminded that at 19 years old I had the good fortune of working in a Piggly Wiggly grocery story as a "checker." Everyday, before we went "on the floor," we were given "reminders" in the form of handouts: "Always greet the customer with a warm, friendly smile." "Never hesitate to say 'thank you.'" "Be particularly helpful to 'a new face.' We want each and every person to come back." "Treat the customer the way you want to be treated when you shop." "Remember, the customer is always right."

How do we instruct our young people about manners and courtesy? Do we tell them, on the spot, "You are supposed to say 'thank you,' after I've completed my purchase"? Or should I hand the salesperson a note that says, "Courtesy Counts"; or "How about a 'thank you?'" Or even, "How about a smile?" One sure way is to ask a salesperson a question to get the employee interested in you. For example, "How was your day today?" "How are you doing these days?" "What's the best feature about your job?" You might even compliment the salesclerk: "What a nice hairdo." "Gosh, your tatto is cool" (they like that one). "I like the way you apply your make-up." For the men: "Great tie." "You have great taste in clothes." If you are at Costco, Wal-Mart, or K-Mart, you can always offer cashiers the welcome comment: "You sure are an efficient cashier."

It's too bad we have to instruct our young people today on courtesy and manners. Of course, you have an option of writing a letter to the company, but how many letters would you have to write?

Although the term "rhetorical analysis" might sound complex and difficult, it is not. In fact, you have probably been analyzing many of your readings for rhetorical devices or for patterns of development without even realizing it. The essay by Orona-Cordova is an example of what the discussion at the end of Chapter 1 is all about: Most essays are developed by incorporating different modes or patterns of development. Here, Orona-Cordova uses **personal narrative,** relating experiences she has had with retail workers, and convincing writing, attempting to convince her reader how she feels about retail workers' lack of courtesy; and she uses **exemplification** to give the reader a full view of her experiences.

There is no doubt about what **issue** Orona-Cordova is discussing in this article. In fact, you can find it pointed out in an early box. However, did you find a stated **thesis?** Orona-Cordova, like many published authors, did not provide the reader with a stated thesis. Instead, she allowed the reader to get to the end of the article without stating her position about the issue. Take a moment and write what you think the thesis might be. If you wrote something like the following, you were able to discover Orona-Cordova's main idea: **Discourtesy by retail workers toward customers arises from several sources, but maybe the customer could help improve the employees' attitude by being friendly to them.**

By recognizing Orona-Cordova's use of implied **thesis, issue,** and **audience** along with the modes she incorporated, you are on your way to being able to complete thorough analysis of future essays. Of course, there are other aspects of writing to be identified as you read other essays, but through the use and understanding of the text, you will be able to discover them.

REFLECTIONS ON COURTESY AND CUSTOMS: SHOULD I BE COURTEOUS IN TODAY'S SOCIETY?

A middle-aged woman, holding a doctorate and living independent of her parents in another city, commented to me that her Mexican-American mother complains that she has become very casual in her manners. She agrees that she is more casual at her home away from her parents than she is when she returns to her parents' home. She has answered the question that introduces this chapter: Should I be courteous in today's society? She constructs her conduct according to the social expectations that she is exposed to at the moment and according to her own personal feelings. Although her mother does not approve of her lack of formality when she first arrives home, her manner gradually changes, adapting to her culture's requirements. However, she is much more comfortable in what she believes to be a less stifling atmosphere.

By now, most of us have already decided how we should act in public, with our friends and families, at our jobs, and in our communities. Most of the time, we act unconsciously; that is, we act without thinking, doing what we've been taught or following our own way. The articles in this chapter express the ideas and attitudes of at least six different authors, displaying traditional Euro-American and multicultural practices. Does reading them influence your thinking or your beliefs about manners? Do they help you answer the question, "Should I be courteous in today's society?" Do they reinforce your already held beliefs or do they give you new ideas to consider? How do you fit into today's society with regard to contact with others?

Reflecting to Write

Personal Narrative

Reflect about your growing-up years. Relate a story about an incident when you performed a particularly courteous act and were rewarded for it. What did it teach you?

Comparison and Contrast

Think about your family's/culture's expectations of courtesy and how they are different from or similar to those of mainstream American society. Write a **comparison and contrast** paper, incorporating **exemplification** and explaining the similarities and differences.

Argumentation

Focus on one of the following statements:

- Americans are more/less courteous now than they were twenty-five years ago.
- Today's young men are not as courteous as they were before the women's movement.
- Rules that tell us how to eat, dress, and talk should/should not be eliminated.

Interview a number of people of various ages, different genders, and different jobs, asking their opinion about one of the questions. Using your findings, write an **argumentative** essay.

Chapter 12

Language: How We Speak to Each Other

One of the major social issues of today is the language that we use in the United States. Many politicians have attempted to pass laws requiring that only English be spoken in federal buildings as well as in all legal matters concerning government business. This has raised the ire not only of those who do not speak English but also of those who empathize with non-English speakers. Recent immigrants who have not yet had the opportunity to learn the language, or the elderly who have difficulty learning a new language would be handicapped by this law and possibly discriminated against by others. On the other hand, maintaining a single official language in the country insures that children who do not know English will be taught it while their minds are physiologically ready to grasp it, and they will have the opportunity to communicate on an equal language level when attempting to apply for jobs and higher education and be relatively fluent in understanding business and legal concerns. Although many doctors and pharmacies, grocery and other stores, restaurants, and other businesses advertise that they speak the language or provide interpreters, many still do not, making transactions difficult between the customer and the service provider.

However, this is not the only concern that language raises in today's society. Have you ever heard older adults complain that they don't understand what the "younger generation" is saying? This "generation gap" in relation to language has been around ever since older and younger generations have been talking to each other. Language is alive; therefore, it changes. Just as individuals change as they grow, they bring new thoughts and ideas to society that must be accommodated by new language. The changes occur in music and in everyday communication. We hear new forms of slang, and those of us who do not keep up with the changing language because we don't use it, or aren't part of the groups that do, are immediately marked as being "old" or "not with it."

But change also occurs in language in the form of technology. We can no longer talk about cars and their needs in the same language we used before everything became computerized. And a "hummer" no longer refers only to a child or someone who hums. Other forms of technological advances have led to increased vocabulary in our language, and if we are to make ourselves understood to technologically up-to-date individuals, we must be able to "speak the language." For example, if you attend a campus that has state-of-the-art equipment, you realize that PowerPoint presentations are preferred to overhead transparencies. You may also be learning through presentations of virtual information, and submitting your assignments by e-mail attachment to your instructor's computer folder instead of handing in a hard copy.

Finally, *how* we communicate with others in our daily living is also an issue of language. The informality of today's society has led to an informality in today's language. Although most of your instructors still insist on "proper" English, you have probably noticed that the world outside the classroom does not. Newspapers, magazines, billboards and other advertisements, television news shows, and other media have modified the language of contemporary America into much faster, more efficient terms to keep up with the fast pace we keep, for example, "e-mails" and ".coms." Most of us do not have time for long letters, so we dash off notes on e-mail to our friends and family. A recent commercial advertising a particular cell phone showed a male and female in a conversation only they could understand as they spoke to each other using one- or two-word phrases.

Language tells a listener a lot about a speaker. In England, language has been used to determine the class one belongs to. For example, you might watch *My Fair Lady,* a musical that depicts Henry Higgins in his work with phonetics to locate the birthplace and class of various individuals attending the theater and selling flowers on the street. While language might not be that subtle in the United States, it continues to indicate certain aspects of a person's education, ethnicity, birthplace, business, entertainment preferences, and even social groups. Listen to the way you talk to the different people you associate with: your friends, parents, grandparents, teachers, ministers, employers, significant others, interviewers, service people, and anyone else whom you come into contact with. Do you change your "language" for the appropriate audience? Why? Do you speak differently on the phone—cell or otherwise—from the way you speak person-to-person? Language can tell us a lot about ourselves if we're listening. What have you heard lately?

TOWARD A NEW POLITICS OF HISPANIC ASSIMILATION: LANGUAGE AND CULTURE

Linda Chavez

In the following excerpt from Out of the Barrio, *(1992), Linda Chavez, president of the Center for Equal Opportunity in Washington, DC, discusses the varying attitudes found among Latinos and non-Latinos concerning the language that they are expected to speak in the United States. Consider for a moment how you feel when you encounter someone who does not speak English. How would you respond to the individual who is a customer or a person looking for directions? Language is complex and involves the emotions and political feelings of many people. To be deprived of one's native language and required to speak someone else's can make some people angry or even resistant to make the change. However, culturally speaking, people from the same ethnic group are not necessarily of a single mind how its members should speak in an English-speaking country. Read Chavez's article and discover the different aspects that she reveals about language and culture of "Hispanics" in the United States.*

Prereading: Consider your language and culture. How would you have to change if you moved permanently to Iran, Zambia, or another non-Western country? What expectations would you have about how your new country should treat you?

Prewriting: What expectations do you have about immigrants who enter the United States?

Vocabulary: Looking up and understanding the following words prior to reading should prepare you for the author's message. Other words will be defined in the margin.

assimilation

forged: formed

alloy: mixture of different things

*A*ssimilation has become a dirty word in American politics. It invokes images of people, cultures, and traditions forged* into a colorless alloy* in an indifferent melting pot. But, in fact, assimilation, as it has taken place in the United States, is a far more gentle process, by which people from outside the community gradually become part of the community itself. Descendants of the German, Irish, Italian, Polish, Greek, and other immigrants who came to the United States bear little resemblance to the descendants of the countrymen their forebearers left behind. America changed its immigrant groups—and was changed by them. Some groups were accepted more reluctantly than others—the Chinese, for example—and some with great struggle. Blacks, whose ancestors were forced to come here, have only lately won their legal rights to full participation in this society; and even then civil rights gains have not been sufficiently translated into economic gains. Until quite recently, however, there was no question but that each group desired admittance into the mainstream. No more. No ethnic leaders demand that their groups remain separate, that their native culture and language be preserved intact* and that whatever accommodation takes place be on the part of the receiving society.

intact: complete, whole

ethnicity: racial, national, cultural origin or background

Hispanic leaders have been among the most demanding, insisting that Hispanic children be taught in Spanish; that Hispanic adults be allowed to cast ballots in their native language and that they have the right to vote in districts in which Hispanics make up the majority of voters; that their ethnicity* entitles them to a certain percentage of jobs and college admissions; that immigrants from Latin America be granted many of these same benefits, even if they are in the country illegally. But while Hispanic leaders have been pressing these claims, the rank and file have been moving quietly and steadily into the American mainstream. Like the children and grandchildren of millions of ethnic immigrants before them, virtually all native-born Hispanics speak English—many speak only English. The great majority finish high school, and growing numbers attend college. Their earnings and occupational status have been rising along with their education. But evidence of the success of native-born

Hispanics is drowned in the flood of new Latin immigrants—more than five million—who have come in the last two decades, hoping to climb the ladder as well. For all of these people, assimilation represents the opportunity to succeed in America. Whatever the sacrifices it entails—and there are some—most believe that the payoff is worth it. Yet the elites* who create and influence public policy seem convinced that the process must be stopped or, where this has already occurred, reversed.

elites: small, privileged group

From 1820 to 1924 the United States successfully incorporated a population more ethnically diverse and varied than any other in the world. We could not have done so if today's politics of ethnicity had been the prevailing ethos*. Once again, we are experiencing record immigration, principally from Latin America and Asia. The millions in Latin immigrants who are joining the already large native-born Hispanic population will severely strain our capacity to absorb them, unless we can revive a consensus* for assimilation. But the new politics of Hispanic assimilation need not include the worst features of the Americanization era. Children should not be forced to sink or swim. The model of Anglo conformity would seem ridiculous today in a country in which 150 million persons are descended from people who did not come here from the British Isles. We should not be tempted to shut our doors because we fear the newcomers are too different from us ever to become truly "American." Nonetheless, Hispanics will be obliged to make some adjustments if they are to accomplish what other ethnic groups have.

ethos: values of a specific group

consensus: general agreement

LANGUAGE AND CULTURE

Most Hispanics accept the fact that the United States is an English-speaking country; they even embrace the idea. A *Houston Chronicle* poll in 1990 found that 87 percent of all Hispanics belived that it was "their duty to learn English" and that a majority believed English should be adopted as an official language. Similar results have been obtained in polls taken in California, Colorado, and elsewhere. But Hispanics, especially more recent arrivals, also feel it is important to preserve their own language. Nearly half the Hispanics in the *Houston Chronicle* poll thought that people coming from other countries should preserve their language and teach it to their children. There is nothing inconsistent in these findings, nor are the sentiments* expressed unique* to Hispanics. Every immigrant group has struggled to retain its language, customs, traditions. Some groups have been more successful than others. A ma-

sentiments: feelings, thoughts, views, attitudes

unique: distinctly characteristic

jority of Greek Americans, for example, still speak Greek in their homes at least occasionally. The debate is not about whether Hispanics, or any other group, have the right to retain their native language but about whose responsibility it is to ensure that they do so.

The government should not be obliged to preserve any group's distinctive language or culture. Public schools should make sure that all children can speak, read, and write English well. When teaching children from non-English-speaking backgrounds, they should use methods that will achieve English proficiency quickly and should not allow political pressure to interfere with meeting the academic needs of students. No children in an American school are helped by being held back in their native language when they could be learning the language that will enable them to get a decent job or pursue higher education. More than twenty years of experience with native-language instruction fails to show that children in these programs learn English more quickly or perform better academically than children in programs that emphasize English acquisition.

If Hispanic parents want their children to be able to speak Spanish and know about their distinctive culture, they must take the responsibility to teach their children these things. Government simply cannot—and should not—be charged with this responsibility. Government bureaucracies given the authority to create bicultural teaching materials homogenize the myths*, customs, and history of the Hispanic peoples of this hemisphere, who, after all, are not a single group but many groups. It is only in the United States that "Hispanics" exist; a Cakchiquel Indian in Guatemala would find it remarkable that anyone would consider his culture to be the same as a Spanish Argentinean's. The best way for Hispanics to learn about their native culture is in their own communities. Chinese, Jewish, Greek, and other ethnic communities have long established after-school and weekend programs to teach language and culture to children from these groups. Nothing stops Hispanic organizations from doing the same things. And, indeed, many Hispanic community groups around the country promote cultural programs. In Washington, D.C. groups from El Salvador, Guatemala, Colombia, and elsewhere sponsor soccer teams, fiestas, parades throughout the year, and a two-day celebration in a Latin neighborhood that draws crowds in the hundreds of thousands. The Washington Spanish Festival is a lively, vibrant affair that makes the federal government's effort to enforce Hispanic Heritage Month in all of its agencies and departments each September seem pathetic by comparison. The sight and sound of mariachis* strolling through the cavernous* halls of the Department of Labor as indifferent

myths: traditional stories of a community

mariachis: group of traditional Mexican musicians

cavernous: cave-like

din: loud noise

federal workers try to work above the din* is not only ridiculous; it will not do anything to preserve Mexican culture in the United States.

Hispanics should be interested not just in maintaining their own, distinctive culture but in helping Latin immigrants adjust to their American environment and culture as well. Too few Hispanic organizations promote English or civics classes, although the number has increased dramatically since the federal government began dispensing funds for such programs under the provisions of the Immigration Reform and Control Act, which gives amnesty* to illegal aliens on the condition that they take English and civics classes. But why shouldn't the Hispanic community itself take some responsibility to help new immigrants learn the language and history of their new country, even without government assistance? The settlement houses of the early century thrived without government funds. The project by the National Association of Latino Elected and Appointed Officials (NALEO) to encourage Latin immigrants to become U.S. citizens is the exception among Hispanic organizations; it should be the rule.

amnesty: general pardon by a government body

Reading for Meaning

1. How does Chavez explain the term "assimilation"? Quote it. Paraphrase it as you understand it.
2. How does Chavez define "the worst features of the Americanization era"? Quote it and explain it in your own words.
3. Chavez asserts that "Hispanics will be obliged to make some adjustments if they are to accomplish what other ethnic groups have." What "adjustments" does she suggest Hispanics have to make in culture and language?

Reading Deeper

1. Whose responsibility is it to maintain a group's native language? Explain what Chavez says about this question.
2. What is NALEO and what is their project? How does Chavez feel about this? Explain.

Reading for Writing

1. Investigate English-only legislation. List points that favor English-only and points that oppose it. Take a position and write a letter to your congressman attempting to persuade him or her to support or not to support English-only legislation the next time it comes up for a vote.

2. Investigate the term "Hispanic." Chavez indicates that "It is only in the United States that 'Hispanics' exist." Research when the term was introduced into our vocabulary and why it came into existence. Interview at least three individuals of different generations and ask them how they feel about the term. Also, look at other terms used to identify Spanish-speaking individuals, what the terms mean literally and figuratively, and which one they prefer and why. Write an essay describing your findings. Be sure to use proper documentation.

SPANGLISH IS HERE TO STAY

Isis Artze

Do you know what "Spanglish" is? If you do, do you approve of it? In addition to the debate about English being the official language of the United States, another debate ensues about the legitimacy of "Spanglish." In the following article, taken from Education Digest, *Sept. 2001. Isis Artze looks at Spanglish, its proponents and its opponents. In academic circles, Spanglish is often referred to as code switching and is recognized as having rules of its own that usually conform to both English and Spanish rules and are used correctly when the speaker is using a mixture of English and Spanish. On the one hand, it is looked at as "degenerate" Spanish by some, but on the other, speakers have been praised in that they are at least knowledgeable of some Spanish and/or English. The fact that they have to switch to Spanish while speaking English, some feel, has many positive elements even though it also indicates an incomplete familiarity with English.*

Prereading: Have you ever been around individuals speaking Spanglish? How do you feel about it?

Prewriting: Have you ever tried to learn a foreign language in school? Did you ever have to substitute English words while you were trying to speak the other language? Write a descriptive paragraph explaining how you felt about having to return to English or combine English with the foreign language to help you communicate and whether doing so was disrespectful to either language.

Vocabulary: Looking up and understanding the following words prior to reading should prepare you for the author's message. Other words will be defined in the margin.

etymologically *idioma casas* **anthropological Anglicisms**

W hether you know it or not, speak it or not, or like it or not, Spang-lish is everywhere. Etymologically, the term combines the words Spanish and English. The *American Heritage Dictionary* defines it as "Spanish characterized by numerous borrowings from English." Nearly 35 million U.S. Hispanics know it as their *idioma*, their language on the streets, and in their *casas*. It is on national magazine covers, on adver-tisements, and is heard in popular song lyrics.

To Ilan Stavans, the foremost scholar of this linguistic phenome-non, it is an anthropological journey. But to its opponents, Spanglish is a threat that must be defused.

In one way or another, Spanglish has been around for nearly 150 years, says Stavans, professor of Spanish at Amherst College in Massachusetts. Asked its future, he says "The future is here," asserting that Spanglish "has already played a dramatic role, not only in the way words are shaped, but also in grammar and construction." If you trace the development of dictionaries in the Spanish-speaking world, it be-comes clear that Spanglish has been silently evolving for quite some time, he says.

Toward the end of the nineteenth century, and in the beginning of the twentieth, he adds, the frequency with which dictionaries of Angli-cisms were published was accelerated: "Words like lasso, rodeo, amigo, mañana, and tortilla made it into English; mister and money, into Span-ish." So why all the recent fuss? For starters, Spanglish has a new status.

cachet: mark of distinction and quality

"Once viewed as degenerate Spanish, Spanglish suddenly has cachet*," says Jennifer Bingham Hull. She points to the tremendous success of *Latina* magazine, whose cover headlines, nearly always in Spanglish, have attracted 200,000 subscribers.

perspective: point of view

Again, look to Stavans for the answer, for his two latest endeavors on the part of Spanglish made it such a hot topic. First, he is teaching a three-credit undergraduate course at Amherst, tracing the development of Spanglish from a literary and anthropological perspective*, "to try to understand what is happening with our language." First offered in fall 2000, it attracted nearly 60 students—noteworthy for a small liberal arts college.

xenophobia: fear of strangers or foreigners

Second, and perhaps more important—Stavans recently completed *The Sounds of Spanglish: An Illustrated Lexicon,* an extensive dictio-nary of Spanglish, being published by Basic Books. "The buzz the course and the dictionary have created on National Public Radio and in newspapers around the globe has brought home to me just how much in-terest Spanglish arouses these days," he says. "But it also generates anx-iety and even xenophobia*. In the U.S., it announces to some people an

hispanizacion: making into Hispanic

overall hispanizacion* of society; abroad, it raises the specter* of U.S. cultural imperialism* and the creation of a 'McLengua.'"

specter: something that haunts or perturbs the mind.

GRAVE DANGER?

imperialism: power, domination or control of a nation over another nation or area

An outspoken Spanglish dissident* is Roberto Gonzalez Echevarria, professor of comparative literature at Yale University, who says, "Spanglish, the composite language of Spanish and English that has crossed over from the street to Hispanic talk shows and advertising campaigns, poses a grave danger to Hispanic culture and to the advancement of Hispanics in mainstream America.

dissident: a person who disagrees with an established belief

"The sad reality is that Spanglish is primarily the language of poor Hispanics, many barely literate in either language. They incorporate English words and constructions into their daily speech because they lack the vocabulary and education in Spanish to adapt to the changing culture around them. Educated Hispanics who do likewise have a different motivation: Some are embarrassed by their background and feel empowered by using English words and directly translated English idioms."

Miami Herald columnist Ana Veciana-Suarez partially echoes this concern: "if we formally sanction* Spanglish, are we allowing proper grammar to take a back seat to convenience? Are we giving the nod of approval to linguistic laziness and ignorance? Will the next step be to excuse our children's lack of verbal achievement? Teach them Spanglish, and teach them to settle for substandard English and menial jobs."

sanction: approve

Stavans responds that, to a certain extent, he agrees: "I don't think the classroom should be used to teach it," explaining that, for now, the only course on Spanglish he advocates is one similar to his own, that is, taught from an anthropological standpoint.

intraethnic: between different cultural groups

LIKE EBONICS?

Veciana-Suarez also compares the recent Spanglish debate to California's Ebonics debate four years ago. And she has a valid point, given Stavans has dedicated considerable time, in his study of Spanglish, to an analysis of Ebonics.

empathy: understanding of another's feelings, situation, or motives

Both are "intraethnic* vehicle[s] of communication, used in the United States . . . to establish empathy* among [groups]," he says. "But the differences with Ebonies [sic] are sharp. For one thing, Ebonics is not a product of *mestizaje,* the cross-fertilization of two perfectly discernible codes; Spanglish is. Spanglish is also not defined by class, as people in all social strata, from migrant workers to politicians, academics, and TV anchors, regularly use it, both in the United States and south of the Rio Grande."

In many ways, Stavans says, Yiddish is closer to Spanglish than Ebonics is: "Like Spanglish, Yiddish was never a unified tongue, but a series of regional varieties. Moreover, while both Yiddish and Spanglish started as intraethnic minority languages, both quickly became transnational verbal codes." The presence of Yiddish in Stavans' own upbringing in Mexico, in a small Jewish enclave*, was crucial to his later fascination with Spanglish he says.

enclave: group living together within a much larger society

Hull also addresses the role of Spanglish in Miami, where it is a predominant language. She says that, on the one hand, the prevalence of Spanglish demonstrates the dexterity* of its users: "For those truly bilingual*, Spanglish can reflect impressive verbal skills as speakers choose from two languages for just the right expression. Switching back and forth between Spanish and English, or 'code switching' as linguists call it, these people will often use Spanish to express emotions and English for analytical thoughts. They also use Spanglish as a shortcut, replacing long Spanish words and phrases with shorter English ones."

dexterity: skillfulness

bilingual: able to speak two languages

On the other hand, she says, the popularity of Spanglish in Miami can reflect a lack of fluency in Spanish: "Though more than half of Miami–Dade County's population is Hispanic, only 3% of its public school students graduate from high school fluent in Spanish. Miami business leaders complain that the prevalence of Spanglish in South Florida is symptomatic of a larger problem they face finding employees who are truly bilingual."

Might Spanglish hinder social advancement? Stavans says the opposite is true: "For Latinos to succeed in the U.S., English has to be learned, but you are worse off if you don't speak Spanglish."

Another common critique is the "purist" view that the Spanish language must be protected. Echevarria says, "Spanish is our strongest bond, and it is vital that we preserve it." He anticipates some will challenge him, comparing development of Spanglish, from Spanish and English, to that of Spanish as a branch of Latin: "I suppose my medievalist* colleagues will say that without the contamination of Latin by local languages, there would be no Spanish (or French or Italian).

medievalist: someone who studies the Middle Ages— 600–1500

naïve: innocent

functional: working

"We are no longer in the Middle Ages, however, and it is naïve* to think that we could create a new language that would be functional* and culturally rich. Literature in Spanglish can only aspire to a sort of wit*

wit: humor, satire

based on a rebellious gesture, which wears thin quickly," he adds, concluding that "those who practice it are doomed to writing not a minority literature but a minor literature."

"Languages are living things," Stavans replies; "they are constantly changing and evolving." It is spoken by everybody, even by those who reject it, he adds, "and if we're using it, it's proof that it's needed." . . .

Reading for Meaning

1. Quote and explain two definitions of Spanglish offered in this essay.
2. List two reasons to use Spanglish that will help keep it in use.
3. What evidence does Stavans give that indicates that Spanglish is needed?

Reading Deeper

1. In serious writing, authors refer to individuals who have credibility to help lend credence to the work. Explain who Ilan Stavans and Roberto Gonzalez Echevarria are and why Artze used their comments.
2. Explain the point Artze is trying to make when she uses the term "'McLengua.'" What does it mean exactly? What does it come from?
3. Echevarria contrasts "poor Hispanics, many barely literate in either language" with "educated Hispanics" who also use Spanglish. Explain how he differentiates between them.

Reading for Writing

1. Although Artze writes a detailed article about Spanglish as a spoken language, there is only minimal information about it as a written language. Find several novels that are written primarily in English but that also have Spanish in them. You might look for novels by Sandra Cisneros, Ana Castillo, Denise Chavez, Rudolfo Anaya, Rolando Hinojosa, or others. Read passages from them and decide whether the use of Spanish in the novel hinders your understanding of the part you read. Write a paragraph about whether Spanish should be used in works that are written for primarily English-reading audiences.
2. In the past, the use of Latin, French, or German was perfectly acceptable in written works because the authors were writing to an "educated" audience who were expected to know the language or how to look up the words to understand them. It also displayed the author's knowledge of foreign works. Today, many individuals who might have

accepted the Latin, French, or German, reject the use of Spanish in literature. Interview five instructors in the departments of English and foreign languages and ask them their opinion about using Spanish in literature for primarily English-speaking readers. Write a brief paper that explains their **position** and add your opinion in the conclusion.

If Black English Isn't a Language, Then Tell Me, What Is?

James Baldwin

Even though this article by James Baldwin was written in 1979, published in the New York Times *and collected in* The Price of the Ticket *(1979) it addresses the issue of Ebonics, one that continues to be of importance to many people inside and outside the African-American community today. After the Oakland Unified School District decided that Ebonics should be used in the classroom to help students learn Standard English, professors, teachers, administrators, activists, and others continue to debate whether or not it should be used in schools. In the following article, James Baldwin traces the history of the language to the slaves to support his assertion that Black English is, indeed, a language rather than a dialect of English.*

Prereading: Consider what Artze says in "Spanglish Is Here to Stay," about Ebonics, Yiddish, and Spanglish and decide how you feel about Ebonics.

Prewriting: Write a paragraph discussing all you know about Ebonics and determine whether or not you believe it should be part of the educational system. Support your position.

Vocabulary: Looking up and understanding the following words prior to reading should prepare you for the author's message. Other words will be defined in the margin.

Guadeloupe   Martinique   Senegal   dialect   Basque countries
Wales   Beat Generation   diaspora

The argument concerning the use, or the status, or the reality, of black English is rooted in American history and has absolutely nothing to do with the question the argument supposes itself to be posing*. The argument has nothing to do with language itself but with the *role* of lan-

posing:
presenting

guage. Language, incontestably, reveals the speaker. Language, also, far more dubiously, is meant to define the other—and, in this case, the other is refusing to be defined by a language that has never been able to recognize him.

submerged: made obscure, covered

People evolve a language in order to describe and thus control their circumstances, or in order not to be submerged* by a reality they cannot articulate*. (And, if they cannot articulate it, they *are* submerged.) A Frenchman living in Paris speaks a subtly* and crucially different language from that of the man living in Marseilles; neither sounds very much like a man living in Quebec; and they would all have great difficulty in apprehending* what the man from Guadeloupe, or Martinique, is saying, to say nothing of the man from Senegal—although the "common" language of all these areas is French. But each has paid, and is paying, a different price for this "common" language, in which, as it turns out, they are not saying, and cannot be saying, the same things: They each have very different realities to articulate or control.

articulate: to say or express clearly

subtly: difficult to understand

apprehending: understanding

inconceivably: not believable

outwit: outsmart

temporal: relating to one's life

What joins all languages, and all men, is the necessity to confront life, in order, not inconceivably*, to outwit* death: the price for this is the acceptance, and achievement, of one's temporal* identity. So that, for example, though it is not taught in the schools (and this has the potential of becoming a political issue) the south of France still clings to its ancient and musical Provençal, which resists being described as a "dialect." And much of the tension of the Basque countries, and in Wales, is due to the Basque and Welsh determination not to allow their languages to be destroyed. This determination also feeds the flames in Ireland for among the many indignities* the Irish have been forced to undergo at English hands is the English contempt for their language.

indignities: acts of humiliating treatment

communal: community

It goes without saying, then, that language is also a political instrument, means, and proof of power. It is the most vivid and crucial key to identity: it reveals the private identity, and connects one with, or divorces one from the larger, public, or communal* identity. There have been, and are, times and places, when to speak a certain language could be dangerous, even fatal. Or, one may speak the same language but in such a way that one's antecedents* are revealed, or (one hopes) hidden. This is true in France, and is absolutely true in England: The range (and reign) of accents on that damp little island make England coherent* for the English and totally incomprehensible for everyone else. To open your mouth in England is (if I may use black English) to "put your business in the street": You have confessed your parents, your youth, your school, your salary, your self-esteem, and, alas, your future.

antecedents: ancestors

coherent: understandable

Now, I do not know what white Americans would sound like if there had never been any black people in the United States, but they would not sound the way they sound. *Jazz,* for example is a very specific sexual term, as in *jazz me, baby,* but white people purified it into the Jazz Age. *Sock it to me,* which means, roughly, the same thing, has been adopted by Nathaniel Hawthorne's descendants with no qualms* or hesitations at all, along with *let it all hang out* and *right on! Beat to his socks,* which was once the blacks' most total despairing image of poverty, was transformed into a thing called the Beat Generation, which phenomenon was, largely, composed of *uptight,* middle-class white people, imitating poverty, trying to *get down,* to get *with it,* doing their thing, doing their despairing best to be *funky,* which we, the blacks, never dreamed of doing—we *were* funky, baby, like *funk* was going out of style.

qualms: uneasiness about a point of conscience

Now, no one can eat his cake, and have it, too, and it is late in the day to attempt to penalize black people for having created a language that permits the nation its only glimpse of reality, a language without which the nation would be even more *whipped* than it is.

skirmish: verbal conflict

I say that this present skirmish* is rooted in American history, and it is. Black English is the creation of the black disapora. Blacks came to the United States chained to each other, but from different tribes: Neither could speak the other's language. If two black people, at that bitter hour of the world's history, had been able to speak to each other, the institution of chattel* slavery could never have lasted as long as it did. Subsequently, the slave was given, under the eye, and the gun, of his master, Congo Square, and the Bible—or in other words, and under these conditions, the slave began the formation of the black church, and it is within this unprecedented tabernacle* that black English began to be formed. This was not, merely as in the European example, the adoption of a foreign tongue, but an alchemy that transformed ancient elements into a new language: *A language comes into existence by means of brutal necessity, and the rules of the language are dictated by what the language must convey.*

chattel: item of property

tabernacle: house of worship

There was a moment, in time, and in this place, when my brother, or my mother, or my father, or my sister, had to convey to me, for example, the danger in which I was standing from the white man standing just behind me, and to convey this with a speed, and in a language, that the white man could not possibly understand, and that, indeed he cannot understand, until today. He cannot afford to understand it. This understanding would reveal to him too much about himself, and smash that mirror before which he has been frozen for so long.

Now, if this passion, this skill, this (to quote Toni Morrison) "sheer intelligence," this incredible music, the mighty achievement of having brought a people utterly unknown to, or despised by "history"—to have

unassailable:
not open to
attack, doubt, or
question

transcended:
gone beyond

patronizingly:
treated as
inferior

sustenance:
support

mediocrities:
item of low
quality

brought this people to their present, troubled, troubling, and unassail-able* and unanswerable place—if this absolutely unprecedented jour-ney does not indicate that black English is a language, I am curious to know what definition of language is to be trusted.

A people at the center of the Western world, and in the midst of so hostile a population has not endured and transcended* by means of what is patronizingly* called a "dialect." We, the blacks, are in trouble, cer-tainly, but we are not doomed, and we are not inarticulate because we are not compelled to defend a morality that we know to be a lie.

The brutal truth is that the bulk of the white people in America never had any interest in educating black people, except as this could serve white purposes. It is not the black child's language that is in ques-tion, it is not his language that is despised: It is his experience. A child cannot be taught by anyone who despises him, and a child cannot afford to be fooled. A child cannot be taught by anyone whose demand, essen-tially, is that the child repudiate his experience, and all that gives him sustenance*, and enter a limbo in which he will no longer be black, and in which he knows that he can never become white. Black people have lost too many black children that way.

And, after all, finally, in a country with standards so untrustworthy, a country that makes heroes of so many criminal mediocrities*, a country unable to face why so many of the nonwhite are in prison, or on the needle, or standing, futureless, in the streets—it may very well be that both the child, and his elder, have concluded that they have nothing whatever to learn from the people of a country that has managed to learn so little.

Reading for Expectations

1. What does Baldwin say is the most "vivid and crucial key to identity"? Why does he say this? What is a communal identity?
2. Select two examples of Black English that Baldwin uses and explain what each means.
3. Baldwin explains how and why new languages come into existence. Explain in your own words what he means.

Reading for Meaning

1. How does Baldwin describe the Beat Generation?
2. What does Baldwin mean when he says that America "would be even more *whipped* than it is" if it penalizes "black people for having cre-ated a language that permits the nation its only glimpse of reality"? Explain.

3. What does Baldwin suggest the importance of a common language would have been to the slaves who were brought to the United States from Africa?
4. Explain what the purpose of Black English was for the slave in relation to his master.
5. Explain Baldwin's conclusion.

Reading for Writing

1. Select several examples of phrases that have come into the English language that are clearly from an ethnicity other than mainstream America. Write a paragraph on each, identifying them, explaining their origin, and discussing what they mean.
2. Identify a point or two that Baldwin makes in his essay and write a letter to Baldwin agreeing or disagreeing with him. Be sure to quote points that he makes in his essay and respond to them.

LOOK. LISTEN. OVER THERE.

Los Angeles Times *Editors*

The informality and speed of our modern life has definitely affected not only the way we live, but it has also affected our language. Too busy to form complete sentences or to elaborate an idea, we shorten our words, use acronyms instead of the words themselves, and generally take less time to communicate with others. And when we run across someone who wants to have a conversation with us, we find them annoying, wanting them to get to the point—bottom line—as soon as possible. Not only has language suffered, but so has our ability to communicate in writing because we often want to write the way we speak—short, choppy, disconnected words that do not always add up to sentences. This is also reinforced in many of the pieces we read.

Prereading: Consider the last time you saw someone you knew as you were walking the opposite direction. Did you ask the individual how he or she was and kept walking—Hey, how are you?—not waiting for a reply? Or did you see the person and say, sincerely or otherwise, "Call me sometime" as you walked quickly toward your destination?

Prewriting: Think of the last time you had a conversation that took more than a few minutes with someone and write your feelings about it. Were you happy to spend time with that person and talk or did you feel rushed to go do something else?

Vocabulary: Looking up and understanding the following words prior to reading should prepare you for the author's message. Other words will be defined in the margin.

discourse   nuance

Have you noticed? Strangest thing. On TV now. Mainly news. Also promos. Sentence fragments. Like this. Short word bursts. Like this. Colorful verbs. Vanished. Whole sentences. Gone. Intelligent discourse. Poof. How? What's happening? Sure, Americans always hurry. Big-time. We hurry; therefore, we are. Gotta go.

But. Now. More TV reporters talking funny. *"President Bush in Georgia today. Campaigning for Republicans."* Cool? Hip? Not! *"West Coast ports. Back at work. Choking on cargo."* Caffeine? New disease? Contagious? Brain burps? Saving cell minutes? Also creeping informality. We've used contractions forever. Slur speech too, dontcha know. Also like abbreviations, acronyms: It's "fax," "e-mail" and "nuke" 'cause they're faster than "facsimile," "electronic mail" and "microwave." Now comes TV Qwik-Speak (QS). QS sounds informed, dramatic, unburdened by elaboration. *"Today. Off the Louisiana coast. An oil slick, miles long. Moving toward shore."* Affectation?* Like torn jeans? Sideways ball caps? Or just lazy?

affectation: a show, pretense

Admittedly, communicating in complete sentences with subjects, verbs and objects, also adjectives, adverbs (and parenthetical asides) takes time. And thought, too. Ears hear words; they don't gulp them like a lunch to-go. Ponder this: whole thoughts and complete sentences involve listeners more. They make us think, allow for connections, perhaps even relate and respond to each other. It's the difference between talking *to* or *at* someone.

apt: suitable

alliteration: two or more words with the same first sound

Careful word choice, apt* alliteration*, clever constructions, metaphors* as warm as the hearth at Grandma's, they all add nuance and lushness to thoughts and ideas. Such exchanges convey beyond words and pictures. They make links, one to one, despite so many rapid, bewildering changes, large and small, all around.

metaphors: comparison of two unlike things without the use of the words "like" or "as"

flagstone: flat paving stones

Word bursts jar. They push people away. Impersonal. Superficial. Distant. Like dashing through a gorgeous forest on flagstones*. You can do it. But what's to feel, savor and remember afterward? Life spans lengthen but time's still short. Especially on TV. Our common cultural touchstone. Where time is sliced too thin for thought izzit better to be fast? Or comprehended?

staccato: very short, quick sounds

Very tiring, speaking staccato*. Also listening. Reading staccato is worst. Eyes can't gulp either. Must stop. QS: wave of the future? Please. Not.

Reading for Meaning

1. Look at the title of this editorial. How does it prepare you for the message? Is it effective? Explain.
2. What do complete sentences and whole thoughts do?

Reading Deeper

1. The authors of this editorial suggest something about informality. What is it? Do you agree?
2. The author compares QS to "torn jeans" and "Sideways ball caps." What is the key to the comparisons? What is the author trying to say?
3. The author compares the impersonal superficial way we talk to "dashing through a gorgeous forest on flagstones." Explain the similarities. Do you think he's correct in his comparison? Explain.

Reading for Writing

1. Consider the last time you read a really long book or article in a magazine. Did you skim it or did you take the time to read it word for word? Write a paragraph about the **differences** between reading a long work and a short one. Give specific examples.
2. Go to your local bookstore and look through articles in various kinds of magazines. Look through magazines designed specifically for young adults, those specifically for women, and those for business people. Look at the length of the articles in each of the magazines. Write down the names of the magazines, title of the articles, who wrote them, and their length. Write a **compare and contrast** essay about the length of the articles, their audience, and what conclusions you came to from your investigations.
3. Using the assignment from #2, look at the ads in the magazines you selected. Analyze them for number of words, kinds of words (nouns, verbs, adjectives), and construction of words (alone, in phrases, in sentences). How do the ads convey their message to the consumer

best—through words or pictures? Write a **descriptive, informative** essay discussing how many words were used in different ads (car ads, make-up ads, clothing ads) and where they were found (magazines for young adults, women, business people, music, etc.). You will have to use **division** and **classification** in your prewriting.

FOR COLLEGIATE WRITERS, IT'S A DOGGIE-DOG WORLD

Mike Bower

The evolution of language is not the only problem students have to contend with. Keeping up with the meaning of everyday words that have been in use since we began oral communication also gives some students difficulty. Mike Bower, writer for the Baltimore Sun, *August 8, 2001, describes problems that have been reported to him by the U.S. editor of the new* Microsoft Encarta College Dictionary. *Using negative information from professors in the field who work daily with student writing, Anne H. Soukhanov created a dictionary that should serve the needs of contemporary students as well as the needs of anyone who requires help with contemporary definitions, spelling questions, or other matters concerning proper English. However, even though Microsoft has produced a resource that answers so many questions, how many students will use it if it is available to them?*

Prereading: Do you know the difference between "there," "their," and "they're"? Do you use them correctly in sentences? Can you identify other words that give you trouble?

Prewriting: Review the last paper you submitted to your instructor. Which words were circled or marked as incorrect? Find the denotative definition or spelling in a dictionary and write it out. Use the correct word in the sentence that was written erroneously. Edit the paper completely, making all the changes needed.

Vocabulary: Looking up and understanding the following word prior to reading should prepare you for the author's message. Other words will be defined in the margin.

lexicographers

Dictionary offers tips on usage, grammar and other areas to address students' declining writing skills.

The first major dictionary of the 21st century is appropriately directed at the deteriorating writing skills of college students.

The *Microsoft Encarta College Dictionary,* published last month [July 2001] by St. Martin's Press, addresses today's students' problems with English grammar, usage, spelling and vocabulary.

How bad is it? Ask any college professor who has to slog through student essays.

That's what the editors of this new dictionary did: They consulted a panel of 80 authorities, including 32 English professors mostly at public universities in 24 states and four Canadian provinces. Examples submitted to the editors will ring bells from community colleges to Harvard:

"Reading *Wuthering Heights,* Heathcliff never fails to make an impression."

"The villain use to be seen lurking on foggy streets late at night."

"In his plight to find the treasure, he perished on the dessert island."

"There's players all over the field."

"Shakespeare's plays had alot of strong women."

"It's a doggie-dog world out there."

"Our society has a dog-eat-dog pecking order."

These are just several examples. Students don't know the difference between "they're," "their" and "there," the professors said. They routinely confuse "its" and "it's." They don't know the difference between "blatant" and "flagrant," "pretext" and "pretense." They think that "although" means "however," as in "Although, everyone did know the murderer."

And because computer spell-checking software doesn't flag words that sound alike but are spelled differently, constructions such as "It prayed on her mind" are handed in uncorrected.

A dictionary, of course, can't solve all these problems, but this one takes a stab at some of them. It features more than 600 usage notes alerting students to common errors. The dictionary also lists words that are often misspelled.

ascendancy: rise

homophones: words that sound the same but are spelled differently

Perhaps most ironic, given Microsoft's role in the ascendancy* of computer spelling checkers, there are 400 notes warning of homophones*. Students looking up "stare," for example, are advised: "Do not confuse 'stare' with 'stair,' which has a similar sound. Beware: Your spell-checker will not catch this error."

Anne H. Soukhanov, editor of the dictionary's American edition, said the panel of professors convinced her to include the spell-check warnings. The spell-check traps are listed in alphabetical order in the front of the dictionary, and Soukhanov said she hopes students will refer to the list first and then look up specific words in the body of the dictionary.

You'd expect a dictionary sponsored by Microsoft to include up-to-the-minute definitions of all things technological and Encarta doesn't disappoint. Computer and Internet words are marked with a lightning-bolt symbol (not "cymbal"), and there's one on almost every page.

Many of them—"bot" for example, the word for a computer program performing routine tasks—have little meaning to Joe Blow, which, by the way, is in the dictionary, along with "Joe Six-Pack." So is "NY-LON," an adjective relating to "a trans-Atlantic lifestyle divided between New York and London, as lived by successful business executives."

("Microsoft" isn't among the book's 320,000 definitions, and Chairman Bill Gates is modestly described as a "U.S. business executive." Steve Jobs, by contrast, is defined as "co-founder of the Apple Computer Co.")

Constructing dictionaries is tricky business. The lexicographers have to decide whether to be descriptive, capturing a moment in a language's history, or prescriptive—making value judgements about the use and spelling of the language.

No dictionary, including the Encarta, is all one or the other, Soukhanov said from her office in Bedford, Va., "but I tend to be on the conservative side."

Her dictionary shows it. It advises against "issues" to denote intentionally unstated emotional or mental problems, as in "He came to see me because he had some issues."

deployed: used

Similarly, "irregardless is a double negative and regarded as non-standard. As such, it should be avoided." And "Like," when deployed* "as a meaningless filler," should be shunned.

Said Soukhanov, "We would never have known about the issue of 'issue' if we hadn't heard from our professors."

tome: a large, scholarly book

In the introduction to the 1,678-page tome*, Soukhanov writes about a "clear and present crisis in many students' use of the English Language." The Encarta is an attempt to help erase the crisis.

For now, it's available only in print.

Reading for Meaning

1. Bower begins his essay with a strong assertion: "The first major dictionary of the 21st century is appropriately directed at the deteriorating writing skills of college students." Does the rest of the essay

support this statement. Explain. Do you agree or disagree with his statement? Explain.

2. Describe and explain the job of lexicographers.

Reading Deeper

1. Find and correct the error in the seven sentences that are quoted after paragraph 4.
2. How do you think Soukhanov would react to "Spanglish"?

Reading for Writing

1. The old cliché, "You can lead a horse to water but you can't make him drink" is quite appropriate in this article. Publishers have published numerous aids, including the dictionary above, that make error correction easy for students; however, they still don't use them. Think of the number of times you have taken advantage of the spell-checker on your computer but you haven't proofread an essay or other assignment before submitting it. Write a **descriptive, exemplification** paragraph about why many students do not take the time to check for errors and use the appropriate resources to correct them in their papers.

2. How many times have you said or heard someone else say, "When I use a dictionary I can't find the way to spell a word I don't know how to spell"? Write a brief **analysis** paper, giving someone directions on how to look up a word in the dictionary so that he or she will be able to spell it correctly.

SILENCE

Maxine Hong Kingston

The following is an excerpt from Maxine Hong Kingston's autobiography, The Woman Warrior: Memoirs of a Childhood Among Ghosts *(1976). Here she writes about her unhappiness in her childhood American school, and she recalls the difference between it and her happiness in her Chinese school. For a woman who depends on language, her early years were painful and distressing to her and her parents.*

Prereading: Consider what life without speaking in school might be like. Choose a day that you are on campus and do not communicate with anyone—friends, professors, staff members, and so forth. It will be different for you from what it might be for a child, but in both cases, communication is usually a necessity.

Prewriting: There has been much written about the use of English immersion and bilingual education in the schools to help children learn English. Look up each of these methods and determine which you think might help an English Language Learner to become comfortable with English. Write a paragraph and support your position.

Vocabulary: Looking up and understanding the following word prior to reading should prepare you for the author's message. Other words will be defined in the margin.

frenum   Sun Yat-sen   Chiang Kai-shek

L ong ago in China, knot-makers tied string into buttons and frogs, and rope into bell pulls. There was one knot so complicated that it blinded the knot-maker. Finally an emperor outlawed this cruel knot, and the nobles could not order it anymore. If I had lived in China, I would have been an outlaw knot-maker.

Maybe that's why my mother cut my tongue. She pushed my tongue up and sliced the frenum. Or maybe she snipped it with a pair of nail scissors. I don't remember her doing it, only her telling me about it, but all during childhood I felt sorry for the baby whose mother waited with scissors or knife in hand for it to cry—and then, when its mouth was wide open like a baby bird's, cut. The Chinese say "a ready tongue is an evil."

tauten: to make tight

I used to curl up my tongue in front of the mirror and tauten* my frenum into a white line, itself as thin as a razor blade. I saw no scars in my mouth. I thought perhaps I had two frena, and she had cut one. I made other children open their mouths so I could compare theirs to mine. I saw perfect pink membranes stretching into precise edges that looked easy enough to cut. Sometimes I felt very proud that my mother committed such a powerful act upon me. At other times I was terrified—the first thing my mother did when she saw me was to cut my tongue.

"Why did you do that to me, Mother?"

"I told you."

"Tell me again."

"I cut it so you would not be tongue-tied. Your tongue would be able to move in any language. You'll be able to speak languages that are completely different from one another. You'll be able to pronounce anything. Your frenum looked too tight to do those things, so I cut it."

"But isn't 'a ready tongue an evil'?"

"Things are different in this ghost country."

"Did it hurt me? Did I cry and bleed?"

"I don't remember. Probably."

She didn't cut the other children's. When I asked cousins and other Chinese children whether their mothers had cut their tongues loose, they said, "What?"

"Why didn't you cut my brothers' and sisters' tongues?"

"They didn't need it."

"Why not? Were theirs longer than mine?"

"Why don't you quit blabbering and get to work?"

If my mother was not lying, she should have cut more, scraped away the rest of the frenum skin, because I have a terrible time talking. Or she should not have cut at all, tampering with my speech. When I went to kindergarten and had to speak English for the first time, I became silent. A dumbness—a shame—still cracks my voice in two, even when I want to say "hello" casually, or ask an easy question in front of the checkout counter, or ask directions of a bus driver. I stand frozen, or I hold up the line with the complete, grammatical sentence that comes squeaking out at impossible length. "What did you say?" says the cab driver, or "Speak up," so I have to perform again, only weaker the second time. A phone call makes my throat bleed and takes up that day's courage. It spoils my day with self-disgust when I hear my broken voice *wince:* shrink come skittering out into the open. It makes people wince* to hear it. I'm back as if from getting better though. Recently I asked the postman for special-issue pain stamps; I've waited since childhood for postmen to give me some of their own accord. I am making progress, a little every day.

My silence was thickest—total—during the three years that I covered my school paintings with black paint. I painted layers of black over houses and flowers and suns, and when I drew on the blackboard, I put a layer of chalk on top. I was making a stage curtain, and it was the moment before the curtain parted or rose. The teachers called my parents to school, and I saw they had been saving my pictures, curling and cracking, all alike and black. The teachers pointed to the pictures and looked serious, talked seriously too, but my parents did not understand English. ("The parents and teachers of criminals were executed," said my father.) My parents took the pictures home. I spread them out (so black and full of possibilities) and pretended the curtains were swinging open, flying up, one after another, sunlight underneath, mighty operas.

During the first silent year I spoke to no one at school, did not ask before going to the lavatory, and flunked kindergarten. My sister also said nothing for three years, silent in the playground and silent at lunch. There were other quiet Chinese girls not of our family, but most of them got over it sooner than we did. I enjoyed the silence. At first it did not occur to me I was supposed to talk or to pass kindergarten. I talked at home and even made some jokes. I drank out of a toy saucer when the water spilled out of a cup, and everybody laughed, pointing at me, so I did it some more. I didn't know that Americans don't drink out of saucers.

It was when I found out that I had to talk that school became a misery, that the silence became a misery. I did not speak and felt bad each time that I did not speak. I read aloud in first grade, though, and heard the barest whisper with little squeaks come out of my throat. "Louder," said the teacher, who scared the voice away again. The other Chinese girls did not talk either, so I knew the silence had to do with being a Chinese girl.

Reading aloud was easier than speaking because we did not have to make up what to say, but I stopped often, and the teacher would think I'd gone quiet again. I could not understand "I." The Chinese "I" has seven strokes, intricacies*. How could the American "I," assuredly wearing a hat like the Chinese, have only three strokes, the middle so straight? Was it out of politeness; "I" is a capital and "you" is a lowercase. I stared at that middle line and waited so long for its black center to resolve into tight strokes and dots that I forgot to pronounce it. The other troublesome word was "here," no strong consonant to hang on to, and so flat, when "here" is two mountainous ideographs. The teacher, who had already told me every day how to read "I" and "here," put me in the low corner under the stairs again, where the noisy boys usually sat.

intricacies: complex; having interrelated parts

After American school, we picked up our cigar boxes, in which we had arranged books, brushes, and an inkbox neatly, and went to Chinese school from 5:00 to 7:30 P.M. There we changed together, voices rising and falling, loud and soft, some boys shouting, everybody reading together, reciting together and not alone with one voice. When we had a memorization test, the teacher let each of us come to his desk and say the lesson to him privately, while the rest of the class practiced copying or tracing. Most of the teachers were men. The boys who were so well behaved in the American school played tricks on them and talked back to them. The girls were not mute. They screamed and yelled during recess, when there were no rules; they had fistfights. Nobody was afraid of children hurting themselves or of children hurting school property. The glass doors to the red and green balconies with the gold joy symbols were left wide open so that we could run out and climb the fire escapes. We played capture-the-flag in the auditorium, where Sun Yat-sen and Chiang Kai-shek's pictures hung at the back of the stage, the Chinese flag on their left and the American flag on their right. We climbed the

teak: hard, yellowish, brown wood

teak* ceremonial chairs and made flying leaps off the stage. One flag headquarters was behind the glass door and the other on stage right. Our feet drummed on the hollow stage. During recess the teachers locked themselves up in their office with the shelves of books, copybooks, inks from China. They drank tea and warmed their hands at a stove. There was no play supervision. At recess we had the school to ourselves, and also we could roam as far as we could go—downtown, Chinatown stores, home—as long as we returned before the bell rang.

Not all of the children who were silent at American school found voice at Chinese school. One new teacher said each of us had to get up and recite in front of the class, who was to listen. My sister and I had memorized the lesson perfectly. We said it to each other at home, one chanting, one listening. The teacher called on my sister to recite first. It was the first time the teacher had called on the second born to go first. My sister was scared. She glanced at me and looked away; I looked down at my desk. I hoped that she could do it because if she could, then I wouldn't have to. She opened her mouth and a voice came out that wasn't a whisper, but it wasn't a proper voice either. I hoped that she would not cry, fear breaking up her voice like twigs underfoot. She sounded as if she were trying to sing through weeping and strangling. She did not pause or stop to end the embarrassment. She kept going until she said the last word, and then she sat down. When it was my turn, the same voice came out, a crippled animal running on broken legs. You could hear the splinters in my voice, bones rubbing jagged against one another. I was loud, though. I was glad I didn't whisper. There was one little girl who whispered.

Reading for Expectations

1. List and explain two experiences Kingston had as a child that made her choose silence in her American school.
2. What characteristics of the Chinese school made speaking easier for Kingston than those of the American school?

Reading for Meaning

1. Why do you think the Chinese say, "'a ready tongue is an evil'"? Explain what you think the saying means. Explain what you think the value of the saying is.
2. Explain the effect of the tongue cutting on Kingston as a child. Was it the effect her mother had intended? Explain.

3. Think of yourself as a kindergarten teacher who received pictures that were all black from a student. What would you say to the parents? How would you convey the seriousness of the situation if they were non-English speaking?

4. How did Kingston cope as a child when she did things that were unusual in the American culture?

Reading for Writing

1. Think about your experiences in elementary school. Which year stands out the most? Were you a shy or an outgoing child? Write a **descriptive, cause-and-effect** paper that discusses your most memorable elementary school year.

2. Kingston talks about her memories of learning to read. Think about the subject that you had trouble with the most when you were in elementary school. Write a **descriptive, cause-and-effect, personal narrative** explaining which subject gave you trouble and how you, your teacher, and/or your parents tried to help you overcome your difficulties. Discuss your feelings about that subject and how you feel about it now.

RHETORICAL ANALYSIS

"Spanglish Is Here to Stay" is an excellent essay to work with for rhetorical analysis. It provides a variety of strategies that the instructional part of this textbook attempts to prepare readers and writers for as they gain more skills. In the left-hand margin there is information that directs you to appropriate chapters in this textbook for discussion about the underlined techniques the author used to write the essay or that comment directly about the techniques the author used.

Spanglish Is Here to Stay

Definition is provided. See Ch. 5, Definition.

Examples are added to help reader. See Ch. 3, Exemplification.

Whether you know it or not, speak it or not, or like it or not, Spanglish is everywhere. Etymologically, the term combines the words Spanish and English. The *American Heritage Dictionary* defines it as "Spanish characterized by numerous borrowings from English." Nearly 35 million U.S. Hispanics know it as their idioma, their language on the streets, and in their casas. It is on national magazine covers, on advertisements, and is heard in popular song lyrics.

Ch. 2,
Description,
author uses
description to
explain who
Stavans is.

Ch. 10,
Persuasion,
evidence to
support topic
sentence

Ch. 3,
Exemplification,
examples to
support
discussion that
Spanish words
are part of
English and
English words
are part of
Spanish.

Ch. 10,
Persuasion,
support from
popular culture,
making
evidence timely

Ch. 5,
Definition,
author uses a
definition or
explanation of
the book.

To <u>Ilan Stavans, the foremost scholar of this linguistic phenomenon</u>, it is an anthropological journey. But to its opponents, Spanglish is a threat that must be defused.

In one way or another, Spanglish has been around for nearly 150 years, says Stavans, <u>professor of Spanglish at Amherst College in Massachusetts</u>. Asked its future, he says "The future is here," asserting that Spanglish "has already played a dramatic role, not only in the way words are shaped, but also in grammar and construction." If you trace the development of dictionaries in the Spanish-speaking world, it becomes clear that <u>Spanglish has been silently evolving for quite some time</u>, he says.

Toward the end of the nineteenth century, and in the beginning of the twentieth, he adds, the frequency with which dictionaries of Anglicisms were published was accelerated: <u>"Words like lasso, rodeo, amigo, mañana, and tortilla made it into English; mister and money, into Spanish</u>." So why all the recent fuss? For starters, Spanglish has a new status.

"Once viewed as degenerate Spanish, Spanglish suddenly has cachet," says Jennifer Bingham Hull. <u>She points to the tremendous success of *Latina* magazine, whose cover headlines, nearly always in Spanglish, have attracted 200,000 subscribers</u>.

Again, look to Stavans for the answer, for his two latest endeavors on the part of Spanglish made it such a hot topic. First, he is teaching a three-credit undergraduate course at Amherst, tracing the development of Spanglish from a literary and anthropological perspective, "to try to understand what is happening with our language." First offered in fall 2000, it attracted nearly 60 students—noteworthy for a small liberal arts college.

Second, and perhaps more important—Stavans recently completed *The Sounds of Spanglish: An Illustrated Lexicon,* <u>an extensive dictionary of Spanglish</u>, being published by Basic Books. "The buzz the course and the dictionary have created on National Public Radio and in newspapers around the globe has brought home to me just how much interest Spanglish arouses these days," he says. "But it also generates anxiety and even xenophobia. In the U.S., it announces to some people an overall hispanizacion of society; abroad, it raises the specter of U.S. cultural imperialism and the creation of a 'McLengua.'"

GRAVE DANGER?

An outspoken Spanglish dissident is Roberto Gonzalez Echevarria, professor of comparative literature at Yale University, who says, "Spanglish, the composite language of Spanish and English that has crossed over from the street to Hispanic talk shows and advertising campaigns, poses a grave danger to Hispanic culture and to the advancement of Hispanics in mainstream America.

"The sad reality is that Spanglish is primarily the language of poor Hispanics, many barely literate in either language. They incorporate English words and constructions into their daily speech because they lack the vocabulary and education in Spanish to adapt to the changing culture around them. Educated Hispanics who do likewise have a different motivation: Some are embarrassed by their background and feel empowered by using English words and directly translated English idioms."

Miami Herald columnist Ana Veciana-Suarez partially echoes this concern: "if we formally sanction Spanglish, are we allowing proper grammar to take a back seat to convenience? Are we giving the nod of approval to linguistic laziness and ignorance? Will the next step be to excuse our children's lack of verbal achievement? Teach them Spanglish, and teach them to settle for substandard English and menial jobs."

Stavans responds that, to a certain extent, he agrees: "I don't think the classroom should be used to teach it," explaining that, for now, the only course on Spanglish he advocates is one similar to his own, that is, taught from an anthropological standpoint.

LIKE EBONICS?

Veciana-Suarez also compares the recent Spanglish debate to California's Ebonics debate four years ago. And she has a valid point, given Stavans has dedicated considerable time, in his study of Spanglish, to an analysis of Ebonics.

Margin notes:

Ch. 1, Reading, bold heading a strategy for reading

Ch. 10, Persuasion, rebuttal argument begins in this paragraph.

Ch. 10, Persuasion, new speaker with popular culture and timely evidence in rebuttal to Stavans's argument

Ch. 1, reading strategy

Ch. 7, analogy

Ch. 7,
Comparison and
Contrast,
extended
analogy
between
Spanglish and
Ebonics

Both are "intraethnic vehicle[s] of communication, used in the United States . . . to establish
empathy among [groups]," he says. "But the differences with Ebonies [sic] are sharp. For one thing,
Ebonics is not a product of mestizaje, the cross-
fertilization of two perfectly discernible codes;
Spanglish is. Spanglish is also not defined by
class, as people in all social strata, from migrant
workers to politicians, academics, and TV anchors,
regularly use it, both in the United States and
south of the Rio Grande."

Ch. 7,
Comparison and
Contrast
analogy

In many ways, Stavans says, Yiddish is closer to
Spanglish than Ebonics is: "Like Spanglish, Yiddish
was never a unified tongue, but a series of regional
varieties. Moreover, while both Yiddish and Spanglish started as intraethnic minority languages, both
quickly became transnational verbal codes." The
presence of Yiddish in Stavans' own upbringing in
Mexico, in a small Jewish enclave, was crucial to
his later fascination with Spanglish he says.

Hull also addresses the role of Spanglish in
Miami, where it is a predominant language. She says
that, on the one hand, the prevalence of Spanglish
demonstrates the dexterity of its users: "For those
truly bilingual, Spanglish can reflect impressive
verbal skills as speakers choose from two languages
for just the right expression. Switching back and
forth between Spanish and English, or 'code switching' as linguists call it, these people will often
use Spanish to express emotions and English for analytical thoughts. They also use Spanglish as a
shortcut, replacing long Spanish words and phrases
with shorter English ones."

Ch. 10,
Persuasion,
transition to
show shift to the
opposing
argument

On the other hand, she says, the popularity of
Spanglish in Miami can reflect a lack of fluency in
Spanish: "Though more than half of Miami-Dade
County's population is Hispanic, only 3% of its public school students graduate from high school fluent
in Spanish. Miami business leaders complain that the
prevalence of Spanglish in South Florida is symptomatic of a larger problem they face finding employees who are truly bilingual."

Might Spanglish hinder social advancement? Stavans says the opposite is true: "For Latinos to suc-

ceed in the U.S., English has to be learned, but you are worse off if you don't speak Spanglish."

Ch. 10, Persuasion, transition to show continuation of an argument

Another common critique is the "purist" view that the Spanish language must be protected. Echevarria says, "Spanish is our strongest bond, and it is vital that we preserve it." He anticipates some will challenge him, comparing development of Spanglish, from Spanish and English, to that of Spanish as a branch of Latin: "I suppose my medievalist colleagues will say that without the contamination of Latin by local languages, there would be no Spanish (or French or Italian).

Ch. 10, Persuasion, rebuttal paragraph

"We are no longer in the Middle Ages, however, and it is naïve to think that we could create a new language that would be functional and culturally rich. Literature in Spanglish can only aspire to a sort of wit based on a rebellious gesture, which wears thin quickly," he adds, concluding that "those who practice it are doomed to writing not a minority literature but a minor literature."

Ch. 10, Persuasion, author ends on strongest argument, indicating her position on the topic.

"Languages are living things," Stavans replies; "they are constantly changing and evolving." It is spoken by everybody, even by those who reject it, he adds, "and if we're using it, it's proof that it's needed." . . .

The references to Chapter 10, Reading and Writing about Persuasion and Argument, clearly indicate that Artze wrote an essay in which she is attempting to convince readers about the importance of and need for Spanglish in contemporary language. Even though her opening sentence, "Whether you know it or not, speak it or not, or like it or not, Spanglish is everywhere" sounds like it will be the thesis, it is not. If you look more closely at the title, "Spanglish is Here to Stay," you will see that it comes closer to being the main point of the essay, but rereading the last sentence of the essay, "It is spoken by everybody, even by those who reject it, he adds, 'and if we're using it, it's proof that it's needed,'" you will see that Stavans asserts his claim about the necessity of the language. However, Artze did not present a one-sided essay, nor did she offer representatives of the opposing side who were unknown in their field. Artze wrote a well-balanced essay presenting important sides of the issue and ending with her main supporter, Stavans, making an important point to convince readers.

REFLECTIONS ON LANGUAGE: HOW WE SPEAK TO EACH OTHER

We have looked at material that discusses language from the perspective of problems and responsibilities of society to the responsibilities of individual students. Some of the material has overlapped, but different perspectives have been covered concerning the politics and academic aspects of language. Very much like other important concerns in society—grammar, sex, zoning, freeway construction, etc.—language does not become a problem until someone points it out to us or until we become consciously involved with it. Then we realize how complex the topic can be.

Regardless of the career we choose, language skills will always follow us, whether in the form of having to write a memo to our boss, a letter to our child's teacher, or a report on an insurance claim. Because we live in a society that requires communication, we will have to speak to answering machines, checkers at grocery stores, customers we perform services for, businesspeople, lawyers, friends, and others who consciously or unconsciously judge us by the language we use. Language can tell us a lot about ourselves if we're listening and/or reading. What have you heard/read lately?

Reflecting to Write

Informative

Interview several international students from different countries. Ask them questions about how they were taught English in their native country. Also ask them what methods were used by their instructors to correct their errors and to teach them differences between the homophones that English has. Write an **exemplification** essay about how students learn English in different countries.

Persuasive

Consider the following scenario: On New Year's Day, your neighbor's children are in the street shooting firecrackers and bottle rockets without adult supervision. It has been an unusually dry December, and you are afraid that the leaves on your roof might catch on fire if a bottle rocket lands on it. Use each of the following as a writing topic:

- In a face-to-face talk with the children's mother, explain the situation and persuade her to keep the children from firing bottle rockets near your property.
- In a letter to your county commissioner attempt to persuade him or her to pass a bill that will make fireworks of any kind illegal in your county.

How do the two discourses differ? How do they sound alike? Discuss the use of language in class after you have written both assignments.

Process Analysis

In a fully developed **descriptive** process paper, discuss the **process** of walking on a treadmill or taking a one-mile walk. Then in an **analysis** paper, give someone directions for walking on a treadmill or for taking a one-mile walk. Or you may do these papers using one of the following pairs:

- Dieting and how to diet
- Painting a room and how to paint a room
- Cooking a meal and how to cook a meal

Compare the language and pattern of development in each. Discuss the use of language and development in class.

Chapter 13

Fashion: How We Look to Each Other

The world of fashion to most of us may be in some elite area like New York or Paris. It seems illusive and expensive, a world that most of us cannot afford, especially if we are talking about haute couture or high fashion. When we watch programs such as the Oscars, many of us tune in early to see what the latest stars are wearing, and we enjoy listening to Mr. Blackwell's analysis of the best and worst dressed stars that night. We want to see what J. Lo is showing off or how beautifully Julia Roberts may be dressed.

On the other hand, when we look in our closets, we realize just how far from the red carpet we are, and reality sets in. But that does not keep us from wanting to dress nicely—if not fashionably. And we have to admit, the American public does, in fact, keep designers like Tommy Hilfiger, Liz Claiborne, Ralph Lauren, and others in business. Although they may be somewhat expensive, they do cater to young adults. And then there are also White Stag, Land's End, and others that are still tasteful but much more reasonably priced. What is it that makes us seek out brand names in clothing, make-up, designer perfumes, shoes, and so forth?

Fashion labels and styles not only make us look good to others, they also tend to give us the self-confidence we need to step into the public eye. Even though we have gone from strict formality in the office to informal Fridays, and there is now an attempt to have informal weekdays, most of us still want to present ourselves in a way that our bosses and coworkers find acceptable. Suits and ties are fine for "businessmen" who work in expensive office buildings, as are matched pantsuits, skirts, suits, and heels for women in high positions, but what does the average college student wear on campus, in temporary jobs, on dates, and out with other students? Anything comfortable is usually the answer, and that usually includes cotton or other "natural" fabrics.

But most of the individuals who are fashion conscious tend to be highly critical of those who are not. Have you ever been "scanned" by someone with a slight sneer on his or her face because of what you are wearing? No doubt your clothes do not measure up in quality or in cost to what the observer is wearing. Your appearance announces who you are to them, and they do not want to be associated with you. Had you been in an expensive outfit, however, the same person might have been more accepting of you. The problem with this shallow method of judging others is that most of us buy into it. How many times have you been concerned about what to wear for an interview or for an important date? We know that we must dress for the moment, the position, the person, or whoever will be observing us at that time. So fashion, in whatever shape or cost, does have an impact on our lives and our psychological well-being.

Think about the last time you went to the store without makeup. If you are a person who wears makeup faithfully, you probably just cringed thinking about that. Or if you are a person who must have your shirt ironed perfectly and a crisp crease in your slacks, you probably would not consider going out without their being done according to your specifications. You are about to put yourself on display for the public and for anyone who might know you. And you certainly wouldn't go out with a stained or torn shirt or pants—unless, of course, they are in fashion. You are defining yourself with your own style, your own fashion, your own identity. These are the markers by which others know you and that you have taken a long time to create.

This chapter includes articles from popular magazines as well as from individuals who have opinions about fashion. They should pique your interest and your curiosity about how much each of us falls into the trap of wearing what society tells us is the "right" thing to wear, smell the way society tells us we should, and construct ourselves the way society tells us is acceptable. In other words, how much of our own identity is constructed according to the way society tells us to be and how much are we actually in control of our identity?

THE BEEFCAKING OF AMERICA

Jill Neimark

The definitions of manhood and womanliness have changed over the years. One approach to the definitions is that of sexuality or how one is constructed biologically. Another approach is from gender or how individuals construct themselves. For centuries, for example, some cultures believed and taught their women that their definition was that of wife and mother. However, many women have chosen to pursue careers, to live a single life, and to have no children rather than to accept traditional roles. Furthermore, the definition of manhood has also changed over the years. Jill Neimark, senior editor of Psychology Today *(1994) points out many of these changes. In addition to her interest in writing about gender issues, Neimark also writes for children.*

Prereading: Look at the title of this article and think about what it means to you. The equivalent of "beefcake" for men is "cheesecake" for women. What is your understanding of each term?

Prewriting: Make a list of about five characteristics that you most admire about men and a list of about five characteristics that you most admire about women. Look at these characteristics and determine if they are similar or different. Write a brief comparison and contrast paragraph using specific examples to develop your ideas.

Vocabulary: Looking up and understanding the following words prior to reading should prepare you for the author's message. Other words will be defined in the margin.

beefcake   Marky Mark   Robert Bly   Renaissance   bourgeoisie
physique   vulnerability   Fabio   sinuous   Charles Darwin
empathy

———

John Wayne. A dusty town in the wild West, and our sweaty, windbitten hero with a bit of a beer belly, rumpled clothing, and an air of absolute indifference to his appearance. Slinging his gun and saving the ranch.

depot: a station

Marky Mark. Urban billboards and bus depots*. A tauntingly insolent beefcake of a boy, smooth skinned, clean shaven, with a tight, carved body that's part tough guy, part Greek god.

Men don't look like they used to. Think of Fabio. Arnold Schwarzenegger. . . .

WHAT'S IN A MAN?

molting: shedding an outer layer

It seems that the whole idea of what it means to be male is molting*. Cultural upheavals from the women's movement to the national emphasis on health and fitness have altered our sense of how a man should act and look. The new male is no longer the unquestioned head of the household, in control of the nuclear family if nothing else. Gender parity* in the workplace has made inroads: today a man may easily have a female boss. Men's health has been given new emphasis ever since several post-World War II studies have found that men were at greater risk of heart disease than women.

parity: equality

According to cultural critic Hillel Schwartz, Ph.D., author of *Never Satisfied,* that awareness of men's physical vulnerability led to a new concern with their bodies. Then, in the 1960s, the Kennedy excitement with amateur sports helped kick off a resurgence* in exercise and jogging. Of late, the phenomenal* rise of self-help groups and popular movements such as Robert Bly's "wild men" has led to a new male awareness of feelings, and growing intolerance of the once typical "tough guy" upbringing. Marks and scars are no longer badges of honor.

resurgence: a sweeping movement

phenomenal: remarkable

As ideals of manhood shift, so has the ideal male body. While it is clearly more masculine—well muscled and sexually potent*—it is paradoxically* feminine as well. Our ideal man is no longer rough and ready, bruised and callused, but, as Schwartz puts it, "as clean skinned and clear complected as a woman." His body is "no longer stiff and upright, but sinuous and beautiful when it moves. Sinuousness didn't used to be associated with manliness." A sexual object, a source of pure visual pleasure, men are increasingly being looked at in ways women always have.

potent: powerful

paradoxically: in contradiction

This fascination with male beauty is not entirely new—consider the ancient Greeks, the beautiful boy of the Renaissance, or Elizabethan noblemen parading the court in revealing tights, silks, satins, and jeweled codpieces*. Charles Darwin himself popularized the idea of women as selectors of plumed* and spectacular male mates. "He was speaking of finches and partridges*," explains historian Thomas Laqueur, Ph.D., author of *Making Sex: Body and Gender from the Greeks to Freud* (Harvard University Press, 1990), "but we generalized to humans. It was known as the peacock phenomenon—the notion of the male as the one with plumage." It wasn't until the rise of capitalism and the bourgeoisie that men renounced flagrant* beauty and adopted the plain suit as a uniform. During the so-called "great masculine renunciation*" men began to associate masculinity with usefulness. Then, notes Laqueur, "gradually women became the bearers of the science of splendor."

codpieces: a pouch worn at the crotch by men in the fifteenth and sixteenth centuries

plumed: decorated extravagantly

partridge: a plump game bird

flagrant: obvious

renunciation: act of rejecting

The consequences of today's shift in male body image are already apparent. The number of men exercising has soared by 30 percent in the last six years alone—8.5 million men now have health club memberships, according to American Sports Data, a research firm. And men spend an average of 90.8 days a year in the club (that's over 2,000 hours). That's nine days a year more than women. . . .

MIRROR MIRROR: WOMEN LOOK AT MEN

For both men and women, male personality is regarded as the most significant quality in attracting a mate. In a sense, this flies in the face of our concern with appearance: it lets us know that no matter how enormous our body obsession, both men and women still rate inner beauty as paramount. . . . [I]ntelligence and sense of humor were rated most important, and sexual performance and physical strength least important.

However, there are intriguing differences, even misconceptions, between the sexes about the important of certain physical characteristics. For instance, men believe an attractive face is more important to women than empathy and the ability to talk about feelings. They also put more emphasis on body build than women do. In general, men judge their physique to be more important than women do. In general, men judge their physique to be more important than women do.

Yet appearance is still only a piece of the pie. Women's sexual response to men is more complex than men's to women. "How odd and unsettling an experience it is," comments Brubach, "to look at all these ads of sexy men sprawling on beds and beaches. I think, 'What a nice chest or legs,' but I don't ever feel that this would be enough material for me to have a sexual fantasy. For most of the women I know sex appeal isn't purely about physical appearance."

David Gilmore [anthropologist and author of *Manhood in the Making*], agrees. His studies of gender and sexuality in tribal and modern cultures have found that for women, "the male image conveys much more than sexual virility. Male power, wealth, dominance, control over other men—all those inspire a response in women. The pure visual image of the handsome man, the languid beautiful male is attractive. But it does not necessarily connect with inner virility, which also turns women on. What's so interesting about this subject is that men today get a double message: The culture tells them, 'Be successful, be the boss of bosses, and women will fall at your feet.' The media tell them, 'Look like a model, and women will fall at your feet.'" . . .

Attractive, self-sufficient women may place higher value on physical features because they have been reinforced for these attributes. Traditionally, beautiful women have been able to leverage their looks to snare a wealthy and powerful man. Now that some women have greater financial independence, they may use that power to seek a stunning mate.

Reading for Meaning

1. Which physical sense is referred to most in this article? Give five examples of how Niemark referred to that sense.
2. What is the purpose of this article? Can you identify the thesis sentence or determine what the thesis is? How does description support the purpose?

Reading Deeper

1. How has the ideal masculine body become more "feminine" according to Neimark? Do you agree or disagree? Explain.
2. What does the following statement mean? "For most of the women I know sex appeal isn't purely about physical appearance." Do you agree or disagree? Explain.

Reading for Writing

1. Choose one of the following topics for an **informative** essay:
   - The use of gym equipment to maintain fitness
   - The changes in men's attitude toward style and fashion in the last two to three years
   - Female bodybuilders

   Using Neimark's article as a model, write an informative essay that has examples in the introduction, bold headings to indicate a major shift in ideas, and descriptive language. Remember that you are not taking sides about these topics; you are presenting information descriptively.
2. In their book on feminist theory, *The Mad Woman in the Attic,* Sandra Gilbert and Susan Gubar assert that when a woman looks in the mirror, she is the reflection of what a man tells her she should look like. Based on your reading, do you think that men see the reflection of what women tell men they should look like? Write a brief paper about what men or women see when they look in the mirror.

STATE OF GRACE

Amy MacLin

Have you ever felt so uncomfortable with yourself that you would like to have a makeover? Today's media is taking many men and women of different ages and incomes and helping them transform themselves, much like Cinderella's fairy godmother did for her. If

*it's good enough for fairy tales, it must be good enough for con-
temporary women and men. But how much of the original personality is changed with the physical? Does a nose job, weight loss,
new hairdos, or other physical alterations change the person? Apparently, many people feel that this "new me" gives them the kind
of self-confidence, poise, and beauty that society expects. The following article, a personal narrative by Amy MacLin, a writer from*
Elle *magazine (Jan. 2004), gives you a firsthand view of how she
took control of her appearance.*

Prereading: Would you consider going through a complete makeover?
How about just a cosmetic makeover in a department store?

Prewriting: Do you believe that where you are from is an obstacle to
being able to get ahead once you graduate? Do you believe that there
are physical aspects about yourself that you must change to be successful in your chosen career or in society? Write a paragraph about
your feelings about yourself.

Vocabulary: Looking up and understanding the following words prior
to reading should prepare you for the author's message. Other words
will be defined in the margin.

Bergdorf   Tocquevillian   Henry Higgins   Eliza Doolittle
Donna Karan

It's been eight years since I left Mt. Juliet, Tennessee, for New York
City, but the people here still treat me as if the price tag is hanging
from my straw hat. The ladies at Bergdorf purr, "What do you think of
the big city?" Bartenders assume I'm the cheerfully immoral type who
takes her Wild Turkey neat. I once had a boss who greeted every single
vacation request with a hearty, "So, you goin' to Billy Bob's weddin'?"

But I was deflated recently when I met a man (English-born,
California-raised) at a party and he wouldn't stop marveling at the way I
still talk. "Are you working-class?" he asked.

I didn't grow up poor, but my parents did—cotton-picking,
mayonnaise-sandwich-eating poor. They worked hard to educate their
only daughter so that she could move up the eastern seaboard and land
on the mastheads of a few fancy magazines: all so some Yankee could
wonder out loud if she was beneath him. It made me doubt the Tocquevillian notion of America as a caste*-blind meritocracy*, and as we say
in Wilson County, it chapped my rear end.

So I wanted to know whether a professional could take the Mt. Juliet
out of the girl: Was there a Henry Higgins for my Eliza Doolittle? Could I

caste: social
class

meritocracy: a
system in which
advances are
based on ability
or achievement

be transformed into a glossy-haired, round-voweled creature from a place where kids played field hockey instead of sniffing glue off the hood of a Camaro? My Fair Lady started out as a filthy flower girl from Tottenham Court Road, which sounds for all the world like a Tennessee trailer park.

For my transformation, I chose New York man-about-town Montgomery Frazier, who, he was quick to inform, is not a stylist but an "image guru." For about $250 an hour, Monty helps a client list of society ladies and Hollywood wives go from where they are to where they want to be with the right dress, the right career move, the right introductions at the right prices.

"I'd like to say I'm manager, marketer, publicist, and stylist, all rolled up into one," Monty said. I told him he was hired.

We met at La Goule, a charming French bistro on Manhattan's Upper East Side. Monty, who is a regular, gets the best banquette* in the house, with a view of Madison Avenue.

banquette: a long upholstered bench

"It's a game!" he says when I congratulate him. (Nervous and unaccustomed to charming French bistros, I had arrived too early and had been pinned against the wall at a back banquette, where I sat putting first one elbow on the table, then the other.)

"They're always so nice to me here," Monty says. " '*Bonjour monsieur*!' Maybe because I always dress a certain way. I guess that's why I do what I do—I look at myself as a canvas."

Bonjour monsieur: a French greeting, "Good day, sir"

At 43, the fair-haired, New Mexico-born Monty has flawless skin the hue and texture of a ripe apricot; I have to physically restrain myself from reaching out to touch his face. He is wearing tweedy Jil Sander trousers with a black cashmere cardigan and black-rimmed specs, because he is having, he tells me, a James Dean meets Italian schoolboy moment. But tomorrow I might find him in mod rocker mode. He knows change is possible for anybody, he says, because he reinvents himself every day.

tartare: French for raw

I order a tuna tartare* as expensive as my shoes and tell him I want him to turn me into a proper lady, then escort me to a ritzy function to see if I "pass," like Eliza at the triumphal ball.

Monty is enthusiastic but stops short when I talk about getting a dialect coach. (He seems to reject the philosophical underpinnings of the transformation entirely, focusing less on diction and class than on adopting a pastel palette and cutting white flower out of my diet.)

"Why would you want to lose your accent?" he says. "It is charming. It is food for conversation."

"Because I feel like people make certain assumptions—"

"People," he says, "can be quite foolish. We live in a global community now—an accent is *interesting*. It makes you memorable. *Embellish* your difference, don't assimilate*!"

assimilate: become similar

"Even in high society?"

sagely: wisely

"In high society," he sagely* replies, "all one needs is quiet grace. Some of the best society ladies are Southern ladies."

I feel as quietly graceful as a canned ham, so I reduce all my existential* despair to this: "What if I knock over my water glass?"

existential:
based on
experience

"It's called being a human being," he says. "As long as you're apologetic and don't do it again on the same day, you're fine."

Over coffee he adds, "Honey, you've got to release your own chain. I see so much more out of you than you can ever see."

The next week I meet Monty at Donna Karan to be outfitted. He is wearing a thick cable-knit sweater in butter cream and wire-rimmed glasses: "Robert Redford with some Jay Gatsby, which is a good look for me."

He introduces me to public relations director Aliza Licht, who has assembled a row of frocks in her airy white office. I have a schoolgirl crush on Aliza; she has long, glorious auburn hair and a diamond ring big enough to serve appetizers on. She is the kind of girl who has always had a pony.

I take a black jersey gown that drapes, Grecianesque, off one shoulder and go into the fitting room. My heart is chugging like a freight train because I am, gentle reader, several funnel cakes past a sample size. I pull. I tug. I suck in. I hope.

And when I look in the mirror, I get it. All that jersey rises to meet me, and I am woman. I tip an imaginary champagne glass to an imaginary Captain of Industry.

Honey, you've got to release your own chain. I walk out to Monty and Aliza.

"You've got it on backward," Aliza says.

"I'm country come to town!" I bellow.

Throughout this experiment I notice that in moments of doubt and confusion, I am the first to remind everyone that I am just off the bus from Dogpatch. If I make the joke before anybody else does, then the shame is mine: I own it.

Monty books a haircut and color for me at the swanky Julien Farel salon. Julien is a darkly handsome Frenchman with his initials stitched on his right breast pocket. I am imagining the two of us in a sun-dappled vineyard when I abruptly apologize for my $15 haircut, a Chinatown special. . . .

I like my new chin-length haircut, which is wispy and layered. Colorist Peter Oon makes my faded red hair a copper penny color with rich-girl blond highlights. Forlornly, I wonder if it will ever look this good again.

Monty invites me to a gala awards ceremony for the Cabrini Mission Foundation, a charitable organization that promotes health care, education, and other social services. I may get to meet Rudy Giuliani*, I tell my mother excitedly.

Rudy Giuliani: former mayor of New York City

"Isn't it wonderful," she says. "Every generation stands on the back of the one before, like the Chinese say. Or is it the Indians?"

On the big night I go back to Julien for a blow-out, then struggle into my gown so makeup artist Randle Doss, a fellow Tennessean, can gussy me up. She draws on smoky drifts of eyeliner while Monty stands by crying, "More! More!"

"Monty," Randle says, "I still want her to look like herself."

I don't know if myself is what I look like when I finally stand in front of the mirror. My hair is more structured than I like it, and Monty has given me a shrug* to put over the Grecian gown—presumably because it's November and cold but also, I fear, because I have the upper arms of a teamster. I feel like a cat in doll clothes.

shrug: woman's small waist-length or short jacket

But also, oddly, fabulous: This is who I am today. I get my mink evening bag and sweep down to the limo.

My original mission, you'll recall was to hobnob in New York society and see if I could pass. But when Monty and I get to the party at Chelsea Piers, I sit down behind my calligraphed* place card, and Monty introduces me to my dinnermates as a writer from ELLE. This strikes me as a great lark until it occurs to me that I actually am a writer from ELLE.

calligraphed: done in fine handwriting— calligraphy

And I realize I don't have to pass, because this-is-who-I-am-today has turned into this-is-who-I-am. Which is a writer from ELLE in Donna Karan with $300 highlights. Who also happens to know all the words to "The Devil Went Down to Georgia."

I'm not the fattest person in the room, so I learn in to ask Monty if I can take off my shrug and he says yes. I feel a rush of affection and want to kiss his apricot cheek. Instead, I ask if well-bred people typically leave some food on their plate. Monty says they do. . . .

My hair has fallen by the time I get to the ladies' room, and I feel sexier: In Montyspeak, I'm Rene Russo in *The Thomas Crown Affair,* after a six-month Ho Ho* binge. I'm fixing my lip gloss when one of the choir girls in regulation plaid, stops at my elbow.

Ho Ho: a Hostess chocolate dessert

"I like your dress," she says softly and turns away.

What I really want to do is run after her: *"It's not mine! This dress is borrowed! Nothing is what it seems! I see so much more out of you than you can ever see!"*

Instead, I just smile and say, "Thank you." But she's already out of sight.

Reading for Meaning

1. What expectations do others have about MacLin? What do you think the indicators are that they are reacting to that show that she is not from "the big city"? Explain.
2. How did MacLin go about making her changes? Explain and describe thoroughly.
3. How does Monty reflect society's expectations of how people should look, speak, and behave?

Reading Deeper

1. Explain what it means to "reinvent" oneself daily. If one is constantly reinventing oneself, is there a "real," consistent individual that a person can say he or she is? Explain your thoughts.
2. How is Monty's attitude about change not exactly what the author was expecting? Explain.
3. How is the following comment—"Monty," Randle says, "I still want her to look like herself"—purely ironic?
4. How does MacLin feel about herself at the end of the article?

Reading for Writing

1. How many "selves" do you have? Which one is the "real" self? Or is there *one* real self that you can call your own? Before you write an essay about your "real" identity, prewrite the characteristics that you think make you uniquely you. Write about the different people you are (student, friend, and so forth) and how the expectations of others (family, society, fashion "gurus," and so forth) help shape you. Write a **descriptive personal narrative** about the various aspects of who you are.
2. Have you ever gone through an experience in which you were expected to dress and behave in a way that was different from your "normal" style? Write a **process personal narrative** explaining how the experience made you feel. Notice that in the above article, MacLin explains her feelings about her transformation as she goes through the process she experienced. Use her article as your model.

"I Feel Silly"

David Plotz

In today's world, men as well as women are taking a lot more time to consider their appearances. In "State of Grace," readers discovered how the author underwent a makeover to make her feel better about herself in the "big city." In the following article (Reader's Digest, 2004), David Plotz explains how he survived a "metrosexual makeover." Never heard of it? Neither had Plotz, but he went through it with the encouragement of those around him. And just as MacLin above, he reveals his feelings along the way.

Prereading: Some people have definite feelings about men having manicures, pedicures, or other typically "feminine" procedures done. What do you think?

Prewriting: How do you feel about men indulging in the beauty treatments that are usually reserved for women? Write a paragraph about what you think men should and should not engage in regarding their appearance.

Vocabulary: Looking up and understanding the following word prior to reading should prepare you for the author's message. Other words will be defined in the margin.

oafish

Here's when I knew I had to change: My two-year-old pointed at the monster in her book and said, "Dada, that wild thing is you." I looked in the mirror: My four-month-old son had spit up milk on my only clean shirt. A line of bicycle grease ran up the right leg of my khakis, my "nice pants," and a splatter of white paint ran down the left. I'd run out of razors and hadn't shaved for a week. My hair looked like I'd stuck my hand in a socket. I could have carried groceries in the bags under my eyes.

Once upon a time, I was a presentable young man. But I married, my journalism career got busy, two children arrived and middle age loomed. My neat, stylish clothes grew ratty. I didn't have to look nice for Saturday night, because Saturday night dates were with our VCR.

Soon after my daughter's comment, my wife, Hanna, and I channel-surfed onto an episode of "Queer Eye for the Straight Guy," the Bravo series in which five hip gay men make over an oafish straight guy with cool clothes, a trendy haircut and chic home furnishings. I was baffled and horrified. Hanna was mesmerized*. "What a great haircut!" she exclaimed. "He's so cute now!"

mesmerized: spellbound

I asked Frank, my best-dressed straight friend, about the show. He told me of a whole world I was missing: straight guys who don't settle for two-minute showers and $10 haircuts, men who style their hair, shop for clothes and get facials. They look great and women love them. There's even a term for these cool groomers: "metrosexuals." I did a little research and found that men are going to spas in record numbers, that the men's skin care industry—who knew there *was* one?—has been growing about ten percent a year for the past five years.

Feeling socially sanctioned, I decide it's time to shape up: I, too, will become a metrosexual. I may not have a life, but I will have a lifestyle.

But I have no idea where to begin. Fortunately, Hanna is thrilled by the project (maybe a little too thrilled) and suggests I start small.

intractable: stubborn

grouting: filling with mortar

I've been cutting my fingernails with the same pocketknife for 18 years. I have hangnails, bloody cuticles, ragged edges, intractable* dirt from working in the garden and grouting* tiles. At Hanna's urging, I make an appointment for a manicure and pedicure.

My "nail technician," Lily Pham, orders me onto a black, throne-like chair and dunks my feet into a warm salt bath. She massages my arches with peppermint oil, nips off the revolting bits of cuticle, makes elegant curves of my jagged toenails, and scrubs off ancient calluses. I feel mighty on my throne, and mighty relaxed.

The manicure doesn't make me feel nearly as kingly, but my devastated nails do become smooth and neat. Lily says men who "don't do hard work" often get polish as opposed to a buff. I don't do hard work. I go for the polish, and soon my nails are glistening.

I take them proudly home to Hanna, who is horrified: "If I went on a date and the guy had polished nails, I'd run screaming from the room." Then she patiently explains that on a guy, buffed nails would be manly and elegant, but polished nails are creepy. I've clearly overstepped some line.

Hanna gives me a pep talk. I need to think bigger. She has me schedule a "cut and color" at Ilo Day Spa, Washington, D.C.'s most elegant hair salon. For years, I've cut my own hair with electric clippers, which leaves me looking like an escapee from a mental hospital. At Ilo, my "colorist," Drake Brown, and "stylist," Kristjún Holt, huddle over my rat's nest. Words like "caramel," "softness," "baliage," and "weight" accompany sweeping motions across my head.

Drake grabs a box of plastic wrap and a cup of Smurf-blue paste—the "lightening product." He paints the paste into my hair with small zigzags, then separates the painted strands with plastic, repeating this dozens of times. I look like the Flying Nun.

When my color sets, Kristjún quizzes me about what kind of shampoo and conditioner I use. I answer, "CVS brand dandruff shampoo, and I don't really know about conditioner." Kristjún looks as thought I've told him I like to torture kittens, but says, "This is why I am here—to help."

He gives me a great haircut: for the first time in years, I feel cool. My blond—excuse me, caramel—highlights give me the air of an urban surfer. Kristjún then sells me a $20 bottle of shampoo, a $16 tube of conditioner, and a $15 jar of "matte" styling paste, and commands me to start blow-drying my hair.

I meet Hanna for lunch, full of swagger*. "You look like some kind of surf freak," she says, recoiling*. I say the color is subtle*. "It's not subtle!" she practically screams. I sag. I'm just not getting the hang of this thing.

swagger: boasting

recoiling: springing back in distaste

subtle: not obvious, not apparent

Maybe I need the surfer complexion to match my surfer hair! I rally and head to Solar Planet, choosing Mystic Tan, a spray coating of self-tanner and moisturizer that produces an even, incredibly natural-looking fake tan.

In practice, the spray tanning is humiliating. I fork over $50 for three sessions, then take my "farmer's tan" body to a private booth. I strip naked, step into another private booth, stand on a metal plate and press a button. Suddenly, three nozzles are spraying me with what feels like ice-cold Sprite. Mercifully, it's over in 30 seconds and my skin has a nice bronze glow.

The day of my haircut and tan, we drive up to New York to visit friends and Hanna's family. My wife's friends ask her quietly if something's wrong with me. My father-in-law mutters about divorce. *They're just jealous,* I hypothesize*.

hypothesize: develop an explanation for

I am, however, having trouble figuring out which hair-care product is which. Is the shampoo the Kérastase Nutritive Bain Satin Facteur Nutrition or the Kérastase Nutritive lait Vital Proteine? Then Hanna sees me blow-drying my hair for the first time ever and bursts out laughing.

I'm used to feeling competent; I know how to write stories, drive a car, play basketball. In this metrosexual world, however, nothing comes naturally. I strive for elegant masculinity but am a buffoon, even to my wife.

I will not be beaten by some "style challenge," however. I head for the Grooming Lounge, a new Washington spa for men. It has dark-wood paneling, leather chairs and a staff that includes many gorgeous women. The customers—lawyerish types in their 40s and 50s—are getting hot lather shaves, messages, haircuts. They gleam with confidence and look like they just strolled off the set of "The Practice."

Erin McGowan, my grooming expert, escorts me back to a private room, lights a candle, turns up the soft jazz and lowers the lights.

I have come for the full monty—eyebrow wax, back wax, nosehair trim—because I've realized that all men on TV have less body hair than I do. I am not a gorilla, but even my light back fur bugs me.

Erin starts by painting hot wax on the area above my nose, tamping it down with a piece of muslin, then tearing the cloth off. I feel like I've been punched in the head, but for the first time since I was 13, I have no monobrow. After she waxes and tweezes the rest of my eyebrows, my eyes look bright and smart.

Then I roll over on my stomach, and she coats my back, neck and shoulders with wax. She rips the wax off, piece by piece. In this magazine, I am not allowed to use the words that describe this pain. Here is an approximation: Imagine someone rubbing a cheese grater up and down your back, then washing you in vinegar. "We normally suggest customers have a beer before their wax," Erin tells me.

My shoulders are now smooth as silk. Erin sells me skin cleanser, moisturizer, shaving oil and gel, nose hair clippers. It's a fortune, but who cares?

Hanna is dumbstruck when she sees me. "Your eyes look good!" And she practically melts when I take off my shirt. "Your back is so smooth and sexy." We're standing in front of a mirror looking at the new me, and she does that thing models do in TV commercials—hugs me from behind then caresses my face. *I've got her.*

I ask Jess, one of my best-dressed friends, to take me shopping. For a few hundred bucks, she outfits me to fit my face: fancy jeans and cowboy shirt from Luck, supercool turtleneck from club Monaco, hipster jacket from Armani Exchange. Wearing my new outfit, I run into a friend I haven't seen for months. Her jaw drops. "Oh my God, you look great! You look so mod!"

That evening when Hanna and I are going out, I am feeling pret-ty snazzy and I criticize her for wearing old boots. "They're embarrassing," I say.

She gasps like *I've* hit her. "Wait, you're criticizing *me* for what *I'm* wearing?"

Despite Hanna's moment of post-waxing weakness, I feel the whole experiment start to blow up in my buffed and smug mug. In two weeks, Hanna points out, I have gone from two grooming products—shampoo and soap—to ten. My bottles and jars use up all her bathroom shelf space. "It's like living with a girl," she gripes.

It takes me longer to get ready in the morning than it takes her. I endlessly stare at myself in the mirror. I obsessively scrub with my face cleanser and inspect my brows. When Hanna hands me our son while I am wearing my new sweater, I hand him back. I don't want him to drool on it. Hanna is getting annoyed by my metrosexuality, and frankly, so am I.

vanity: excessive pride in one's appearance

intolerable: unbearable

My vanity* is becoming intolerable*, even to me. It's not that I don't like looking good, because I do. And it's not that I'm not selfish, because I am. But I can't justify wasting all this energy and money when there are gutters to clean and children to diaper. I'll keep the conditioner and the face cleanser—my skin and hair really do look better—but I'll give up the tanning, the pedicures, the facials.

Maybe, just maybe, though, Hanna will treat me to another back wax one of these days. This morning, I noticed the hair on my shoulders is sprouting back already.

Reading for Meaning:

1. What led Plotz to become concerned about his appearance?
2. Define "metrosexual."
3. What is the effect of having Plotz sit in a "thronelike" chair at the manicure and pedicure salon?
4. In the MacLin article, Monty is MacLin's guru. Who acts as one for Plotz? How does he take the advice?

Reading Deeper

1. Why do you think Plotz was "horrified" at what he saw on "Queer Eye for the Straight Guy"?
2. Why do you think Plotz had to identify his "best-dressed" friend as "straight"? Why couldn't he just say, "my best-dressed friend"?
3. Why do you think Plotz had to feel "socially sanctioned" before he could improve his appearance?
4. From the way Plotz has described himself, why do you think his wife was "thrilled" with his decision to become a "metrosexual"?
5. How do individuals who know nothing about "metrosexual" makeovers react to Plotz's new look? Are they all the same?
6. When he describes the spa, how does he describe the surroundings? How does he describe the female staff? How would a feminist read this?
7. What problems result from Plotz's adventures in metrosexuality? List them.

Reading for Writing

1. Consider the last time you had your hair cut. Compare and contrast that experience with the one that Plotz describes. Write a personal narrative describing the similarities and differences.
2. If you were Plotz's style guru, what advice would you offer him? Write a letter to him offering advice for self-improvement. Make suggestions for things that you know work because you've used them.

High Heels Scare Me

Anne Perrin

Shoes have always been a matter of concern to all people, mainly as something that protects our feet. However, as fashion demands more and more stylish shoes for women, doctors, as well as the women who wear the shoes, have discovered that instead of protecting our feet, shoes can sometimes injure them by their design. From tennis or walking shoes to high heels, shoes have changed drastically over the years and have come to mean different things to different people. In the following narrative, Anne Perrin, instructor at the University of Houston and North Harris College, recalls the small selection she had to choose from when she was growing up and contrasts them with the rather large and surprising array of shoes that have come on the market.

Prereading: Look at the shoes you are wearing right now. Are you wearing them for comfort or for some other reason? Notice the shoes of others in your class. Why do you think they bought the shoes they are wearing?

Prewriting: Have you ever bought a pair of shoes that were really nice and then realized that you couldn't wear them because they hurt your feet? Write a paragraph describing your favorite pair of shoes.

Vocabulary: Looking up and understanding the following words prior to reading should prepare you for the author's message. Other words will be defined in the margin.

Salvador Dali   Amazonian

I remember when buying shoes was an event to look forward to, a special occasion all its own that often signaled a major upcoming event. For the opening of school, you went one day with all your brothers and sisters to the local shoe store, sat in the same chair you sat in the year before, and had your foot measured with a gray metal object resembling a large oceanic* amoebae*. You felt important—family funds were going to be expended on your behalf. People were interested in your needs. All you had to do was sit there and be waited on. When the shoe salesman promptly announced to the whole store that your foot had grown a whole size and that he would have to go to the "far back" to see if they even carried your new size, your mother would give you that look that indicated a confirmation of her own diagnosis. It always seemed that the

oceanic: coming from the sea

amoeba: a protozoan with an unclear, changeable form

bigger my feet got, the longer he took in the "back." In the meantime, my little brothers were oblivious to my drama, having by this time found every foot measuring device in the store and hidden them behind the store displays, and my younger sister was shaking the gum machine and shoving her fingers up the opening trying for a "red" glob of gum to come out. Somehow, the salesman always managed to find a pair and would come back with only one shoe box, pull out the new shoes, discard wads of tissue paper, then cram my feet into the new Buster Browns and announce a perfect fit. Not to be shown up, my mother would always insist that I had to "walk" around then pinch my toes through the shoes so hard my toenail hurt for days. Only her pronouncement of a "fit" would seal the deal.

Back then shoes meant something. Black and white Buster Browns meant elementary school. Penny loafers meant high school. That first pair of high heels meant prom. It was the same for my brothers. To own a pair of loafers meant you could have the car for a drive and stay out later. When the oldest brother got a pair of men's shoes that laced up and had that design punched into the leather on top, he knew he was grown up for sure. It was a simple life. The shoe salesperson was always a man, and, even though my mother stopped going with me years ago, I still pressed on the toes of my shoes to confirm a fit. I just didn't kill my toes in the process.

I am afraid of shoe departments now. Terribly afraid. I want my old life back and see little hope of its returning in the near future. This fear first came about last year when I went with a friend to the local mall for some high heels for work. Years ago I had gotten used to the salesperson, male or female, simply asking me my "size"—no measuring, no sitting like a queen in a chair waiting for one's subjects to pay homage. Instead, I am supposed to wander before table upon table of shoes all arranged like a Venus Flytrap—the more you wander around, the more ensnared* you get and can't find your way out. Also, there are sections now: the women-of-tone are grouped around the running shoe tables while those subscribing to the motto, the-bigger-the-hair-the-better-the-woman, are circling the late evening and prom shoes tables. All I wanted was some nice business high heels.

ensnared:
caught

What I got was a vinyl cushioned sofa in the high heel section across from the perfume counter and a sales teenager who promptly handed me some nylon booties for my feet and disappeared, never to be seen again. I took my tennis shoes and socks off and slipped on my booties then took a look around. Cold sweat began to form. To my left was a pair of high heels like a bad Salvador Dali painting. The top part looked like an old pair of high-top tennis shoes I once owned for P.E.

only this shoe looked like the gym shoe had been stretched to twice its length. Instead of white canvas and laces, this shoe was lime green. The shoe still had crisscross lacing but the heel was a four-inch spike. What was I supposed to do in these? How was I supposed to respond? Gym was gym and prom was prom. What happened. I had visions of Kathy Simons, the best basketball player at my old high school, dribbling down the court on these things and breaking her neck.

I quickly recovered and looked to my right. There I saw a pair of red vinyl shoes with toes so pointed they looked just like a pie server with four-inch clear acrylic heels that had a red and white striped pole inside that spun when you walked. Was I supposed to set up a barber shop or something? Where was I supposed to put my toes in these things? One pair had the shape of my old Buster Browns but was made of green plaid and had a sole three inches thick. My school day memories were shattered. One pair had camouflaged mesh on top and pointed toes so vicious they could pierce the armor of an Abrams tank; the heel was four inches tall and covered with black vinyl. One pair had the soles of a tennis shoe but the top of a business shoe. I was confused. I wanted my mother.

I looked over at the men's shoe selection and saw men my age in the same dilemma. One man was with his teenaged son who was trying to talk his father into buying a pair of men's business shoes that laced and had the design pattern on top, only these shoes were made of orange vinyl. The father's face had the same look on it I saw once on a man who had just been told that his wife had not had twins—she had had quintuplets. Another man was holding a pair of work boots with glow-in-the-dark shoelaces. They were on their own—I had my own misery. I quickly looked away just in time to see a nylon bootie slide like a snapped rubber band off my left foot and go sailing across the aisle, smashing into the perfume counter. I pretended I saw nothing.

At that moment, my friend brought over a yellow vinyl boot, pointed-toes and four inch spikes with a top part that zippered up to the calf. You can hurt yourself with those shoes. I tried to imagine how I would have to act in those shoes and started slowly backing up on my vinyl cushion. It was then that I saw "the" boot.

I was dumbfounded. Black vinyl, the queen mother of all pointed toe shoes, 4-inch spike and zipped up to the thigh. My friend and I both saw it at the same time, and I walked over to the table with just my one bootie on, circling it like cult ritual. I had visions of an Amazonian woman named Helga wearing a lot of black leather, holding a whip and talking in a deep voice to a lot of men who were all begging to be put in the "time out" corner. I thought you had to order those boots from catalogs with brown wrappers. I wanted my Buster Browns; I wanted squashed toes again. I realized deep down in my soul that I just wasn't woman enough for that boot.

At the moment of my greatest misery, a salesperson came up and asked if I needed help. I began to stammer something about low-heeled business shoes, and I remember feebly mumbling "black" or "navy." She looked at my feet and said, "I'm guessing you wear a size 8." I almost passed out. Then she told me she might have a pair of shoes that I might like but that it was in the "far back" of the store and would take a few extra minutes to get. I started to feel better.

Reading for Meaning

1. What kind of shoes does Perrin go to the store looking for? What kind does she ask for after looking around?
2. Describe the difference between tennis shoes Perrin remembers and tennis shoes that she sees while she is shopping.
3. Who are the women-of-tone? How do you know?

Reading Deeper

1. How do the memories of shopping for shoes when she was younger affect the feelings she has when she is shopping for business shoes? Explain.
2. What point is Perrin making when she writes about men's shoes? Explain.

Reading for Writing

1. Write a **personal narrative describing** your shopping trips to get shoes when you were younger and your parents/guardians had to go with you.
2. Times have changed, and so have the salespeople and the mode of shopping for shoes. Write a **comparison and contrast** essay **describing** how shoe shopping used to be years ago and how it is now. If you don't remember what it used to be like, visit an exclusive, expensive shoe store pretending to be looking for shoes. Let the salesperson wait on you and help you with your selections. Then write the **descriptive, compare and contrast** paper that uses the experience of shopping for shoes in an expensive shoe store and in a department store or in a shoe store like Payless or DSW.

WHY PRETTY ISN'T PRETTY ENOUGH ANYMORE

Susan Dominus

Following the latest fashion trends is one thing. Changing one's appearance so that one's clothing, hair style, makeup, perfume, and shoes meet the demands of the designers is another. However, going through plastic surgery is a more drastic method that men and women have been using to improve their appearance for society and for their own feelings of self-confidence. Now that enhancement through the use of Botox and lasers has come onto the market, the cost and definition of plastic surgery have changed drastically, making the procedures more affordable. But the cost and, in some cases, the risks of more radical forms of plastic surgery, such as breast implants and liposuction for both men and women, still remain deterrents to many. In this article from Glamour (2002), Susan Dominus explains how even the natural beauty of stars is not quite enough for today's demanding society. Although this article is written specifically about women, there are others that explain that some men who are dissatisfied with their strenuous workouts because they are still unable to increase the size of calves, chest, or thighs are considering having or have elected to have these procedures done also.

Prereading: Consider your own body and face. Are you satisfied with them? Would you like a little more bulk here or there to give you a more fit looking body? Are you willing to go through plastic surgery to enhance your face or body?

Prewriting: Think about men and women who are considered "beautiful people." Ralph Lauren uses many of them in his ads for his fashions, and they can be seen on television commercials. Write a paragraph about how the use of these models leads individuals to consider or reject procedures available through plastic surgery.

Vocabulary: Looking up and understanding the following words prior to reading should prepare you for the author's message. Other words will be defined in the margin.

augmentation   liposuction   vanity   collagen   silicone

In our new nip-and-tuck world, young women are remaking everything from their lips to their inner thighs with cosmetic surgery. Even perfectly gorgeous Audrey [Hepburn] and Marilyn [Monroe] wouldn't have held up to today's sky-high standards! *Glamour* investigates the plastic surgery problem—and what it means for you.

Once a month, Lee, a 29-year-old banker in Atlanta gets together with eight of her oldest friends to catch up over a few bottles of red wine. They talk about things women have been bonding over forever, like men, work, sample sales. But lately, a new topic has been headlining the gatherings: their breasts. Specifically, the work they've had done on them. Two of Lee's friends have had cosmetic surgery on theirs, and as for Lee, she just had an augmentation—which her friends were eager to see in close detail. Three glasses of wine into their most recent get-together, off came Lee's top, to cheers all around. "A few of them were like, 'Can we touch 'em?' " says Lee. "I said, 'Sure, what do I care?' I love them."

Lee and her friends aren't wealthy, older ladies who lunch, nor are any of them strippers or even aspiring sitcom stars. They're career women in their twenties and thirties, and they're hardly unique. "I see plenty of young, middle-class women who might decide to have a procedure instead of a vacation," says New York City plastic surgeon Philip Godfrey, M.D., echoing doctors around the country. The number of women getting their physiques cut-and-pasted has surged 128 percent in the past six years, with countless more craving the procedures: A whopping 83 percent of the 7,701 readers who responded to an online *Glamour* poll said they'd like to have work done, with breast enhancement and liposuction topping their lists.

You don't need to have LASIK surgery to see that plastic surgery has gone mainstream. Safer than ever, it's also cheaper: Breast implants that might have cost $10,000 in 1994 can now be found for half the price. If even that's too much, you could always put yours on layaway (available through some surgeons' offices) or turn directly to lending agencies that target the surgery market—some of which promise revolving credit so you can go ahead with the next procedure while you're still recovering, financially and otherwise, from the first. With costs dropping, so are patients' ages; doctors report that half the women who are getting implants are under 34, as are a third of those getting liposuction.

Some part of me used to feel a little sorry for women who got implants instead of shrugging off their anxieties or pulling on a padded bra like the rest of us—*sheesh,* didn't they have any self-esteem? But lately when I spot the happy owner of another impressively protruding pair at the gym, I've started to wonder if she might know something I don't about giving your ego a lift. Maybe there's something to all those ads for plastic surgery, the ones that pitch their product as a vehicle of self expression, even self-love: "Be your best," encourages one Web ad. "After all, you're worth it," assures another (never mind that they haven't met you). It's enough to make those of us still wearing padded bras think, *Sheesh,* where's *my* self-esteem?

Women are buying and coming out, eager to display the way they've taken control of their bodies. Instead of entering doctors' offices through private doorways, patients talk about their fabulous surgeons over brunch—recommending them as they do hairstylists—or throw themselves parties just to celebrate their recently endowed busts (giving new meaning to the words "hostess with the mostest").

The stigma that used to overshadow plastic surgery is, evidently, history. TV stars, whether anchors or actors, once went to great pains to hide work they've had done; now people are stars *because* of their plastic surgery, on programs like *Extreme Makeover,* ABC's second-most popular reality show, and *Nip/Tuk,* a fictional FX Network drama in the same vein (and one of the cable's most successful new shows). Even primetime's everywoman, *Everyone Loves Raymond*'s Patricia Heaton, has come clean about her real-life beauty tools: breast reduction and tummy tuck. The reason she got them? "Vanity, pure vanity," she's said, cheerfully.

I can acknowledge that for the woman racked with anxiety over her thighs, liposuction may feel like liberation; for the woman who has always despised her lips, collagen feels like confidence. Sure, plastic surgery can be good for *a* woman. The tougher question: is it good for women in general?

OUR BODIES, OUR SELF-RESPECT

There *is* an argument to be made for the positive power of surgery. For one thing, it makes us a little more equal: Why should thin thighs be limited to those lucky enough to be born with thin-thigh genes? And for individuals, it can be an act of empowerment. To hear doctors tell it, patients are more confident than ever. "I used to see a lot of boyfriends come in with their girlfriends and say, 'We were thinking about a D-cup,'" says Gerald Imber, M.D., a plastic surgeon in New York City. "I never hear that anymore—it's more about what the women want." Tina Diaz, a manicurist in her thirties who's had implants, says she often listens to what clients complain about men who don't want them to go under the knife. "I tell them, 'Don't forget, it's *your* body,'" says Diaz. It's enough to make your head spin; so now men who love their girlfriends' bodies in all their imperfections are the oppressors?

We assume that women typically get plastic surgery to make themselves look younger and sexier, but people have complicated reasons for undergoing complicated procedures. In Sara's case, the surgery made her feel older, more womanly. Others decide to change their physical selves to match the person they feel they are inside; someone with an unfortunate nose may feel it's preventing people from noticing her winning personality. . . .

While we've been taught to believe that looks shouldn't matter, let's face it, they do, probably to no one more than ourselves. How we feel about our appearance is thought to account for one-third of our level of self-esteem, says David Sarwer, Ph.D., a psychologist with the Center for Human Appearance at the University of Pennsylvania. In other studies, of the 80 to 90 percent of women who said they were satisfied with their plastic surgery, the majority also reported a boost in body image following the first year of surgery, results that most psychoanalysts would envy.

THE UGLY SIDE OF CHASING BEAUTY

In fact, plastic surgery starts looking a lot less attractive once you consider what you've given up when you go under the knife. "Sure, we can progressively trade in the bodies we start out with for newer, more perfect versions . . . but isn't there something precious and special about the ones we came into this world with?" notes Naomi Wolf, author of *The Beauty Myth,* the groundbreaking 1991 book about how the world's preoccupation with female appearance holds women back. "I hate to see us losing our individuality. I *like* the way old people look."

We surrender certain things when we want to remake ourselves into Gwyneth Paltrow's sister (younger sister, that is): The bittersweet pleasure of seeing your family history in the mirror, not to mention the history *you've* made—the smile that made your best friend want to meet you, the legs that carried you across the finish line.

Another downside: All this self-improvement is bound to disfigure our beauty ideals. More choices are a positive thing, yes. But the reality is, we're all choosing the same chiseled nose, sculpted thighs and tasteful 36C's. "I'm 40," says Wolf. "Maybe in 20 years, in America facelifts will have become so absolutely normative that I'll be considered a freak if I don't get one, and that's not good. At a certain point, you have to be superhuman to resist the coercion." In Hollywood, plastic surgery's already practically a job requirement. "It's rare that you go into an audition where most of the women haven't done something to augment their boobs," says *Judging Amy*'s Jessica Tuck. She's held out, but that doesn't mean she's found success without big breasts: She just carries rubber bra fillers around. "I call them boobs in a box. I put 'em on for auditions when I need to look fab-u-chichi and chuck them off when I go home. And believe me, I've gotten called back for many more auditions with them than without."

. . . Good grief—isn't it enough that women do everything men do, and in heels, as was once said of Ginger Rogers? Do we also have to fit in time for spot lipo, brow-lifts, and collagen touch-ups? It's rare that a patient has one procedure and considers herself a finished work of art. Part of that dissatisfaction lies in the imperfection of the process itself: Get saline breast implants now, for instance, and you'll probably need them fixed up in seven to 10 years. One study found that 30 percent of silicone implants rupture* within five years, which didn't stop manufacturers from recently requesting that the FDA reconsider its 10-year ban on them. And plastic surgery sometimes requires that you swap one imperfection for another—heavy thighs for puckered, post-lipo skin, imperfectly shaped breasts for ones with scars. "When you get plastic surgery, you never look better, you simply look different," contends *Nip/Tuk* creator Ryan Murphy. "And now you're announcing to the world the reasons why you hate yourself—you're sort of billboarding your own self loathing."

Even women with enviable good looks want surgery. "My breasts were perfectly fine, but I basically got implants because my best friend was about to get them," says Lee. "I knew I'd be jealous when I saw them." A friend of Tuck's told her she regretted getting liposuction after hearing the plastic surgeon begin to joke, as he started the suction, "This will be the easiest $10,000 I ever made." He thought she was already plenty thin, and only then did she realize he was right. The race for perfection starts to look like the worst kind of competition—the kind no one feels she's won. . . .

rupture: burst open

Reading for Meaning

1. How has the attitude about breast enhancement changed over the years? Explain.
2. Explain how TV has added to women's desire to have makeovers.
3. Why would boyfriends go to plastic surgeons with their girlfriends? Explain.
4. Why are men being referred to as "oppressors" when they don't want their girlfriends to have plastic surgery?
5. Even though there are positive points about having cosmetic surgery, Dominus includes the "down side." Explain several negative points about the different procedures.

Reading Deeper

1. Why do you think there has been an increase in the number of women who want to undergo cosmetic surgery? Explain.
2. Explain why larger breasts make some women feel better about themselves. Where have women gotten the idea that "the larger the breast the better the woman"?
3. Do you agree that "At a certain point, you have to be superhuman to resist the coercion" to get a facelift? Explain.
4. If scientists have found that silicone implants rupture after several years, why do you think the manufacturers have asked the FDA (Federal Drug Administration) to reconsider the ban so that they can continue to use them? Explain.

Reading for Writing

1. Write a letter to your mother and tell her that you are considering cosmetic surgery and which procedure you are getting. Explain to her why you think it is important for you to go through this procedure. You will be writing a letter to **convince** her to believe that what you are doing is best for you.
2. Find a copy of this article in the December 2002 issue of *Glamour* and look at the suggestions that are made to enhance Audrey Hepburn's and Marilyn Monroe's beauty and figure. Read the comments at the bottom of each picture. Consider the fact that these comments were made by doctors who practice medicine today. Write an essay that **takes a position** on whether or not you agree with their suggestions.

RHETORICAL ANALYSIS

Susan Dominus's article, "When Pretty Isn't Pretty Enough" investigates the reasons why women elect to have plastic surgery. Rather than presenting what could simply be a research paper with facts and statistics, Dominus becomes personally involved and brings the reader into the conversation with direct references to "you" in the article. Whether a patient goes to her doctor for breast implants or for liposuction, Dominus describes her as having feelings of self-hatred, dissatisfaction with her body, and low self-esteem. Dominus looks at different sides of the beauty issue, and even though this is an informative, expository essay, it both supports and negatively critiques it, leaving the readers to make a decision about how they feel about it. In the left-hand margin there are notes that direct you to appropriate chapters in this textbook for discussion about the underlined techniques the author used to write the essay or that comment directly about the techniques the author used.

Ch. 2,
Description,
topic

Ch. 3,
Exemplification

Ch. 4, Narrative,
thesis

Ch. 4, Narrative,
creates a tone
within the full
paragraph to
establish a
rapport with
readers and
shows that these
women are
ordinary just
like the readers

Ch. 10,
Persuasion, uses
quotation from
expert to give
author

Ch. 10,
Persuasion, uses
statistics for
support and as
evidence

Ch. 9, Causal,
uses cause and
effect

When Pretty Isn't Pretty Enough

In our new nip-and-tuck world, young women are remaking everything from their lips to their inner thighs with cosmetic surgery. Even perfectly gorgeous Audrey [Hepburn] and Marilyn [Monroe] wouldn't have held up to today's sky-high standards! *Glamour* investigates the plastic surgery problem—and what it means for you.

Once a month, Lee, a 29-year-old banker in Atlanta gets together with eight of her oldest friends to catch up over a few bottles of red wine. They talk about things women have been bonding over forever, like men, work, sample sales. But lately, a new topic has been headlining the gatherings: their breasts. Specifically, the work they've had done on them. Two of Lee's friends have had cosmetic surgery on theirs, and as for Lee, she just had an augmentation—which her friends were eager to see in close detail. Three glasses of wine into their most recent get-together, off came Lee's top, to cheers all around. "A few of them were like, 'Can we touch 'em?'" says Lee. "I said, 'Sure, what do I care?' I love them."

Lee and her friends aren't wealthy, older ladies who lunch, nor are any of them strippers or even aspiring sitcom stars. They're career women in their twenties and thirties, and they're hardly unique. "I see plenty of young, middle-class women who might decide to have a procedure instead of a vacation," says New York City plastic surgeon Philip Godfrey, M.D., echoing doctors around the country. The number of women getting their physiques cut-and-pasted has surged 128 percent in the past six years, with countless more craving the procedures: A whopping 83 percent of the 7,701 readers who responded to an online *Glamour* poll said they'd like to have work done, with breast enhancement and liposuction topping their lists.

You don't need to have LASIK surgery to see that plastic surgery has gone mainstream. Safer than ever, it's also cheaper: Breast implants that might have cost $10,000 in 1994 can now be found for half the

Ch. 10,
Persuasion, uses
compelling
evidence
throughout the
remaining
paragraph to
support topic
sentence

Ch. 4, Narrative,
uses tone and
first person to
establish rapport
with reader

Ch. 10,
Persuasion, uses
persuasive
quotations as
compelling
evidence

Ch. 7,
Comparison,
uses comparison

Ch. 3,
Exemplification,
various
examples in
paragraph

Ch. 4, Narrative,
use of first
person

price. If even that's too much, you could always put yours on layaway (available through some surgeons' offices) or turn directly to lending agencies that target the surgery market—some of which promise revolving credit so you can go ahead with the next procedure while you're still recovering, financially and otherwise, from the first. With costs dropping, so are patients' ages; doctors report that half the women who are getting implants are under 34, as are a third of those getting liposuction.

Some part of me used to feel a little sorry for women who got implants instead of shrugging off their anxieties or pulling on a padded bra like the rest of us—*sheesh,* didn't they have any self-esteem? But lately when I spot the happy owner of another impressively protruding pair at the gym, I've started to wonder if she might know something I don't about giving your ego a lift. Maybe there's something to all those ads for plastic surgery, the ones that pitch their product as a vehicle of self expression, even self-love: "Be your best," encourages one Web ad. "After all, you're worth it," assures another (never mind that they haven't met you). It's enough to make those of us still wearing padded bras think, *Sheesh,* where's *my* self-esteem?

Women are buying and coming out, eager to display the way they've taken control of their bodies. Instead of entering doctors' offices through private doorways, patients talk about their fabulous surgeons over brunch—recommending them as they do hairstylists—or throw themselves parties just to celebrate their recently endowed busts (giving new meaning to the words "hostess with the mostest").

The stigma that used to overshadow plastic surgery is, evidently, history. TV stars, whether anchors or actors, once went to great pains to hide work they've had done; now people are stars *because* of their plastic surgery, on programs like *Extreme Makeover,* ABC's second-most popular reality show, and *Nip/Tuck,* a fictional FX Network drama in the same vein (and one of the cable's most successful new shows). Even primetime's everywoman, *Everyone Loves Raymond*'s Patricia Heaton, has come clean about her real-life beauty tools: breast reduction and tummy tuck. The reason she got them? "Vanity, pure vanity," she's said, cheerfully.

I can acknowledge that for the woman racked with anxiety over her thighs, liposuction may feel like liberation; for the woman who has always despised her lips, collagen feels like confidence. Sure, plastic surgery can be good for *a* woman. The tougher question: is it good for women in general?

Our Bodies, Our Self-Respect

There *is* an argument to be made for the positive power of surgery. For one thing, it makes us a little more equal: Why should thin thighs be limited to those lucky enough to be born with thin-thigh genes? And for individuals, it can be an act of empowerment. To hear doctors tell it, patients are more confident than ever. "I used to see a lot of boyfriends come in with their girlfriends and say, 'We were thinking about a D-cup,'" says Gerald Imber, M.D., a plastic surgeon in New York City. "I never hear that anymore—it's more about what the women want." Tina Diaz, a manicurist in her thirties who's had implants, says she often listens to what clients complain about men who don't want them to go under the knife. "I tell them, 'Don't forget, it's *your* body,'" says Diaz. It's enough to make your head spin; so now men who love their girlfriends' bodies in all their imperfections are the oppressors?

We assume that women typically get plastic surgery to make themselves look younger and sexier, but people have complicated reasons for undergoing complicated procedures. In Sara's case, the surgery made her feel older, more womanly. Others decide to change their physical selves to match the person they feel they are inside; someone with an unfortunate nose may feel it's preventing people from noticing her winning personality. . . .

While we've been taught to believe that looks shouldn't matter, let's face it, they do, probably to no one more than ourselves. How we feel about our appearance is thought to account for one third of our level of self-esteem, says David Sarwer, Ph.D., a psychologist with the Center for Human Appearance at the University of Pennsylvania. In other studies, of the 80 to 90 percent of women who said they were satisfied with their plastic surgery, the majority also reported a boost in body image following the first year of surgery, results that most psychoanalysts would envy.

The Ugly Side of Chasing Beauty

In fact, plastic surgery starts looking a lot less attractive once you consider what you've given up when you go under the knife. "Sure, we can progressively trade in the bodies we start out with for newer, more perfect versions . . . but isn't there something precious and special about the ones we came into this world with?" notes Naomi Wolf, author of *The Beauty Myth,* the groundbreaking 1991 book about how the world's preoccupation with female appearance holds women back. "I hate to see us losing our individuality. I *like* the way old people look."

We surrender certain things when we want to remake ourselves into Gwyneth Paltrow's sister (younger sister, that is): The bittersweet pleasure of seeing your family history in the mirror, not to mention the history *you've* made—the smile that made your best friend want to meet you, the legs that carried you across the finish line.

Another downside: All this self-improvement is bound to disfigure our beauty ideals. More choices are a positive thing, yes. But the reality is, we're all choosing the same chiseled nose, sculpted thighs and tasteful 36C's. "I'm 40," says Wolf. "Maybe in 20 years, in America face-lifts will have become so absolutely normative that I'll be considered a freak if I don't get one, and that's not good. At a certain point, you have to be superhuman to resist the coercion." In Hollywood, plastic surgery's already practically a job requirement. "It's rare that you go into an audition where most of the women haven't done something to augment their boobs" says *Judging Amy*'s Jessica Tuck. She's held out, but that doesn't mean she's found success without big breasts: She just carries rubber bra fillers around. "I call them boobs in a box. I put 'em on for auditions when I need to look fab-u-chichi and chuck them off when I go home. And believe me, I've gotten called back for many more auditions with them than without."

. . . Good grief—isn't it enough that women do everything men do, and in heels, as was once said of

Ginger Rogers? Do we also have to fit in time for spot lipo, brow-lifts, and collagen touch-ups? It's rare that a patient has one procedure and considers herself a finished work of art. Part of that dissatisfaction lies in the imperfection of the process itself: Get saline breast implants now, for instance, and you'll probably need them fixed up in seven to 10 years. One study found that 30 percent of silicone implants rupture within five years, which didn't stop manufacturers from recently requesting that the FDA reconsider its 10-year ban on them. And plastic surgery sometimes requires that you swap one imperfection for another—heavy thighs for puckered, post-lipo skin, imperfectly shaped breasts for ones with scars. "When you get plastic surgery, you never look better, you simply look different," contends *Nip/Tuk* creator Ryan Murphy. "And now you're announcing to the world the reasons why you hate yourself—you're sort of billboarding your own self loathing." . . .

Even women with enviable good looks want surgery. "My breasts were perfectly fine, but I basically got implants because my best friend was about to get them," says Lee. "I knew I'd be jealous when I saw them." A friend of Tuck's told her she regretted getting liposuction after hearing the plastic surgeon begin to joke, as he started the suction, "This will be the easiest $10,000 I ever made." He thought she was already plenty thin, and only then did she realize he was right. The race for perfection starts to look like the worst kind of competition—the kind no one feels she's won. . . .

Even though this is only part of the article, it is clear that Dominus is attempting to present various sides of the questions inherent in plastic surgery. She points out the positive sides that have helped women afford makeovers, but she also points out the negative that deal with society making women feel more at ease with themselves because they don't conform to society's idea of beauty. Which would you choose?

REFLECTIONS ON FASHION: HOW DO I CONSTRUCT MYSELF?

The fashion industry, as well as many cosmetic surgeons, are making millions of dollars on men's and women's desire to improve their looks—looks that, in some cases, do not need improvement. On the other hand, when spending a few dollars on a dress or suit for a special occasion is what is needed for someone to feel good about himself or herself and to feel that he or she makes a good impression on others, what's the harm? Unfortunately, some individuals spend so much time trying to improve the outer appearance that they forget the inner qualities that are also important.

How we construct ourselves and our appearances in our different roles is essential to our well-being and will continue to be an important part of everyone's growing-up process, even for those who claim that they don't care about their appearance and declare that they dress for comfort. We cannot escape the conditions that society places on us to look "appropriate" for certain situations: interviews, certain jobs, social events on a grand scale, and other events. How many times have we heard the old cliché you can never make a first impression twice? Remembering that and that our appearance is part of our performance of who we are at that moment in public or in private should help us try to be "ourselves" as much as possible—even if we are from cities or towns that are not prestigious or glamorous. So, just how much of our own identity is constructed the way society/fashion/cosmetic surgeons tell us to be and how much are we actually in control of our identity?

Reflecting to Write

Personal Narrative

Think about the time you first started wearing makeup and heels, or if you're a male, started looking for the right shirt to show off your chest development or decided to accept or reject the "ghetto" or other looks. Write a **descriptive, personal narrative** explaining how you became fashion conscious and/or conscious of your own fashion style.

Do you have an individual whom you admire for his or her fashion or physique? Arnold Schwarzenegger came to the United States with the intention of becoming a bodybuilder. Are there any particular bodybuilders, male or female, whom you admire? Write a **personal narrative** explaining whom you feel is a role model or someone whom you would like to emulate because of his or her fashion savvy or physique. Be as **descriptive** as possible about what this person stands for.

Informative

There have been many exercise gurus in the media or who have produced DVDs to entice men and women to follow their programs for fit bodies. For example, Jack LaLanne was an early TV exercise role model and still appears on talk shows to encourage viewers to keep fit. Others such as Richard Simmons and Jane Fonda have also made their name in fitness programs. Investigate these and/or other fitness specialists who have made exercising an important part of some people's daily routines. How did they get started? What is their "secret" to success? How much money are they making from the public? How many people are successful in becoming fit and staying fit with their plans? These are some questions you might consider answering as you investigate the topic and write an **informative exemplification** paper. Don't forget to document your material.

Go to the library and find the section of old periodicals. Look either at the collections they have on the shelves or at microfiche versions. Find old issues of magazines like *Ladies Home Journal, Redbook,* or others that were published in the 1800s. Compare the advice the staff writers give to women about fashion and looking good with the advice contemporary magazines give their readers. Write a **comparison** or **contrast** essay explaining what you find. Be sure to get the names of the articles and the magazines as well as the dates they were published. Be as **descriptive** as possible.

Anne Perrin's article, "High Heels Scare Me," widens the discussion of fashion to the shoe industry. Investigate when tennis shoes became designer shoes endorsed by basketball stars and how this helped to raise the prices. Look at tennis shoes for young children and see which characters are stamped on the canvas and soles. Write an **informative exemplification** paper on the changes in tennis shoes for comfort, purposes, and trends. Be sure to document the material you use.

Another fashion statement young people seem to have discovered but that has been around for decades is tattooing. Many times body piercing is used in conjunction with tattooing. Write an **informative descriptive** paper that explains the interest young people have in these "new" fashion areas, what they stand for, whom they attract, and the benefits and risks attached to them. You might want to interview individuals who have had body piercing and/or tattoos. Be sure to document any material you use.

Chapter 14

The Media:
How We Are Influenced

What exactly do we refer to when we use the term "the media" in its broadest sense? According to *Merriam-Webster Collegiate Dictionary* online, media refers to "the agencies of mass communication" or, in other words, radio, television, newspapers, magazines—anything that communicates news and information to the general public. We are bombarded daily, in different forms, with information that we might or might not want to know. The media also alert us to "breaking news," information about incidents that might be of great importance to the public: the September 11 attack, the earthquake in Iran, the release of paroled criminals, the kidnapping of children, and so forth. When highly volatile news happens, members of the media begin what appears to be a feeding frenzy, trying to be "first on the scene" with "exclusive interviews" from the police, witnesses, victims, relatives, and friends so they can provide up-to-the-minute coverage. Who can forget the coverage of Princess Diana's accident and death?

With all these different reporters, anchors, and writers, how is the general public supposed to know which one to believe? And whose slant on the story is the most accurate? For example, on the cover of the September 24, 2001 issues of *Time* and *Newsweek,* there is a picture of Ground Zero. *Newsweek*'s photograph features three firemen raising the American flag with the captions "After the Terror" and "God Bless America." Above the photo are four small shots of the twin towers of the World Trade Center. *Time,* on the other hand, presents a slightly dusty President Bush waving a small American flag, with workers in the background rubble, a worker in the foreground reaching out to him, and a firefighter and man in a suit and tie standing behind him. The captions for this issue are "One Nation, Indivisible," and "America digs out—and digs in." Obviously, both of these special issues are about the September 11 attack, but each is sending a different political message. How do you interpret the messages?

273

In subtle and not so subtle ways, the media influence their readers and viewers. Whether it is through political, feminist, religious, or other belief structures, the media present the "facts" in a way that appeals to some but offends others. But what is the responsibility of the reporters, anchors, and writers. And what is the responsibility of the public?

In the following articles, we will look at attitudes that span a continuum from complete avoidance of television to the belief that television should have even more influence than it already has. A *Newsweek* writer asserts that the media do not, in fact, have the kind of influence critics claim. On the other hand, large corporations must believe that the media do have influence or they would not spend almost $2.25 million for a 30-second commercial during the Super Bowl to advertise their products. Knowing that they have an enormous national and international audience, they not only spend millions for airtime, they also spend enormous sums to produce sometimes multiple commercials for their product. To determine how much the general public is influenced would take research most of us do not have the time or interest to complete. Therefore, we should begin on a smaller scale, asking ourselves how much the media influence us and our friends and families. Do we "tune out" completely? Do we choose only those who agree with our leanings? Do we listen to those who oppose our beliefs so we can better understand how to respond to them? Or do we just criticize the media offering suggestions for change? There is no single right or wrong answer. There is just what we feel comfortable with. What do you do?

Why We Tuned Out

Karen Springen

There are several ways to deal with the programs children watch on television and the amount of time they spend watching TV: not allow television watching at all, monitor the time and the programs they watch, use it as a reward for special accomplishments, or give total freedom to their desire to watch television. Each has its own benefits and drawbacks, and parents usually choose one of these options. In the following article from Newsweek *(Nov. 11, 2002), Karen Springen explains that she and her husband chose the first option.*

Prereading: If you had to make the decision about whether to let your children or younger siblings watch television, what would you do?

Prewriting: How much discussion about television programs did you have with your friends when you were in elementary and middle school? Did you ever feel left out when you didn't watch a program everyone else watched? Write a descriptive paragraph discussing how watching or not watching popular television programs affected your life in school.

When Jazzy was 1 year old, her babysitter asked if TV was OK. We thought about it, and we said, "No."

"What's your favorite TV show?" our girls' beloved ballet instructor asked each pint-size dancer in her class. Our oldest daughter, Jazzy, didn't know how to answer. She shrugged. Her moment of awkwardness results from a decision my husband, Mark, and I made five years ago. We don't allow our kids to watch TV. Period. Not at home, not at friends' houses; and they don't watch videos or movies either. We want our daughters, Jazzy, now nearly 6 and Gigi, 3, to be as active as possible, physically and mentally. So when a babysitter asked whether Jazzy, then 1 year old, could watch, we thought about it—and then said no.

inquisitive: curious

When we look at our inquisitive*, energetic daughters, we have no regrets. And our reading of the research makes us feel even better. Nielsen Media Research reports that American children 2 through 11 watch three hours and 16 minutes of television every day. Kids who watch more than 10 hours of TV each week are more likely to be overweight, aggressive and slow to learn in school, according to the American Medical Association. For these reasons, the American Academy of Pediatrics recommends no TV for children younger than 2 and a maximum of two hours a day of "screen time" (TV, computers or video games) for older kids. We are convinced that without TV, our daughters spend more time than other kids doing cartwheels, listening to stories and asking such interesting questions as "How old is God?" and "What makes my rubber ducks float?" They also aren't haunted by TV images of September 11—because they never saw them.

Going without TV in America has its difficult moments. When I called my sister, Lucy, to make arrangements for Thanksgiving, she warned that her husband was planning to spend the day watching football. We're going anyway. We'll just steer the girls toward the playroom. And some well-meaning friends tell us our girls may be missing out on good educational programming. Maybe. But that's not what most kids are watching. Nielsen Media Research reports that among children 2–11, the top-five TV shows in the new season were "The Wonderful World of

Disney," "Survivor: Thailand," "Yu-Gi-Oh!," "Pokémon," and "Jackie Chan Adventures."

Will our happy, busy girls suffer because they're not participating in such a big part of popular culture? Will they feel left out in school when they don't know who won on "Survivor"? "Kids are going to make fun of them," warns my mother-in-law. A favorite child psychiatrist, Elizabeth Berger, author of *Raising Children with Character,* cautions that maintaining a puritanical* approach may make our kids into social outcasts. "Part of preparing your children for life is preparing them to be one of the girls," she says. "It's awful to be different from the other kids in fourth grade."

puritanical: sternly moral

Our relatives all watch TV. So did we. I was born in 1961. The year Newton Minow, then the chairman of the U.S. Federal Communications Commission, called television a "vast wasteland." But I loved it. My sister, Katy, and I shared a first crush on the TV cartoon hero Speed Racer. Watching "Bewitched" and "The Brady Bunch" and, later, soap operas gave us an easy way to bond with our friends. Am I being selfish in not wanting the same for our children?

So far, our daughters don't seem to feel like misfits. We have no problem with the girls enjoying products based on TV characters. The girls wear Elmo pajamas and battle over who can sit on a big Clifford stuffed animal. From books, they also know about Big Bird, the Little Mermaid and Aladdin. And they haven't mentioned missing out on "Yu-Gi-Oh!" cartoon duels. Dr. Miriam Bar-on, who chairs the American Academy of Pediatrics committee on public education, says I'm helping our kids be creative, independent learners and calls our decision "awesome." And Mayo Clinic pediatrician Daniel Broughton, another group member, says that "there's no valid reason" the girls need to view television.

As the girls grow older, we can't completely shield them from TV anyway. We'll probably watch Olympic rhythmic gymnastics; the girls love it. And if Jazzy's favorite baseball team, the Cubs, ever make the World Series, we'll tune in. Last Monday Jazzy's music teacher showed "The Magic School Bus: Inside the Haunted House." Though "Magic School Bus" is a well-regarded Scholastic product, I still cringed, wondering why the kids weren't learning about vibrations and sounds by singing and banging on drums. But I kept silent; I'd never require my kids to abstain in school. Like Jean Lotus, the Oak Park, Ill., mom who founded the anti-TV group the White Dot and who also reluctantly allows her kids to view TV in school, I'm wary of being seen "as the crusading weirdo." But some public ridicule will be worth it if I help get even a few people to think twice before automatically turning on the tube. Now it's time for me to curl up with the girls and a well-worn copy of *Curious George.*

Reading for Meaning

1. How was Springen raised with respect to television watching when she was growing up?
2. How will Springen deal with the television issue when her children grow older?

Reading Deeper

1. In Springen's reply to her well-meaning friends that her children are missing out on some "good educational programming," she replies in the article, "But that's not what most kids are watching." This is known as a *red herring,* a logical fallacy that shifts the argument to something other than the topic at hand. How would you respond to this comment? She also asks a rhetorical question, "Am I being selfish in not wanting the same for our children?" Respond and support your answer.
2. What is the reason for Springen's listing of the top five shows children watch? Does it support her argument for why her children should not watch television? Explain.

Reading for Writing

1. List the reasons Springen gives for not allowing her children to watch television. List the reasons that others gave her for letting her children watch TV. Make a third list of reasons that you might use to persuade Springen to allow her children to watch television or to encourage her to maintain her position. Take a position and write a **persuasive** essay about allowing children to watch television.
2. Find a copy of the November 11, 2002 *Newsweek* and read the article that precedes this one, which is also about television. Write a commentary about *Newsweek*'s position on television viewing based on this article and the one you found. Support your belief by **comparing and contrasting** the two articles. Be sure to use documentation for any material you might have quoted.
3. Write a **letter** to Springen expressing your point of view, supported by facts and opinions, about what you think about her decision. Since

this article was written in 2002, it would be interesting to see if she is still maintaining a strict control over her daughters, who are now several years older.

THE MONEY SHOT

Ken Gordon

The media are constantly bombarding us with commercials for fashion, food, drink, makeup, automobiles, deodorant, and other "necessities" of our lives. When we drive to campus and work, billboards advertise these and other commodities, sometimes marring beautiful scenery or even signal lights or signs. In the last few years, some of these commodities have found their way into movies and television programs, causing many individuals to become disgusted with the products and to feel as if they are a captive audience when all they wanted was to relax and enjoy a program without commercials. Ken Gordon, writer for Psychology Today *(2003), explains how many viewers have become complacent about "product placement" in TV and film. He does, however, note that there are many of us who continue to be upset by the intrusion.*

Prereading: Are you one of the people who don't even notice that products are being advertised in television programs and movies? Does it make any difference to you that they are there?

Prewriting: Does the number of commercials annoy you while you are watching your favorite television programs? Would you prefer to have more products embedded in the programs without interrupting the story line? Write a paragraph explaining your answer.

Vocabulary: Looking up and understanding the following words prior to reading should prepare you for the author's message. Other words will be defined in the margin.

discreet   TiVo

grimace: make a facial expression showing disgust or disapproval

subtle: not obvious

cameo: a brief appearance

Product placement has become a bit like air pollution. We may grimace* or cough when we catch a whiff, but most of the time we shrug it off as part of the cost of living in modern society.

But lately, brand-name products are more and more likely to make less and less subtle* cameos* in both TV and film. The new NBC drama *Las Vegas* gives prominent play to the Mandalay Bay Casino, which let the network film for free. Even less discreet: Last summer's *The Restaurant,* which gave as much air time to Mitsubishi and American Express as to the reality show's handsome chef.

On the other hand, marketers and their kin claim that they're just defending themselves against clicker-thumbing, TiVo-wielding viewers. Frank Zazza, CEO of a placement valuation company called iTVX, says

aesthetic: pertaining to good taste

placement has even become an aesthetic* necessity in this branded society. Imagine, he says, an episode of *CSI Crime Scene Investigation* without recognizable products: "They find a clue, and where's the clue? In a can of soda. They lift up the can and it says 'soda.' It doesn't work."

What does all this product-enhancing programming do to an audience? Does Johnny Six-pack object to being brand-handled? Armond Aserinsky, director of the Aspen Institute for Media Psychology, thinks most of us don't even notice. "The bulk of people who watch TV and go

impervious: unaffected

to the movies are quite impervious* to much of what they're shown," Aserinsky says. "It all looks good. And it's damned fast."

Assault people with too many absurd placements, though, and they may rebel. Stuart Fischoff, a media psychologist at California State University, Los Angeles, says the mall scene of Steven Spielberg's *Minority Report*—crowded with shots of the Gap and other retailers—caused a

tsunami: tidal wave

screening audience to respond with a wave of outrage and finally a tsunami* of dismissive* hilarity.

dismissive: not considered seriously

Even consumer insurrection* doesn't mean that advertisers have failed, says Brian Wansink, a marketing professor at the University of Illinois-Urbana: "My guess would be within a week, any sort of negative effect—'That was sort of shameless'—would turn into 'Dr. Pepper, that's

insurrection: open revolt

sort of cool.'" Cultural critic Mark Crispin Miller, author of *Boxed In: The Culture of TV,* agrees: "A placement that attracts a lot of negative attention, spurs a lot of ridicule, etc., still may work at getting folks to buy." There is, Miller reminds us, "a profitable difference between people hating a commercial and not buying what was advertised."

Fischoff suggests that our responses to product placement may

engenders: creates

have something to do with age, since younger people are more accustomed to being deluged by ads. That's not always true, though. Andy Denhart, 26, who runs a Web log about reality TV, complains, "*The Restaurant*'s product placement is lazy and inorganic and only engenders*

contempt: bitter scorn

contempt* from the audience because the products constantly interrupt the story." On the other hand, Nancy K. Austin, a 53-year-old writer,

churlishness: lack of civility or graciousness

found the churlishness* and psychodrama of the show more annoying than the marketing—at least catching the episode in which the boss

balky: stubborn

charmed the balky* bartender with a free Vespa scooter. "Was Vespa a product placement, too, right along with American Express?" asks

ciao: Italian greeting or farewell

Austin. "Maybe it was, but all I could think was Ciao*, baby! I can't help it; I'm a total sucker for Vespas."

Reading for Meaning

1. List some reasons why TV programs must have brand-name items in their scenes.
2. Gordon contrasts younger and older viewers' impressions of "product placement." Explain the differences between the two.

Reading Deeper

1. What is the reason for objecting to advertising, or, as Gordon puts it, "product placement," in TV programs and film?
2. Since the viewing public is not obliged to buy products, whether they are in advertisements or on programs and film, why are people so bothered about the products' appearances?

Reading for Writing

1. Watch a full night of television on the network channels and on the cable channels, if you have access to them. List the names of the programs and the products that you see on them. Which programs have the most number of products? Write a brief review of the evening's watching, noting the kinds and names of products that appeared and which programs used them. Express your opinion about how they were shown.
2. Watch several movie videos or DVDs that have been recently released, looking specifically for product placement. Take the name of the product, company, or brand name that is being advertised and explain how they were being shown. Were they part of the action or just scanned in the background by the camera? What is your reaction to them? Write a brief **convincing** essay about the position you have taken on product placement in movies. Use the movies you watched as part of your supporting ideas.

THE LIMITS OF MEDIA POWER

Robert J. Samuelson

Because most of the information that people get today is from media, it is difficult to deny that media have a direct influence on the way we think and behave. Whether the form is television, mag-

azines, or newspapers, media in their various formats present views about the economy, the labor market, wars in various parts of the world, crime, and so forth to all who pay attention to what they are saying. Of course, we do not have to rely on only one source. That is why there are so many different newspapers and magazines: They provide a different slant to the news. It then depends on whom we as readers and listeners want to believe. In the following article, Robert J. Samuelson, a writer for Newsweek *(Oct. 6, 2003), denies the power of media to shape public opinion single-handedly but agrees that members of the media enjoy the myth about the power they wield.*

Prereading: Consider how you get the news of the day. Do you listen to the radio as you drive to campus or work? Do you read the newspaper? Do you watch CNN or local news? Do you listen to your friends' rendition of the events?

Prewriting: Write a paragraph explaining the importance of the media in your life and how they help you determine what you believe about what is going on in your community, city, country, and world.

Vocabulary: Looking up and understanding the following words prior to reading should prepare you for the author's message. Other words will be defined in the margin.

adversity   complicit   mythology

---

unsolicited: not requested

In my business, you receive a lot of unsolicited* advise and abuse. Some years ago a reader proposed that I "drop dead." Another well-wisher later suggested that "the best thing you could say is nothing at all." One of these tirades* arrived last week. Sandwiched between incoherent* political musings and stories about the family cat were some wickedly funny insults ("You act like you're selling stock shares in Idiots-R-Us!") and, surprisingly, some important questions. Why are the media so negative? Or in my case, why am I talking down the economy? This general complaint is, I suspect, fairly widespread among the public and deserves a serious answer.

tirade: long, angry, negative speech

incoherent: unclear

indictment: accusation

The indictment* is straightforward. If the mass media dwell on the worst, it's said, we will make the worst come true. We will poison public opinion and create a self-fulfilling pessimism*. If people are constantly told the economy is going to the dogs, it will go to the dogs. The merchandising of anxiety and fear will spread anxiety and fear. Commentators like me (said the reader) "run around telling everyone, 'Woe is us, the sky is falling.'" I plead not guilty.

pessimism: gloomy view; hopelessness

What prompted this outburst was a recent column ("The Creaky Job Machine," Sept. 22 [2003]) pointing out—I am hardly alone—that the economic "recovery" has yet to reach the labor market. By one government survey, jobs are still dropping; by another, the unemployment rate has barely receded. I could take refuge in the facts. The White House Council of Economic Advisers (which can't be accused of bad-mouthing the economy) has compared the present recovery with all those since 1960. At a similar stage in earlier recoveries, non-farm jobs were up about 1 percent; this time, they've declined by almost 2 percent.

expedient: most efficient; quick

But the facts represent an expedient*—and partly dishonest—defense. They may be true, but they skirt the harder question of why I emphasized poor job performance when I could have been more optimistic or chosen a more heartening subject altogether. For example: although the present unemployment rate (6.1 percent) has risen sharply since late 2000 (3.9 percent), it's still much lower than the peak rates of the recessions of 1990–91 (7.8 percent) or 1981–82 (10.8 percent). Why not make that point? Or why not examine recent economic improvements: stocks, exports and corporate computer spending are all up.

collateral: accompanying

In the news business, the toughest decisions often involve determining what's "news" and what isn't. I focused on the poor job picture precisely because it contrasts with other economic improvements (readers, I thought, might wonder why) and because it fits my own outlook (to wit: the 1990's boom and stock "bubble" left much collateral* damage; but recovery will be slow and unsatisfying). But readers don't know my thought processes and could legitimately suspect other motives: sensationalism—highlighting the grimmest news I could find; or politics—trying to make George W. Bush look bad. Whatever the motive, stories like this can seem hellbent on sowing gloom and doom, which might kill the recovery.

The real defense is that we're not powerful enough to do that. Of course, we're not innocent of all the charges leveled against us; on some, we're repeat offenders. We're suckers for the latest political, intellectual or cultural fads, though these aren't always of the negative variety (social problems, health hazards, political feuds and economic setbacks). We can also be boosters for unrealistic crusades and utopian fantasies. Remember the media's Internet infatuation! We're regularly drawn to anything that seems new, different, controversial, engaging and entertaining. But we cannot single-handedly shape public opinion, especially as it affects the economy.

spontaneously: happening without cause or reason

The present situation offers stunning proof. If ever bad news should have mattered, it's been in the last three years. Editors and reporters didn't have to contrive adversity. It arrived spontaneously*: the popping of the stock bubble, September 11, corporate scandals, steady layoffs, the war in Iraq. By all logic, confidence should have collapsed. It hasn't. In previous recessions, consumer spending often dropped; in this one, it actually increased. Americans didn't abandon the mall. They took advantage of lavish auto "incentives." They bought new homes and, with interest rates low, refinanced mortgages on old ones. Despite the weak labor market, most Americans think their jobs are safe. (A Gallup poll in August asked respondents whether they were worried about being fired; 81 percent said no, 19 percent said yes. The results in 1997 were almost identical—80–20.)

People just don't heed the media that much. What they absorb represents one factor in what they believe and how they behave. Their experiences, habits, views and prejudices count for more. They trust their judgments, not ours. Because the media are everywhere—and inspire much resentment—their influence is routinely exaggerated. The mistake is in confusing visibility with power, and the media are often complicit in the confusion. We embrace the mythology because it flatters our self-importance. The truth is that we echo, amplify, influence and refine public opinion but rarely create or manipulate it. In a democracy, that's just fine.

Reading for Meaning

1. How does Samuelson suggest that the media influence the country's economy? Explain. How does Samuelson respond to this?
2. What are the possible motives readers of Samuelson's article might accuse him of for reporting only the worst possible scenarios of the economy?

Reading Deeper

1. What is the job of the White House Council of Economic Advisers?
2. If the media cannot "shape public opinion" alone, what are the other factors that might do so?
3. Samuelson asserts that a mistake in made in "confusing visibility with power." What does that mean?

Reading for Writing

1. Samuelson asserts that media "cannot single-handedly shape public opinion." Take a position on this statement and write an **argumentative** essay supporting or opposing it. Be sure to document any material that you use.
2. Consider your own reliance on the media for news about the economy, job stability, war reports, and so forth. Write a **response** to

Samuelson's article explaining how the media influence your opinions. You may do this as a **personal narrative** or as a **letter** to Samuelson. Be sure to give specific incidents.

Signs of Intelligent Life on TV

Susan Douglas

In the previous articles, we saw how the media influence their readers and viewers. In this article originally published in Ms. *(May/June 1995), Susan Douglas discusses how some television programs are a reflection of the influence of feminism and their reaction to it. Although many people shy away from being called feminists or want nothing to do with feminism, any time someone agrees that women should be given equal rights, pay, and opportunities as men are given, they adhere to the principles of feminism. Douglas looks at the status women have been allowed to have in these prime-time programs and looks at the impact they have had. She also critiques the way the characters of both the men and women have been developed by the directors.*

Prereading: Whether you are a man or a woman, do you consider yourself a feminist? Why?

Prewriting: How do you feel about Diane Sawyer, Barbara Walters, and other women who have important positions on television news programs? How do you feel about women as anchors on local television news? How do you feel when women reporters cover football or basketball games, sports usually involving men specifically? Write a paragraph about how you feel about women's roles in television broadcasting.

Vocabulary: Looking up and understanding the following words prior to reading should prepare you for the author's message. Other words will be defined in the margin.

**pundits   Diane Sawyer   Charles Manson   Connie Chung
Tonya and Nancy**

When the hospital show *ER* became a surprise hit, the pundits who had declared dramatic television "dead" were shocked. But one group wasn't surprised at all.

Those of us with jobs, kids, older parents to tend to, backed-up toilets, dog barf on the rug, and friends/partners/husbands we'd like to say

diurnal: daily

ideological:
concerned with
ideas, belief

escapist:
provides
diversion or
escape of the
mind to purely
imaginative
activity or
entertainment

resonates: has
an effect and
evokes response

précis:
summary of
facts

phallic:
masculine,
sexual

weimaraners:
large dogs from
Germany

percussive:
drum-like
sounds

more than "hi" to during any diurnal* cycle don't have much time to watch television. And when we do—usually after 9:38 p.m.—we have in recent years been forced to choose between Diane Sawyer interviewing Charles Manson or Connie Chung chasing after Tonya [Harding] and Nancy [Kerrigan]. People like me, who felt that watching the newsmagazines was like exposing yourself to ideological* smallpox, were starved for some good escapist* drama that takes you somewhere else yet resonates* with real life and has ongoing characters you care about.

When *NYPD Blue* premiered in the fall of 1993 with the tough-but-sensitive John Kelly, and featuring strong, accomplished women, great lighting, bongo drums in the sound track, and male nudity, millions sighed with relief. When *ER* hit the air, we made it one of the tube's highest rated shows. Tagging farther behind, but still cause for hope, is another hospital drama, *Chicago Hope.*

All three shows acknowledge the importance of the adult female audience by featuring women as ongoing characters who work for a living and by focusing on contemporary problems in heterosexual relationships (no, we haven't achieved everyday homosexual couples on TV). More to the point, hound-dog-eyed, emotionally wounded yet eager-to-talk-it-through guys are center stage. So what are we getting when we kick back and submerge ourselves in these dramas? And what do they have to say about the ongoing project of feminism?

For those of you who don't watch these shows regularly, here's a brief précis*: *NYPD Blue* is a cop show set in New York City and has producer Steven Bochoco's signature style—lots of shaky, hand-held camera work, fast-paced editing (supported by the driving, phallic* backbeat in the sound track), and multiple, intersecting plots about various crimes and the personal lives of those who work in the precinct. Last season there were more women in the show; and last season there was John Kelly.

This year, the show is more masculinized. Watching Bobby Simone, played by Jimmy Smits, earn his right to replace Kelly was like witnessing a territorial peeing contest between weimaraners*. Bobby had to be as sensitive and emotionally ravaged as Johnny, so in an act of New Age male oneupmanship, the scriptwriters made him a widower who had lost his wife to breast cancer. But Bobby had to be one tough customer too, so soon after we learn of his wife's death, we see him throwing some punks up against a fence, warning them that he will be their personal terminator unless they stop dealing drugs.

ER has the same kind of simultaneous, intersecting story lines, served up with fast-tracking cameras that sprint down hospital corridors and swirl around operating tables like hawks on speed. And there are the same bongo drums and other percussive* sounds when patients are

Valium: trademark drug used to calm anxiety and tension

rushed in for treatment. *Chicago Hope* is *ER* on Valium*: stationary cameras, slower pace, R&B instead of drumbeats. It's also *ER* on helium or ether, kind of a *Northern Exposure* goes to the hospital, with more off-beat plots and characters, like a patient who eats his hair or a kid whose ear has fallen off.

Whenever I like a show a lot—meaning I am there week in and week out—I figure I have once again embraced a media offering with my best and worst interests at heart. Dramatic TV shows, which seek a big chunk of the middle- and upper-income folks between 18 and 49, need to suck in those women whose lives have been transformed by the women's movement (especially women who work outside the home and have disposable income) while keeping the guys from grabbing the remote. What we get out of these twin desires is a blend of feminism and antifeminism in the plots and in the female characters. And for the male characters we have an updated hybrid* of masculinity that crossbreeds decisiveness, technical expertise*, and the ability to throw a punch or a basketball, with a soft spot for children and a willingness to cry.

hybrid: object that is a product of two different things

expertise: specialized knowledge or skill

On the surface, these shows seem good for women. We see female cops, lawyers, doctors, and administrators, who are smart, efficient, and successful. But in too many ways, the women take a backseat to the boys. In *NYPD Blue,* for example, we rarely see the women actually doing their jobs. The overall message in the three shows is that, yes, women can be as competent as men, but their entrance into the workforce has wrecked the family and made women so independent and hard-hearted that dealing with them and understanding them is impossible. Despite this, they're still the weaker sex. . . .

The Ariel Syndrome—Ariel was the name of Walt Disney's little mermaid, who traded her voice for a pair of legs so that she could be with a human prince she'd seen from afar for all of ten seconds—grips many of the women, who have recurring voice problems. Watch out for female characters who "don't want to talk about it," who can't say no, who don't speak up. They make it even harder for the women who do speak their minds, who are, of course, depicted as "bitches."

One major "bitch" is the wife of *ER*'s Dr. Mark Greene (Anthony Edwards). He's a doctor who's barely ever home, she's a lawyer who lands a great job two hours away, and they have a seven-year-old. Those of us constantly negotiating about who will pick up the kids or stay late at work can relate to this. The problem is that *ER* is about *his* efforts to juggle, *his* dreams and ambitions. We know this guy, we like him, we know he's a great doctor who adores his wife and child. Her, we don't know, and there's no comparable female doctor to show the woman's side of this equation. As a result when conflicts emerge, the audience is primed to want her to compromise (which she's already done, so he can stay at the job he loves). When she insists he quit his job and relocate, she sounds like a spoiled child more wedded to a rigid quid pro quo than to flexibility, love, the family. It's the conservative view of what feminism has turned women into—unfeeling, demanding blocks of granite.

One of the major themes of all three shows is that heterosexual relationships are a national disaster. And it's the women's fault. Take *NYPD Blue.* Yes, there's the fantasy relationship between Andy Sipowicz (Dennis Franz) and Sylvia Costas (Sharon Lawrence), in which an accomplished woman helps a foul-mouthed, brutality-prone cop with really bad shirts get in touch with his feelings and learn the pleasures of coed showering. While this affair has become the emotional anchor of the show, it is also the lone survivor in the on-going gender wars.

It looks like splitsville for most of the show's other couples. Greg Medavoy (Gordon Clapp) infuriates Donna Abandando (Gail O'Grady) by his behavior, which includes following her to see whom she's lunching with. She's absolutely right. But after all the shots of Greg looking at her longingly across the office (again, we're inside his head, not hers), the audience is encouraged to think that she should give the guy a break. By contrast, her explanations of why she's so angry and what she wants have all the depth and emotional warmth of a Morse code message tapped out by an iguana. Of course Greg doesn't understand. She won't help him.

venomous: poisonous; spiteful

In this world, female friendships are non-existent or venomous*. And there is still worse sludge gumming up these shows. Asian and Latina women are rarely seen, and African American women are also generally absent except as prostitutes, bad welfare moms, and unidentified nurses. In the *ER* emergency room, the black women who are the conscience and much-needed drill sergeants of the show don't get top billing, and are rarely addressed by name. . . .

veneer: thin layer

liberalism: political view that is not conservative

One of the worst things these shows do, under a veneer* of liberalism* and feminism, is justify the new conservatism in the United States. The suspects brought in for question on *NYPD Blue* are frequently threatened and sometimes beaten, but it's O.K. because they all turn out to be guilty, anyway. Legal representation for these witnesses is an unspeakable evil because it hides the truth. After a steady diet of this, one might assume the Fourth Amendment, which prohibits unreasonable research and seizure, is hardly worth preserving.

So why are so many women devoted to these shows? First off, the women we do see are more successful, gutsy, more fully realized than most female TV characters. But as for me, I'm a sucker for the men. I want to believe, despite all the hideous evidence to the contrary, that

patriarchy: the rule of society by males only

some men have been humanized by the women's movement, that they have become more nurturing, sensitive, and emotionally responsible. I want to believe that patriarchy* is being altered by feminism. Since I get zero evidence of this on the nightly news, I want a few hours a week when I can escape into this fantasy.

bizarre: incredibly odd

hoist: to raise or haul up

petard: part of a saying "hoist with one's own petard" meaning hurt by one's own scheme

Of course, we pay the price for this fantasy. TV depicts "real men" being feminized for the better and women masculinized for the worse. The message from the guys is, "We became the kind of men you feminists said that you wanted, and now you can't appreciate us because you've forgotten how to be a 'real' woman." It's a bizarre* twist on the real world, where many women have changed, but too many men have not. Nevertheless, in TV land feminism continues to hoist* itself with its own petard*. Big surprise.

Reading for Meaning

1. What reason does Douglas give for the big surprise that programs such as *ER, Chicago Hope,* and *NYPD Blue* were successful when they came out?
2. How are men being portrayed in these programs?
3. Even though women are being given more important jobs in these shows than ever before, there is a down side. Explain it.

Reading Deeper

1. Explain how a television show can be at once feminist and antifeminist. Use specific examples.
2. Explain what having a "voice problem" means in terms of women.
3. Explain how the "conservative view" of feminism describes women.
4. Define what Douglas means when she says men say that women have forgotten "how to be a 'real' woman." What is a "real" woman in this sense?

Reading for Writing

1. Douglas explains that she watches these programs to see men who have characteristics that she prefers over the characteristics that she sees being portrayed "on the nightly news." Explain the difference between what she wants from men and what she believes to be a more "realistic" view of men's characteristics. Do you agree with her assessment of men? Write an **informative** essay incorporating **description, personal narrative,** and **comparison** and **contrast** to tell readers what you think men are like.

2. Douglas indicates that women who speak their mind are "depicted as 'bitches'" in these programs. Unfortunately, many individuals who do not necessarily watch these programs also categorize women who are assertive, self-confident, career-oriented, in control, and so forth as "bitches." Explain how you think this description has come into being. Write an **informative** essay, incorporating **definition** also.

3. This article is obviously somewhat dated in its reference to the episodes in these programs. Watch one or two of the programs for 2–3 weeks and decide if what Douglas was seeing several years ago is still true for today's episodes. Of course, some of the characters will change—Dr. Greene in *ER*, Bobby Simone in *NYPD Blue*, and others are no longer part of the programs—and *Chicago Hope* is no longer on, but look for the attitudes that Douglas discusses. Write an article that critiques the way men and women are depicted in one of these programs.

OPERATING ON ACCURACY

Claudia Kalb

Reality TV has made a name for itself in programs such as Survivor, The Bachelor, *as well as others. However, the producers of* ER *use resources such as professional doctors to help ensure that the details in the program are not only realistic but also accurate. The idea that programs of this kind do not influence viewers is hard to believe considering the polls taken after several of the shows have aired. In this article, Claudia Kalb, writer for* Newsweek *(Sept. 30, 2002), examines the technical aspects of* ER *and how it has influenced other medical programs to follow its lead.*

Prereading: Do you watch *ER* or any other medical program? What do you think about it?

Prewriting: Have you ever been to an emergency room? Write about the experience. If you have not, find a friend or member of your family who has been and ask the individual to recall the experience. Write about the scenario that he or she shared with you.

Vocabulary: Looking up and understanding the following words prior to reading should prepare you for the author's message. Other words will be defined in the margin.

osteopath   jargon

I t's a Thursday morning on the set of *ER* and actress Alex Kingston (Dr. Elizabeth Corday) is tripping over her lines. "I need 30 'migs' per kilo of methylprednisolone," she says, rushing to a gunshot victim. "Entry wound left mid-, sterno . . . cleido . . . uh . . . I'll never get that," she says, smiling at Jon Fong, an osteopath and one of *ER*'s on-set medical advisers. "Dr. Jon" sounds it out: "Sterno-cleido-mas-toid." Soon, everyone, including Noah Wyle (Dr. John Carter) and director Richard Thorpe, begins chanting together: "Sterno-cleido-mas-toid. Sterno-cleido-mas-toid." Thorpe even kicks into a jig to pound the jargon into Kingston's head. Finally, she gets it—and Thorpe shouts the magic words: "Cut. Let's print."

excruciating:
very intense

ER, one of television's most successful dramas ever—despite, or perhaps because of, its excruciating* medical accuracy—has long been the envy of Hollywood. This week [September 2, 2002], as the show kicks off its ninth season, two new medical dramas will fill prime-time slots on CBS and ABC. Like *ER, Presidio Med* and *MDs* have added doctors to their production staffs as gatekeepers* of the truth in a fictional world. At the same time, the shows have become targets of health organizations, which have become increasingly aware that medical drama is an ideal conduit* for public-health education.

gatekeepers:
persons who
control access to

conduit: a
connection that
brings things
together

Studies suggest that viewers take medical info they see on TV seriously. The Kaiser Family Foundation found that half of *ER*'s regular viewers—which number more than 20 million—say they gained new knowledge about health issues from the show. After one scene on human papilloma virus, awareness of sexually transmitted disease jumped from 24 to 47 percent. In May, Robert Blendon, a Harvard public-health researcher, surveyed responses to *ER*'s season finale, about a smallpox scare. He was pleased to find that the number of viewers who learned that smallpox vaccine can prevent the disease—even after exposure—rose 18 percent. "If we had an attack," says Blendon, "that would be the biggest public-health message" to relay.

Those kinds of numbers have prompted groups like the Centers for Disease Control and, most recently, the American Association of Health Plans (managed care's trade group), to knock on Hollywood's door. In July [2002] the AAHP hired the William Morris Agency to improve its image. High on the list: a meeting with the writers of *MDs,* which pits do-good doctors against number-crunching execs in a San Francisco hospital. The danger is that special-interest groups will present one-sided information that makes it on air. But the AAHP says it's building bridges, not pushing agendas. And others, like Kaiser and the CDC, which has its own Hollywood unit, agree. "Our goal is to get accurate health information out," says the CDC's Vicki Beck. "We don't control the content."

For the creative side, the priority, by far, is making the characters compelling. "Medicine," says *ER*'s supervising producer, Dr. Joe Sachs, "is the wallpaper." Still, being accurate and timely bolsters* the drama and relevance of storylines. That's where medical types like Sachs, who also has a film degree, come in. At a recent writers' meeting, he was joined by medical supervisor Dr. Mark Morocco, a former actor, who stumbled in still wearing scrubs after an all-night shift at a real ER at UCLA. Starbucks lattes and popcorn helped keep him awake, as did the medical nitpicking he and Sachs did on that week's script. (Should a negligent* parent "shake" or "whack" a kid?) Morocco revels* in TV's power: "Imagine how many patients we'd have to see to reach the number of people we get on a bad night on *ER*."

The new shows have their own docs onboard. Two of *MDs*' writers are, in fact, M.D.s. "We want to be as accurate as possible," says executive producer Marc Platt. And *Presidio Med* (produced by a team from *ER*), set in a San Francisco clinic, also has two physicians writing. One, Lisa Zwerling, says she debated working in TV until a mentor said: "This is the public-health opportunity of a lifetime."

In the end, what really matters to Hollywood is ratings. That means having viewers like Marcy Jaslow, 15, who was treated by Morocco at UCLA for an eye allergy, "You work for *ER*?" she shrieked when told about his day job. "Oh my God, I *love* that show!" Just what the doctor ordered.

bolsters
supports

negligent:
careless

revels: takes
great pleasure in

Reading for Meaning

1. What kind of details does Dr. Morocco look for in *ER*? Why?
2. There are at least two different expectations in the medical shows. Who represents the different groups that express them?

Reading Deeper

1. Why have the different networks added doctors to their production staffs? What is the effect of this move?
2. What is at least one of the positive effects that have come from *ER*?
3. While there are those who say that media are unable to influence society, how does *ER* prove them wrong? Explain.

Reading for Writing

1. Watch either reruns of *ER* on a cable channel or the season shows on a network channel. Select one of the doctors whom you enjoy the most, and using at least one episode of *ER*, select the "doctor's" actions, words, and bedside/lack of bedside manner that attract you to him or her as an authentic doctor. Write a characterization of the "doctor" as a real doctor. Would you want to go to him or her for your medical needs? Explain why.

2. Visit a real ER in a hospital. Interview a nurse or several nurses when they are not busy, and ask them about the routine in their ER. Ask them their opinion about how *ER* is different from or the same as their emergency room situations. Write a **comparison and contrast** essay using a real emergency room setting and one depicted on television.

RESISTING THE FALSE SECURITY OF TV

Tom Shales

Sometimes it is difficult for us to consider TV as providing viewers with a "false sense of security" in light of the coverage we are exposed to of events like the September 11 attack, the war in Iraq, the California mudslides, the earthquake in Iran, and so forth. If there is a natural disaster, a terror warning, a school shooting, or anything of significance to viewers, satellites and technology have made it possible for viewers to see the events almost as they are happening, and then to view them over and over again. On the other hand, TV also provides mindless programming to allow individuals to escape from the problems of the world. We can actually have it both ways: agitated and calmed. However, Tom Shales, a Pulitzer Prize–winning media critic who writes for The Washington Post *(2004), critiques television for not doing enough to make the viewing public continue to feel the anger and outrage that we felt on September 11.*

Prereading: Have you forgotten the events of September 11? Do you need the media to remind you continuously about the horror of that day and the rage we should feel toward the terrorists? How do you think you would feel if the events were shown repeatedly to you?

Prewriting: Do you think that television and other forms of media influenced you to think or feel a particular way about the September 11 attack? Write a paragraph explaining what you think.

Vocabulary: Looking up and understanding the following words prior to reading should prepare you for the author's message. Other words will be defined in the margin.

therapeutic   banality   Tommy Lasorda

J eez, I'm cranky. Even for me. But I seem to have a lot of company. People are just incredibly ticked off. They're alternately irked and furious. These are times that really try men's souls, and women's too. We've never lived through anything exactly like this before, and so we don't know quite how to behave.

carp: complain

intrinsic: belonging to the nature of a thing

We look to television for cues, but this is new to television, too. As usual, it's easier to carp* about what TV is doing than to come up with an alternative course of action. I do think there's an intrinsic* reassurance in the fact that TV just keeps going, keeps pouring out the sitcoms and the dramas, the huff and the fluff, the schlock and the slop.

trivial: unimportant

I have referred to this as "the therapeutic effect of banality." It's like: "Oh, look, honey. Kellogg's has a new cereal with strawberries in it." Or "Oh boy, kitty litter that sparkles." These trivial* and distracting messages come with trivial and distracting television programs attached: Somebody's pregnant on *Friends,* and somebody's leaving *Judging Amy,* and the brothers are battling again on *Frasier.* If you want to be reminded of the war on terrorism in prime time, you can go to Fox News or CNN or watch one of the network newsmagazines. But do you?

A JOLT TO REALITY

. . . Very high on the list of things I think everybody is desperate to see are Demonstrations of American Competence. In their way, well-produced TV shows fill that bill, and that may be part of the reassurance factor. We still produce the best commercial TV shows in the world, by God; we've mastered that.

But there are things more profoundly satisfying than a first-rate episode of *ER.* Chief among them, recently, was a short walk taken by the president of the United States—the short walk from the dugout to the pitcher's mound at Yankee Stadium, where George W. Bush threw out the first ball in Game 3 of the World Series.

TAUNTING THE TERRORISTS

It looked like a good, healthy throw, too—no sissy pitch from Bush. It also looked as though the president were wearing a bulletproof vest under his jacket, because there was an odd bulkiness to it, and he had it zipped up to the top. No one could quibble with the wisdom of taking such precautions. It did nothing to hinder the bracing, bolstering* effect of seeing him out there essentially taunting* the terrorists, jeering at them, giving a thumbs-up, and hurling that ball.

bolstering:
supporting

taunting:
making fun of

Of course, Fox had to screw things up a little bit with its enormous electronic billboards in the stadium. In any wide shot with the pitcher on the right, home plate on the left, the screen was dominated by one of these new superimposed* banners: "Ally's back, tomorrow night on Fox." This was not only obnoxious*, it was apparently ineffective, as Ms. McBeal returned for a new season with ratings that were definitely mediocre*, banner or no banner.

superimposed:
placed on top of

obnoxious:
offensive

mediocre: of
low quality

During an actual commercial break, viewers saw one terrific spot, part of a campaign called "Live Brave." Tommy Lasorda looked into the camera and said, "You wanna fight terrorism? Go to a ballgame!" And then he barked out a few ways in which going out to the ballpark had the effect of giving the finger to Osama bin Laden.

"PLAY BALL"

Major League Baseball sponsored another great commercial: "We mourn. We heal. We stand united. We play. But we never forget." The last line was over a photo of the World Trade Center as it stood until the morning of September 11. Up in the stands, meanwhile, fans unfurled a banner: "USA fears Nobody. Play Ball." You have to be moved. You have to be impressed.

Every network, of course, simply must put a label on its continuing coverage, a superficial way of making that coverage distinctive. "America on Guard," "America Fights Back," "America Recovers," whatever. The titles could be more descriptive: "America Gets Sick and Tired of the FBI Telling Us to Be on High Alert While the President Tells Us to Go About Our Business as Usual."

Over on CNN, and probably on other cable networks too, Robert Culp pops up now and then selling something called the American Guardian Homeguard Preparedness Kit. It consists mainly of a videotape ("How to shoot your neighbor if he breaks into your shelter"), plus a "survival pack" that looks like the stuff you find in the bathroom of a good hotel. It sells for $39.95, and dialing the 800 number to order it may be, Mr. Culp solemnly intones, the most important phone call you will ever make. Yes, the practice of cashing in on a crisis is very much with us, and for us this crisis has probably only begun.

What should TV do that it isn't doing? I wish I knew. One thing worries me about TV's ability to banish thoughts of the war and the peril* we face and the vicious obscenity of the September 11 attacks: Are we going to use television like Prozac to lull us into a false security—perhaps even a tolerance, an acceptance, of an appalling and treacherous* evil?

We need to stay angry. We need to remember the horror of that day in September. It was said in the days immediately following that the images of the airplanes crashing into the towers and the towers collapsing, and of people leaping from windows to escape the murderous heat, were being cheapened through overexposure, that they were being shown too often. And the networks largely pulled them from the air.

But there's a danger in not showing them, too, isn't there? In pretending it didn't happen? Maybe those images should be replayed every now and then—brought out of the library and shown to us in all their horror, just so there is absolutely no possibility that we might forget.

Of course it will make us uncomfortable. It should. If TV lets us get too comfortable, the war will be over. And we will have lost.

peril: danger

treacherous: not to be trusted

Reading for Meaning

1. What were the differences between coverage of the September 11 attacks on the various television stations? What suggestion does Shales make to improve those differences?

2. How did President George W. Bush appear to be "taunting" the terrorists?

Reading Deeper

1. Why does Shales criticize commercials at the time of the September 11 attacks?

2. If going to the ballpark provides good escape and relief from terrorism for some people, why can't watching "trivial" sitcoms do the same for those who do not appreciate certain sports? Why can't Americans have a slogan, "Watch TV," that is just as meaningful as "Play Ball"? Explain the difference.

Reading for Writing

1. Shales suggests that "Maybe those images should be replayed every now and then—brought out of the library and shown to us in all their horror, just so there is absolutely no possibility that we might forget." This is what the Holocaust Museum has done in every city where one has been established. Write an **informative** essay that explains the benefits and the drawbacks of continuing to display the horrors of historical events.

2. Think back to the coverage of September 11 and the events that surrounded that day. There is no question that they were repeated numerous times. Write a **personal narrative** about what you remember about that day, your feelings about how the coverage was handled then, and what you think now about the way coverage was handled.

3. Tom Shales is, in effect, suggesting that television be even more influential on viewers' lives, thoughts, and attitudes than it already is. What do you think about this? If this were to be done, then whose attitudes would be shown to us to influence us? What happens when conflicting views are shown? Whose beliefs are we supposed to be influenced by? Whose beliefs will get privileged? Should we give airtime to those who want to spread anti-American beliefs? If we don't, do we violate First Amendment rights? How would this affect the Patriot Act? There are a lot of issues to consider when suggesting that television keep the viewing public "uncomfortable." Write an essay to **convince** readers what you feel about the responsibility of television to influence viewers about political topics. Include what you think might be the effects of this kind of influence.

RHETORICAL ANALYSIS

Karen Springen provides an excellent example of a personal narrative that incorporates negotiation and compromise in discussing her husband's and her position on allowing their daughters to watch television. In this article from *Newsweek,* readers find that even though they know how she feels, they don't know what made her feel this way or how the facts she reports affect her decision to ban television from her home. This article provides several strategies about personal narrative, negotiation, and compromise that are discussed in Chapters 4 and 10. In the left-hand margin there are explanations that direct you to appropriate chapters in this textbook for discussion about the underlined techniques the author used to write the essay or that comment directly about the techniques the author used.

Why We Tuned Out

When Jazzy was 1 year old, her babysitter asked if TV was OK. We thought about it, and we said, "No."

Ch. 4, Narrative, Personal Narrative

"What's your favorite TV show?" our girls' beloved ballet instructor asked each pint-size dancer in her class. Our oldest daughter, Jazzy, didn't know how to answer. She shrugged. Her moment of awkwardness results from a decision my husband, Mark, and I made

Main point, assertion of the essay

Support for decision

five years ago. We don't allow our kids to watch TV. Period. Not at home, not at friends' houses; and they don't watch videos or movies either. We want our daughters, Jazzy, now nearly 6 and Gigi, 3, to be as active as possible, physically and mentally. So when a babysitter asked whether Jazzy, then 1 year old, could watch, we thought about it—and then said no.

Ch. 10, Persuasion relevant evidence to support her position

When we look at our inquisitive, energetic daughters, we have no regrets. And our reading of the research makes us feel even better. Nielsen Media Research reports that American children 2 through 11 watch three hours and 16 minutes of television every day. **Kids who watch more than 10 hours of TV each week are more likely to be overweight, aggressive and slow to learn in school, according to the American Medical Association.** For these reasons, the American

Ch. 10, Persuasion Fact

Ch. 10, Persuasion support for claim

Ch. 10, Persuasion support for decision

Academy of Pediatrics recommends no TV for children younger than 2 and a maximum of two hours a day of "screen time" (TV, computers or videogames) for older kids. We are convinced that without TV, our daughters spend more time that other kids doing cartwheels, listening to stories and asking such interesting questions as "How old is God?" and "What makes my rubber ducks float?" They also aren't haunted by TV images of September 11—because they never saw them.

Going without TV in America has its difficult moments. When I called my sister, Lucy, to make arrangements for Thanksgiving, she warned that her husband was planning to spend the day watching football. We're going anyway. We'll just steer the girls toward the

Ch. 10,
Persuasion
opposition to
her argument

Ch. 10,
Persuasion
rebuttal, another
red herring

Ch. 10,
Persuasion
another point
for the
opposition

Ch. 10,
Persuasion
paragraph
devoted to
points from the
opposition

Ch. 4, Narrative
use of personal
experience

Ch. 10,
Persuasion
compelling
evidence that
supports
narrator's
position

Ch. 10,
Persuasion
compelling
evidence

Ch. 1, Reading
author calls
attention to
word through
the use of
quotation marks

playroom. And some well-meaning friends tell us <u>our girls may be missing out on good educational programming.</u> Maybe. But that's not what most kids are watching. <u>Nielsen Media Research reports that among children 2-11, the top-five TV shows in the new season were "The Wonderful World of Disney," "Survivor: Thailand," "Yu-Gi-Oh!," "Pokémon," and "Jackie Chan Adventures."</u>

<u>Will our happy, busy girls suffer because they're not participating in such a big part of popular culture?</u> Will they feel left out in school when they don't know who won on "Survivor"? "Kids are going to make fun of them," warns my mother-in-law. A favorite child psychiatrist, Elizabeth Berger, author of *Raising Children with Character,* cautions that maintaining a puritanical approach may make our kids into social outcasts. "Part of preparing your children for life is preparing them to be one of the girls," she says. "It's awful to be different from the other kids in fourth grade."

<u>Our relatives all watch TV. So did we. I was born in 1961.</u> The year Newton Minow, then the chairman of the U.S. Federal Communications Commission, called television a "vast wasteland." <u>But I loved it. My sister, Katy, and I shared a first crush on the TV cartoon hero</u> Speed Racer. Watching "Bewitched" and "The Brady Bunch" and, later, soap operas gave us an easy way to bond with our friends. <u>Am I being selfish in not wanting the same for our children</u>?

So far, our daughters don't seem to feel like misfits. We have no problem with the girls enjoying products based on TV characters. The girls wear Elmo pajamas and battle over who can sit on a big Clifford stuffed animal. From books, they also know about Big Bird, the Little Mermaid and Aladdin. And they haven't mentioned missing out on "Yu-Gi-Oh!" cartoon duels. <u>Dr. Miriam Bar-on, who chairs the American Academy of Pediatrics committee on public education, says I'm helping our kids be creative, independent learners and calls our decision "awesome." And Mayo Clinic pediatrician Daniel Broughton, another group member</u>, says that "there's no valid reason" the girls need to view television.

Ch. 10,
Persuasion
compromise for
negotiation

As the girls grow older, we can't completely shield them from TV anyway. <u>We'll probably watch Olympic rhythmic gymnastics; the girls love it. And if Jazzy's favorite baseball team, the Cubs, ever make the World Series, we'll tune in</u>. Last Monday Jazzy's music teacher showed "The Magic School Bus: Inside the Haunted House." Though "Magic School Bus" is a well-regarded Scholastic product, I still cringed, wondering why the kids weren't learning about vibrations and sounds by singing and banging on drums. But I kept silent; I'd never require my kids to abstain in school. Like Jean Lotus, the Oak Park, Ill., mom who founded the anti-TV group the White Dot and who also reluctantly allows her kids to view TV in school, I'm wary of being seen "as the crusading weirdo." But some public ridicule will be worth it if I help get even a few people to think twice before automatically turning on the tube. <u>Now it's time for me to curl up with the girls and a well-worn copy of *Curious George*</u>.

Ch. 4, Narrative
author returns to
narrative to
complete essay

This article was obviously written by a mother who is deeply concerned about exposing her daughters to television. However, even though she provides facts she has discovered in her research about children and their television habits, she fails to take any middle-ground stance until she compromises in the last paragraph. Even though many children watch television many hours a week, what is preventing her from limiting the time her daughters watch it? She also mentions the enjoyment she had sharing her television-watching experiences with her sister and wonders if she is being selfish now by denying her daughters access to television. This article is quite thought provoking and written to appeal to an audience of parents who are also concerned about the amount of time their children spend in front of the television and the kind of programming they watch. Is her either-or, all-or-nothing approach to television watching one that you agree with? Is her compromise enough to make you agree with her position?

REFLECTIONS ON THE MEDIA: HOW MUCH DOES THE MEDIA INFLUENCE ME?

From the time you were born, you have been exposed to the influence of the media in one form or another. Depending on parental controls, you probably had some access to TV when you were a child, and you probably listened to the radio as you were growing up. The old cliché, no man is an island, is quite accurate in today's society where we can discover what is happening in various parts of the world at almost a moment's notice.

But how do we protect ourselves from comfortably adopting the opinions of others? At some point we have to learn how to sift through the rhetoric of commentators and find the right answers about issues that will affect our lives. Learning how to listen closely for rhetorical fallacies and generalizations helps. Realizing when one's fundamental beliefs are being questioned or criticized by well-meaning writers or reporters also helps. Learning how to distinguish a well-supported argument from one that is filled with unsupported assertions, especially when written, helps us question those who are generally accepted because of their famous name or popular positions. In the 1800s, Ralph Waldo Emerson wrote in his book *Self-Reliance,* "Nothing is at last sacred but the integrity of your own mind." Watching whom we allow to influence it is an activity that lasts a lifetime.

Reflecting to Write

Personal Narrative

Keep a television **journal** for one week, recording everything you watch on television, even when you are surfing through the commercials during your favorite shows. Sometimes you stop and watch something interesting on CNN or the Food Network or Discovery for those few minutes. Record the name of the programs, the time you watched them, and your responses to them. Then write a paper **analyzing** your TV-watching patterns. Draw conclusions about when you watch television, why you watch it, and why you watch the programs you watch. This is a **process** paper based on your personal experiences.

Follow your normal television-watching pattern for one week. Then, using Susan Douglas's article as your model, determine which programs you like to watch best and why you like them. Write an **in-**

formative personal narrative explaining which characteristics of each show that you *absolutely will not miss* are important to you.

Informative

Interview several instructors or other older adults who read newspapers and/or magazines regularly. Ask them questions such as the kinds of periodicals they read, how often they read them, and why they read those as opposed to others of the same nature. You might also ask them about how much they feel influenced by the periodicals they read. After interviewing at least five different adults of different age groups, write a paper discussing the influence of written media on older adults. You might want to use **division** and **classification** as a primary pattern of development.

During election years, newspapers and newsmagazines lean toward one or more candidates running for office. The 2003 election of the governor of California is a prime example, especially in light of the numerous candidates for the position. In the 2004 presidential election, the media definitely took sides. Find several newsmagazines, *Newsweek, Time, U.S. News and World Report,* and others whose writers write about political topics. Examine whom they supported and how they did it in their writings. How did they attempt to convince their reading public to vote for their choices? Write an **informative analysis** of their approach to the election. Did they discuss the issues? Did they "sling mud" at the opponents? What was their style and is it effective for you as a reader?

One of the criticisms about programs like *ER* is that even though the writers and directors appear to be more liberal in their approach to strong women, the victims of accidents who die, or who are shot or injured severely and do not recover are women rather than men. Watch several episodes of *ER* or *NYPD Blue* re-runs and determine the ratio of male to female survivors on the programs. What does this say about the directors' feelings about women? Write an **informative** essay about your findings. Be sure to document the material you use.

Chapter 15

Health: How We Care for Ourselves

Regardless of how old or how young we are, health is a subject that concerns all of us. Usually, we don't even think about our health until something stops us—often because we don't have time to get sick. In a society that is so technologically and medically attuned to our bodies, our health should be better than it has ever been. Scientists have found the causes and cures of many diseases—not the common cold, but who's counting?—and are conducting research to find cures for cancer, Alzheimer's disease, diabetes, and other disabling conditions. Even if we can't or don't want to see a doctor for a minor but uncomfortable condition, we have access to pharmacies with free consultations that do not replace a doctor's advice, and aisles and aisles of over-the-counter drugs at reasonable prices. Although some individuals, including doctors, have turned to approved herbal medications and others have successfully used homeopathic treatments, hypertension, cancer, obesity, and mental health conditions are problems that require professional attention and the cooperation of the patient. All kinds of treatments—exercise, specialized diets, chemotherapy, surgery, special medications, and so forth—are usually available to us. However, we cannot extend our healthy state and our life span unless we take care of ourselves. And that is part of what this chapter is about—caring for ourselves with the knowledge and skills that we have.

The other part involves problems that occur in other countries that do not have the resources of First World nations. The World Health Organization oversees and monitors epidemics such as AIDS and SARS that plague countries around the world and disseminates information to other health organizations so they can keep the public aware and advised about possible spread and/or contamination. Without such organizations, many countries would not have the information they need to begin protecting their residents.

But information is not the only preventive medicine. Many countries are already in dire need of technical and medical aid to prevent disease and treat their ill citizens. They look to the United States and to other industrialized countries to help them care for their people. Not only are adults ill, but the more vulnerable of the population: children and elderly. But without aid from other countries, developing nations do not have the resources to help themselves. Even in the United States, many of our children and elderly do not have access to adequate nutrition, medical care, and drugs because of the cost and because they do not have insurance that will pay for their care.

Health is a complex issue that creates concern for local, state, and federal governments and agencies when budgets are already bursting with other demands. At least one article in this chapter discusses the need to help other countries help themselves, but many may ask what will happen to the sick and elderly in our own country? Thus, health is a political issue that involves us all. How we care for ourselves and for others is a major problem that all of us face daily.

You Can Lead a Man to Tofu, But Can You Make Him Eat It?

Carolyn Lamborn O'Neill

Many of us consider changing our eating habits around New Year's Day. Our resolution is to lose x number of pounds. Although we may begin with good intentions, many of us lose the resolve in our attempt, and we return to our old habits. In this article, found in the new magazine At Heart, *Carolyn Lamborn O'Neill does not tackle the task of weight loss; she is interested in being heart healthy. While that may lead to weight loss, it means changing one's way of eating for a lifetime. And as she discovers, change only comes from within.*

Prereading: Have you ever decided to go on a diet? How well did it work? Have you ever considered changing your eating habits completely for a lifetime instead?

Prewriting: Write down all you know about cholesterol, heart disease, heart attacks, salt, high blood pressure, and obesity without looking the terms up in a dictionary.

Vocabulary: Looking up and understanding the following words prior to reading should prepare you for the author's message. Other words will be defined in the margin.

tofu   cholesterol   soy

Today, a heart healthy diet isn't just about eating less fat and cholesterol. A diet high in soy, fiber, and fruits and vegetables may even reduce "bad" cholesterol. But can real people eat like this? The author experiments with her husband.

I've been married long enough—just about 2 months—to know that you can't make people change their lifestyle. Of course, that's unless they really want to. But, I also know that my husband's diet is far from heart healthy.

Both of us have normal cholesterol levels. But, heart disease runs in our families. So, we made a deal. We would both follow American Heart Association (AHA) diet guidelines for 1 week. At the week's end, my husband could decide for himself. Would he continue to eat healthy?

CAN YOU EAT YOUR WAY TO GOOD HEALTH?

A big part of eating well is what you *don't* eat. For healthy people with low risk of heart disease, the AHA recommends limiting:

- Total fat to < 30% of calories
- Saturated fat and trans fat (combined) to < 10% of calories
- Dietary cholesterol to < 300 mg
- Salt to < 1 teaspoon (2400 mg) per day

If you have high cholesterol and/or other problems that put you at risk for heart disease, you need to watch what you eat. For some people, diet and exercise may not be enough. Talk to your doctor about additional treatment options.

Saturated fats can raise levels of bad cholesterol in your blood. Trans fats can raise your cholesterol levels, too. Read food labels. Track how much fat, cholesterol, and salt you eat.

Good health is also about the kinds of food you *should* eat. Choose lower-fat options. For example, skim milk is better that whole-fat milk.

CHOLESTEROL: LESS IS MORE

Your body needs some cholesterol to function. But, too much is a major risk factor for heart disease.

Your body makes all the cholesterol it needs. That's why eating a lot of foods high in cholesterol can raise your levels. You may have high cholesterol and not know. Even if you eat well and exercise.

THE IMPORTANCE OF LIMITING SALT

Limit salt. This is especially true for people with high blood pressure. Salt causes the body to retain fluids. so, your heart has to work harder to pump blood through the body. This can be dangerous for your heart.

Examples of high-salt foods include some frozen dinners, processed deli meats, and canned soups. Salt content is listed on food labels. Track your daily intake.

Lean, skinless meats are better than fattier cuts. And, eat plenty of fruits and vegetables. All these foods are good choices.

STRATEGY FOR SUCCESS

Know how to eat well. It's the first step. But, a trip to the grocery store is definitely the second. My advice: give yourself plenty of time. Once you start reading labels, you'll see how quickly fat adds up. Butter? Eleven grams of fat, 8 mg of saturated fat, and 30 mg of cholesterol *per tablespoon*.

You'll also find a whole new world of foods. More grocery stores now carry tofu (soy protein). Also soy milk, soy cheese, and meat substitutes made from soy. These are all easy ways to include soy in your diet.

There are several butter-like spreads that even promise to lower cholesterol. These spreads are made with *plant sterols*. Plant sterols are found in fruits and vegetables. Look for these spreads in the butter and margarine section. (Warning: read labels carefully. Some margarines contain trans fats.)

You'll also need to rethink eating habits. Brown rice is a better choice than quick-cooking rice. Whole-grain bread is a rich source of fiber. (Hint: soft, white sandwich bread is *not*.)

WHOLE-GRAIN TOAST WITH PLANT-STEROL SPREAD ON THE SIDE, PLEASE.

My first strategy was substitution. Out went the whole milk and butter. In came low-fat cheese. Olive oil was the only fat left standing. (Canola oil is another good choice).

The spreads made with plant sterols were the easiest to adopt. OK. So they don't taste the same as butter. But, all the brands that I tried tasted fine with my whole-grain toast. Another easy switch was low-fat mayo.

I knew my greatest challenge would be getting my husband to eat soy protein. Instead of fighting the tofu battle, I bought soy "chicken" patties and "cheese" slices. (I removed both from their wrappers and stored them in plastic bags. I told him that they were soy *after* he had eaten them.)

EATING WELL IN THE REAL WORLD

So what did my husband decide after 7 days of eating healthy? Absolutely nothing. He had forgotten that we were following a more healthy diet. The fact is, food that is good for you tastes good, too. Whole-grain foods and fresh vegetables have a lot of flavor. Using fresh herbs instead of salt boosts the taste of food.

Soy chicken has become a favorite quick-fix dinner. But, I did not create a vegetarian husband in 7 days. Nor do I want to. We live in the real world. And, we still eat a real steak once in a while.

indulge: yield
to desires

Eating well is a way of life. It's not about a single meal. The AHA suggests you look at how you eat over time. This is more important than watching each bite you put in your mouth. The key is moderation. Indulge* from time to time. But, make it the exception, not the rule. It turns out even a true meat-and-potatoes man can live with that.

Reading for Meaning

1. What are possible sources of cholesterol?
2. List the things that can raise cholesterol levels in the blood.
3. Why did O'Neill and her husband decide to follow the AHA guidelines?

Reading Deeper

1. What did O'Neill discover two months after she had been married? Is this true only about eating healthy? Explain and give examples.
2. O'Neill explains that the key to eating well is moderation. What does she mean by this? How does she defend indulgence?

Reading for Writing

1. Although many individuals have decided to remove animal and animal products from their diets, there is quite a bit of controversy about

maintaining a vegetarian or a vegan diet. Examine the different arguments, including medical recommendations, concerning these kinds of diets, and ultimately, this way of life. Write an **informative** paper that **defines** vegetarian and vegan, describes the eating habits involved with each group, explains the benefits and drawbacks of each, and arrives at a conclusion about what you think of the beliefs and activities.

2. O'Neill talks about the problems that the overuse of salt can create in one's physical condition. According to her figures, we should not have more than one teaspoon of salt a day in our food. Visit your local grocery store and look at the dietary labels for the salt content in each of the following products:

   - Canned vegetables that are not labeled low sodium
   - Canned vegetables that are labeled low sodium
   - Canned meat such as Spam, chicken, and ham
   - Fully cooked hams
   - Country-cured hams
   - Canned soups not labeled low sodium
   - Canned fish, such as tuna, salmon, and sardines
   - Canned soups labeled low sodium
   - Packaged deli meats
   - Cheeses
   - Potato chips and corn chips
   - Salted nuts

   Write a **descriptive** essay discussing the use of salt in packaged foods and how it might affect our health.

Is Stress Making You Fat?

Meryl Davids Landau

In case you haven't noticed, stress occurs in everyday life. We work under deadlines, our children are sick, we have a test and a paper due on the same day, and the list goes on. Taken individually, they are things we can live with. In fact, many individuals believe that they work best under stress and that they get more accomplished when there are deadlines rather than when they have free time. When someone tells them to relax, they become more "stressed-out" because they don't have time to relax in their schedule. There are, however, major stress events in our lives, such as divorce, death of a parent or spouse, loss of a job, a move, and so forth. When those start adding up, we need to be aware of our health. In Meryl Davids Landau's article from Glamour *(2002), she explains that stress can not only be bad for your blood pressure, but it can also make you eat! Will putting on a few pounds make you feel even more stress to keep your weight down?*

Prereading: What things in your life are causing you stress? Have you noticed if you have gained any weight with the increased stress level you're under?

Prewriting: Do you work better when you have lots of time to complete projects or when you are under a tight deadline? How do you behave with those around you when you have to complete a project? Reflect on the last time you had a project due—whether at work or in class—and think about how you felt while you were completing it. Write a **descriptive** paragraph about how you reacted to the stress the project caused. Ask those close to you to characterize your behavior during that time. Do their opinions agree with how you remember your activities? Write a paragraph considering these questions about how you react to stress.

Vocabulary: Looking up and understanding the following words prior to reading should prepare you for the author's message. Other words will be defined in the margin.

rampages   obesity

There's a scientifically proven reason you munch like a madwoman when stress has you by the neck. *Glamour* has the latest news on how to stop.

It feels like a fact of life, almost too obvious to state: When you're stressed, you eat. Deadlines and crazy days beget vending-machine rampages and glazed-doughnut sprees. This we know. But here's the surprise: The problem probably isn't just your willpower—it's your hormones, too. New research shows that when you're under stress, your body is flooded with chemicals that can increase cravings. One recent study from Yale University in New Haven, Connecticut, found that women who had high levels of the stress hormone cortisol in their systems downed double the amount of sugar and fat as their peers.

Having your own orange-alert day? You're not alone: About 50 percent of American women report being stressed fairly often, with 28 percent feeling under the gun almost daily, according to a Roper ASW report. And 65 percent of Americans are now overweight, according to the Centers for Disease Control and Prevention in Atlanta. "It's no coincidence that obesity levels and stress rates are both up," says Jim

Manganiello, a psychologist in private practice in Charlottesville, Virginia. "The two are absolutely linked." *Glamour* consulted leading experts to find out how you can pull yourself out from the stress-fat quicksand.

*WHAT'S BEHIND YOUR CRAVINGS

squelching:
squashing,
silencing

The first step to squelching* your cravings, say experts, is understanding what scientists call your fight-or-flight response to stress. The moment you get anxious, whether because of a real threat (a bus is about to hit you) or simply anxiety (Will I get the job?), a chemical alarm triggers the release of cortisol and other hormones into your bloodstream. And even though the danger (real or imagined, your body can't tell the difference) may end suddenly, it can take hours for cortisol levels to return to normal. And the problem with that? High levels of cortisol can increase your appetite, says Elissa Epel, Ph.D., and assistant professor of psychiatry at the University of California at San Francisco.

"When cortisol levels are high, it's never a carrot stick that does it for you—you want Ben & Jerry's," says Pamela Peeke, M.D., an assistant professor of medicine at the University of Maryland School of Medicine in Baltimore and a leading expert in the study of stress and weight. That's because "sweet, fatty foods are calorie-dense and a good source of instant energy for the body," Epel explains. These cravings are your body's way of making sure you replace any calories you'd burn off while you're busy fighting—or fleeing—to protect yourself.

The problem, however, is that most of us aren't literally running for cover, so we're not burning off those extra calories that our bodies demand we eat. When 38-year-old technical writer Marcy Robb of Pittsburgh went back to work after taking seven weeks off for maternity leave, she constantly worried that her baby wouldn't fare well without her. As a result, "I was practically mainlining cheese Danishes from Au Bon Pain," Robb says. "They were so satisfying, but afterward, I'd feel let down. I realized that stress was making me eat, and that stressed me out more."

And get this: Muffins and Mallomars may even taste better to us when we're faced with difficult times, says Kelly Brownell, Ph.D., director of the Yale Center for Eating and Weight Disorders. Brownell's preliminary research shows that stress might actually enhance the flavor of sweet, fatty foods.

Wondering if you're someone who might experience cortisol spikes? The answer is simple, says Dr. Peeke. If you can't resist temptation on torturous days but can pass them by at other times, you're a stress eater and need to tame your cravings.

*WHERE DOES STRESS FAT GO?

vexing:
bothersome,
irritating,
annoying

Another of cortisol's more vexing* qualities is the way it conspires with the hormone insulin to promote fat storage in your stomach. When you're stressed, cortisol and insulin levels may rise. If they stay up for several hours, they can overstimulate an enzyme responsible for packing fat specifically into cells deep inside your abdomen, says George Chrousos, M.D., chief of the pediatric and reproductive endocrinology branch at the National Institutes of Health in Bethesda, Maryland, and a leading stress researcher.

Why, when you're stressed, is fat more likely to go to your middle than, say, to your thighs? Fat in the abdomen is easier to convert to instant energy than fat stored elsewhere—and instant energy is exactly what your stressed-out body, thrown into a state of "emergency" by hormones such as cortisol, believes it needs, says Dr. Chrousos. But remember, when the emergency doesn't require, say, scrambling out of the way of a bear, but exchanging e-mails with an angry boss, you don't burn off your ab fat. Hello, potbelly. . . .

And this belly fat carries health risks—so many that Dr. Peeke has dubbed it toxic weight. Carrying extra pounds around your abdomen has been linked to heart disease, hypertension, and type II diabetes. . . .

*IS STRESS EATING A "WOMAN THING"?

Although researchers aren't sure if cortisol affects women more than men, they do know that women struggle more with eating under stress, says Dr. Peeke. A recent University of Minnesota study of about 1,800 obese people confirmed that women feel much less confident about controlling their eating when under the gun than men do. Women are also heavily influenced by that four-letter word: diet. In a study of 62 normal-weight women last year by the University of British Columbia in Vancouver, those most preoccupied with limiting calories had cortisol levels that were 18 percent higher than those who were less calorie-obsessed. "If every time you're faced with food you think, Should I eat this? Should I order something light? What about dessert? You're hitting your body with stress, regardless of what you end up eating," explains study co-author Susan I. Barr, Ph.D. Instead, Barr suggests, choose what your body really craves and eat it with no regrets—even if it's two Mallomars. (Put those cookies on a plate, close the box and sit down to eat them; doing so will help keep you from downing the whole box, experts say.)

*YOUR STRESS-STOPPING OPTIONS

So what works to reduce stress eating? Exercise, researchers say—and not just because it burns calories. Any regular activity that gets your heart rate up (from walking to spinning class) will increase the production of "feel good" chemicals in your brain that can help reduce some of the detrimental* effects of cortisol spikes, says Shawn Talbott, Ph.D., author of *The Cortisol Connection*. Exercise can also help stop a cortisol surge—and reduce cravings—at the moment it hits. A quick run up the stairs may be all you need to help get rid of the excess cortisol, Talbott says.

detrimental: causing harm or injury

Besides exercise, there are some surprisingly simple ways to take a swipe at stress and the hormones that make you binge. For one, connect with your friends. Finnish researchers recently found that women who lack emotional support have a greater tendency to use food for coping. Mood-lifting, mind-body activities like yoga, massage and meditation are also important because they help stop stress signals from going to the brain, says Bruce S. Rabin, M.D., medical director of the University of Pittsburgh Medical Center Healthy Lifestyle Program. So can yukking it up and doing your best to be optimistic. Getting eight hours of sleep is also a key—cortisol levels can be higher when you don't get the shut-eye you need, Dr. Rabin says.

If you're struck by a cortisol-induced craving during the late afternoon (or the "corti-zone" time, as Dr. Peeke calls it, because this is the toughest time of the day for women to resist noshing), reach for a snack that has the sweetness you crave along with filling protein. Examples: a small container of yogurt topped with blueberries or strawberries, one-fourth cup hummus with carrot sticks, string cheese and a pear.

Even if life has you on a tension treadmill, you can choose to override cravings when you feel them about to strike. That's what Marcy Robb did. "I knew that trying to lose my post-pregnancy weight on top of being stressed about returning to work was just too much for me. So I joined Weight Watchers for help on how to choose healthier foods and squeeze exercise into my schedule," she says. Robb reports that she's now a steady 130 pounds, a healthy weight for her 5'5" frame.

maverick: independent-minded, refusing to go along or conform with rules

The good news is that while maverick* hormones may influence your appetite, whether you act on them is totally up to you. Think of it this way: Day in and day out, you're taking on challenges—angry-boss challenges, dating-world challenges, crazy-family challenges. If you can conquer these big tasks in life, then what's a little cookie got over you?

Reading for Meaning

1. What natural condition increases an individual's desire to eat when under stress? Explain.
2. Explain the fight-or-flight response to stress and how it helps to make some individuals fat.
3. Explain the function of sweets and fats in relation to the fight-or-flight response.
4. What are the risks of building up "belly fat"?
5. List the suggestions given to ease stress and hormones that might make us fat.

Reading Deeper

1. What is the relation of stress to obesity? Explain how stress and obesity are affecting Americans.
2. Even though many individuals crave sweets during times of stress, what options are suggested that are sweet but good for us?

Reading for Writing

1. Most people today are concerned with fitness and healthy eating; however, there are those of us who continue to snack on not-so-healthy food, given the opportunity. Look at your own eating habits and keep an eating journal in which you record the food, including snacks, you eat for a week. Be sure to record the time you eat and the activities you were doing while you were eating (watching TV, studying, typing a paper, and so forth). Write an **informative** paper that analyzes your eating habits and arrives at conclusions about whether or not stress makes you eat more than normal.
2. Consider how you handle stress. Make a list of all the stressful things in your life. Now, make a list of all the ways you deal with them. Are you successful? Write a **process** paper that describes how one can live a stressful life and still be able to cope with the problems and deadlines. Use examples from your own life to support your assertions.

THE LAST TIME I WORE A DRESS

Daphne Scholinski

When fashion dictates what we should look like and what we should wear, some are damaged by their refusal to adhere to the gender requirements. Although this article is not specifically about what one should and should not wear, Daphne Scholinski provides a personal narrative that reveals what being required to wear a dress did to her. By giving society the authority to determine what we should be based on our gender, some individuals automatically take away our right to make decisions about our choices. In other words, when we "choose" to wear what fashion "experts" tell us to wear, we have allowed them the authority to control what we think and believe about ourselves. Scholinski's book The Last Time I Wore a Dress *(1997), gives details about her treatment for Gender Identity Disorder for which she was treated because she failed to comply with the strictly enforced gender roles society enforces.*

Prereading: Consider your own wardrobe. How many "designer" labels do you have? Did you buy them because they fit better than other brands or because of peer or other pressure?

Prewriting: In the past, there was a traditional routine for little girls' clothing. They were identified from birth by the use of pink blankets and distinguished from boys in their blue blankets. Little girls then wore other identifying markers: dresses, jewelry, ribbons and bows, and so forth. Many mothers have become less concerned about this tradition and have moved away from gender identifying clothing. In a paragraph, state your position on the tradition and explain your thoughts.

Vocabulary: Looking up and understanding the following words prior to reading should prepare you for the author's message. Other words will be defined in the margin.

superficial   scrutinize   femininity   diagnosis

Room 304 was pale white. Bed A, my bed, had white nubby polyester sheets and a white blanket. A nurse with keys jangling on her belt wore floor-gripping white shoes and a white coat like a doctor. I told her I didn't need to be here. "Uh-huh," she said. I told her my parents were divorced and my sister needed me at home very much and my father had a lot of problems. My mother, too. She said, "Hold out your arm."

"No needles," I said, and she said, "Just a pulse." She grabbed my wrist with unnecessary force and wrote my pulse in my chart on a clipboard. Same with my temperature. I could see she was going to write down everything so I told her my boyfriend was killed by the police on his birthday and died in my arms, blood everywhere, but there was nothing I could do to save him.

"Oh really?" she said. She looked at me with concern. I said, "Yeah," and shrugged as if it were no big deal.

Later, through the door at the nurses' station that split—top-half open, bottom-half closed—I told her, "When I get out of here, I'm going to be a rock musician. It's all set up. I've got a contract."

"Oh really?" she said.

I mentioned that I was lucky to be alive considering that when I was twelve a car hit me and broke both my legs and my right arm, fractured my pelvis and my skull and I had to lie in traction.

"Oh?" she said.

When my mother visited, she told the nurses I had an active imagination.

Lies: I told them for the flash of concern on the nurse's face, the look of interest. What I really meant, what I wanted to say, I couldn't find the words for.

My second day in I met my psychiatrist, Dr. Browning. We were supposed to meet at 10 A.M. but 10 A.M. came and went and he breezed onto the unit in his white coat and black shoes at 10:25, no explanation, never mind an apology. It was understood that I was free all the time and that whenever he cared to arrive I'd sit in a room and tell him my deepest feelings. So we did not get off to a good start and I was not inclined to like doctors in the first place, since they acted superior. When I grew bolder, I delivered the greeting a lot of patients gave their doctors: "Well, if it isn't Dr. Sigmund Fraud."

On the hallway, one side was double rooms, the other side was singles and some of these had been left mostly bare so they could be offices. We entered one. Two chairs with cushions on the back beside a coffee table; I think it was old furniture from the lounge.

Dr. Browning had wire-rimmed glasses which made his dark eyes look bigger than they were. I looked at his eyes but he did not look at mine; if he caught my glance, he turned away and I knew that to him I was a specimen, a thing he was studying.

We sat down. He crossed his left knee over his right and adjusted his yellow legal pad so it balanced on his left thigh. All settled in, he asked, "Do you know why you're here, Daphne?"

Why should I make it easy for him? Besides, I wanted to hear him explain me to me, "No." He started in about my problems at school, cutting class, miserable grades, threatening a teacher. He said I was failing school and a thought popped up, How come no one ever says school is failing me? I didn't say this. He continued peering at me through his wire-rimmed glasses. I had a problem with authority figures, he said, and I thought, Okay, this is cool, I can admit to this. I said, Yeah, yeah, I know.

He asked me about problems at home and I told him my father hit me, my mother doesn't want me around, and he scribbled away, flipping up pages as he went. We moved along to drugs and alcohol and I exaggerated my use because doctors always like to hear about youth and drugs.

His pen paused in its scratching and I thought I could throw him a question for a change. I asked him what my diagnosis was. I knew this was a major deal; it was like being a Disciple or a Latin King; it was your identity in the hospital; when the doctor looked at you, he didn't see you, he saw *paranoid* or *schizophrenic*.

Dr. Browning said I had a multiple diagnosis because of the complexity of my situation. I liked the sound of that: the complexity of my situation. One of the diagnoses was Conduct Disorder, which made sense to me, I've never been one to lie about my bad behavior. He said another diagnosis was Mixed Substance Abuse, which I knew to be a stretch of the truth but what did I care if he thought I had a drug problem.

He rolled his pen between his fingers for a moment. He said the other diagnosis was something called Gender Identity Disorder, which he said I'd had since Grade 3, according to my records. He said what this means is you are not an appropriate female, you don't act the way a female is supposed to act.

I looked at him. I didn't mind being called a delinquent, a truant, a hard kid who smoked and drank and ran around with a knife in her sock. But I didn't want to be called something I wasn't. Gender screw-up or whatever wasn't cool. My foot started to jiggle, I couldn't stop it. He was calling me a freak, not normal. He was like the boys in Little League calling out tomboy, tomboy, and Michelle who pinned me down for the red lipstick treatment. He was like the boys who yelled, *Let me see your titties,* when I rode shirtless on my bike in the wind.

Actually, Dr. Browning was worse. He had an official name for me.

He was saying that every mean thing that had happened to me was my fault because I had this gender thing. I knew I walked tough and sat with my legs apart and did not defer to men and boys, but I was a girl in the only way I knew how to be one.

He clicked his pen and slipped it in the pocket of his white coat. I knew the matter was settled, that nothing would make him change his mind. Anything I said now would be written in my chart as *defensive behavior.*

Michael Reese Hospital & Medical Center
Date: 9/11 Fellow's Admission Note

1st psychiatric admission for this 14½ year old SWF brought by both parents after referral from outside MHC. History obtained from parents, patient, past evaluation records. Presenting Problems include:

1. Violent Behavior @ home and a pattern of abusive behavior towards authority figures.
2. Multiple drug use.
3. School failure and multiple school suspensions and expulsion from a Chicago High School.
4. Family problems, parents separated and unable to establish secure, consistent provision of home for child.

History is very long and complicated and the problems which led to hospitalization basically began 3 yrs ago, with parents' separation. Since then there has been an escalation of pt's behavioral acting out with the above problems becoming evident. During past year there have been two episodes of violent behavior in mother's home, school failure and a problem of shoplifting and petty stealing. Heavy use of multiple drugs is noted by both parents and admitted by patient.

Past history of development milestones is unremarkable. A Gender Identity Disorder has been present since Grade 3. The patient has been in various treatments since Grade 3 as well. There is no family history of psychiatric illness.

No major medical problems are noted.

Mental Status: frightened, anxious young woman appearing her stated age, who although dressed as a tomboy was sexually provocative.

No thought disorder noted.

Rate, rhythm, conduct of speech, normal.

Affect depressed, frightened, consistent with conduct of thought.

Impression: Patient's behavior has been out of control for some time now and parents have been unable to establish limit setting. There are severe psycho social stressors with parents' separation and apparent emotional abandonment of child. She seems to be an unhappy, frightened girl who has a great deal of secondary depressive affect, primitive rage, a permissive superego and grandiose expectations. I like her, however, and she had several strengths.

Initial diagnosis:

1. Conduct disorder, Socialized, Unaggressive vs. Identity Disorder (Borderline Disorder of Childhood)
2. Gender Identity Disorder
3. Mixed Substance Abuse.

Initial Treatment Plan filled out.

————, M.D.

Time turned solid, like a wall. Who knew what time it was? I never saw a patient wearing a watch. One clock was at the nurses' station, to keep track of shifts, the other was in the lounge so we'd know when our tv shows were coming on. Afternoons we watched *All My Children, One Life to Live, General Hospital,* one soap opera slopped into the next. We'd turn the channel if the news appeared; we never saw newspapers. The first term of the Reagan administration passed while I was locked up. The only thing I knew about Reagan was that his economic plan was to blame if we ran out of Styrofoam cups or if we didn't have enough staff to do an activity.

Outside, time mattered. Inside we didn't want to know how much time was passing us by. We knew it was going slowly, but it was going. In seclusion, especially, time was a wall that closed in; we scratched at it with a plastic spoon.

On 3 East and West, the older people were the scariest; they were us if we weren't careful. We called Margaret "the incredible shrinking woman" because her wheelchair swallowed her up. Someone walking by would say, "My, Margaret, you're looking smaller today," and she'd raise her head and scowl. We'd have these one-way conversations with her. She'd pee and shit in her chair and when an attendant came to clean her, she'd let loose with "No contact! No contact!" She sat in her shit for hours. The smell was subtle at first. We'd sniff and think, what's that smell? It grew stronger until it gagged you. She was the oldest, so she was entitled.

Daytime the older ones parked in front of the television; you could walk right up and turn the channel and no one would make a peep.

Even the younger ones looked old, if they had the big-time diagnosis: paranoid schizophrenia or manic depression. Pacing and screaming, they'd worn themselves out.

Bob was twenty-two and busy. He paced the halls so hard his tee shirt had sweat-rings under the arms.

"Hi, Bob," I said.

"I am Jesus," he said. "I know it's hard to believe, but I am Jesus."

A couple of times I paced with him, down the long corridor and back, for exercise. As we turned the corner he asked, "Have you accepted me as your savior?" He wasn't mean about it. Just curious.

I wanted to help him. I was always this way, helping my friends. I thought of myself as a roving counselor. It kept people a nice distance away from my problems. Being in the mental hospital was a boon for my counseling skills, although after a while I got confused. For instance, the more I talked to Jesus, the more I liked him, and the less crazy he seemed. Zealous, but not dangerous. I could imagine him in the outside world, preaching. He'd probably help some people.

This posed an interesting dilemma: If I thought he was sane, what did that make me? Mental hospitals are rife with this kind of debate. Are people like Bob simply more sensitive than the rest of us? Bombarded with information, the delusional find it hard to function in the world, but is that their fault or the world's? The staff discouraged this sort of questioning. They liked the line between sane and insane to be perfectly clear.

"I used to hear voices," I told Jesus. This wasn't true, but I didn't want him to feel alone. Plus, I wanted to fit in. "I've come to realize they have no power over me. They're just voices, Bob."

"Hmm," he said, considering this. He wasn't convinced but my interest made us friends. He told me his visions—what he and John the Baptist had been up to. Listening to him was like going to the movies, without the pictures; it was a great distraction. He said the twelve apostles were in the area. I asked, "So have they gotten in touch with you?" and he said he hadn't heard from them in a while but they had a plan. They were going to have a reunion at a bar on Rush Street in Chicago.

Bob took anti-psychotic meds mixed with orange juice in a tiny, plastic cup. He let me have a sip but it tasted gross.

The other famous person in the unit was Jimi. I asked him, "What's your name?" and he said, "Jimi." That's all I knew about him for a while. Another patient told me that it was Jimi as in Jimi Hendrix. He was white, twenty-five years old, with a wispy brown mustache. I didn't like him as much as Jesus, maybe because I took music more seriously than religion. In music therapy, Jimi was confronted with a guitar. He picked it up and strummed a few lame notes, his eyes closed, his fingers fluttering.

"Don't you know you're dead?" I asked him.

"Am not," he said. He cocked his head and listened to music that was entirely different from the noise we heard.

Jimi could seem totally normal. We'd be in the lounge having a regular conversation about the nurses and he'd say, This is just like what happened at one of my concerts. And I'd think, What? And then, Whoa.

None of the crazy people knew they were insane. I'd sit around thinking, I am so sane in comparison to these folks, and then a flicker of a thought would reach my brain. Maybe I don't know I'm insane. They don't know they're insane, so why should I know? Maybe I don't realize I'm walking around saying I'm Patsy Cline.

At this point I liked to go to my room, turn on my cassette player and listen to music so loud I'd max out the volume and make the machine vibrate.

Choosing our meals for the next day became a time-consuming activity. We sat on the cushy seats in the lounge and studied the piece of folded white paper that came up from the cafeteria. The words on the menu were fuzzy, as if they'd been typed on a very old typewriter, and next to each word—French toast, Jell-O, meatloaf—was a dash for us to check off.

The anorexics, Julie and Lisa, spent at least an hour huddling over their menus, adding up the calories. Snooty—that was Julie, with her cheekbones sticking out. If she liked you, she gave you a glossy black-and-white photo of her face with her name on the bottom—her modeling headshot. Fifteen, with her nose in *Cosmopolitan*. Pen in hand, she filled out the *Cosmo* questionnaires diligently. *Your romance I.Q.* If she licked a stamp, she counted the glue in her required daily calorie intake.

Lisa spoke with a British accent, I don't know where she was from, but it was a real accent. Instead of saying butt, she said bum. She pulled at her thighs—there was nothing there but bones. She said, "Yuck." I thought, If you get any thinner, when I exhale I'm going to blow you across the room. In front of the nurse she said, "I'm going to have to put on some weight." Actors, all of us. When we horsed around, sat on each other's laps in the lounge, Lisa's tailbone was like a dagger.

With lunch or dinner we could order one can of soda. Every once in a while, I'd order two cans of Mountain Dew, and sometimes they'd appear on my tray when the nurse pulled it out of the metal rack. I imagined a worker down in the kitchen saying, Oh, okay.

I never drank my soda. By the time the staff at Michael Reese ordered me transferred to another hospital, I must have had two hundred cans of it in my bathroom cabinet. Stacked-up cans in neat rows, it was comforting to look at them. I'd use the soda to trade for a deck of cards, or cigarettes. I'd keep track of inventory. I'd think, I'm running low on Tab and I know Julie likes Tab and someone brought her a box of candy, which she'll never eat, so I'll order up a Tab and trade.

When the hospital transferred me out, the staff never gave me my soda. I spent a long time collecting that soda and I could have taken it to the next hospital and used it for leverage.

When we were bored, somebody might go up to the nurse's station and ask for the green volume of the *Diagnostic and Statistical Manual of Mental Disorders,* third edition. The nurse would hand it through the split door—she didn't care if you borrowed it. Somebody would page through it on the couch and a couple of us would come around, just the younger patients, and ask, "Hey, would you look up paranoid schizophrenic?" The person holding the book would look that up and we'd read from the manual. Then we'd flip to the last entry in the book, zoophilia. Sex with animals, *ha ha.* Someone would ask, "What are you here for?" We looked up anorexia for Julie and Lisa. Manic depression?

Borderline personality? Obsessive-compulsive? I didn't tell anyone about my gender thing. I said I was in for Conduct Disorder.

We placed bets that we could get a new diagnosis added on. No money, just a dare.

Danny was a Disciples gang member but from a different part of Chicago, so I'd never known him. His voice was pure. Handsome, the only black teenage boy on the unit. He sang "Precious Blood" and then slid into a Luther Vandross number. In the hallway, he taught us how to break-dance; on the linoleum, we spun around on our butts—our bums, as Lisa put it. Out-of-control behavior was what Danny was in for—or maybe his parents just wanted him out of the gang. He always seemed fine to me.

He bet he could get hallucinations written on his chart. This was tricky. It had to be convincing, so he started out small. "Did you hear that?" he asked, and we shook our heads, no.

Heather was the rich girl on the unit, tight Guess jeans and a pink Izod polo shirt. Super bratty. Baby fat in her cheeks, blond hair she sucked in her mouth. I don't know why she was in, I guess her parents couldn't handle her or maybe she'd tried suicide. Her first day on the unit, her old boyfriend brought her a stuffed brown bull with white horns and a black nose. Big animal, three feet high, a couple of feet long, a foot wide. The next morning I snuck into her room and threw the bull on her bed where she was sleeping. She roared out of the room saying, "Who did this?" I was back in my room, la, la, la, all innocent. The housekeeper told on me. After a while Heather throught it was funny so we were best friends.

She looked the way my doctors wanted me to look, smooth and girly. I asked my father and his girlfriend to send me Izod shirts and button-down collars, like hers. Mostly I wore jeans and tee shirts that said Led Zeppelin or Pink Floyd, nice and ratty.

"Why do you wear clothes like that?" Columbia, the attendant, asked me.

Even in her white nurse pants, Columbia looked hip. "It's such a shame," she said. "You could fix yourself up to look pretty."

Everything she said made me feel ugly. I said, "Whatever."

Heather decided to go for split personalities. She had a role model in Anne, who lived downstairs where security was higher. Anne was a legend. First thing on the unit, you heard this muffled screaming from downstairs: that was Anne. She had eight personalities. Columbia said Anne had attacked an attendant, hurt him, and she'd attacked patients, too, with her bare hands. Anne's screaming grew loud like the 'L' train rumbling by when we took the elevator down to the activities room. When Danny pinched Heather's butt in the elevator, Columbia said, "You don't want to go live with Anne, do you?" She wasn't kidding.

Heather figured split personalities was a snap. One second she was her usual spoiled, be-bop self, demanding, "Give me my diet Sprite," and the next—after a few transitional moments—she was a mewling three-year-old with her thumb in her mouth.

I bet I could get anorexia written on my chart. The anorexics were psyched. The more anorexics, the better—the less attention anyone would be paying to what they weren't eating.

First thing to do to fake anorexia was to stand at dinner, one foot jiggling. I knew this from Julie and Lisa. We ate, and jiggled, and talked about the negative calories in chewing lettuce. They told me how many calories were in each forkful of broccoli.

I arranged my face in an expression of fascination. "Really?" I said.

I watched what food Julie and Lisa left behind on their plates and tried to leave a little bit more.

"Did you hear that?" Danny asked. He ran up to a nurse's aide. "Did you hear that?" He ran into his room and huddled on his bed, like he was really scared.

Heather put her thumb in her mouth. "Mommy," she said. The nurse's aide gave her a glance.

In therapy, Dr. Browning asked me, "Are you not feeling well?"

I said, "I think I'm fat." And I knew *tendencies toward anorexia* had made it onto my chart.

Danny quit the hallucinations after a while. You didn't want to go too far with that, or you'd end up swallowing a cupful of medication that might be more than you'd bargained for.

Heather grew tired of being a three-year-old. She shifted out of being three gradually, so the nurses would be on edge, waiting for the other personality to come back.

Even if we'd looked up Gender Identity Disorder, I don't think anyone would have tried to fake it. We knew the rules: pacing, screaming, hallucinating and vomiting were okay. Not okay was walking around with a scarf in your hair, for a boy, or being like me, a girl who never felt comfortable in a dress.

Reading for Meaning

1. Since Scholinski is being told that she is hospitalized for various reasons, including drug and alcohol use, what is the point of the title? Why does she start her essay talking about makeup and feminine characteristics?

2. Scholinski was diagnosed with "Conduct Disorder" and "Mixed Substance Abuse." She didn't mind being called a "delinquent, truant, a hard kid who smoked and drank and ran around with a knife in her

sock." To her, these characteristics are "normal." Not being normal is being a "gender screwup . . . a freak, not normal." Based on her beliefs about her conditions, what can we say about what society is telling us? Explain.

Reading for Deeper Meaning

1. When Scholinski says, "This is how I learned what it means to be a woman," is she talking only about wearing makeup? What else could she be referring to?
2. Define femininity according to the characteristics Scholinski gives. Do you agree with them? Explain.
3. Scholiniski tells us that her treatment cost one million dollars. What was she being treated for?

Reading to Write

1. Consider your choice of attire. You might be a person who likes to dress up or you might be someone who would rather not have to wear heels and "feminine" clothing if you're a woman or a suit and tie if you're a man. Write a **descriptive, personal narrative** about growing up and being told what you must wear because of your gender. Include how you felt, where you were going, what you ended up wearing, and how you feel about dress now that you are able to choose your own clothes.
2. Today's styles have become much more unisex in their approach. Women and men both wear Dockers, jeans, "sweats," and other casual apparel. On the other hand, when dressing for a big event, such as your parents' anniversary party, a New Year's Eve party at an expensive hotel, a bar mitzvah, and so forth, men and women have to observe the appropriate dress code. Write a **process analysis** paper giving directions to a young man or woman who is uncomfortable dressing up about how to dress for a "big event" and how to dress for an evening with his or her friends.

SWEET, ELUSIVE SLEEP

Karen Springen and Pat Wingert

How well and how long do you sleep at night? Insomnia, the inability to sleep, keeps many people up for various reasons. This affects their physical, mental, and emotional health, making them unable to process information efficiently, irritable, and frequently paranoid. Numerous studies have been conducted on people's sleeping patterns and on dreams. In the following article (News-week, Aug. 9, 2004), Karen Springen and Pat Wingert discuss an increasingly recurring problem in today's society: sleep disorders and dreams.

Prereading: Think about how well you sleep in general and how well you slept last night. Do you normally wake up refreshed or are you reluctant to begin the day? Does the amount of sleep you get affect your ability to function?

Prewriting: Think about the most vivid dreams you've had and write a **descriptive** passage about one or two of them. Were they happy dreams or unpleasant ones?

Vocabulary: Looking up and understanding the following words prior to reading should prepare you for the author's message. Other words will be defined in the margin.

REM sleep   insomnia   dreams   sleep deprivation
sleep disorders   anxiety   depression   limbic system

You toss, you turn, you worry. What happens when insomnia disrupts your night—and your dreams.

Earlier this summer, Mike Trevino, 29, slept nine hours in nine days in his quest to win a 3,000-mile, cross-country bike race. For the first 38 hours and 646 miles, he skipped sleep entirely. Later he napped—with no dreams he can remember—for no more than 90 minutes a night. Soon he began to imagine that his support crew was part of a bomb plot. "It was almost like riding in a movie. I thought it was a complex dream, even though I was conscious," says Trevino, who finished second.

Trevino's case may be extreme, but it raises important questions: If we don't sleep (or sleep enough), what happens to our dreams? And if we don't dream, what happens to us? These are not purely academic or *existential:* based on experience *existential* questions. Nearly 40 percent of Americans report getting fewer than seven hours sleep on weekdays and nearly 60 percent say they experience some kind of insomnia at least several nights a week, according to a National Sleep Foundation poll. "Sleep may be essential for life," says Jerry Siegel, a neuroscientist at UCLA's Center for Sleep *optimum:* the greatest degree attainable under specified conditions Research. "It's certainly essential for optimum* brain function."

For those of us who are stressed, anxious and working too hard, insomnia only makes things worse. When our worries wake us in the middle of a REM cycle, issues that might have been resolved through dreams are left hanging. Dreams tend to get more positive as the night wears on, and waking up too soon interrupts this process. "People who are sleep deprived are often irritable," says Rosalind Cartwright, chairman of psychology at Rush University Medical Center in Chicago. "They haven't worked through the bad feelings."

Clincial depression interferes with healthy sleeping—and dreaming. In a study published this month, Eric Nofzinger and his colleagues at the University of Pittsburgh found that depressed dreamers crank up their limbic systems more than other dreamers. "The brain of depressed dreamers doesn't shut off," he says. "It keeps ruminating* about things, which makes it hard for the person to get to sleep—or if they do, it wakes them up in the middle of the night to work on all the problems they have."

ruminating: going over in the mind repeatedly, casually or slowly

Rats eventually die when they don't get any REM sleep. Humans don't. Yet the drive to dream is relentless. Some studies have shown that when humans are deprived of REM, they begin to have vivid, REM-like dreams during their non-REM phases. After days of not sleeping, people begin to do something like dreaming while awake, as Trevino's experience shows, says Cartwright.

bank: deposit, save

You can't bank* sleep or REM either—although the body seems eager to try. When people who are sleep deprived finally do hit the pillow, they have what scientists call "rebound REM": extra-long REM cycles, which can lead to hypervivid dreams and even nightmares, says UCLA's Siegel. "The REM sleep during the rebound is more intense psychologically."

If you know you have trouble sleeping, here's what to do: Find out if you have a physical problem such as sleep apnea (which interrupts breathing during sleep). If you're physically fine, go to bed and get up at a regular time every day, stay away from caffeine and alcohol before bedtime, develop sleep rituals and avoid bright lights in the bedroom. Good sleep produces good dreams. "You'll work better, feel sharper, actually be more creative," says Cartwright. No wonder they say that dreams are sweet.

Reading for Meaning

1. What happens to rats when they are deprived of REM sleep? Does that happen to human beings?
2. What is a "'rebound REM'"? Explain.

Reading for Deeper Meaning

1. Explain what the authors mean by "Good sleep produces good dreams."
2. How are people suffering from depression and sleep-deprived individuals similar? List two ways.

Reading for Writing

1. Keep a dream diary for a week. Even though you might think you don't dream or that you forget your dreams when you wake up, make a serious effort to remember them. After one week of recording your dreams, read them and determine if the assertion, "Good sleep produces good dreams" is true for you or not. Explain in a **descriptive** and **cause-and-effect** paragraph.

2. Some people claim to be "a morning person" while others claim vigorously that they are not. Determine when you function best and what this means in relation to your sleep pattern. Write a **descriptive personal narrative** explaining what kind of person you are and what happens when your pattern is disrupted.

THE KEYS TO CAREGIVING

Julie Scelfo

Since the late President Reagan was diagnosed with Alzheimer's disease, more and more attention has been given to finding a cure for it and developing drugs that can reverse or slow its progress. In the following article, however, Julie Scelfo looks at the often forgotten person in this disease: the caregiver who spends endless hours, days, and even years taking care of a loved one. Scelfo also provides easy suggestions to caregivers to help them care for themselves.

Prereading: Do you or does someone you know care for an adult who needs constant supervision and attention? Think about the time dedicated to working with such a dependent person. How much time does the caretaker devote to matters other than caring for the dependent person?

Prewriting: Write a paragraph describing your understanding of what being a caregiver entails.

Vocabulary: Looking up and understanding the following words prior to reading should prepare you for the author's message. Other words will be defined in the margin.

Alzheimer's disease   immune system   AARP   respite

O ut of guilt, loyalty and love, the Helpers often neglect to help themselves.

More than 20 million Americans are now hitched to a routine as relentless as tending to a newborn. Caregivers experience interrupted sleep, restricted liberty and emotional strain. New research indicates that caregiving can lead to negative health effects, including depression, a weakened immune system, even premature death. Common sense dictates that caregivers should give themselves breaks, but often, motivated by a mix of love, guilt, loyalty and tenacity, they don't do what's good for them. Here, some guidelines to avoid total burnout.

Ask for help. Caregivers are often overprotective of their loved ones and refuse to allow other people to provide relief. "Carry around a list," says Bonnie Lawrence of the Family Caregiver Alliance, so when friends and family ask, "How can I help?" you can respond with specific requests: mow the lawn, go to the grocery store, pick up a prescription. Don't be shy about asking a friend to sit with your mother for an hour just to give you time to make dinner. Enlist a social worker to help you navigate the confusing array of long-term-care options. *To find local assistance, see* eldercare.gov *or call Eldercare Locator at 800-677-1116.*

Get support. Caregiver-support groups and online bulletin boards can help answer questions and relieve social isolation. AOL offers a live "Caregivers Corner" chat—an especially good resource for people who wake at odd hours or can't leave home. Ask your local chapter of the Alzheimer's Association (800-273-3900 or www.alz.org) to pair you up with another caregiver for social outings with your charges. *For bulletin boards and support-group information, call or e-mail the Family Caregiver Alliance (800-445-8106;* caregiverhelp@caregiver.org*). Check out chat groups and message boards on* AOL.com.

Change your habits. Instead of getting frustrated, adapt. "You have to have a new definition of what's normal," says AARP's Elinor Ginzler. "If they're sleeping from 2 until 4 in the afternoon, you should nap then, too." Play games the ailing person used to enjoy—backgammon, bridge—but with no winning or losing. If getting dressed provokes issues of pride or power struggles, replace zipper-and button-close pants with elastic or Velcro waistbands. *For more ideas, see* AARP.org/life.

Take a break. Find opportunities to give yourself time off. If there's one 30-minute TV show that holds Dad's attention, use that time to sit alone on the porch. Take advantage of adult day-care centers (which provide medical supervision) to catch dinner and a movie with friends. Hire respite care-professionals who come to your home so you can leave for a few hours. In San Francisco, the Family Caregiver Alliance holds a weekend camp for people with Alzheimer's. The patients enjoy scheduled activities, and you'll get to relax, knowing they're receiving one-on-one care. *Contact Eldercare for adult day-care and adult* *day-health-center referrals, or Family Caregiver Alliance for respite-care and weekend-camp information.*

Reading for Expectations

1. What symptoms can caregivers suffer from?
2. What reasons do many caregivers give for not wanting to let others take care of the dependent person? Do you know others? List them.

Reading for Meaning

1. Why does Scelfo provide phone numbers and URLs in this article?
2. How can an online chat group help a caregiver? Why can this be preferable to talking with family members who know the ailing person?

Reading for Writing

1. Offer to serve as a caregiver for a friend or relative for one hour a week for two weeks. After each session, write a **descriptive** paper including how you felt for that hour to reflect your responses to caregiving. Try to choose a time when the person you will care for is not sleeping or watching television. Make it an active caregiving session.
2. Complete some research on Alzheimer's disease and write a short **informative, expository** paper with documentation that tells the symptoms, progress, and needs of Alzheimer's patients.

WHERE LIVING IS LETHAL

Geoffrey Cowley and Karen Springen

The United States is known as an industrialized country, and, as such, we are among the wealthiest countries in the world. Because of this, we have state-of-the-art medical technology; however, we still have children dying because of inability to access the health-care system. Consider the problems of individuals, children especially, who live in nonindustrialized countries whose social services are dependent on the generosity of other countries for their care. In this article from Newsweek *(Sept. 22, 2003), Geoffrey Cowley and Karen Springen investigate the difficulties that children in "poor countries" have to live with and reveal the number of deaths that occur simply because of a lack of inexpensive vaccines.*

Prereading: Consider what your life might be like if you did not have access to your doctor when you need him or her.

Prewriting: In 2004, the supplies of flu vaccine became quite low or they were not available at all. There were also times when it was rationed out only to special populations. Write a paragraph considering what life might be like here without availability of drugs such as antibiotics, vaccines, or other life-saving medications.

Vocabulary: Looking up and understanding the following words prior to reading should prepare you for the author's message. Other words will be defined in the margin.

moribund   neonatal   vermin   contaminated   vulnerable   UNICEF

To experience childhood as Americans knew it a century ago, you don't have to travel very far. Just 700 miles from Miami, on Haiti's desolate Central Plateau, obesity and food allergies and attention deficit disorder are unheard of. In this part of the world, a healthy child is one who escapes death from tetanus or tuberculosis—someone like 14-year-old Moula. When the boy's family carried him to Dr. Paul Farmer's frontier clinic in the village of Cange two years ago, he had a raging fever and a ballooning abscess on his back. Farmer's team saved his life by treating the TB and other infections that were devouring his spine. But they couldn't restore life to his legs—and they knew he wouldn't survive in his mountaintop settlement without them. So Moula lives in the clinic now. He wheels around behind the *auxiliary** nurses, coaxing moribund children to hang on, and he seems to feel he's the luckiest guy alive. When I met him last March, he had just been given a new wheelchair. His smile could have lit an office building.

auxiliary: extra, support

In a sense, Moula *is* lucky. Kids like him still die in *droves** in Haiti—and Angola and Afghanistan and Bolivia and dozens of other poor countries. Worldwide, nearly 11 million children perish before their 5th birthdays every year. They don't die because science has yet to find treatments for their conditions. Most die for lack of clean water, adequate nutrition and the most basic medical necessities—skilled birth attendants, 50-cent vaccines, antibiotics that were developed eight decades ago. "We know what to do," says Dr. Robert Black of Johns Hopkins University's Bloomberg School of Public Health. "We have interventions that are proven. What we haven't done is commit the resources needed to deliver them."

droves: large masses

Children's lot is clearly improving by many measures. The overall death rate for kids younger than 5 has dropped by 30 percent since 1980.

Some countries (Cuba, Brazil, Bangladesh) have made even greater strides. And bold initiatives by Bill Gates and other philanthropists have helped create a new sense of urgency and possibility. But obscene *disparities:* disparities* persist. Kids born in South Asia and sub-Saharan Africa still die at differences 20 to 30 times the rate of kids in the industrialized world. In fact 90 percent of the world's childhood deaths—roughly 9.7 million a year—now occur in 42 developing countries. And 99 percent of the victims are poor.

What exactly is killing all these kids? Birth complications and neonatal infections are the biggest scourges, together killing 3.2 million children in the 42 hardest-hit countries each year. Diarrhea and pneumonia claim an additional 2.1 million lives each, followed by malaria, AIDS and measles. But none of these conditions kills at random. In a sense, everyone of them is a symptom of poverty. Poor kids, wherever they live, encounter more than their share of health hazards—more crowding, more vermin, more contaminated water—and inadequate diets leave them doubly vulnerable to whatever hazards they confront. "More than half of the deaths in children can be attributed to under-nutrition alone," says Black. "What finally kills the child may be pneumonia, but if the child were well nourished, he never would have developed it in the first place." The final blow is a lack of adequate health services. Kids in poor countries are not only more exposed and more susceptible to disease. Once sick, they often go untreated.

dynamic: immense energy or force

This dynamic* plays out incessantly in the hills of central Haiti. Farmer started his clinic there in the mid-1980s, while studying medicine and anthropology at Harvard. His patients were landless peasants who'd been forced off their farms and onto the barren hillsides by a U.S.-sponsored hydroelectric-dam project. Thanks to his vision, tenacity* and fund-raising acumen*, the Clinique bon Saveur is now a thriving community center with a school and a 104-bed hospital. Partners in Health, the relief group he founded with Harvard in 1987, now operates in seven countries. Traversing* the shaded grounds at dawn, Farmer is mobbed by supplicants* who have walked for days to get there and camped on the pavement once they arrive. "Feel my stomach," they plead. "Can you fix my hands?" "Please, look at my baby."

tenacity: stubbornness

acumen: ability to grasp and comprehend combined with keen practical judgment

traversing: crossing

supplicants: people who ask humbly

The medical staff works 16-hour days to avoid turning anyone away, and it has achieved astounding results. In the region served by Zanmi Lasante (Creole for Partners in Health), infant mortality now stands at one third Haiti's national rate. The interventions that make the biggest difference are often simple ones: sterile birth kits; antibiotics for typhoid; milk, zinc and vitamin A to combat malnutrition. Policy analysts estimate that these and other basic measures could save 6 million children a year—all for the price of a few aircraft carriers.

potable: fit to drink

Unfortunately, the gap between possibilities and realities is growing ever wider. As World Bank health consultant Davidson Gwatkin observes, "The more you need health care, the less likely you are to receive it." Some 46 percent of children are still born without skilled attendants in the neediest countries. Fewer than half have access to potable* water and only 5 percent of those who are high risk of malaria sleep under insecticide-treated mosquito nets. Vaccination rates are actually falling throughout sub-Saharan Africa. In that region, according to UNICEF, the proportion of kids immunized against measles fell from 62 percent in 1990 to 50 percent in 1999, as government priorities shifted.

commodity: an economic good

Political will is the key commodity*. For all the talk of leaving no child behind, the United States has yet to commit more than a 10th of 1 percent of its gross domestic product to foreign health assistance. And as a global task force noted recently in *The Lancet,* U.S. development aid for child survival has declined in the past few years. Even within the United States, 12 million children still live in poverty, 9.2 million lack health insurance, and federal rules bar immigrant children from receiving public-health benefits until they've been here five years. "The consequences of this neglect are painful and expensive," says Irwin Redlener, president of the nonprofit Children's Health Fund and associate dean of Columbia University's Mailman School of Public Health. "We've made a mockery of our rhetoric. It turns out not to mean very much in terms of real dollars and services."

Dollars and services are important. But like many doctors who serve the poor, Farmer dreams of something more fundamental. The ultimate challenge is not just to manage the symptoms of poverty, he says, but to change the social arrangements that perpetuate it. His clinic is set up to handle 35,000 patients a year, but it took in nearly 200,000 destitute peasants in 2002—even as Haiti struggled to meet interest payments of foreign debts incurred by past dictators. His efforts may inspire awe, but as he is first to admit, they are stopgaps.

Reading for Meaning

1. List the reasons why children in poor countries die before they reach their fifth birthday.
2. List the countries that have made strides in improving the lot of children.

Reading Deeper

1. Cowley and Springen indicate five conditions that kill children in the "hardest-hit" countries. List them. What do the authors mean when they say that these conditions are not "random"? What does random mean?
2. The authors mention "leaving no child behind." What are they referring to? Why do they mention it here?

Reading for Writing

1. Cowley and Springen have written an effective argument for the need for aid to children in poor countries. However, consider the other side of the issue in terms of the economy of the nations. What would the effects be on the country and the families if even one-half of the children who die at birth are saved? Make a list of the **effects** that those added children would have on the nation. Write an **informative** paper that makes suggestions for helping the "developing countries" once millions of the children are saved. Consider looking for information about what is already being done to help. Can you offer other suggestions? Be sure to document any material you use.
2. At a time when social services are being cut in many states because of budget deficits, care to the poor, including to children, is being cut. On the other hand, not to cut it would mean having to cut other areas, such as education (student loans, grants, scholarships and so forth), aid to the elderly, defense, the prison system, aid to the disabled, and so forth. Who deserves the money and who can do without it? Assume the role of governor of your state and write a **persuasive** paper to the residents of your state that supports cutting or not cutting aid to the poor mentioning some of the other areas that are in the budget.

RHETORICAL ANALYSIS

The following essay by Carolyn Lamborn O'Neill offers a variety of rhetorical techniques, reading strategies, and patterns of development. By beginning in a personal narrative mode, O'Neill announces that she is going to write about improving health by explaining how to do it—process and analysis—from her own attempts and experiences. As she proceeds, readers discover that she is not only explaining how to be heart-healthy, but she is also attempting to convince and persuade. At the end of the essay, she reveals that she is actually negotiating with the reader rather than saying that following her method is the only way to improve one's health. In the left-hand margin there is material that directs you to appropriate chapters in this textbook for discussion about the underlined techniques the author used to write the essay or that comments directly about the techniques the author used.

**You Can Lead a Man to Tofu,
But Can You Make Him Eat It?**

Ch. 4, Narrative begins with personal experiences

Ch. 1, Reading reading technique

Ch. 4, Narrative uses box technique as a transition from personal narrative to informative pattern of development

By using second-person, the author pulls the reader into the essay.

Ch. 1, Reading bullets used as reading technique

Ch. 10, Persuasion use of persuasive language

Ch. 8, Process how-to passage

Chpts. 8, Process and 9, Causal use of cause and effect and process analysis

Today, a heart healthy diet isn't just about eating less fat and cholesterol. A diet high in soy, fiber, and fruits and vegetables may even reduce "bad" cholesterol. But can real people eat like this? The author experiments with her husband.

I've been married long enough—just about 2 months—to know that you can't make people change their lifestyle. Of course, that's unless they really want to. But, I also know that my husband's diet is far from heart healthy.

Both of us have normal cholesterol levels. But, heart disease runs in our families. So, we made a deal. We would both follow American Heart Association (AHA) diet guidelines for 1 week. At the week's end, my husband could decide for himself. Would he continue to eat healthy?

CAN YOU EAT <u>YOUR</u> WAY TO GOOD HEALTH?

A big part of eating well is what you *don't* eat. For healthy people with low risk of heart disease, the AHA recommends limiting:

- Total fat to < 30% of calories
- Saturated fat and trans fat (combined) to < 10% of calories

---

CHOLESTEROL: LESS IS MORE

Your body needs some cholesterol to function. But, too much is a major risk factor for heart disease.

Your body makes all the cholesterol it needs. That's why eating a lot of foods high in cholesterol can raise your levels. You may have high cholesterol and not know. Even if you eat well and exercise.

THE IMPORTANCE OF LIMITING SALT

Limit salt. This is especially true for people with high blood pressure. Salt causes the body to retain fluids, so your heart has to work harder to pump blood through the body. This can be dangerous for your heart.

Examples of high-salt foods include some frozen dinners, process deli meats, and canned soups. Salt content is listed on food labels. Track you daily intake.

- Dietary cholesterol to < 300 mg
- Salt to < 1 teaspoon (2400 mg) per day

If you have high cholesterol and/or other problems that put you at risk for heart disease, <u>you need to watch what you eat</u>. For some people, diet and exercise may not be enough. <u>Talk to your doctor about additional treatment options</u>.

<u>Saturated fats can raise levels of bad cholesterol in your blood. Trans fats can raise your cholesterol levels, too.</u> Read food labels. Track how much fat, cholesterol, and salt you eat.

Good health is also about the kinds of food you *should* eat. <u>Choose</u> lower-fat options. For example, skim milk is better that whole-fat milk. Lean, skinless meats are better than fattier cuts. And, <u>eat</u> plenty of fruits and vegetables. All these foods are good choices.

Know how to eat well. It's the first step. But, a trip to the grocery store is definitely the second. My advice: give yourself plenty of time. Once you start reading labels, you'll see how quickly fat adds up. Butter? <u>Eleven grams of fat, 8 mg of saturated fat, and 30 mg of cholesterol *per tablespoon*</u>.

You'll also find a whole new world of foods. More grocery stores now carry tofu (soy protein). Also soy milk, soy cheese, and meat substitutes made from soy. These are all easy ways to include soy in your diet.

There are several butter-like spreads that even promise to lower cholesterol. <u>These spreads are made with *plant sterols*. Plant sterols are found in fruits</u>

Chs. 8, Process and 10, Persuasion use of persuasive and process analysis language

Ch. 1, Use of box is reading technique

Chs. 8, Process and 10, Persuasion persuasive and process analysis language

Ch. 1, Reading and 8 Process informative material and reading technique

Ch. 1, Reading and 8 Process informative material and reading technique

and vegetables. Look for these spreads in the butter and margarine section. (Warning: read labels carefully. Some margarines contain trans fats.)

Ch. 7, use of contrast

You'll also need to rethink eating habits. Brown rice is a better choice than quick-cooking rice. Whole-grain bread is a rich source of fiber. (Hint: soft, white sandwich bread is *not*.)

WHOLE-GRAIN TOAST WITH PLANT-STEROL SPREAD ON THE SIDE, PLEASE.

Ch. 1, reading technique

Chs. 4, Narrative and 8, Process personalizing the procedure and telling what she did

My first strategy was substitution. Out went the whole milk and butter. In came low-fat cheese. Olive oil was the only fat left standing. (Canola oil is another good choice).

The spreads made with plant sterols were the easiest to adopt. OK. So they don't taste the same as butter. But, all the brands that I tried tasted fine with my whole-grain toast. Another easy switch was low-fat mayo.

Chs. 4 and 8, Narrative and Process process based on personal narrative

I knew my greatest challenge would be getting my husband to eat soy protein. Instead of fighting the tofu battle, I bought soy "chicken" patties and "cheese" slices. (I removed both from their wrappers and stored them in plastic bags. I told him that they were soy *after* he had eaten them.)

EATING WELL IN THE REAL WORLD

So what did my husband decide after 7 days of eating healthy? Absolutely nothing. He had forgotten that we were following a more healthy diet. The fact is, food that is good for you tastes good, too. Whole-grain foods and fresh vegetables have a lot of flavor. Using fresh herbs instead of salt boosts the taste of food.

Ch. 10, Persuasion concluding thesis

Soy chicken has become a favorite quick-fix dinner. But, I did not create a vegetarian husband in 7 days. Nor do I want to. We live in the real world. And, we still eat a real steak once in a while.

Eating well is a way of life. It's not about a single meal. The AHA suggests you look at how you eat over time. This is more important than watching each bite you put in your mouth. The key is moderation.

Ch. 10,
Persuasion

Ch. 10,
Persuasion
compromise at
the end for a
negotiation

Indulge from time to time. But, make it the exception, not the rule. It turns out even a true meat-and-potatoes man can live with that.

O'Neill incorporated personal narrative, contrast, informative, process analysis, persuasion, and cause-and-effect patterns of development in her essay. She provides a lot of factual information about cholesterol, fat, and salt to support her assertions. She also uses eye-catching boxes, font sizes, bold print, and section divisions to keep the reader interested. Finally, she compromises with her audience, admitting that regardless of the suggestions she made, she and her husband still "live in the real world" with temptations to eat food that is not normally considered healthy—such as steak. However, she also admits that rather than conforming to a strict regimen, "moderation" is the key and "indulgence" is permitted from time to time.

REFLECTIONS ON HEALTH: HOW IMPORTANT IS MY HEALTH AND THE HEALTH OF OTHERS TO ME?

The scope of health problems in the United States as well as around the world is staggering. We become concerned when obesity or hypertension become part of our medical vocabulary—and rightly so; however, the antitheses of these conditions—malnutrition, starvation, infections, and so forth—are part of the medical vocabulary of parents of tens of millions of dying children in poor countries. This is not to say that the United States does not experience serious health problems. We experience different ones. And regardless of the expert care and state-of-the-art medical technology we have, there will always be patients whom we cannot save from diseases such as cancer or pneumonia. AIDS is on the rise, SARS has not been stopped yet, cancer is not under control, and Alzheimer's and many other diseases that lead to death continue to plague us. The responsibility of the government to provide funds for research is one answer; but another answer lies in our own responsibility to care for ourselves. Another problem is affordable insurance, but with rising costs for premiums, employers cannot always afford to pick up the entire cost.

Thus, health will continue to be a complex issue that each of us must handle for ourselves and our loved ones. As parents, we are concerned about our children; as children, we are concerned about our aging parents; as residents of the United States, we are concerned about the health of our country; and as citizens of a larger community, we are concerned about the health of the world. It radiates from one small circle to one that encompasses millions of lives. As a social issue, health will always be with us.

Reflecting to Write

Personal Narrative

Just how healthy do you think you are? Keep a health journal for one week. In it record the following aspects of your health:

- Amount of exercise you did each day
- Amount of salt intake you had daily (don't forget that salt is in canned products, chips, processed food, etc.)
- Number of vegetables you ate each day
- Number of fruits you ate each day
- Amount of fiber you ate each day
- Number and kind of snack foods you nibbled on each day
- Amount of cholesterol you ate each day
- How much sleep you got each night

At the end of the week, **analyze** your **journal** for the healthy things you are doing and the not-so-healthy things. Write an informative report about your own health habits concerning rest, food, and exercise. Explain if this reflects your typical behavior. Arrive at some conclusions.

Collaboration

Get a group together that consists of at least three or four students. Each group member will conduct interviews with ten women, asking them about their thoughts about mammograms. Ask them if they know about the latest panel's determination about the benefits and lack of benefits from having mammograms. If they are willing to share, ask them for their age. It will help give you additional information. Finally, ask them if they would still consider having a mammogram even if the benefits are small. Collect your data, which should consist of answers from 30 to 40 women. Even though it is a small sampling, determine how these women feel about mammography. Write an **informative** paper about their feelings and experiences with mammograms.

Service-Learning Projects

Find out when the next Breast Cancer Awareness Walk will take place in your community or nearby community. Volunteer to walk and collect commitments from others for donations for the distance you walk. As you do, distribute a brochure or talk seriously to the individuals you approach informing them about breast cancer. During the event, talk to survivors of the disease as well as to family members who are there and others. After the Walk, write a **personal narrative** reflecting on what you learned about breast cancer, the effects on families, and anything else you learned from your experience. Share your discoveries in class.

In groups, create a brochure for middle-school or high school students giving them statistics and measures that can be used to prevent AIDS. Be sure to remember the age of your audience and create a brochure that will be age-appropriate. Create an oral presentation that you can take to a middle school or high school group—a health class, an extracurricular organization, a PTO meeting, and so forth—and get permission from the principal to address the group and to hand out the brochures. Be sure that you are completely informed about AIDS and can answer questions the students might have. After the presentation, write a **personal reflective** paper describing your experiences and what you learned from them. Include any comments from students who made a particularly strong impact on you. Share your experiences with the class.

This assignment can also be done with work at an Alzheimer's facility or other assisted-living facility that has a unit specifically devoted to caring for Alzheimer's patients. The brochure, however, will be related to Alzheimer's disease and the audience is geriatric patients and their families.

Informative

Find a copy of the made-for-television HBO production *Normal.* This is a story about the difficulties encountered by a man who realizes that he is uncomfortable as a man, and he is in the process of becoming transgendered. Among the many difficulties he encounters is his mental health. Much like Scholiniski in her article, "The Last Time I Wore a Dress," the main character is misunderstood and humiliated. Research the topic of transgendered individuals and write an **informative** paper discussing the mental health aspect of their process toward changing their sexual identity.

Investigate the benefits and drawbacks of universal health care. Many European countries have gone to this form of medical benefit for their people, and some states are beginning to consider adopting a form of universal health care. After you have made a prewriting chart of the benefits and drawbacks, determine your **position** and write an essay that informs the reader of all sides. Do not try to convince your reader, but definitely let your reader understand the important positive and negative issues involved in moving from what we currently have to universal health care.

Chapter 16

Recreation: How We Play

Although there are many forms of recreation, playing with dolls has had a significant impact on the lives of both girls and boys over the years. For little girls, playing with dolls has helped train them for the roles of girlfriend, wife, and mother as Emily Prager and Gary Cross suggest. Dolls have helped to instill a sense of nurturing of and responsibility for the baby dolls little girls have cradled, fed, and diapered. Dolls were dressed, undressed, combed, and talked to, providing companions when no one else was around. Thus, dolls have played and continue to play an important role in many little girls' lives.

And then came Barbie. The doll immediately became one of the most controversial toys little girls played with. As several authors suggest, Barbie was simultaneously liberating and oppressive, with physical characteristics that were at once admired by little girls whose sense of womanly beauty, identity, and self-esteem were gradually developing; however, Barbie's physical endowments were impossible to achieve. But Barbie not only influenced little girls and their mothers, she created an image in little boys' minds about what women were supposed to look like and how they were supposed to behave.

Little boys, however, did not escape playing with dolls, regardless of how insistent Hasbro was that G.I. Joes were not dolls. The G.I. Joe figure became a popular icon prior to the Vietnam War but changed later. Just as Barbie influenced thousands of little girls, G.I. Joe influenced little boys. G.I. Joe taught them about manhood and instructed them in the ways of combat. And like the moms who gave Barbies to their daughters, many dads gave G.I. Joes to their sons.

Over the years, dolls have come and gone, competed with Barbie and G.I. Joe, changed to meet the needs of the growing, diverse population, and continued to influence youngsters as they grow up. Whether little boys are given dolls and baby carriages and little girls are given G.I. Joes and trucks, their "femininity" and "masculinity" will continue

"Toys" *by Linda Daigle*

to be determined by society, parents, and peers. Which dolls/toys did you play with when you were growing up and how influential were they on the person you are today?

WHY BOYS DON'T PLAY WITH DOLLS

Katha Pollitt

What is the difference between a doll and an action figure? Is it gender? What did you play with when you were a child? In today's world of unisex identification, manufacturers have continued to make many of their toys gender specific; however, many parents now offer trucks to little girls and dolls to little boys. Any gender identification in toy selection becomes as serious a "sin" as requiring pink for girls and blue for boys in today's sexist-conscious world. In fact, many hospitals have switched from pink and blue blankets to yellow or other colors that are not gender-identifying. On the other hand, Katha Pollitt (Seeing and Writing, 1995) *explains that it makes little difference what parents do to relieve socially accepted gender roles for their children because they'll be exposed to them in everyday life anyway.*

Prereading: Think about the toys you played with when you were growing up. Did you have dolls, action figures, or other gender-specific toys?

Prewriting: When were you first aware that, because you were a male or female, you had to do things differently from your opposite-sex friends? Write a paragraph recalling the incident and express your feelings about the discovery.

Vocabulary: Looking up and understanding the following words prior to reading should prepare you for the author's message. Other words will be defined in the margin.

prenatal   cognitive   macho   determinist theory   stereotype

---

It's twenty-eight years since the founding of NOW [National Organization for Women], and boys still like trucks and girls still like dolls. Increasingly, we are told that the source of these robust preferences must lie outside soceity—in prenatal hormonal influences, brain chemistry, genes—and that feminism has reached its natural limits. What else could possibly explain the love of preschool girls for party dresses or the desire of toddler boys to own more guns than Mark from Michigan?

True, recent studies claim to show small cognitive differences between the sexes: He gets around by orienting* himself in space; she does it by remembering landmarks. Time will tell if any deserve the hoopla with which each is invariably* greeted, over the protests of the re-

orienting: locating in a particular direction

invariably: constantly

searchers themselves. But even if the results hold up (and the history of such research is not encouraging), we don't need studies of sex-differentiated brain activity in reading, say, to understand why boys and girls still seem so unalike.

The feminist movement has done much for some women, and something for every woman, but it has hardly turned America into a playground free of sex roles. It hasn't even got women to stop dieting or men to stop interrupting them.

innate: natural, instinctive

Instead of looking at kids to "prove" that differences in behavior by sex are innate*, we can look at the way we raise kids as an index to how unfinished the feminist revolution really is, and how tentatively it is embraced even by adults who fully expect their daughters to enter previously male-dominated professions and their sons to change diapers.

inflict: impose

I'm at a children's birthday party. "I'm sorry," one mom silently mouths to the mother of the birthday girl, who has just torn open her present—Tropical Splash Barbie. Now, you can love Barbie or you can hate Barbie, and there are feminists in both camps. But *apologize* for Barbie? Inflict* Barbie, against your own convictions, on the child of a friend you know will be none too pleased?

Every mother in that room had spent years becoming a person who had to be taken seriously, not least by herself. Even the most attractive, I'm willing to bet, had suffered over her body's failure to fit the impossible American ideal. Given all that, it seems crazy to transmit Barbie to the next generation. Yet to reject her is to say that what Barbie represents—being sexy, thin, stylish—is unimportant, which is obviously not true, and children know it's not true.

grotesque: bizarre, very strange

Women's looks matter terribly in this society, and so Barbie, however ambivalently, must be passed along. After all, there are worse toys. The Cut and Style Barbie styling head, for example, a grotesque* object intended to encourage "hair play." The grown-ups who give that probably apologize, too.

obnoxious: highly disagreeable

How happy would most parents be to have a child who flouted sex conventions? I know a lot of women, feminists, who complain in a comical, eyeball-rolling way about their sons' passion for sports: the ruined weekends, obnoxious* coaches, macho values. But they would not think of discouraging their sons from participating in this activity they find so foolish. Or do they? Their husbands are sports fans, too, and they like their husbands a lot.

Could it be that even sports-resistant moms see athletics as part of manliness? That if their sons wanted to spend the weekend writing up their diaries, or reading, or baking, they'd find it disturbing? Too antisocial? Too lonely? Too gay?

Theories of innate differences in behavior are appealing. They let parents off the hook—no small recommendation in a culture that holds moms, and sometimes even dads, responsible for their children's every misstep on the road to bliss and success.

psychic: mental

They allow grown-ups to take the path of least resistance to the dominant culture, which is always less psychic* effort, even if it means more actual work: Just ask the working mother who comes home exhausted and nonetheless finds it easier to pick up her son's socks than make him do it himself. They let families buy for their children, without *too* much guilt, the unbelievably sexiest junk that kids, who have been watching commercials since birth, understandably crave.

chafe: irritate by rubbing against

But the thing the theories do most of all is tell adults that the *adult* world—in which moms and dads still play by many of the old rules even as they question and fidget and chafe* against them—is the way it's supposed to be. A girl with a doll and a boy with a truck "explain" why men are from Mars and women are from Venus, why wives do housework and husbands just don't understand.

paradox: contradiction

The paradox* is that the world of rigid and hierarchical sex roles evoked by determinist theories is already passing away. Three-year-olds may indeed insist that doctors are male and nurses female, even if their own mother is a physician. Six-year-olds know better. These days, something like half of all medical students are female, and male applications to nursing school are inching upward. When tomorrow's three-year-olds play doctor, who's to say how they'll assign the roles?

ideology: set of ideas

With sex roles, as in every area of life, people aspire to what is possible, and conform to what is necessary. But these are not fixed, especially today. Biological determinism may reassure some adults about their present, but it is feminism, the ideology* of flexible and converging sex roles, that fits our children's future. And the kids, somehow, know this.

That's why, if you look carefully, you'll find that for every kid who fits the stereotype, there's another who's breaking one down. Sometimes it's the same kid—the boy who skateboards *and* takes cooking in his after-school program; the girl who collects stuffed animals *and* A-plusses in science.

inculcating: teaching by repetition

Feminists are often accused of imposing their "agenda" on children. Isn't that what adults always do, consciously and unconsciously? Kids aren't born religious, or polite, or kind, or able to remember where they put their sneakers. Inculcating* these behaviors, and the values behind them, is a tremendous amount of work, involving many adults. We don't have a choice, really, about *whether* we should give our children messages about what it means to be male and female—they're bombarded with them from morning till night.

Reading for Meaning

1. Why don't women discourage their sons from participating in sports? How do the mothers feel about their sons' "passion for sports"?
2. How are women complicit in maintaining the idea of manliness for their sons? Why do they do it?

Reading Deeper

1. How do "theories of innate differences in behavior" let "parents off the hook"? What does this mean? Do you agree? Explain.
2. Think about TV commercials in terms of being sexist. Explain how they are and use specific examples that you have seen in the last week.

Reading for Writing

1. Go to a local toy store and analyze it for the way it is organized. Are gender-specific toys together? What about different categories of toys like games? How are they organized? How are electronic games organized? Write a **division** and **classification** essay, **describing** how the store is organized, if there are any sexist overtones to it, and draw conclusions about it.
2. Go to a local toy store and watch a parent and child customer as they shop. How does the parent deal with the child? Does the parent encourage the child to go to a particular set of toys or to gender-specific toys? How does the child react to the parent's prompting? Does the child indicate any desire to go elsewhere? What is the result of the toy store visit? Write a **descriptive** paper explaining the parent child interaction in the toy store. Explain whether the parent seems to be more feminist or more traditional and how the child responds. Draw conclusions.

MACHO IN MINIATURE: HISTORY OF G.I. JOE DOLLS

Ed Liebowitz

Toys have been part of children's lives for centuries. Some have been quite simple. How many times have you seen your son/ daughter or brother/sister pick up a stick and favor it over his/her many more expensive toys? On the other hand, many toys are more sophisticated—interactive toys for toddlers, computer games, remote-controlled cars and airplanes—the list goes on. However, there is always one toy that children return to—the doll. But the term "doll" has a negative connotation for male children. To refer to the highly popular figure of G.I. Joe as a doll raises the ire of many men and the eyebrows of some women. In the following article, originally published in the Smithsonian *magazine, Ed Liebowitz gives readers a historical account of the G.I. Joe figures. And he begins with the argument about what exactly to call this toy.*

Prereading: Does it matter to you if G.I. Joe is called a doll or an action figure or a toy? Is there a meaning to the name that you object to or to the one that you prefer?

Prewriting: When you hear the name G.I. Joe, what images, beyond the figure itself, does it evoke in your mind? Write a paragraph that describes these images.

Vocabulary: Looking up and understanding the following words prior to reading should prepare you for the author's message. Other words will be defined in the margin.

ubiquitous   adversaries   paradox

For nearly 40 years, G.I. Joe has been on America's front lines—in toy boxes from coast to coast.

"Don't you dare call G.I. Joe a doll!" Hasbro toy company president Merrill Hassenfeld charged his sales force at the 1964 Toy Fair, in New York. "If I overhear you talking to a customer about a doll, we're not shipping any G.I. Joes to you."

G.I. Joe was a doll, of course, but Hassenfeld's designers had done all they could to make him the toughest, most masculine doll ever produced. Ken, companion of the glamorous and by then already ubiquitous Barbie, sported Malibu shorts and a peaches-and-cream complexion. The inaugural 1964 G.I. Joe, as preserved in the *Smithsonian*'s social history collection at the National Museum of American History (NMAH), cuts a radically different figure. In his khaki uniform and combat boots, he stands an imposing 11½ inches tall. A battle scar creases his right cheek, and an aluminum dog tag dangles from his neck. Hasbro would furnish him with M-1 rifles, machine guns, bayonets and flame throwers—a far cry from Barbie's purses and pearls.

articulation: having a hinge or pivot connection

While Barbie had little articulation* in her limbs, G.I. Joe debuted as "America's Moveable Fighting Man," with knees that bent and wrists that pivoted to take better aim at any enemy. "Barbie is pretty stiff, with her feet perpetually deformed into high-heeled shoes," says Barbara Clark Smith, a curator of social history at NMAH. "She's essentially a model for viewing by others. She relates back to the historic restrictions of women's physical movement—to corsets and long skirts. While Joe is active, Barbie is pretty inflexible, waiting to be asked to the prom."

G.I. Joe was the concept of Larry Reiner, an executive at the Ideal Toy Company, one of Hasbro's competitors. But when Ideal balked at Reiner's soldier-doll—as recounted in Vincent Santelmo's *The Complete Encyclopedia to G.I. Joe*—Reiner took his brainstorm to Hasbro. Initially, Merrill Hassenfeld had grave reservations, but his product development director, Done Levine, overcame them. (As for Reiner, he never really cashed in on his idea. He signed for a flat fee, amounting to $35,000 from Hasbro, but neglected to negotiate a royalty agreement that could have earned him tens of millions.)

colleagues: fellow members of a group

"When the country's not at war," Levine told his colleagues*, "military toys do very well." Ironically, G.I. Joe came out the same year—1964—that President Lyndon Johnson used the Gulf of Tonkin incident to up the ante in Vietnam. Until that war tore the country asunder*, G.I. Joe thrived. Sales reached $36.5 million in 1965. That was also the year that Joe gained some black comrades* in arms, although the face of the African-American G.I. Joe doll was identical to that of his white counterpart*, merely painted brown. Joe got a new mission and a new uniform. The original had been modeled after the infantrymen, sailors, marines, and pilots of World War II and Korea—the war of dads and grandads. In 1966, Hasbro outfitted Joe for Vietnam, giving him a green beret, an M-16 and the rocket launcher of U.S. Army Special Forces.

asunder: into separate pieces or parts

comrades: friends, companions

counterpart: one that is similar to another

adrift: without direction or purpose

But according to Santelmo, orders for Joe ground to a near halt in the summer of 1967 as the little guy found himself adrift* in the same hostile home front as veterans returning from Vietnam. Some consumers even called G.I. Joe's Americanism into question. Since 1964 G.I. Joe heads had been produced in Hong Kong, then shipped to Hasbro's U.S. plants to be fastened atop American bodies. His uniforms came from Hong Kong, Japan and Taiwan. One angry mom wrote to Hasbro to say that "the true American soldier is not outfitted with clothes made in Asia." Another, quoted in the *New York Times* magazine and from the other end of the political spectrum, asked, "If we're going to have toys to teach our children about war . . . why not have a G.I. Joe who bleeds when his body is punctured by shrapnel*, or screams when any one of his 21 moveable parts are blown off?"

shrapnel: fragments from an explosive

In 1967, Hasbro had introduced a talking G.I. Joe, and the doll predictably barked battle commands. In reality, however, he was not so resolute, and under continued cultural cross fire, he abandoned the battlefield entirely in 1969. Joe had begun his existence by closeting his identity as a doll; now, he would survive by stowing his uniform and becoming, in effect, the greatest draft dodger in U.S. toy history. Hasbro

freelance:
person who sells
services without
a long-term
contract

attributes:
characteristics

bionic: normal
biological
capability
enhanced by
electronic or
electro-
mechanical
devices

pygmy: race of
dwarfs

Neanderthal: a
crude or boorist
person

extraterrestrial:
occurring
outside the earth
or its
atmosphere;
superhuman

quagmire:
difficult
situation

amorphous:
shapeless

cabal: group of
people who plot
to do an act

prankish:
mischievous

surreptitiously:
secretly

indignities:
humiliating
treatment

repackaged Joe as a freelance*, civilian adventurer. As Joe drifted into the '70s, the round "Adventure Team" medallion he wore was more peace sign that dog tag. He sprouted big fuzzy hair and a bush beard that would never make it past a Marine barber. And he took on all sorts of trendy attributes*, from a Bruce Lee-like kung fu grip to Six-Million-Dollar-Man-style bionic* limbs.

On his far-flung travels away from battle zones, the AWOL soldier found new foes to fight. He did combat with giant dams, spy sharks, pygmy* gorillas, massive spiders, white tigers, boa constrictors, mummies, and abominable snowmen—anyone and anything, it seems, but actual U.S. military adversaries. Having conquered the natural and unnatural world, G.I. Joe found new opponents in outer space—"The Intruders," dumpy Neanderthal* space aliens who looked like a race of squat Arnold Schwarzeneggers. Against them, Joe risked death by squeezing; a toggle on the intruder's back lifted beefy arms to ensnare the man of action in an extraterrestrial* bear hug.

But if Joe got caught in the Vietnam quagmire*, it was the OPEC oil embargo in 1976 that almost did him in for good. Petroleum, of course, is the major component of plastic, of which the figures, vehicles and most of G.I. Joe's equipment were made. "As a result," writes Santelmo, "Hasbro found that it would have become economically unfeasible for the company to continue producing such large-scale action figures at a price that the public could afford." G.I. Joe shrank from almost a foot high to a mere three and three-quarter inches. Although he returned, in his pygmy incarnation, to limited military action in the early years of the Reagan administration, the downsized Joe continued to be far more preoccupied fighting amorphous* enemies like Golobulus, Snow Serpent, Gnawgahyde, Dr. Mindbender and Toxo-Viper, a destroyer of the environment.

Then came the Persian Gulf War and, with it, a renewal of patriotism. And when crude oil prices dipped after that conflict, Joe swelled to his earlier size. But new antagonists included a group calling itself the Barbie Liberation Organization (BLO). In 1993, this cabal* of prankish* artists bought several hundred "Teen Talk" Barbies and Talking G.I. Joe Electronic Battle Command Dukes, switched their voice boxes and surreptitiously* returned them to toy stores. Brushing Barbie's long blond hair, an unsuspecting doll owner might hear Barbie cry out: "Eat lead, Cobra," or "Attack, with heavy firepower." G.I. Joe suffered similar indignities*. The BLO sent the *Smithsonian* a "post-op" G.I. Joe, who, in his best Barbie soprano voice, warbles such memorable phrases as "Let's plan our dream wedding," "I love to try on clothes" and "Ken's such a dream."

insignia: badge of identification on clothing

In today's patriotic climate, G.I. Joe once again stands ready to take on anything from al-Qaida to the axis of evil. A 10th Mountain Division Joe, released recently, wears the same uniform, insignia* and battle gear as American troops who served in Bosnia and Afghanistan, while another Joe does duty as an Army Ranger. "Currently on the shelves you'll find representatives of four branches of service," says Derryl DePriest, Hasbro's marketing director. "We bring G.I. Joe into a very realistic format—the clothing, the stitching and the shape of the helmet all pay homage [to the actual troops in the field]."

curator: administrator of a museum

preeminent: outstanding

aspire: to desire strongly

Like many toys nowadays, America's miniature fighting man is a product of the factories of the People's Republic of China. But no matter his size, color or country of origin, Joe's role as political weather vane will likely continue for many a campaign to come. "Joe challenged and confirmed traditional gender roles," curator* Clark Smith observes. "He challenged the preconception that boys wouldn't play with dolls, while he clearly reinforces the notion of the man as warrior." Smith believes he will remain America's preeminent* playtime paradox. "He reflects the changing and confused thinking of what we want boys to aspire* to, what we want men to be—and whether we want to admit what battles we're really in."

Reading for Meaning

1. Compare and contrast Barbie and G.I. Joe physically and culturally.
2. Why did Larry Reiner receive only $35,000 for G.I. Joe from Hasbro?
3. What is the relationship of war to sales of G.I. Joe and other military toys?
4. After leaving the battlefield, whom did Joe do battle with?
5. Why did Joe become a three and three-quarter-inch figure? Explain. Why did he "grow up" again years later? Explain.
6. How does Hasbro make Joe look authentic? Explain.

Reading Deeper

1. Why did Hasbro decide to change G.I. Joe into other personalities in 1969?
2. According to Clark Smith, Joe has done more than provide a "doll" for little boys to play with. He "reflects the changing and confused thinking of what we want boys to aspire to, what we want men to be—and whether we want to admit what battles we're really in." What exactly does Smith mean by that? Explain.

Reading for Writing

1. Liebowitz raises the question of whether or not G.I. Joe should be called a doll. Look up the definition of "doll" and write a **definition** paragraph using both **denotative** and **connotative** definitions. Take a position on the question of Joe as "doll." If you think he should not be called a doll, suggest what he should be called. Write an essay that attempts to **convince** the reader of your position.

2. Looking at the historical development of Joe and his other personalities, explain what the concept of being a man was in the 1960s, how it's changed over the years, and what it is today. Has Joe kept up with these changes? Write an **informative** essay focusing on G.I. Joe as a model for the changing definition of manhood. Or you might say that G.I. Joe is *not* a model for the changing definition of manhood. Defend your position.

OUR BARBIES, OURSELVES

Emily Prager

Several generations of contemporary women grew up with the Barbie Doll as one of the main icons of womanhood, a figure that little girls wanted to look like and be like. And little boys grew up looking at the Barbie doll thinking that that was what little girls should be like. The image and the message sent by this seemingly innocent toy created a gender role for women that was difficult for them to see beyond. In Emily Prager's article (Interview Magazine, *Dec. 1991),* this New York Times *columnist reveals her surprise and relief when she discovers the "truth" about Barbie's creator.*

Prereading: Did you have a Barbie Doll when you were growing up? Did you have other dolls? Which one(s) did you prefer playing with? Why?

Prewriting: Would you give a female child a Barbie Doll for a present? Explain in a paragraph why you would or wouldn't.

Vocabulary: Looking up and understanding the following words prior to reading should prepare you for the author's message. Other words will be defined in the margin.

Zsa Zsa Gabor   phallic

eclectic: from
various sources

I read an astounding obituary in the *New York Times* not too long ago. It concerned the death of one Jack Ryan. A former husband of Zsa Zsa Gabor, it said, Mr. Ryan had been an inventor and designer during his lifetime. A man of eclectic* creativity, he designed Sparrow and Hawk missiles when he worked for the Raytheon Company, and, the notice said, when he consulted for Mattel, he designed Barbie.

If Barbie was designed by a man, suddenly a lot of things made sense to me, things I'd wondered about for years. I used to look at Barbie and wonder. What's wrong with this picture? What kind of woman designed this doll? Let's be honest: Barbie looks like someone who got her start at the Playboy Mansion. She could be a regular guest on *The Howard Stern Show.* It is a fact of Barbie's design that her breasts are so out of proportion to the rest of her body that if she were a human woman, she'd fall flat on her face. If it's true that a woman didn't design Barbie, you don't know how much saner that makes me feel. Of course, that

ameliorate:
make better

subliminally:
below one's
conscious level

epitome: ideal
example

doesn't ameliorate* the damage. There are millions of women who are subliminally* sure that a thirty-nine-inch bust and a twenty-three-inch waist are the epitome* of lovability. Could this account for the popularity of breast implant surgery?

I don't mean to step on anyone's toes here. I love my Barbie. Secretly, I still believe that neon pink and turquoise blue are the only colors in which to decorate a duplex condo. And like many others of my generation, I've never married, simply because I cannot find a man who looks as good in clam diggers as Ken.

The question that comes to mind is, of course, did Mr. Ryan design Barbie as a weapon? Because it *is* odd that Barbie appeared about the same time in my consciousness as the feminist movement—a time when women sought equality and small breasts were king. Or is Barbie the dream date of weapons designers? Or perhaps it's simpler than that: Perhaps Barbie is Zsa Zsa if she were eleven inches tall. No matter what, my discovery of Jack Ryan confirms what I have always felt: There is something indescribably masculine about Barbie—dare I say it, phallic. For all her giant breasts and high-heeled feet, she lacks a certain softness. If you asked a little girl what kind of doll she wanted for Christmas, I don't think she'd reply, "Please, Santa, I want a hard-body."

totemic:
serving as a
symbol of

On the other hand, you could say that Barbie, in feminist terms, is definitely her own person. With her condos and fashion plazas and pools and beauty salons, she is definitely a liberated woman, a gal on the move. And she has always been sexual, even totemic*. Before Barbie, American

ineffably:
indescribably

jodhpurs:
riding slacks
fitting tightly at
knees and
ankles

portfolios:
itemized list of
investments

mantra:
formula of
words designed
to produce a
certain effect

ominous:
threatening

truncated:
shortened by
cutting off

obscenity:
indecency

dolls were flat-footed and breastless, and ineffably* dignified. They were created in the image of little girls or babies. Madame Alexander was the queen of doll makers in the fifties, and her dollies looked like Elizabeth Taylor in *National Velvet.* They represented the kind of girls who looked perfect in jodhpurs*, whose hair was never out of place, who grew up to be Jackie Kennedy—before she married Onassis. Her dolls' boyfriends were figments of the imagination, figments with large portfolios* and three-piece suits and presidential aspirations, figments who could keep dolly in the style to which little girls of the fifties were programmed to become accustomed, a style that spasm-ed with the sixties and the appearance of Barbie. And perhaps what accounts for Barbie's vast popularity is that she was also a sixties woman, into free love, and fun colors, anti-class, and possessed of a real, molded boyfriend, Ken with whom she could chant a mantra*.

But there were problems with Ken. I always felt weird about him. He had no genitals, and, even at age ten, I found that ominous*. I mean, here was Barbie with these humongous breasts, and that was OK with the toy company. And then, there was Ken with that truncated* unidentifiable lump in his groin. I sensed injustice at work. Why, I wondered, was Barbie designed with such obvious sexual equipment and Ken not? Why was his treated as if it were more mysterious than hers? Did the fact that it was treated as such indicate that somehow his equipment, his essential maleness, was considered more powerful than hers, more worthy of the dignity of concealment? And if the issue in the mind of the toy company was obscenity* and its possible damage to children, I still object. How do they think I felt, knowing that no matter how many water beds they slept in, or hot tubs they romped in, or swimming pools they lounged by under the stars, Barbie and Ken could never make love? No matter how much sexuality Barbie possessed, she would never turn Ken on. He would be forever withholding, forever detached. There was a loneliness about Barbie's situation that was always disturbing. And twenty-five years later, movies and videos are still filled with topless women and covered men. As if we're all trapped in Barbie's world and can never escape.

God, it certainly has cheered me up to think that Barbie was designed by Jack Ryan. . . .

Reading for Meaning

1. What kind of dolls came before Barbie? Describe what they looked like.
2. Why did Prager have problems with the Ken doll? Were the problems limited to Ken or did they include Barbie? Explain.

Reading Deeper

1. Why is it a relief to Prager that a man instead of a woman designed Barbie?
2. What messages does the Barbie Doll send to little girls and to little boys? Explain.

Reading for Writing

1. Madame Alexander has been called the "queen of doll makers." Find a Madame Alexander doll in a toy store or doll store and examine her. Write a **descriptive** passage about all the details of this doll. Then go to the section of Barbies and look at all the different Barbie styles in the store. Write a **descriptive** passage about the Barbies. Decide which doll you would prefer giving to a child and why you chose that doll. In the remainder of the paper discuss your decision.
2. Draw a model for a new doll/figure that represents what you think a doll for little girls should look like. Be sure to include the clothes the doll/figure will wear. Give a name to the doll/figure. And write a **descriptive** ad that would be used to attract consumers—children and adults—to buy the new doll/figure.

BARBIE, G.I. JOE, AND PLAY IN THE 1960s

Gary Cross

Although the two preceding articles discuss Barbie and G.I. Joe independently, the following article by Gary Cross is one in which the author compares and contrasts the two toys in ways that you might not have considered when reading the other ones. In this section, Cross, author of Kids' Stuff: Toys and the Changing World of American Childhood *(1997), shows how society impacts on toys as well as how toys impact on society.*

Prereading: What was the last toy an adult gave you when you were still a child? Did you like it? Did you play with it?

Prewriting: If you could give a child any toy you'd like him or her to have, what would you choose? Would you ask the child what he or she would like? Write a paragraph about what toy you would choose to give and why.

Vocabulary: Looking up and understanding the following words prior to reading should prepare you for the author's message. Other words will be defined in the margin.

icon   conscripted   Benjamin Spock

Television and the new business climate in the toy industry alone did not transform the meaning of play. Toys were changing because American society was changing. By looking at the two most important trend-setting toys we can find clues to these changes. Much has been written about Barbie and G.I. Joe as icons of popular culture. But Barbie and G.I. Joe were also toys, and like other toys they were mostly given to children by adults.

Barbie began her career as a stiff plastic dress-up figure. Ruth Handler often claimed that she invented Barbie to fill a void in girls' play. Girls wanted a less cumbersome and more fun version of the fashion paper doll. In using paper dolls as a model, Mattel was in effect redirecting doll play away from the friendship and nurturing themes of the companion and baby dolls that had predominated* since the 1900s. In the nineteenth century paper dolls were used to display the latest styles and to portray royalty and famous actresses, especially in magazines devoted to fashion. They were associated with an adult world of quasi-aristocratic consumption*. They had little to do with domestic or friendship themes. Paper dolls and their focus on fashion were an important part of girls' play in the first half of the twentieth century, but they were only a minor part of the toy business.[1]

Mattel, however, put fashion doll play at the center of the industry. The idea of making the paper fashion doll three dimensional was hardly new. Even the association of doll play with consumption was not innovative. It had been built into the concepts of dolls from Patsy to Toni. But Barbie was not a child doll dressed in children's fashions. Rather Barbie was in the shape of a young woman with very long legs and an exaggerated hourglass figure. She looked neither like the little girl who owned her nor like the little girl's mother. She was neither a baby, a child, nor a mother but a liberated teenager, almost a young woman. Handler admitted that even in this her creation was not so original. She "borrowed" the look from a German dress-up doll she and her daughter Barbara had noticed on vacation in Switzerland. But she marketed it on a grand scale at a perfect point in the history of American childhood: at the end of the 1950's.[2]

Barbie was an early rebel against the domesticity that dominated the lives of baby-boom mothers. It may not be surprising that some of the first generation of Barbie owners became feminists in the late 1960s and 1970s. The revolt against, at least, the momism of the feminine mystique* was played out with Barbie, who never cared for babies or children. But Mattel's doll was also an autonomous teenager with no visible ties to parents in a time when the earliest of the baby boom generation were just entering their teens. This crop of teenagers, coming of age in a

predominated: exerted control

consumption: wasteful spending

mystique: air of mystery or reverence

more affluent* United States, had more choices than their parents had had and were freer of adult control. To the eight-year-old of 1960, Barbie represented a hoped-for future of teenage freedom. It was this attraction of Barbie that long survived the maturation of the baby-boom generation. It is also not surprising that when Mattel market-tested Barbie it found that mothers were not nearly so positive about the doll as were their daughters. Mothers recognized that this doll was a break from the tradition of nurturing and companion play and that girls apparently welcomed it.

Despite all this, Barbie hardly "taught" girls to shed female stereotypes. Rather she prompted them to associate the freedom of being an adult with carefree consumption. With her breasts and slender waist, Barbie came literally to embody the little girl's image of what it meant to be grown up. At the same time, in her contemporary fashions, she represented the up-to-date. Barbie did not invite children to be Mommy, nor was she the child's friend in a secret garden of caring and sharing. She was what the little girl was not and, even more important, what her mother was not. She was a fashion model with a large wardrobe designed to attract attention. Instead of teaching girls how to diaper a baby or use floor cleaners, Barbie play was an education in consumption— going to the hairdresser and shopping for that perfect evening gown for the big dance. Even when she had a job (model, stewardess, or later even a doctor), her work and life had nothing to do with the jobs of most women. Barbie was never a cashier at Wal-Mart or a homemaker.

If Barbie taught that freedom meant consumption, the Barbie line was designed to maximize parents' real spending. Playing consumer required that Barbie have a constantly changing wardrobe of coordinated clothing and accessories. Clothing sets were often much more expensive than the "hook," the doll itself. The first Barbie advertising brochure featured, for example, a Barbie-Q Outfit, Suburban Shopper, Picnic Set (with fishing pole), Evening Splendor (complete with strapless sheath), and even a Wedding Day Set. By the early 1960s Barbie had play environments, for example the Barbie Fashion Shop and Barbie Dream House.[3]

Barbie's glamour required constant purchases of dolls and accessories. Playing grown up meant that Barbie had to have a boy friend, Ken (introduced in 1961). Because Barbie seemed to be six to seven years older than her owners, Mattel introduced in 1964 a little sister, Skipper, with whom the children could identify. . . .

Mattel even succeeded in persuading little girls to "trade in" their old Barbies for a discount on a new look in 1967. Adults found this strange—voluntarily parting with a "loved" doll. But the girls saw it differently: they were simply trading in an old model for a new, much as their parents traded in their flashy 1959 Chevys for the more sedate look of the 1960s models. Barbie's environment—clothes, hair, playsets, and friends—changed with adult fashion. But Barbie's face and shape remained a constant symbol of growing up. Thus Mattel created that elusive and contradictory prize—an ephemeral* classic—and in doing so reshaped the play of American girls. A doll that mothers at first disliked became the doll that mothers had to give their daughters.[4]

ephemeral: lasting only a short time

Hasbro's G.I. Joe mirrored the success of Barbie by becoming a perennial* fad. It achieved this feat, at first not by challenging expectations of fathers as Barbie broke with the doll culture of mothers, but by affirming the values and experiences of many fathers. Like so many other contemporary toys, G.I. Joe was inspired by a TV series, an action-adventure show, *The Lieutenant* (1963), that was supposed to appeal to adult men. But the program failed even before the toy appeared. G.I. Joe was not tied to any specific media personality or story. He represented the average soldier, evoking* memories of fathers' experience in World War II and the Korean War. The original G.I. Joe of 1964 shared with Barbie the critical feature of being a dress-up doll, although marketed as "America's Moveable Fighting Man." At twelve inches, half an inch taller than Barbie, G.I. Joe was suitable for costuming in the uniforms of four American military services (sold separately). Again like Barbie, G.I. Joe was accessorized*. Hasbro adopted what was often called the "razor and razor blade" principle of marketing. Once the boy had the doll, he needed accessories—multiple sets of uniforms, jeeps, tents, and weaponry.[5]

perennial: yearly

evoking: calling to mind

accessorized: given additional objects for beauty, convenience, or effectiveness

Still, Joe was not simply a boy's version of Barbie. The obvious historical precedent was the cast-metal soldier, very different from the paper doll. Miniature soldiers had been part of boys' play for centuries. The object was to reenact the drama of present and past battles. G.I. Joe added to this traditional game by giving boys articulated* figures with a man's shape and musculature*. The Joes were a major improvement over cheap and impersonal soldiers that stood on bases. Joe took the play beyond the traditional deployment* of infantry, cannon, and cavalry. Detailed "Manuals," accompanying the doll, marched "Joe through basic training up to combat readiness," showing the boy how to pose his toy to crouch in a trench or throw a grenade. Joe changed war games from the pleasure of acting the general—arranging soldiers and weapons on a field of battle—to playing the soldier, the G.I. whom the boy dressed and posed. This probably made war play far more appealing to young children because they could identify with the individual soldier. Joe may have contributed to the decline of other forms of boys' play, at least temporarily, insofar as erector sets almost disappeared and Tinkertoys and Lincoln Logs were relegated* to preschoolers in the G.I. Joe era.[6]

articulated: joints that move, moveable parts

musculature: muscle system

deployment: spreading out troops over an area

relegated: sent to another place

Nevertheless, the early G.I. Joe did not challenge traditional war play as Barbie displaced baby doll and companion doll play. G.I. Joe's success was based on a boy's identity with the all-male world of heroic action aided by modern military equipment and gadgetry. The play was conventional, featuring males bonding in adventure. This was a woman-less world. Boys rejected the idea of a female nurse when it was introduced to the G.I. Joe line in 1965. These boys could play war the way their fathers might have fought it in World War II or in Korea. And they could dress their Joes in battle gear similar to that worn by conscripted uncles or older brothers serving their two-year stints in the army of the mid-1960s. The object was not the clash of enemies (as would be the case with later action figures). Even though boys made their Joe dolls fight each other, Hasbro offered soldiers from only one side. The point was to imitate the real world of adults in the military. G.I. Joe still connected fathers with sons.

Again in contrast to Barbie, G.I. Joe went through major changes. By 1967 as the Vietnam War heated up and adults such as Benjamin Spock attacked war toys, sales decreased. Beginning in 1970 Hasbro responded by transforming the "fighting" Joes into an "Adventure Team." Joes searched for sunken treasure and captured wild animals. As the Vietnam War wound down to its bitter end in 1975, it was awkward to sell military toys glorifying contemporary jungle warfare. While veterans of World War II and even Korea might enjoy giving their sons toys that memorialized their own youth, the situation for fathers who had reached manhood during the Vietnam era was very different. Most of these men wanted to forget the Vietnam War (whether they fought in it or opposed it), not to give their sons toys recalling this military disaster or any real war.

In 1976, with the Vietnam War in the past, G.I. Joe became "Super Joe" and shrank to eight inches (because of higher costs for plastic). He no longer could be dressed. He returned to the role of a fighter, but he did not rejoin the ranks of enlisted men. He no longer was part of a world that fathers, uncles, or older brothers had ever experienced. Instead he was a high-tech hero, no longer connected to a troublesome reality. His laser beams and rocket command vehicles helped him fight off aliens, the Intruders. Added to his team was Bullet Man, the first of a long line of superhumans. The object of play was to pit good guys against bad guys, not to imitate real military life. But even these changes could not save Joe. From 1978 to 1981 the "Great American Hero" disappeared from store shelves to be pushed aside by an even more fantasyful line of toys based on George Lucas's *Star Wars.*[7]

With Barbie little girls combined growing up with feminine consumerism. This gave Barbie a permanent aisle of hot-pink packages in every serious toy store. G.I. Joe began as a celebration of an all-male world of realistic combat. But Joe encountered deeper contradictions in the 1960s than did Barbie and was forced to flee into fantasy. Still, both toys became models for toy play and consumption that still prevail today. They did so by breaking away from the world of parents.

Endnotes

[1]Ruth Handler, *Dream Doll* (Stamford, CT: Longmeadow Press, 1994), chs. 4–5; Rebecca Harnmell, "To Educate and Amuse: Paper Dolls and Toys, 1640–1900" (M.A. thesis, University of Delaware, 1988, University Microforms International, Ann Arbor, 1989).

[2]Handler, *Dream Doll;* A. Glen Mandeville, *Doll Fashion Anthology and Price Guide,* 4th ed. (Cumberland, MD: Hobby House, 1993), 1–33; K. Westenhouser, *The Story of Barbie* (Paducah, KY: Collector Books, 1994), 5–15; Billy Boy, *Barbie: Her Life and Times* (New York: Crown, 1987), 17–28, 40–44.

[3]Mattel, "Barbie, Teen-Age Fashion Model," "Barbie, Teen-Age Fashion Model, and Ken, Barbie's Boy Friend (He's a Doll)," "Exclusive Fashions by Mattel," book 3 (Hawthorne, CA: Mattel, 1958, 1960, 1963). All in the Strong Museum.

[4]Billy Boy, *Barbie,* 92; Mandeville, *Fashion Anthology,* 41–43, 69–71; Ron Goulart, *The Assault on Childhood* (Los Angeles: Sherbourne, 1969), 26.

[5]"Fact Sheet: Hasbro's G.I. Joe, A Real American Hero," Hasbro Press Kit, Feb. 1993, TFC, Box 3; Susan Manos and Paris Manos, *Collectible Male Action Figures* (Paducah KY: Collector Books, 1990), 8–9.

[6]"G.I. Joe, Action Soldiers: America's Moveable Fighting Man" (Pawtucket, RI: Hasbro, 1964), Strong Museum.

[7]Manos and Manos, *Male Action Figures,* 20–33, 38–43; Vincent Santelmo, *The Official 30th Anniversary Salute to G.I. Joe* (Iola, WI: Kreuse, 1994), 17–18, 66–72, 75–97, 325, 343, 412–413).

Reading for Meaning

1. What is the difference between paper dolls of the 1800s and those in the 1900s? Explain.
2. What is the history of the creation of Barbie? Who was her creator? Where did she get her idea?
3. In what ways was G.I. Joe similar to Barbie? Explain. How was he different?
4. Explain what the "manuals" that came with G.I. Joe were for.

Reading Deeper

1. Explain Cross's explanation of Barbie being closer to a feminist reading than a traditional one. In other words, what does Cross say Barbie represented to young girls in the 1960s that more traditional interpretations do not discuss?
2. What does Cross mean by the final sentence in his essay?

Reading for Writing

1. Cross wrote a classic subject-by-subject, comparison-and-contrast essay and also added some point-by-point similarities and differences about both Barbie and G.I. Joe. Analyze this essay by making a chart that lists each of the points of similarity he makes about the two toys and each of the points of difference he makes. Be sure to document where you got each of the points. Then go to the two articles that precede this one and add other points that those authors made in their essays that also show similarities and differences not included in Cross's article. Be sure to document the points. Write a paper using selected points from the articles to **convince** a friend (male or female) that either a Barbie doll or a G.I. Joe figure is an excellent gift to buy a child.
2. In both articles about G.I. Joe, the authors give important dates and wars that had an effect on the sale of G.I. Joe. Create a timeline that gives important dates and events that deal with the Women's Movement and write an **informative** essay that explains how the events had or did not have an impact on women's attitude toward Barbie.

BABY

bell hooks

Not only is the issue of gender-specific toys important, so, too, is the issue of ethnicity as reflected in toys. This is an age when society is becoming more sensitive in recognizing the wide diversity of populations that have moved into the United States. From ethnic-specific Hallmark cards to ethnic-specific aisles in the grocery stores to completely ethnic-specific grocery stores, the different nationalities and ethnicities that compose our country are finally being acknowledged. On the other hand, some say that manufacturers are exploiting the "new markets" by advertising to them specifically. bell hooks, cultural critic and feminist, presents a personal narrative discussing her life as a child growing up amid Barbies and Baby. This article comes from her book Bone Black *(1996).*

Prereading: Consider the toys you played with when you were growing up. Were any of them reflective of your ethnicity? Were you aware of the ethnicity of your toys?

Prewriting: Consider giving a child a doll. Would you give that child a doll that is clearly from an ethnicity different from the child's ethnicity? Why or why not? Write a paragraph explaining your answer.

————

We learn early that it is important for a woman to marry. We are always marrying our dolls to someone. He of course is always invisible, that is until they made the Ken doll to go with Barbie. One of us has been given a Barbie doll for Christmas. Her skin is not white white but almost brown from the tan they have painted on her. We know she is white because of her blond hair. The newest Barbie is bald, with many wigs of different colors. We spend hours dressing and undressing her, pretending she is going somewhere important. We want to make new clothes for her. We want to buy the outfits made just for her that we see in the store but they are too expensive. Some of them cost as much as real clothes for real people. Barbie is anything but real, that is why we like her. She never does housework, washes dishes, or has children to care for. She is free to spend all day dreaming about the Kens of the world. Mama laughs when we tell her there should be more than one Ken for Barbie, there should be Joe, Sam, Charlie, men in all shapes and sizes. We do not think that Barbie should have a girlfriend. We know that Barbie was born to be alone—that the fantasy woman, the soap opera girl, the girl of *True Confessions,* the Miss America girl was born to be alone. We know that she is not us.

My favorite doll is brown, brown like light milk chocolate. She is a baby doll and I give her a baby doll name, Baby. She is almost the same as a real baby. She comes with no clothes, only a pink diaper, fastened with tiny gold pins and a plastic bottle. She has a red mouth the color of lipstick slightly open so that we can stick the bottle in it. We fill the bottle with water and wait for it to come through the tiny hole in Baby's bottom. We make her many new diapers, but we are soon bored with changing them. We lose the bottle and Baby can no longer drink. We still love her. She is the only doll we will not destroy. We have lost Barbie. We have broken the leg of another doll. We have cracked open the head of an antique doll to see what makes the crying sound. The little thing inside is not interesting. We are sorry but nothing can be done—not even mama can put the pieces together again. She tells us that if this is the way we intend to treat our babies she hopes we do not have any. She laughs at our careless parenting. Sometimes she takes a minute to show us the right thing to do. She is too terribly fond of Baby. She says that she looks so much like a real newborn. Once she came upstairs, saw baby under the covers, and wanted to know who had brought the real baby from downstairs.

She loves to tell the story of how Baby was born. She tells us that I, her problem child, decided out of nowhere that I did not want a white doll to play with, I demanded a brown doll, one that would look like me. Only grown-ups think that the things children say come out of nowhere. We know they come from the deepest parts of ourselves. Deep within myself I had begun to worry that all this loving care we give to the pink and white flesh-colored dolls meant that somewhere left high on the shelves were boxes of unwanted, unloved brown dolls covered in dust. I thought that they would remain there forever, orphaned and alone, unless someone began to want them, to want to give them love and care, to want them more than anything. At first they ignored my wanting. They complained. They pointed out that white dolls were easier to find, cheaper. They never said where they found Baby but I know. She was always there high on the shelf, covered in dust—waiting.

Reading for Meaning

1. Why should Barbie not have a girlfriend according to hooks? What does that indicate about her feelings about real famous women? What do you think leads to this belief?
2. Why did hooks want a doll that was brown?

Reading Deeper

1. Discuss the difference between Baby and Barbie in terms of real life situations for young women.
2. According to hooks, adults don't realize that children have reasons for what they say and think. How does she support this in her essay?
3. Are there any hints in the story prior to the last paragraph that already made you think that the narrator was the "problem child"? List them.

Reading for Writing

1. In the 1950s and into the 1960s, the Dick and Jane readers were used to teach children how to read in public schools. Later they were

criticized for being sexist and for not reflecting the diverse student population of the classroom. How does this criticism relate to what hooks is talking about in her essay? Write a **division** and **classification** essay about manufacturers' production of predominantly white dolls for a diversely populated society. You might want to conduct research in popular toy stores or in toy departments in department stores. Find the number of ethnically marked dolls, the ethnicity they belong to, their gender, the neighborhood the store is in, and anything else that might have an impact on the kinds of toys available.

2. Consider the issue of gender roles and ethnicity. What part do dolls play in shaping children's identity in terms of gender roles and self-esteem? Go to a toy store and look specifically for the doll section. What do the dolls of the dominant society do and how are they portrayed? What do dolls of the various ethnicities do and how are they portrayed? What messages are little girls getting about themselves as women from the dolls they play with? Write an **informative** essay explaining your findings and your conclusions.

Just Play? Who Knew?

Los Angeles Times *Editorial*

Go back to your growing up years. How much of it was controlled by your parents or guardians? Did you have music lessons or ballet or other activities that were structured and took away from your play time with your friends? Do you remember if you resented that time or if you enjoyed it? In the following Los Angeles Times *(Nov. 2, 2002) editorial, the author looks at a new study that praises unstructured play time for children and talks, ironically, about the ways children's toy manufactures can still profit from it.*

Prereading: When you see children on a playground or at a park, are they normally playing children's games with each other or are they playing in supervised, structured activities guided by adults?

Prewriting: What are the benefits of having children participate in supervised, structured activities? What are the drawbacks? Write a **comparison and contrast** paragraph discussing the benefits and drawbacks of structured activities.

Vocabulary: Looking up and understanding the following words prior to reading should prepare you for the author's message. Other words will be defined in the margin.

blather   spatial   entrepreneur

Just when parents finally had their children's schedules figured out for maximum success skills, along comes this new blather about unstructured play.

Up to now, it's been soccer practice Tuesday afternoons and games on Saturday mornings (remember, 80% of L.A. children can't hack the test for the President's Council on Physical Fitness). Monday is private tutoring in standardized test-taking skills. Wednesdays are for afterschool piano lessons, which have been linked to better spatial reasoning (whatever that is, we're sure it will come in handy for the SAT's in 10 years). Scouts on Thursdays for socialization. Meeting of the Primary School Reading to the Literate Club on Fridays (all the top universities are looking for community service these days). And Sunday school, of course, something for the spiritual side.

The latest thinking, though, is that the kids have been overscheduled. All these childhood experts are praising recess and play and the importance of letting kids just hang around, making up their own games or imagining things. It's been the subject of studies at Case Western Reserve and the University of Michigan.

This isn't just about meaningless stuff like letting kids have fun and enjoy life. No, this is important. It turns out that unstructured play, the kind that doesn't need instruction or adults to organize it or expensive equipment, is thought to develop creativity and problem-solving ability, perceptual and cognitive* and social skills, every psychologically correct thing you can name. It seems that all parents ever needed for their kids to get into Harvad was to give them an empty packing box as a toy. Despite all their effort, once again the clueless parents have been depriving their children of an important developmental tool. There's just no winning.

cognitive: a process by which knowledge is gained

Or is there? Those Saturday afternoons are still free, and it can't be long before some entrepreneur takes advantage of that slot to offer Unstructured Play Class at the community center at $49 for the series, $13 per drop-in. The advanced class in Guided Imagination would cost a little more.

The Back to Basics children's toy catalog is bound to come out with its Vintage-Style Brown Cardboard Box to foster unstructured play skills, with the large size selling for just under $100.

Then again, we could all just wait for new studies to say that letting kids watch hours of TV with a remote control in hand fosters quickreaction skills and small-motor development.

Reading for Meaning

1. What are the findings from the new study at Case Western Reserve and the University of Michigan?
2. What does the author of this article wittily suggest will come out on the market to help parents with the findings?

Reading Deeper

1. What tone does the author use when starting to write about the new classes and toys to help children with their unstructured time? Do you agree with the tone? Explain.
2. What is the importance of recess at school? Explain.

Reading for Writing

1. Take a position on what this editor is saying and write a **response** to the editor of this article. Develop your position and support it.
2. According to the editor, children are "overscheduled." If we take the author's word, then there must have been a study at some point that indicated that children's time should be structured. Without going to the library or the Internet for research, suggest what benefits could come from structuring children's time and getting them into all the activities that the author mentions. Write an essay supporting the structuring of children's time with activities and the benefits that can come from them. Draw conclusions at the end.

RHETORICAL ANALYSIS

Editorials usually provide authors with opportunities to address their readers, to convince or persuade them or to give an opinion about some newsworthy event. In this editorial, the author seizes on the new study about children's playtime and uses **satire,** a literary device to poke fun at something with the intent of change, to present his or her views. To do this, the editor also uses **irony,** a tone that can be humorous, and that says one thing but means another, to convince readers about how he or she feels about the study. In the left-hand margin there is information that directs you to appropriate chapters in this textbook for discussion about the underlined techniques the author used to write the essay or that comments directly about the techniques the author used.

Just Play? Who Knew?

Ch. 2,
Description use
of contrast to
introduce topic
and author's
attitude

Just when parents finally had their children's schedules figured out for maximum success skills, along comes this new _blather_ about unstructured play.

Up to now, it's been soccer practice Tuesday afternoons and games on Saturday mornings (remember, 80% of L.A. children can't hack the test for the President's Council on Physical Fitness). Monday is private tutoring in standardized test-taking skills. Wednesdays are for after-school piano lessons, which have been linked to better spatial reasoning (whatever that is, we're sure it will come in handy for the SAT's in 10 years). Scouts on Thursdays for socialization. Meeting of the Primary School Reading to the Literate Club on Fridays (all the top universities are looking for community service these days). And Sunday school, of course, something for the spiritual side.

Ch. 10,
Persuasion
support for first
part of assertion
in first sentence

Chs. 7
Comparison and
10, Persuasion
introduction of
new position
through
transition

The latest thinking, though, is that the kids have been overscheduled. All these childhood experts are praising recess sand play and the importance of letting kids just hang around, making up their own games or imagining things. It's been the subject of studies at Case Western Reserve and the University of Michigan.

Ch. 5, Definition
use of definition

Use of satire
and ironic tone.
See discussion
that precedes
the article.

This isn't just about meaningless stuff like letting kids have fun and enjoy life. No, this is important. It turns out that unstructured play, the kind that doesn't need instruction or adults to organize it or expensive equipment, is thought to develop creativity and problem-solving ability, perceptual and cognitive and social skills, every psychologically correct thing you can name. It seems that all parents ever needed for their kids to get into Harvard was to give them an empty packing box as a toy. Despite all their effort, once again the clueless parents have been depriving their children of an important developmental tool. There's just no winning.

Use of irony.
See discussion
in above
paragraph.

Or is there? Those Saturday afternoons are still free, and it can't be long before some entrepreneur takes advantage of that slot to offer Unstructured Play Class at the community center at $49 for the

Satire of popular culture. See discussion that precedes the article.

series, $13 per drop-in. The advanced class in Guided Imagination would cost a little more.

    The Back to Basics children's toy catalog is bound to come out with its Vintage-Style Brown Cardboard Box to foster unstructured play skills, with the large size selling for just under $100.

Conclusion satirizes studies. See discussion that precedes the article.

    Then again, we could all just wait for new studies to say that letting kids watch hours of TV with a remote control in hand fosters quick-reaction skills and small-motor development.

In this short editorial, the author incorporates irony and satire, as well as the definition of at least one term, to convince readers that universities and other funding agencies are spending thousands of dollars on topics such as children's playtime, which parents already understand. However, the author is also addressing an audience that usually falls for every new study that comes out telling parents how to raise their children in the best way possible. These parents want the best for their children and don't want them to be left behind academically or socially.

REFLECTIONS ON RECREATION: WHAT ARE YOUR ATTITUDES ABOUT HOW CHILDREN PLAY AND WHAT THEY PLAY WITH?

So where do you stand on giving gender- and/or ethnic-specific toys? Are children looking for reflections of themselves in their toys as they were in the books they were learning to read from when the Dick and Jane series was in use? The relationship between toys and children is symbiotic—each benefits from the well-being of the other; therefore, it "pays" for the toy industry to listen to children and their parents. But there is more to consider. Politics, family values, feminism, the economy, wars, regional values and needs, traditional attitudes, liberal attitudes, movies, and so forth contribute to the ever-evolving industry.

    Observe the children around you and see what kinds of games they play and the toys they play with. How different are they from you when you were a child? How similar? Are sidewalks still decorated with hopscotch squares? Do children play jacks or marbles anymore? Does the nostalgia of children playing innocent games ever make you feel the way Robert Frost did in his poem "Birches"? Recreation, like much of society, has changed and will continue to change as we make new discoveries, leave the past behind, and become more technologically sophisticated. But it looks like Barbie and G.I. Joe will continue to follow children as they grow up. For some, that can be quite comforting.

Reflecting to Write

Persuasive/Convincing

There are some children who grow up believing that dolls are useless; in other words, they have no function. Write an essay that attempts to **convince** a child that dolls are not "useless" and that they do serve a purpose. Be **descriptive** and use names of dolls that are on the market today to make your points.

Argumentation

G.I. Joe and Barbie are gender-specific toys. However, in light of the desire of many individuals to move away from giving toys that are traditionally given to boys or girls because of gender, decide whether or not you might give your son a Barbie doll and/or your daughter a G.I. Joe toy. Write an **argumentative** essay trying to **convince** your reader why you would or would not give a son a Barbie doll and/or a daughter a G.I. Joe toy.

Informative

Go to the Internet and look up Madame Alexander dolls. Get information about their origin, popularity, where they can be purchased, how expensive they are, who buys them and for what reasons, and what has made their popularity endure. Write an **informative descriptive** essay about Madame Alexander dolls. Try to get pictures of various models to present to the class.

Go to the Internet and/or the library and find information about baby dolls. They, like the Barbie doll, have changed over the years. Trace the development of the baby doll from its origins to contemporary baby dolls. Write a **descriptive informative** paper about the evolution of baby dolls and their popularity.

Interview five to ten women of different ages, generations, and ethnicities about the toys they grew up playing with. Ask them about the dolls they had, their favorite toys, whether they had dolls that reflected ethnicities, and what toys they give to their children, grandchildren, or other children in their families. Write an **informative** paper tracing the differences in attitude toward dolls in women of different ages and ethnicities.

Using the above prompt, interview five to ten men, asking them about the dolls/action figures they played with when they were young.

Get permission to visit a day-care center in your area. Visit the areas in the center for each of the age levels of children that the center takes. Examine the different toys and dolls that they provide for the children. Look at the complexity of the games and toys for age-specific children. What kinds of games do the caregivers play with the children? How much free play are they given? How interactive are the different age groups with children of their own age? Write a **descriptive informative** essay about how the day care you visited uses dolls, toys, and games to help children develop motor skills, socialization skills, gender identification, and their imagination.

G.I. Joe and Barbie are both cultural artifacts that say something about the culture of the United States in relation to what parents teach or taught their children about gender. Write an **informative** essay describing how toys reflect the belief that Americans have about men and women today. You might want to visit a toy store to look at their merchandise before you begin your essay.

Chapter 17

Sports: How We Compete

Sports are fun. Sports help many of us get exercise we otherwise would not get. Sports help us meet new people, whether we are participants in a game or spectators along the sidelines or in the bleachers. Sports even enable students to get their education through scholarships, and, if we are fortunate and talented enough, sports may help them get a job playing for a major professional team. Yes, sports have provided countless viewers and participants hours of pleasure, friendly competition, bonding with teammates and family, and winning answers in trivia games.

Sports have also contributed to good sportsmanship. According to *Merriam-Webster's Collegiate Dictionary* online, sportsmanship is "conduct (as fairness, respect for one's opponent, and graciousness in winning or losing) becoming to one participating in a sport." That's an interesting definition to consider, especially in light of what spectators see on television or from the bleachers—teammates piling onto the field to fight, as was the case at the end of the 2002 and 2003 Hawaii Bowl, and in many baseball and basketball games. For some viewers, it is disappointing; for others, it is expected and anticipated. In fact, violence is also expected in ice hockey games because some spectators believe it makes the game exciting. Furthermore, coaches and managers aren't exempt from displays of temper and many have been ejected from the game for confrontations with referees, umpires, and other game officials. If you've ever sat in the stands of a high school sports activity, you've probably heard the parent-critic-coaches yelling the "correct" calls or plays that should be made. These examples, which are numerous, unfortunately overshadow the spirit of competition and provide negative examples of the meaning of sportsmanship while the "good sports" get little notice, like the coaches who have stopped a game in which their teams are winning by numerous points rather than continue to run up the score. On the other hand, there are coaches, spurred on by enthusiastic fans, who will allow their team to accumulate unneeded points against a team that is clearly out of its league.

In addition to on-field activities, off-the-field activities have also caused eyebrows to rise. Questions about equity in school and college sports, integrity of coaches, managers, and players, and criminal activity by players off the field or court have received extensive coverage in the media. Pete Rose, Kobe Bryant, and Eddie Griffin are names usually associated with excellence in their fields; however, their names have recently been tied to illegal incidents. In Bryant's case, no decision regarding his guilt or innocence was made in court, with Bryant and the accuser settling out of court, but many fans and observers have passed their judgment.

Sports used to be associated with images of innocence and youth—baseball, mom, and apple pie. Clear spring days watching young athletes compete on the track, cool fall afternoons and evenings cheering at football games, hot summer days watching tennis players compete—these are exciting events and times that linger with us. Unfortunately, other events frequently tend to intrude on the joy of the game, the pleasure derived from winning, and the lessons learned from losing. How do you feel about sports today?

A Train Wreck Called Title IX:
Effect of Title IX on Men's College Sports

George F. Will

Title IX comes from the Education Amendments of 1972, and it has caused controversy since it was first passed. The next two articles show only two authors who feel strongly about the way it has been interpreted and implemented, but there have been many more authors with divergent opinions. If you do not have an opinion about Title IX, read both articles before you make up your mind. In the following article, George Will, writer for Newsweek *(May 27, 2002), takes on the issue of Title IX from a perspective that the author who follows him does not appreciate. Read both articles and determine which author makes more sense to you.*

Prereading: Do you take sides in an argument about gender issues based on who is conducting the argument—a male or a female? Do you have any feelings about men's and women's sports?

Prewriting: Think about the sports program at your high school. Did the women have as much access to, interest in, and attendance at their activities as the men had in their sports? Did you go to any of the women's sports activities? Write about the support your high school gave to women's sports as compared to men's sports.

enactment:
making into law

adumbrated:
briefly outlined

besotted: drunk
on specific
kinds of ideas

lunacy:
insanity; foolish
act

proportionality:
corresponding
size

immutable:
unchanging

presaged:
warned

exempted:
excused

autonomous:
independent

perverse: not
right or good

construed:
defined

non sequitur:
conclusion that
does not follow
from the premise

dogma: rules of
a belief system

On this 30th anniversary of the enactment* of Title IX, the law prohibiting sexual discrimination in education, consider this: has even more nonsense been written about Title IX than has been committed in its name?

Title IX, as adumbrated* by ideology-besotted* Education Department regulation writers, has produced this lunacy*:

Colleges have killed more than 400 men's athletic teams in order to produce precise proportionality* between men's and women's enrollments and men's and women's rates of participation in athletics. And Title IX has given rise to a huge "gender equity" industry of lawyers, sensitivity-trainers and consciousness raisers.

The industry prefers the word "gender" to "sex" because "sex" suggests immutable* differences, while "gender" suggests differences that are "socially constructed" and can be erased by sufficiently determined social engineers. The story of the policy train wreck that Title IX has become in the hands of such engineers, and of further misadventures that may be coming, is told in a timely book, *Tilting the Playing Field: Schools, Sports, Sex, and Title IX* by Jessica Gavora, a senior policy adviser at the Justice Department.

The U.S. soccer players who won the 1999 Women's World Cup were called "daughter of Title IX," and when the WNBA began playing in 1997, arenas displayed THANKS TITLE IX! banners. This propaganda pleased people who believe all progress comes from government. But throughout the 1970s, the years of the most rapid growth of participation of girls in high-school sports, which presaged* the growth of women's college sports, Title IX was, Gavora says, unenforced and unenforceable because no athletics regulations had been written.

The first Title IX implementing regulations for athletics were written in 1979, and through most of the 1980s athletics were exempted* from Title IX coverage. By which time, the women of the 1999 soccer triumph and of the WNBA were already excelling in their sports. By 1979, one in four high-school girls were participating. Since then, the Title IX "revolution" has made the number one in three. Clearly, autonomous* cultural change, not Congress, produced the increase in female participation, which carried over into college athletics, where the real Title IX revolution has been perverse*.

Gavora says the "ever-mutating" Title IX has been construed* on the basis of a non sequitur*: if there is unequal participation when there is discrimination, there must be discrimination where there is unequal participation. Title IX fanatics start from the dogma*—they ignore all that pesky evidence about different male and female patterns of

cognitive:
factual
knowledge

cognitive* abilities, and brain structure and function—that men and women are identical in abilities and inclinations.

Confronted with evidence of what Gavora calls "the sportsmania gap"—men care more about playing sports—the fanatics say: This is the result of historical conditioning, which colleges must combat. Colleges must not just satisfy women's demands for sports, they must create demands. Until it is created, statistical proportionality often can be achieved only by cutting men's teams. Leo Kocher, University of Chicago wrestling coach, explains the Alice in Wonderland logic:

"Say there's a school that has equal numbers of boys and girls and it decides to offer 200 athletic opportunities. If they have 100 girls who want to play sports and they have 1,000 boys who want to play sports, the law says you must give 100 opportunities to those 100 girls and you must give 100 opportunities to those 1,000 boys. In the end, 100 percent of the girls are fully accommodated but only 10% of the boys are taken care of."

Between 1992 and 1997, 3.4 men's positions on college teams were cut for every woman's spot created. UCLA's swimming and diving team, which has produced winners of 22 Olympic medals? Gone. University of Miami's? Going. As are hundreds of men's gymnastics, wrestling, baseball, track and other teams.

androgyny:
having both
male and female
characteristics

Under what Gavora calls Title IX's "affirmative androgyny*," it is illegal to accept the fact that men and women have different interests, abilities and zeal regarding competition, or that young men have distinctive needs for hierarchy and organized team activities. As Gavora says, Title IX feminists seem to think "young girls aren't worthy of respect and admiration unless and until they act like young boys." And until women have their consciousnesses "raised" by social engineering, they need not be thought of as individuals, but merely as malleable* raw material.

malleable:
capable of being
shaped or
influenced

And now some Title IX imperialists want to extend it from locker rooms to classrooms: If participation in sports must mirror the sexual composition of the student body, why not participation in the engineering department? And why not in extracurricular activities other than sports—debating, orchestra, choir, cheerleading?

Title IX has become, Gavora says, the "codification of feminism" and "the story of this law is in many ways the story of the women's movement." A depressing story.

Reading for Meaning

1. What exactly does Will mean by the "lunacy" that Title IX has produced? List the "offenses" he states that have arisen from Title IX.

2. What term does Will use to refer to the supporters of Title IX? What does this say about his attitude toward Title IX? Can you give any other supporting quotations that further display his attitude about Title IX? List at least three.

Reading Deeper

1. Will struggles with the idea that identity is constructed rather than something that never changes. In fact, he uses the terms "sex" and "gender" to indicate this struggle. Explain the difference between "sex" and "gender" and what your belief is about whether identity is permanent or changing. Give examples. Do you agree with Will or disagree with him? Explain.
2. Will calls the "story of the women's movement" "a depressing story." Some women would agree with him. Would it be for the same reasons? Explain how a feminist would read that comment and how Will actually means it.

Reading for Writing

1. Will complains that women are getting preferential treatment to the detriment of men. However, nowhere in his article does he mention that the federal funds given to institutions were not being used "equally" for both men and women. Instead, he simply complains that because of Title IX, women are now getting more than men. Write a one-page **letter** to the editor of *Newsweek* responding to Will's article.
2. In the following passage, Will is guilty of committing a logical fallacy called a slippery slope or the domino theory, in which the writer predicts that if one thing happens then it will immediately happen in other areas. For example, "If participation in sports must mirror the sexual composition of the student body, why not participation in the engineering department? And why not in extracurricular activities other than sports—debating, orchestra, choir, cheerleading?" If Title IX was written to ensure that federal moneys are being spent equally for men and women in funded colleges and universities, should the areas Will mentions NOT be considered for equal opportunity for both sexes? Do you believe that universities and colleges funded by federal dollars should have equal opportunity for both sexes? Take a **stand** on this and write a well-developed argumentative essay to **convince** your audience about your position.

THE MYTHS OF TITLE IX

Maria C. González

*Now that you have read one perspective about Title IX, here is an-
other one that is a basic rebuttal of Will's position. Although
Maria González is not responding directly to the Will article, she
does address several of the issues Will brings up. Before you make
a decision about where you stand on the issue, read the following
article by Dr. Maria González, associate professor in the Department of English and a member of the Gender Equity Subcommittee
of the University Athletic Committee at the University of Houston.*

Prereading: Think about what you know about Title IX based on your
reading of George Will's article. Consider what he says.

Prewriting: Make a list of points from Will's article that oppose Title IX.

Vocabulary: Looking up and understanding the following words prior
to reading should prepare you for the author's message. Other words
will be defined in the margin.

pundit   non-revenue   quota   compliance   equitable   NCAA

always get frustrated when some right-wing pundit attacks Title IX
for destroying men's sports. The accusation that Title IX is unfair to
non-revenue male sports programs, like wrestling, is false. To accuse the
expansion and development of more athletic opportunities for women as
a blow to the sports opportunities for men rings very hollow once one
seriously begins to look at the issues involved.

Title IX is often incorrectly identified as the law requiring equal
opportunities for women to play sports. Its actual wording does not
specifically identify sports at all. Below is the actual language from the
Education Amendments of 1972:

> No person in the United States shall, on the basis of sex, be ex-
> cluded from participation in, denied the benefits of, or be subjected
> to discrimination under any education program or activity receiv-
> ing Federal financial assistance.

This federal civil rights statute requires equal opportunity for women in
education programs that receive federal funds. Many states have similar
requirements for the funds they give to universities and colleges. The
law was originally designed to prevent the discrimination women faced
before Title IX. Most law schools, engineering programs, and medical
schools did not allow or required low and strict quotas for women in

their programs. The federal government understood that it was unfair to keep women out of educational programs and to limit their opportunities just because they were of a different gender. Before 1972, a law school or medical school could deny admittance to a woman just because she was a women no matter what her test scores or grades were. There were many all-male engineering programs in the country, and even today, the field is heavily dominated by men. This law was originally about trying to make sure women had the same educational opportunities as men had in order to become professionals.

In 1979, the Office of Civil Rights within the Department of Education clarified Title IX for athletics. The clarification became known as the Intercollegiate Athletics Policy Interpretation and formed the basis from which compliance of the law would be defined. The three major areas under review were identification of sports being offered to both genders, determination of whether they were receiving similar amounts in scholarship, and determination of whether the sports' infrastructures supported them equitably. The first two categories were easy to measure: Were a similar number of sports programs offered to both genders, and did they receive a similar number of scholarship offerings? The third category, program infrastructure, involves all the coaching support, training support, and facilities available to the sporting programs. The policy simply stated that all these items needed to be equitable but not necessarily the same. Hence, the other part of this policy was the compliance issue. How do you measure equity and know you have complied with the rules and regulations of Title IX?

Compliance of any civil rights law is often the hardest thing to do for any bureaucracy. It was the process of applying the spirit of Title IX to athletics that began all the trouble, according to some pundits. They have accused Title IX of requiring the elimination of certain sports programs for men. This is false. The compliance in the law does not require *enhancement:* the elimination of any program. It requires the enhancement* of opportunities for the historically deprived gender and working toward equity in sports programs. Institutions did not have to have a fifty-fifty split on all parts of their programs; they simply had to prove they were working toward that goal. The trouble came when athletic departments realized that they only offered maybe 10 percent to 25 percent of their athletic budgets and programs to women. They were way out of line with the concept of equity. When the total number of participating student athletes is 200 and only 20 of those 200 are women, a program has a compliance problem. When a university offers ten major sports programs and only three are for women and all the rest are only for men, it has a compliance problem. When the budget for an athletic program is $1 million and only 10 percent goes to women's sports, the university has a compliance problem. When students attend a university or college where 56 percent of the students are women and only 10 percent of the university's student athletes are women, the university has a compliance problem. These were many of the issues that universities and colleges were facing in the 1980s and 90s. They had allowed their athletic programs to become enormous but really serve only one gender. Hence, Title IX began the wonderful expansion of sporting opportunities for women and girls. This included opportunities at the kindergarten to twelfth grade level as well because Title IX includes the public school system in the country.

The National Wrestling Coaches Association has attempted to sue the Department of Education, claiming discrimination against men. Their case was thrown out of court but they are appealing, of course. What the wrestling coaches fail to understand is that universities would rather cut their programs and hand those resources over to build some sort of women's sports programs than to cut men's football or basketball, which are the programs with the majority of resources. The decision of a university to direct their athletic resources is left to the discretion* of its internal decision-making bodies. Nowhere in the language of Title IX or NCAA policy does it say how to meet compliance issues. It simply requires colleges and universities to attempt to create more equitable opportunities for women to participate in sports.

discretion: free decision or choice within certain legal bounds

In 2002, the Bush administration commissioned a special review of Title IX and its impact on collegiate* athletics. The commission members were mostly individuals who believe in the old myths* about Title IX. They, like many others, actually believed Title IX was discriminating against men's sports programs. What they discovered was that even after years of attempting to create equitable opportunities in sports for women, 64 percent of athletic budgets went to men's sports programs and only 32 percent to women's. And that while many more athletic opportunities are now available to women, still only 43 percent of athletic scholarships in the nation went to women. The sad truth is that the commission discovered that women's sports did not cause the elimination of wrestling programs. It was the unwillingness of universities to contain the ever increasing budget demands of football and basketball. The funding priorities remained football and basketball, and sports like men's wrestling or track became less important. In many cases, universities decided to allow less audience-attracting sports programs to carry the full burden of developing opportunities for women in sports. If the National Wrestling Coaches Association should be suing anyone, it should be suing the National Football Coaches Association for being unwilling to take on any of the burden of Title IX and expanding the opportunity for women in sports.

collegiate: college

myths: an unfounded or false notion

Reading for Meaning

1. Who makes the decisions about how Title IX money is spent?
2. Explain the difference between equal and identical.

Reading Deeper

1. What exactly is Title IX supposed to do? Explain.
2. Explain two myths of Title IX that people have believed and are, in fact, false.

Reading for Writing

1. Investigate the number of sports at your university/college or at the university/college close to you. If the institution is public, the budgets for the sports should be accessible to the public. Determine how much is spent on women's sports and how much is spent on men's sports. Find archival information about which sports were offered prior to Title IX. Has Title IX made a difference in women's sports in that particular institution? Write an **informative** essay discussing how the money is distributed among the different sports. Arrive at conclusions.

2. Make a list of points supporting Title IX from the González article. Using the list you made opposing Title IX from the Will article in the prewriting, determine your position on Title IX. Write an **argumentative** article attempting to **convince** the reader that Title IX has hurt men's athletics or has not hurt men's athletics. Be sure to document the material you use.

PETE ROSE—AMERICA'S ANTIHERO

John Harty III

The topic of sports has many aspects that evoke loyalty, excitement, and even a sense of patriotism. And those players who have made a name for themselves by their talent, courage, and triumphs tend to live in the minds of those who follow sports. For example, baseball, sometimes known as our national sport, has produced many individuals of whom we can be proud and who can act as role models for our children. We even take our children to Cooperstown, New York, to visit the Baseball Hall of Fame so we can point out the great legends of the game. In 2003, Pete Rose, a player with enormous talent, admitted to a crime he committed so that he could be allowed to be placed in the Hall of Fame. This controversy has ignited debates inside and outside baseball. In the following article, John Harty III, assistant professor of English at Prairie View A&M University, not only explains Rose's situation, but he also uses another example of a sports hero who was prevented from being honored in the Hall of Fame.

Prereading: How much do you know about baseball? Did you play softball when you were a youngster? Did you follow a particular baseball team or baseball player?

Prewriting: For decades, professional and amateur athletes have been discovered taking steriods or other illegal drugs to enhance their performance or committing crimes such as assault, rape, and so forth. In some cases, prizes have been stripped from Olympic athletes and teams. Do you think a major athlete, amateur or professional, should be honored/recognized in a public way for his or her achievements in the game if he or she has participated in illegal activities? Write a paragraph stating and supporting your position.

Vocabulary: Looking up and understanding the following words prior to reading should prepare you for the author's message. Other words will be defined in the margin.

antihero   hustle (v)   tragic flaw   Joe DiMaggio   Lou Gehrig
integrity

Pete Rose is baseball's Peter Pan, the perpetual man–boy in a base-ball uniform who refused to grow old. Mr. Rose's nickname is Charlie Hustle, a name which would be almost ludicrous* to give to any other player. Rose, even as an aging superstar, did the little things, too, such as hustling out a hit that surely would end up an easy out, hustling on and off the field, and playing each of his five positions (first base, second base, third base, left field, and right field) with the vigor of a young player who had just reached the Major Leagues.

ludicrous: ridiculous

The *American Heritage Dictionary* also defines "hustle" as a noun; slang: "An illicit or unethical way of doing business or obtaining money; a fraud or deceit." Pete Rose did not and does not take steriods, drugs, and does not smoke or drink alcohol. But he has one Tragic Flaw. He is an addicted gambler with a tendency to let gambling ruin his life. He has lost hundreds of thousands of dollars betting over the years. Even as the manager of the Cincinnati Reds, he recently confessed for the first time in his best-selling book, *Prison without Bars* (Rodale Press, 2004), that he gambled to retain the thrill that he could no longer get as he did on the playing field:

- As Rookie of the Year in 1963
- In five positions in All-Star games
- In four league championships with Cincinnati
- In two winning World Series with Cincinnati
- In two pennants with the Philadelphia Phillies
- In one World Series Championship with the Phillies
- By connecting for 4,256 hits
- In breaking the immortal Ty Cobb's record
- In hitting for 44 games straight for the longest hitting streak in the National League (the longest, of course, is held by Joe DiMaggio for 56 games as the all time record while he played for the American League's New York Yankees).

The Baseball Hall of Fame, also known as Cooperstown, for the New York town where it is located, honors players for "the numbers they put up," but the rules of election also include the following: "Voting shall be based upon the player's record, playing ability, integrity, sportsmanship, character, and contributions to the team(s) on which the player has played."

Commissioner Bart Giamatti ruled in 1989, the first year Pete Rose became eligible for the Hall of Fame, that Rose was ineligible. Giamatti, a former member of Yale's English Department and also the former President of Yale, subsequently* died from a heart attack shortly after rendering* the Rose decision. Many attributed* this to the enormous stress he was under on ruling about Pete Edward Rose.

subsequently: following in time; later

rendering: delivering

attributed: explained by giving a cause

Rose lied about his gambling for 14 years. With only a year of eligibility left to get into the Hall of Fame under regular voting (a Veterans Committee could eventually elect him in the future), Mr. Rose, with writer Rich Hill, decided to tell it like it is, thus gaining for his honesty, Rose hopes, one last shot at the Hall of Fame, and, aw shucks, why not make a million-dollar book advance along the way.

illiterate: unable to read or write

Rose's exclusion from the Hall of Fame has brought back the memory of another legendary group banned from baseball. In 1919 the notorious Black Sox scandal took place. The legendary and illiterate* Shoeless Joe Jackson was a member of that group that took $5,000 as a bribe to throw the World Series against Cincinnati. He then proceeded to hit .375 and make several outstanding plays. Judge Kennesaw Mountain Landis banned Jackson from baseball. The disgraced Jackson spent his working life from then on as the owner of a liquor store. The refrain* from that day was, "Say it isn't so, Joe."

refrain: a recurring phrase or saying

punitive: inflicting or involving punishment

Judge Landis wished to clean up baseball, and his punitive* actions brought baseball back into America's limelight. Much the same *resuscitate:* bring back to life

thing has happened to Pete Rose in an American business that wishes to be squeaky clean. Although his six-month prison sentence for income tax fraud was not a part of the ban decision (it took place after he had already been banned from baseball), the prison sentence did little to resuscitate* Rose's image. Baseball fans have already enshrined* Pete Rose in their "Hall of Fame." Yet Rose, of course, wants the immortality of being in the real Hall so that future generations will hear about his playing days. If he fails to make the Hall in 2004, his final chance comes by the distant voting of the Veterans Committee.

enshrined: to put in a shrine

Commentators have pointed out that if admittance into the Hall over the years had been made with a "morals clause," the numbers in the Hall would be much lower. Joe DiMaggio and Lou Gehrig are giant exceptions whose characters off the field were as strong as their playing talents on the baseball diamond. As Mickey Herschowitz pointed out in the *Houston Chronicle:* "Of course, you should know the Hall includes among its membership drug addicts, drug dealers, drunks, wife abusers, a bigamist*, and at least two players who fixed a game and several guilty of putting on airs." And one must remember that O. J. Simpson remains a member of the Pro Football Hall of Fame.

bigamist: a person married to more than one person

Baseball Commissioner Bud Selig has recently stated that he has not read *Pete Rose: My Prison without Bars* and has declined to comment on what he might do about the Rose decision. Many fans hope for a split decision: Rose will not be allowed to manage or coach in baseball again. However, Rose did "put up the numbers" (most resoundingly* the record for hits—4,256 of them) and should be enrolled in baseball's Hall of Fame.

resoundingly: loudly, emphatically

He has two final chances: one in the final year of his eligibility (2004) and another in the Veterans Committee selection. But the odds are that Pete Rose will not make it into the Hall of Fame. He might well be remembered as is Shoeless Joe Jackson and the attendant association with a lack of integrity*. If Rose is a victim, he is a victim of something America has emphasized over the years since Rose's early playing days: accountability.

integrity: firm observance of a code of moral or ethical standards

Reading for Meaning

1. List the different achievements Rose had during his baseball career.
2. What offense did Rose commit that kept him from being inducted into the Hall of Fame?

Reading Deeper

1. What is a "morals clause" and what does it do?
2. Explain what is meant by hitting ".375" in baseball. Who did it?

3. How can one be referred to as a "victim" of accountability? Is this good or bad? Explain.

Reading for Writing

1. How do you think Harty feels about Rose's failure to be allowed into the Hall of Fame? Does he support the decision or does he oppose it? Quote specific passages that make you believe that he supports or opposes the decision.
2. Find the name and address of the current baseball commissioner and write a **letter** supporting or opposing the induction of Pete Rose into the Hall of Fame. Be sure to give specific reasons for your position.

No BLOOM ON THIS ROSE

Fay Vincent

In the following article from Time *magazine (Jan. 9, 2004), Fay Vincent takes another perspective about Pete Rose's desire to be enshrined in the Hall of Fame. Do not make up your mind about whether he should or should not be admitted until you have read this article also.*

Prereading: Did you know who Pete Rose was before reading or hearing about him in this class? What did you know? What did you think about him?

Prewriting: What would you tell a youngster who is enthusiastically involved in baseball about Pete Rose? Write a description of what you know at this point about him.

Vocabulary: Looking up and understanding the following words prior to reading should prepare you for the author's message. Other words will be defined in the margin.

redemption   credentials   Joe Torre   Dusty Baker

———

B aseball is a game of errors and redemption. It is a game that keeps track of mistakes and features them as part of the official line score—runs, hits, errors. Pete Rose made the ultimate error by betting on baseball while he was managing the Cincinnati Reds in the late '80s. Although he consistently denied his guilt, he accepted a lifetime ban from the game. For the next 14 years, Rose continued to publicly deny that he had ever bet on baseball. The arrival last week [January 12, 2004] of his new book, in which he finally confessed, stunned the baseball world. Rose wants to persuade that world that his admission should redeem him and thus restore him not just to the game but ultimately to the Hall of Fame.

There is only one capital crime in baseball, and the reason for that is historic. In 1919 gamblers rigged* the World Series, and the guilty players were tossed out of baseball for life by the first commissioner, Kenesaw Mountain Landis. That middle name tells you all there is to know about how tough he was, and ever since it has been clear that anyone who bet on a game in which he was a participant would be banished from baseball for life. No one has ever been reinstated, not even the hapless* "Shoeless" Joe Jackson, who for years begged Landis to be reinstated* and whose cause has drawn support largely because Jackson was illiterate* and almost surely had what lawyers would describe a "diminished capacity" to comprehend the consequences of his actions.

Against that backdrop, Rose presents a difficult case. His credentials for the Hall of Fame are superb*—no player has had as many career hits—but before he can be voted on by the baseball writers (who initially have the power to grant that ultimate honor), he must be reinstated in the good graces of the game. Only the commissioner has that authority. And no commissioner thus far has seen fit to pardon anyone, because the lifetime ban has been an almost perfect immunization* against the gambling virus. Rose has not made things easy for himself. His book is like the player he was. He was known as Charlie Hustle, and he hustles through brief moments of remorse and apology. In what may be the most remarkable statement in the book, he writes, "I'm sure that I'm supposed to act all sorry or sad or guilty now that I've accepted that I've done something wrong. But you see, I'm just not built that way . . . Let's move on." It's as if the ordinary rules of public apology do not apply because he is different.

Rose is a product of our culture. We teach our business moguls*, our movie stars and our Pete Roses that the rules of conduct, and even our laws, do not apply to them as they do to the rest of us. During Major League Baseball's investigation of Rose in 1989, one of his lawyers argued to me that "Pete Rose is a national institution. He doesn't think baseball can afford to take him on."

Rose obviously wants to be reinstated both to manage again and to join his peers in Cooperstown, N.Y. Since he last managed, the salaries of top managers like Joe Torre and Dusty Baker have risen to levels Rose could only have dreamed about when he was in the dugout. Money is what makes Rose hustle, and he would dearly love to command the big money now available to managers. But how can Commissioner Selig

rigged: to control by deceptive or dishonest means

hapless: unlucky

reinstated: allowed back in

illiterate: unable to read or write

superb: excellent

immunization: protection from or resistance to

mogul: very rich or powerful person

ever trust Rose not to fall back into his old betting ways? I will be astonished if Pete ever puts on a manager's uniform again.

As things stand now, I see little reason to reinstate Rose. He has not made the slightest effort to redeem himself, and no tight-lipped confession can compensate for the damage he has done to the game and those around it. He surely has no case for being let back on the field as a manager. As for keeping him off the field but allowing him to be a candidate for the Hall of Fame, I would not, as commissioner, take the risk. By reinstating him, I would be watering down the antigambling deterrent* that has been effective for more than 80 years. Such a decision would not be popular, perhaps, but there are times when a public-opinion poll does not produce a principled result. Rose alone has kept himself out of the Hall of Fame. That honor should go to honorable players, umpires, executives and managers. If it is not in Pete Rose to be sorry or sad or to feel guilty, then it should not be in Commissioner Selig to feel merciful. For most of us, the premise of forgiveness is contrition*. So, as Rose put it himself, "Let's move on."

deterrent: act that prevents or discourages someone from acting

contrition: being sorry

Reading for Meaning

1. What is Rose's intention in his new book? How does Vincent feel about it?
2. What reasons are given for taking "Shoeless" Joe Jackson's side in reinstating him to the game of baseball? Do you think these are reasonable? Explain.

Reading Deeper

1. Vincent creates a simile in the third paragraph comparing a lifetime ban from baseball to an immunization. Explain.
2. Explain Rose's attitude about gambling in his book.
3. What do you think Vincent means by "the rules of conduct, and even our laws, do not apply to them as they do to the rest of us." Explain and decide if you agree or disagree with that statement.

Reading for Writing

1. Using both the Vincent and the Harty articles, determine your position on this debatable topic and write an **argumentative** essay attempting to **convince** your reader that he or she should believe your side.
2. Gambling, like alcoholism and drug abuse, is an addiction. Look up Web sites about gambling as an addiction. Find statistics, definitions,

effects, and so forth about it, and write an **informative** essay about gambling and the many ways people gamble.

Double Standards

Deroy Murdock

Even though the federal government protects individuals against discrimination on the basis of color, sex, religion, or national origin, there are still many places that legally prohibit people of certain sex, color, or religion from participating in their organization. How is this possible? The groups are privately owned and do not accept funding from the federal government. For example, if you apply to teach at a school that is aligned with a particular religion, that school may refuse to hire you on the basis of your religion if your religion is different from the institution's. And it is perfectly legal. The following article takes issue with the "discrimination" that women feel as they are not allowed to participate in the Augusta National Golf Tournament. Read the article below by Deroy Murdock and then the one following it by Deborah Rhode before you make up your mind about your feelings.

Prereading: How do you feel about men and women being segregated from one another in schools, places of recreation, clubs, or specific organizations?

Prewriting: Have you even been discriminated against for any reason? Sometimes it's as subtle as being watched while you are shopping in a store or as obvious as being refused entrance to a place you want to go. Write about your experience and how you felt.

Vocabulary: Looking up and understanding the following words prior to reading should prepare you for the author's message. Other words will be defined in the margin.

**Augusta National Golf Club   Junior League   ACLU   Boy Scouts
Jim Crow   Spelman College   Daughters of the American Revolution**

----

excoriated:
censured
severely

Feminists who demand that Augusta National Golf Club admit women should think twice. If they succeed, men may try to gain entry to places now open only to females.

Located outside a small town in Georgia, Augusta National has been excoriated* for its males-only membership policy. After the National Council of Women's Organizations planned to target sponsors of

preemptively:
action that is
done before
others can do it;
done by oneself
first

Augusta's 2003 Masters championship, the club preemptively* asked several companies to withdraw their support from the golf classic.

"Any entity that holds itself out as publicly as they do ought to be open to men and women alike," NCWO chair Martha Burk tells me. "It does not reflect well on the club and its tournament, which is the crown jewel of golf, to be identified with discrimination."

Augusta, in turn, released a poll on November 13 that shows Americans disagree with Burk. Among 800 Americans surveyed between October 30 and November 4, by WomanTrend, a division of the polling company, 74 percent agreed that "Augusta National has the right to have members of one gender only." Asked whether the club was correct not to cave under Burk's pressure, 72 percent of males concurred*, while 73 percent of women agreed. (The poll's margin of error is +/−3.5 percent.)

concurred:
agreed

"These are extraordinarily high numbers, especially when you consider how aggressive the campaign against the club has been," said WomanTrend president Kellyanne Conway. "What's also striking is how few women support Ms. Burk's demands."

It would be easier to take Burk seriously if she directed some of her wrath at other discriminatory establishments. Though far less controversial, there are venues where men are forbidden. If women penetrate Augusta, how will they bar males from all-female institutions?

Start with the 68 member campuses of the Women's College Coalition. Such schools as Barnard, Mount Holyoke, and Smith offer top drawer, liberal arts instruction. Men need not apply. With 296 chapters in America, Canada, Mexico, and England, the Junior League's active dedicated associates perform community service projects. Its Web site explains that they also "share ideas and build networks for information exchange" when they gather. There are some 193,000 Junior League members—not one of them male. Women even have their own golf course, albeit* abroad. Since its 1924 launch, the Ladies Golf Club of Toronto has had only female members. As *Sports Illustrated*'s Rick Reilly discovered, men may play there, but only when invited by members. Women sneered at Reilly, who was stunned by the separate but unequal amenities* for male guests: a poorly appointed locker room and a gravel-covered parking lot behind the clubhouse. "This joint makes Augusta seem like the ACLU," Reilly wrote in *SI*'s September 16 edition.

albeit: even
though

amenities:
something that
leads to
comfort,
convenience, or
enjoyment

The vital principle here is freedom of association. As the First Amendment states, "Congress shall make no law . . . abridging . . . the right of the people to peaceably assemble." These words reflect the right of Americans to associate privately with whomever we wish, and not with others, for whatever reasons.

sector: a
subdivision of
society

There is no such freedom in the public sector*. Since Americans are equal before the law, government schools, for instance, cannot discriminate on the basis of sex (although some exceptions apply in cases of military education). Public golf courses may not bar women (or men) from their fairways. If the CIA implemented a "men only" hiring policy, it would be sued at once, and rightly so.

Those who do not understand this distinction may wind up reducing everyone's liberties.

For example, gay rights activists have pressured the Boy Scouts to hire gay scoutmasters despite the group's ban on homosexual leaders. But if the Boy Scouts must employ those who clash with their teachings, must New Jersey's Mountain Meadow summer camp do likewise? Mountain Meadow is a place where gay parents can take their kids for outdoor recreation. Should it be forced to hire heterosexual camp counselors who might frown on Tommy's two daddies?

segregation: separation of race, class, or ethnic group by discriminatory means

What about Jim Crow? Southern states and cities imposed laws that required the segregation* of private facilities. Thankfully, the civil rights movement got those regulations killed.

But what if a private group opens its doors only to blacks (or only to whites)? It should be legally free to do so. Should it be ridiculed or even boycotted? Americans are free to do those things, too. But the First Amendment's free-association clause ultimately protects the right of private groups to define themselves as narrowly as they like.

Freedom of association keeps every organization from resembling every other. While public institutions should accept all classes of citizens (including GIs—gay and straight—who clutch their weapons and not other soldiers) private outfits and facilities should remain free to craft their membership rosters as they desire. That includes Spelman College and the Daughters of the American Revolution. Until feminists welcome men into all-female establishments, they should embrace freedom of association. Otherwise, they may learn the hard way that what's good for the gander* is good for the goose, too.

gander: adult male goose

Reading for Meaning

1. The second sentence of this article, "If they succeed, men may try to gain entry to places now open only to females" sounds like a threat. Can you explain why the tone of this sentence is important to the message of the article? How does the last sentence reflect the same tone and idea?

2. Explain what "freedom of association" means in this article.

Reading Deeper

1. The very first word in this article refers specifically to "feminists." Who does this word include? Can a man be a feminist? Explain.

2. In the following sentence, "If women penetrate Augusta, how will they bar males from all-female institutions?" Murdock makes the assumption that women want to bar males from all-female institutions. Is that what this article is about? Explain your answer.

Reading for Writing

1. In at least one academic conference that invites men and women to participate and to present papers annually in the United States, there is usually one session given by the feminists of the organization that prohibits male presence. Consider the points that can support this practice and the points that can oppose it. Write an **argumentative** essay, taking a **position** and defending it. Be sure to include the different sides of the argument.

2. Think about when you were younger. Did you ever want to play a sport that only the members of the opposite gender played? Or were you part of a class in which someone chose members for teams? Were you allowed/chosen to participate? If not or if you were not chosen until last or almost last, how did you feel? Write a **personal narrative describing** the incident and how you felt.

TEE TIME FOR EQUALITY

Deborah Rhode

In the following article, Deborah Rhode presents a position that counters that of the preceding article. Whether or not you agree with Murdock's position as he stated it in "Double Standards," read the following article and make up your mind.

Prereading: What do you know about golf? Why do you think women have not been allowed to play it for so long?

Prewriting: Find a brief history of golf and write a response to the underlying philosophy men had about it when it was first played. You might give a little bit of the history as context for your response.

Vocabulary: Looking up and understanding the following words prior to reading should prepare you for the author's message. Other words will be defined in the margin.

exclusion   Tiger Woods   tee times

For many women lawyers, golf is only partly about golf. It is also about status, networks, and exclusion. Golf has long been a source

of inequality for women—often to the indifference of men. The extent
of insensitivity was brought home this summer when Tiger Woods was
asked to comment on the exclusion of women from Augusta National
Golf Club, the site of the prestigious* Masters tournament. According to
Woods, Augusta's members, including many top executives from Fortune 500 companies, were "entitled to set up their own rules the way
they want them."

prestigious:
commanding
position in
people's minds

It seems unlikely that Woods would have made a similar statement
a decade ago, when he would have been excluded from many clubs like
Augusta because of the color of his skin. His response, and those of
other defenders of club policies, speaks volumes about this nation's different tolerance for racism and sexism.

"It's just the way it is" no longer flies as an excuse to bar golfers of
color. In 1990, a famous flap* ensued when the Professional Golfer's
Association's annual championship was scheduled for Shoal Creek, an
Alabama country club that discriminated against blacks. After civil rights
groups threatened to picket* the tournament and to boycott* its sponsors,
some sponsors withdrew more than $2 million in advertising revenues*.

flap: state of
excitement

picket:
demonstrate or
protest

Within weeks, Shoal Creek accepted its fist black member, and
within months, the nation's four major golf organizations adopted anti-
discrimination policies. These policies prohibit the organization from
holding a tournament at a course that excludes individuals based on
race, sex or national origin.

boycott:
combine with
others to abstain
from buying,
using,
patronizing, etc.
as a means of
coercing or
intimidating

Augusta, which independently administers the Masters, is not
bound by these policies, and none of its corporate sponsors pulled their
support after learning of its gender bias. Even Hewlett-Packard (one of
the corporate sponsors), whose female CEO would be barred from membership, was "unavailable for comment" when contacted by the *New York
Times.* A request by the National Council of Women's Organizations
that Augusta admit a woman before next year's tournament provoked
defiance by its chairman, William Johnson: "We will not be bullied,
threatened or intimidated. . . . We do not intend to become a trophy in the
[council's] display case."

revenues: total
income
produced by a
given source

WHY IT MATTERS

Should women care? To many women's rights activists, discrimination
by private golf clubs is not high on the agenda compared to, say, domestic violence or the feminization of poverty. For many individuals who
care about social equality, the goal should be trying to do in—not get
in—these bastions of male privilege.

Yet gender bias on the golf course should not be omitted from the feminist wish list. Such discrimination has public consequences; it keeps professional women out of the informal networks where business and mentoring relationships are forged*. According to the National Golf Foundation, about two-thirds of male executives now play golf. For women lawyers, lack of access to these potential clients is a significant problem. In an increasingly competitive practice climate, a broad client base is often crucial to professional power, status and economic reward.

forged: brought into being by effort

Although few clubs now exclude women entirely, many discriminate in tee times and membership privileges like access to the "men's grill." Even public courses, which legally are barred from discrimination often get away with it. In her research for *The Unplayable Lie,* a book about women and golf, Marcia Chambers documented countless instances of female players being refused tee time during peak hours, only to find that male colleagues* calling later had no difficulty gaining access.

colleagues: fellow workers in a profession

Despite these indignities*, many professional women who are short on time, interest or innate* athletic ability are nonetheless learning to play golf. More than 1 million women begin each year, according to Suzanne Woo's recent book, *On Course for Business: Women and Golf.* So it is all the more irritating when these women still are not invited, or entitled, to join their male colleagues' game.

indignities: humiliating treatment

innate: belonging to from birth

As long as golf is a source of both economic and symbolic inequality, it should be a focus of professional concern and social reform. Strategies include pickets, boycotts and enforcement or enactment of statues withholding tax or liquor-license privileges from clubs that discriminate. Some women have also brought successful lawsuits under public accommodations laws that prohibit discrimination by private clubs that offer services or facilities to non-members.

Few golf courses still retain the sign, legendary until five years ago, at the Royal St. George's Club in Britain: "Women and dogs prohibited." But women are not yet equal partners in this sport and until that changes, they will not be truly equal colleagues in the professional world outside it.

Reading for Meaning

1. How is golf more than just a game to women? Explain at least two ways.
2. Why do some feminists not see equality on the golf course as an important issue to pursue? How does Rhode feel about it? Explain.

Reading Deeper

1. Why do you think Tiger Woods was interviewed about the discrimination against women as practiced at Augusta? Was his answer what was expected? Explain.
2. Why is it surprising that Hewlett-Packard did not pull its support for the Augusta tournament after learning of gender discrimination? Explain.

Reading for Writing

1. Now that you have read both articles, determine which side you support. Write your own **argumentative** essay using points from both articles to argue your **position.**
2. Interview five male and five female students on campus and five male and five female professionals off campus about their views on discrimination against women in sports. Write an **informative** essay discussing the position that the interviewees take about the subject.

RHETORICAL ANALYSIS

Maria González begins her argumentative, persuasive essay with a definitive statement about what she believes. By stating her thesis and her informed opinion at the outset, there is no doubt in the reader's mind where this article is going and what it will support throughout the essay. She then moves on to use historical background, exemplification, and statistics to provide compelling evidence to support her point. Since she is writing an argumentative essay, González brings in the oppositions' points and methodically refutes them. In her conclusion, she reviews the issues she discussed and ends on a note that supports her points. In the left-hand margin there is information that directs you to appropriate chapters in this textbook for discussion about the underlined techniques the author used to write the essay or that comments directly about the techniques the author used.

The Myths of Title IX

Maria C. González

Ch. 10, Persuasion begins with personal opinion and targets a specific group

I always get frustrated when some right-wing pundit attacks Title IX for destroying men's sports. The accusation that Title IX is unfair to non-revenue male sports programs, like wrestling, is false. To ac-

Ch. 10,
Persuasion
thesis/claim is
last sentence
and mentions
the issues
without naming
them

cuse the expansion and development of more athletic opportunities for women as a blow to the sports opportunities for men rings very hollow once one seriously begins to look at the issues involved.

Title IX is often incorrectly identified as the law requiring equal opportunities for women to play sports. Its actual wording does not specifically identify sports at all. Below is the actual language from the Education Amendments of 1972:

Ch. 5, use of
definition

No person in the United States shall, on the basis of sex, be excluded from participation in, denied the benefits of, or be subjected to discrimination under any education program or activity receiving Federal financial assistance.

This federal civil rights statute requires equal opportunity for women in education programs that receive federal funds. Many states have similar requirements for the funds they give to universities and colleges. The law was originally designed to prevent the discrimination women faced before Title IX. [Most law schools, engineering programs, and medical schools did not allow or required low and strict quotas for women in their programs. The federal government understood that it was unfair to keep women out of educational programs and to limit their opportunities just because they were of a different gender.] **Before 1972, a law school or medical school could deny admittance to a woman just because she was a woman no matter what her test scores or grades were. There were many all-male engineering programs in the country, and even today, the field is heavily dominated by men.** This law was originally about trying to make sure women had the same educational opportunities as men had in order to become professionals.

Ch. 9, Causal
use of cause and
effect in
brackets

Ch. 3,
Exemplification
use of
exemplification
in bold

Ch. 10,
Persuasion use
of historical
background for
support

In 1979, the Office of Civil Rights within the Department of Education clarified Title IX for athletics. The clarification became known as the Intercollegiate Athletics Policy Interpretation and formed the basis from which compliance of the law would be defined. **The three major areas under review were identification of sports being offered to both genders, determination of whether they were receiving similar amounts in scholarship, and determination of**

Ch. 1, Reading
announces and
lists the points
as a reading
technique in
bold

Ch. 10,
Persuasion asks
a specific
question that the
author will
answer with
evidence

Ch. 10,
Persuasion
points out
opposing point
of view

Ch. 10,
Persuasion
rejects the point
and supplies
support for her
position

Ch. 10,
Persuasion
provides
compelling
evidence
through
statistics
indicated by
wavy line

Ch. 3,
Exemplification
use of
exemplification
for support in
bold

whether the sports' infrastructures supported them equitably. The first two categories were easy to measure: Were a similar number of sports programs offered to both genders, and did they receive a similar number of scholarship offerings? The third category, program infrastructure, involves all the coaching support, training support, and facilities available to the sporting programs. The policy simply stated that all these items needed to be equitable but not necessarily the same. Hence, the other part of this policy was the compliance issue. <u>How do you measure equity and know you have complied with the rules and regulations of Title IX</u>?

Compliance of any civil rights law is often the hardest thing to do for any bureaucracy. It was the process of applying the spirit of Title IX to athletics that began all the trouble, according to some pundits. <u>They have accused Title IX of requiring the elimination of certain sports programs for men</u>. **This is false.** <u>The compliance in the law does not require the elimination of any program. It requires the enhancement of opportunities for the historically deprived gender and working toward equity in sports programs. Institutions did not have to have a fifty-fifty split on all parts of their programs; they simply had to prove they were working toward that goal</u>. **The trouble came when athletic departments realized that they only offered maybe 10 percent to 25 percent of their athletic budgets and programs to women. They were way out of line with the concept of equity. When the total number of participating student athletes is 200 and only 20 of those 200 are women, a program has a compliance problem. When a university offers ten major sports programs and only three are for women and all the rest are only for men, it has a compliance problem. When the budget for an athletic program is $1 million and only 10 percent goes to women's sports, the university has a compliance problem. When students attend a university or college where 56 percent of the students are women and only 10 percent of the university's student athletes are women, the university has a compliance problem.** These were many of the issues that universities and colleges were facing in the 1980s and 90s. They had allowed their athletic programs to become enormous but really serve only one gender. Hence, Title IX began the wonderful expansion of sporting opportunities for women and girls. This included opportunities at the kindergarten to twelfth grade level as well because Title IX includes the public school system in the country.

Ch. 10, Persuasion another issue to support her claim/thesis

The National Wrestling Coaches Association has attempted to sue the Department of Education, claiming discrimination against men. Their case was thrown out of court but they are appealing, of course. What the wrestling coaches fail to understand is that universities would rather cut their programs and hand those resources over to build some sort of women's sports programs than to cut men's football or basketball, which are the programs with the majority of resources. The decision of a university to direct their athletic resources is left to the discretion of its internal decision-making bodies. Nowhere in the language of Title IX or NCAA policy does it say how to meet compliance issues. It simply requires colleges and universities to attempt to create more equitable opportunities for women to participate in sports.

Ch. 10, Persuasion use of background to support her point in bold

In 2002, the Bush administration commissioned a special review of Title IX and its impact on collegiate athletics. The commission members were mostly individuals who believe in the old myths about Title IX. They, like many others, actually believed Title IX was discriminating against men's sports programs. What they discovered was that even after years of attempting to create equitable opportunities in

Ch. 10, Persuasion use of statistics to provide compelling evidence indicated by wavy line

sports for women, 64 percent of athletic budgets went to men's sports programs and only 32 percent to women's. And that while many more athletic opportunities are now available to women, still only 43 percent of athletic scholarships in the nation went to women. The sad truth is that the commission discovered that women's sports did not cause the elimination of wrestling programs. It was the unwillingness of universities to contain the ever increasing budget demands of football and basketball. The funding priorities remained football and basketball, and sports like men's wrestling or track became less important. In many cases, universities decided to allow less audience-attracting sports programs to carry the full

Ch. 10,
Persuasion
concludes with
a review of the
issues
mentioned in
the claim and
supports the
claim

burden of developing opportunities for women in
sports. If the National Wrestling Coaches Association
should be suing anyone, it should be suing the National Football Coaches Association for being unwilling to take on any of the burden of Title IX and
expanding the opportunity for women in sports.

REFLECTIONS ON SPORTS

What Exactly Is the Purpose of Sports?

Sports, in general, can be controversial; however, when gender equity is added, the topic becomes even more controversial. Although there are those who seem to believe that some women do not enjoy playing sports, there are many female athletes who have won personal as well as worldwide recognition for their contributions to their sports. The increasing competitiveness and precision of women's sports should reveal to critics that women are serious contenders. In May 2003, Annika Sörenstam was the first woman to compete in the men's Professional Golf Association (PGA) Tour's Bank of America Colonial event. In 1973, Billy Jean King competed against Bobby Riggs, a world champion tennis player in the 1930s who claimed that even at her relatively young age, she could not beat him at tennis. Women are not *getting serious* about sports. Women *have been serious* about athletics for decades but have been pushed aside repeatedly. During World War II, women formed the first professional female baseball league, which was the subject of the movie, *A League of Their Own,* released in 1992.

Unfortunately, women's achievements have not been as publicly recognized as other issues. Many athletes' use of illegal drugs, their gambling, and their involvement in criminal activity have smudged the image of the All-American player—sort of like waking up and discovering that the boy next door is really the serial killer you've been hearing about for months. It just isn't something you want to think about. For most of us, athletes and sports have been something we have grown up with and have enjoyed, and want to pass that love of sports on to our children. Sports are, in fact, a way to build character, but sports are also a way in which character has been stripped away. It is up to us as participants and as spectators to determine which role we want to play in sports as they grow into bigger and better games, like the extreme games that demand even more skill and athletic endurance. Where do you stand on this social issue?

Reflecting to Write

Argumentative

A high school football coach once defended the irate actions of one of his angry football players by saying, "You can't judge [the player's] character by his actions on the sideline. He was reacting to what was going on on the field." If one of the messages we send players and parents is that participation in sports builds character, how do we reconcile the message with justification of violent/angry reactions during or after a game? Write an **argumentative** essay **defining** character and taking a **position** on whether or not the role of violence in sports contributes to character building inside and outside the game.

Once women began competing, they progressed into a territory dominated by men: golf. Even though they created the Women's PGA, some women have wanted to compete in the men's PGA. This has created a controversy over whether women should be allowed to compete against men in a traditionally all-male sport or whether they should be restricted to their own association. Conduct research in this area and list the points that support and oppose the issue. Make an informed decision about your position and write an **argumentation** essay trying to **convince** your reader about whom women should or should not play with.

Personal Narrative

Think about a sport that you actively participated in while you were in high school or that you actively participate in now. What was the most exciting moment you had in that sport? Write an **informative personal narrative describing** the moment.

Think about a sports activity that you attended as a spectator and at which you were annoyed by another spectator who was rude and critical of the coach, the players, the officials, or any other part of the game. Write a **descriptive narrative** discussing his or her actions and how you and or the other spectators reacted to his or her behavior.

Informative

Go to your local high school and attend one or two men's and one or two women's at-home basketball games. Write an **informative** essay, **comparing** and **contrasting** the number of fans present, the quality of the playing, the enthusiasm of the fans, the enthusiasm of the cheerleading, the presence of administrators, and so forth. Draw conclusions about the popularity of men's and women's basketball at that particular high school.

Investigate the number of athletic scholarships awarded at a local high school. Ask the administrator who gives you the information for a breakdown of men's and women's scholarships awarded. Also ask for the amount of money awarded to men and women for those scholarships. Finally, ask for a record of athletic scholarships awarded in the last ten years to men and women from that school. Write an **informative comparison and contrast** essay about the equity of scholarship money provided to men and women in the last ten years in that high school.

Chapter 18

Safety and Security:
How We Protect Ourselves

Most of us want to feel safe and secure in private and in public. That feeling, however, is becoming harder and harder to experience since the September 11th attacks on the World Trade Center Twin Towers and the Pentagon. Now we are periodically reminded that we have a false sense of security and that we must be on alert. Every few weeks and during holidays or special events, we are reminded of our vulnerability by new color-coded alerts. However, this is not much different from the mid-1900s. Many of us still remember the weekly Friday air-raid signal sounding at noon and the close encounter we had in the 1960s with Castro and the Bay of Pigs. In fact, if we look closely in some of our towns, we can still find the air-raid horns rising above a street in neighborhoods, at major intersections, or in other public areas. Not much has changed, but it seems like everything has changed. Desire for that sense of personal security for ourselves and our families is the same, but the threat hanging above our heads, like the sword of Damocles, remains mysterious and from an unknown source.

This global fear, however, should not let us forget that many of us, regardless of age, simply want to feel safe among our peers, in our classrooms, and in relationships. The basic need for safety and security is a primary condition identified by Abraham Maslow on the second level of his Hierarchy of Needs, following the most basic needs of air, water, food, and shelter and so forth. Maslow believes we need these elements to help us develop into individuals who can perform at peak levels. If we are worried about belonging, being loved, or feeling self-esteem, Maslow believes we cannot reach our peak of self-fulfillment. Whether we are safe in our homes, in our classrooms, in our cars, or in the special places we go for a sense of security, we must be able to feel safe and at ease to be the best we can be.

On the other hand, we have the power to make others feel comfortable or uneasy, needed or unnecessary, attractive or common, loved or ignored. Each of us influences, to different degrees, the people around us. And while we can't *control* others' feelings or attitudes, a recent survey reported that 76 percent of its respondents said that a smile is one of the most important assets coworkers can have to be successful. A smile says many things to those who see it, including, "I'm safe. I won't hurt you." Or it can say, "You're okay. I like you." How many people have you helped to feel safe today?

The Beach

Stella Thompson

How we protect ourselves sometimes means more than self-defense in the traditional sense. Sometimes we have a vulnerability that demands protection from the outside world, from individuals who are cruel and intentionally want to hurt us, or simply from situations where we know that we will come away with battered feelings. Sometimes there are quiet places we can go either to soothe feelings of fear or to heal from pain. In the following essay, Stella Thompson, professor of composition and literature at Prairie View A&M University, adopts the persona of a young person trying to find comfort in a world full of pain.

Prereading: Have you ever been teased or made fun of to the point that you were truly hurt? How did you cope with the pain?

Prewriting: Most of us have an "escape plan" for times when we are hurt by those around us. Write a descriptive paragraph explaining your "plan" and the place you go to feel "safe."

Vocabulary: Looking up and understanding the following word prior to reading should prepare you for the author's message.

sanctuary

I go to the beach when I feel lonely. I go there to find myself, my authentic self. I like the word authentic. Mrs. Williams used that word in class last Wednesday when she was talking about the expensive book she found in an antique shop. I keep thinking about that book, thinking about how important it is to be found.

When I go to the beach, I feel like Mrs. Williams' book, found. That's a strange feeling. Sitting on the sand with my feet pointing at the water, I lean back on my elbows and stare. It almost seems like I'm looking at forever. People don't usually walk along the beach where I like to go, but the strange thing is that I don't feel lonely there. I never really stopped to think about being lonely on the beach until last Wednesday. After class, I drove to the beach, just to think. Monday and Tuesday weren't good days. Just about anything bad that you can image happened between Monday and Wednesday. After that last quiz, the second one in a week, I couldn't wait to get off campus. I'm usually a good student, but last week was not a good week.

At the beach I just sat on the sand and listened. Brian always asks me what I hear. He says he can't hear anything but noise. I can't imagine why he thinks water, wind, and birds are noise. People are noise. People who don't like your hair or your shoes or your shirt. That's noise. People who laugh when you don't know the answer or when you drop something. If someone laughs at Brian, he just yells, "Shut up!" I guess it doesn't bother him. He doesn't like staying at the beach very long. He usually says, "Let's go," ten minutes after we get there.

I watched a kid building a sandcastle one day. He didn't seem to notice that he was alone. He just kept building. I think he must have felt like I do when I sit on the sand and just stare at the world. The birds make their sounds, and I hear the wind, but I don't usually think too much about the sounds. I watch the water. It's like a friend. It seems to know when to come closer and when I need more space. When I walk along the edge of the water, I feel free. I can splash my clothes or get sand in my hair and no one laughs at the way I look. If gulls laugh, I think they laugh with me, not at me.

The wind sometimes shifts, catching me by surprise. When I take along a book, the pages try to turn the wrong way. I guess that's sort of like when I sit in a classroom, wondering what I want to do with my life. Some days the pages of my life just seem to turn the wrong way. My little brother teases me that I should just become a beach bum. He knows how much I like the beach. I keep thinking about Mrs. Williams' book and about the woman at the beach, with an extra shirt tied around her waist. Some people seem to plan ahead. They must carry around a mental checklist, with room for notes about the weather, about the traffic— maybe even about what they will have for dinner.

That woman just disappeared over a sand dune. I'm not sure that she even saw me. I don't know if she saw the sand or the sky. I don't talk very much, but I feel like I have interesting conversations when I go to the beach. Mrs. Williams would laugh if I told her about my imaginary conversation with the heron. I don't think herons spend much time talking about what they don't like about each other, the way people do. Herons seem more dignified. Maybe they think there are more important things in the world than what you're wearing.

I always feel angry when I see people throw trash on the beach. They may think that someone else will pick it up, but they probably just don't think at all. I almost stepped on a broken bottle today. My shoes were wet, so I pulled them off. I wonder if someone tossed that bottle on the sand, or if it just drifted there with the tide. Trouble happens that way. Sometimes people cause problems, by doing something wrong or by not doing something right. Other times, things just happen, and it's no one's fault at all. I don't guess you can protect yourself, in either case. Maybe I should just keep my shoes on all of the time. Signs don't make any difference. "No littering" doesn't mean anything. I watch people throw their trash all over the place, even under the litter sign.

I don't think the world is really such a bad place. People just have a bad week once in awhile. I guess everyone does, but maybe we make things worse for ourselves and others when we don't take responsibility for making things better. When I watch the tide bring things in, sometimes a sea skeleton or a scrap of paper or cloth, I think about where those things started their journey. They wash ashore and become part of a new place. I have a shelf of treasures at home. The pieces of shells and driftwood are good company when I can't go to the beach. They remind me that everything has a story, and I don't feel so lonely.

I visited a bird sanctuary once. The field glasses were fun. I could see things that I would have missed. One man pointed out a rare bird with an interesting name. He said I was lucky to see it in a lifetime. I guess people don't know what they miss when they aren't looking. I liked the sanctuary. I like that word. My beach feels like a sanctuary. I go there to sort out my thoughts and to decide who I really am. I don't usually take field glasses. That might be a good idea. I could follow the gulls farther. They disappear so fast.

Mrs. Williams read a poem to the class a few weeks ago. It was about four blind men and an elephant. I thought the poem was funny because each man thought a different part of the elephant was the whole animal. I told my dad about the poem, but he didn't laugh. He just said people are like that. I guess I know what he meant. We see something and think we understand it better than anyone else. Most of the time we are wrong. Usually there is at least one person who knows more than we do.

Authentic is probably the right word for the real elephant, not for the part we think we understand. I don't think I'll ever see an elephant at the beach. If I ever do, I hope I'll remember to look at the whole animal.

Mrs. Williams found a picture that she liked, in that book from the antique shop. She brought the book to class to show us the picture. It was a picture of a little girl looking through a telescope at the stars. We wrote poems about the picture. Everyone wrote something different. I never could think of the right words, but I wanted to say that the stars the little girl was looking at were the same stars I saw at the beach after my family's last picnic.

Some things, like stars, don't change with the tides. Some things do. Life is complicated. I like to think that life is like things that I can understand. Mrs. Williams calls that thinking in metaphors and similes. Sometimes, when things get tense, Dad says, "Go with the flow," and Mom answers, "but then drop anchor." I guess they're both right, on different days. Mrs. Williams says that growing up is a lot like flying a kite. You have to learn how to hold the string. That seems like a simple thing, but it took me a long time to learn. I ruined a lot of kites. One day Dad said he was glad I wasn't practicing driving.

When I'm sitting on the sand at the beach, life seems simpler. I can almost write that poem about the stars when I hear the surf and the gulls. I forget about the ketchup I dropped on my shirt at lunch, and I think about how the beach would look if everyone enjoyed it as much as I do. When you value something, you don't destroy it, or try to make it into something else. You just like it the way it is, for what it is. People should be treated like that, authentic. I don't mean that something can't be improved. Change can be good. When I'm hungry or thirsty, I think the beach would be nicer with a food court or two, or a water fountain, but maybe not.

Reading for Meaning

1. Why does the narrator go to the beach?
2. What constitutes "noise" in the narrator's mind? Describe.
3. What makes the narrator angry? Explain why.
4. The narrator thinks "Maybe I should just keep my shoes on all of the time." Is the narrator speaking literally or metaphorically? comparing unlike things? Explain what the narrator is talking about. Does the narrator do this again anywhere in the narrative? Explain.

Reading Deeper

1. Why is it important "to be found"? What does the narrator mean by that statement? Explain.
2. Brian and the narrator do not seem to have much in common. Describe what each likes. Why do you think the narrator asks him to go to the beach? Explain.

3. The narrator describes the setting through the use of **personification,** giving human characteristics to nonhuman things. Give three examples of personification and explain how thinking about the things in that way makes the narrator feel.
4. How is the narrator different from the woman on the beach and others like her? Give examples.
5. Is the narrator in fashion? How do you know? Explain.

Reading for Writing

1. Thompson uses a style of writing called **interior monologue.** Even though interior monologue is not usually structured quite so well as this narrative is, it is still a style that is used to tell a story. Reread the narrative and look carefully for the images or words or thoughts that are repeated and that tie the essay together. For example, look for the word *lonely* and see when it is used. Is a sense of loneliness or not feeling lonely a theme in the narrative? Look for other themes and overarching ideas, and explain how they make it cohesive. Write an **analysis** of the narrative, explaining how Thompson creates unity and cohesion in this **personal narrative** without the rigid structure usually expected in a written work.
2. The narrator in this personal narrative finds safety and security by going to the beach. Where do you find yours? What do you look for in a safe place? Write a **descriptive personal narrative** discussing the place where you go when you need to get away from the world for a little while. You may use a traditional structure or you may use **interior monologue.** For the latter, use Thompson's narrative as your model.
3. Who is the narrator of this narrative? Is the narrator male or female? Reread the narrative, marking it for gender-specific indicators—hints that might make you think the narrator is male or female. Take a **position** about which gender you think wrote the narrative, and write a well-supported essay defending your choice.

THREADING THE INVISIBLE LINE

Elline Lipkin

Just how safe are we in today's society? Do you have burglar bars on your windows in your home? Do you have a security system? How important is it for you to have a sense of safety and security in your personal environment? Many of us believe we are safe until we or someone we know is attacked or injured in some unex-

pected way. In the following article, Dr. Elline Lipkin, assistant professor at the University of California, Berkeley with a degree in Creative Writing from the University of Houston, presents a personal narrative integrated with information from various sources that discuss safety in our lives.

Prereading: There was a time in recent American history when many people slept with their windows open and did not lock their doors at night. There was a time when strangers could knock on a person's door and be greeted with hospitality. What do you think about these events?

Prewriting: What did you parents or guardians tell you when you were young about talking to strangers or taking candy from strangers? Did you pay attention to them? Write a paragraph explaining what you would say to a young child about strangers today.

Vocabulary: Looking up and understanding the following words prior to reading should prepare you for the author's message. Other words will be defined in the margin.

chaos   prostate cancer   Parkinson's disease   calamity   cortex
reptilian

---

negotiated: succeeded in getting through

maelstrom: violent whirlpool

furtive: secret

deli: short for delicatessen, who sells ready-to-eat foods

assuaged: helped make easier

venture: do something dangerous or risky

Years ago, when I first moved to New York City, I was terrified. After I negotiated* the airport's maelstrom* of quick-moving chaos, navigated past all those fast-moving walkers, made my way to the borrowed apartment where I was staying (gripping the cab's seat as it barreled along the city's blocks), fumbled with the front door's many locks (I had yet to live anywhere where it was standard to have multiple locks on the door; three was considered average), I finally arrived. I felt amazed I had simply made it there alive. The only problem was, I was afraid to go outside.

My first three days in the city consisted of furtive* runs to the corner deli* to buy orange juice, milk, and one of their special sandwiches, cut in two, so I could have one half for lunch, one half for dinner. This meant I didn't have to go out again. Little assuaged* me as the sights, smells, and sounds of the city roared up around the apartment I was hunkered down (or up) in as I kept myself hostage trying to adjust to the over-stimulation, the extrasensory sway of it all.

Inside, I studied my subway map, a neighborhood diagram the owner of the apartment had left, guidebooks, anything that might help me comprehend where I had landed, until, after a few days' adjustment, I finally felt able to go out. I'd venture* a slightly longer walk beyond the deli, try walking quickly down a new block, step into a new store, until finally, I led up to a quick subway run.

sheepishly: with embarrassment

Years later, I look back at that time period a little sheepishly*. It was all so new, so different, so loud, that it was all I could do to make my short ventures out and then retreat to a controlled environment where I felt safe again. Gradually, the streets, with all their fast-paced activity, started to feel safe as I walked them and nothing bad seemed to happen. Each trip was like a deposit in an account of well-being as I built up my confidence, although entering the subway, with its closed cars, still always caused a bubble of anxiety to rise. . . .

accosted: approached and spoken to in a threatening way

Then, one Sunday morning, I remember reading the *New York Times* and drawing a sharp breath as I read about two roommates who were walking home in Chelsea, a neighborhood not far from where I lived, when they were accosted* by a man who forced them into the stairwell of their building where they were both brutally robbed and raped. The story was disturbing enough to me, but what I couldn't shake from my thoughts was the idea that I just knew that they had felt safe. How many times had I ventured onto what I felt was a "questionable" block because I was with a friend? The strength in numbers that having an escort meant an invisible veil of untouchability cloaked us from harm was part of my thinking then—surely, since I was not alone, nothing bad could happen. More than learning the shocking details of their attack, realizing that being accompanied by another was not protection enough was what shook me up that morning. It left me turning the question over and over in my mind: When are we really ever safe in reality versus safe in feeling? And what should we put our faith in, if we can't trust that we are safe when we think we are? Is being safe, truly, just a matter of dumb luck?

subtext: indirect meaning, beneath the surface

assessing: measuring

In the Jaunary/February 2004 issue of *The Atlantic,* Cullen Murphy explores the insurance industry in "Looking for Trouble: Get a Life—At Your Own Risk," but the subtext* to the article is the impossibility of truly assessing* risk hand-in-hand with the very human need to try. Murphy points out that we're almost constantly bombarded with conflicting information about the safety and danger of eating certain types of food, doing certain types of activities and more. Figuring out one's "risk load," he writes, is obviously beyond the ordinary person's capacity. For example, he offers that "people who are short have a greater risk of dying from stroke, but tall men are more likely to develop prostate cancer." Murphy mentions that it's not surprising that "people who suffer from depression have a greater likelihood of heart disease,

disposition: one's mood

but a sunny disposition* isn't necessarily a happy alternative: optimists are more likely than pessimists to be involved in automobile accidents (because they don't give themselves enough time to get to where they're

buffs: fans

gallstones:
pieces of hard,
crystal matter
formed in the
gallbladder

simulated:
giving the
appearance or
effect of

rationalizing:
giving reasons
for; justifying

hypervigilant:
extremely
cautious and
careful

trepidation:
fear, uncertainty

phenomenon:
something that
happens that can
be seen or felt

cumbersome:
difficult to
handle because
of its large size

going and end up speeding).'' And on it goes. Sports buffs* are obviously at greater risk for injuries, but apparently are less likely to develop gallstones*. Coffee-drinkers risk increased blood pressure, but decreased risk for Parkinson's disease. . . . All of this left me to wonder again: How can we ever really know what's safe?

After I had been in New York City about a year, a friend raved to me about a self-defense course she had taken. Working with instructors who dressed up in elaborate padding in order to mock-mug the participants, she claimed the course was actually effective because you practiced techniques of self-defense in simulated* scenarios rather than learning how to fend off an invisible attacker. More importantly, she said, it made her feel safe as she walked around the city late at night. I was hesitant to accept the reality of how little I knew about self-defense, rationalizing* that walking around in a hypervigilant* state was enough. Still, the story of the roommates rattled around in my head. When the same friend sent me a card with the start date of the next session and informed me she had paid the tuition as a gift, I had no reason to refuse. With trepidation*, I went. . . .

In a January 2004 article in *The New Yorker,* writer Malcolm Gladwell explores this mystifying disconnect between actually being safe and feeling safe by looking at the phenomenon* created by the S.U.V. Gladwell considers the recent rise in popularity of the cumbersome* vehicle and why people decide to buy one versus a more compact car. S.U.V. buyers, he writes, "thought of big, heavy vehicles as safe: they found comfort in being surrounded by so much rubber and steel." In fact, Gladwell concludes, after visiting various car testing centers, speaking with automotive experts, and consulting the latest statistics, this is utterly false. Citing the work of a cultural anthropologist G. Clotaire Rapaille, whose specialty, he says, is, "getting behind the rational—what he calls 'cortex'—impressions of consumers and tapping into their 'reptilian' responses," Gladwell reports that when S.U.V. buyers thought about safety, they were thinking about something "that reached into their deepest unconscious." Rapaille tells him that people think safety is connected to their surroundings being round and soft, hence air bags were crucial in making drivers "feel" safe. Rapaille was also able to pinpoint the contradictions between real safety and the feeling of safety through other means. He says, "there's this notion that you need to be high up. That's a contraction, because the people who buy these S.U.V.'s know at the cortex level that if you are high there is more chance of a rollover. But at the reptilian level they think that if I am bigger and taller, then I'm safer. That you can look down is psychologically a very powerful notion."

The oddest contradiction of all came in this report that drivers feel safer when there is a cup holder attached to the dash. "What was the key element of safety when you were a child?" Rapaille asks. "It was that your mother fed you, and there was warm liquid. That's why cup holders are absolutely crucial for safety. If there is a car that has no cup holder, it is not safe. If I can put my coffee there, if I can have my food, if everything is round, if it's soft, and if I'm high, then I feel safe." I was struck again by how the feeling of safety and the rituals we enact to try and keep this feeling near us can eclipse* what the reality is, as best it can ever be known.

eclipse: cover; hide

Gladwell goes on to offer more examples about "the puzzle of what has happened to the automobile world: feeling safe has become more important than actually being safe." He tests the response times and maneuverability of a silver 2003 Chevrolet Trailblazer—a 5,000 pound S.U.V.—alongside a shiny blue two-seater Porsche Boxster convertible. To his amazement, while getting into the Boxster, he didn't initially feel safe (he describes feeling as if he was sitting in a go-cart). While taking it through numerous handling tests, he felt he had perfect control, in contrast to the response times of the bulky Trailblazer. Are the best cars the biggest and heaviest vehicles on the road? he asks, and answers himself, "not at all." Gladwell continues, "The S.U.V. boom represents, then, a shift in how we conceive of safety—from active to passive." While most people use the standard of size as a measuring stick for safety, that is to feel safe, what they should think of in terms of actually being safe is how the car handles. Herein lies an essential contradiction again.

Gladwell describes a Jetta as a "nimble" car designed to obey the driver's most subtle command. Yet the car "is so small and close to the ground and so dwarfed by other cars on the road, that an intelligent driver is constantly reminded of the necessity of driving safety and defensively," he writes. "The S.U.V. embodies the opposite logic. The driver is seated as high and far from the road as possible. The vehicle is designed to overcome its environment, not to respond to it." He continues, "Jettas are safe because they make their drivers feel unsafe. S.U.V's are unsafe because they make their drivers feel safe. That feeling of safety isn't the solution; it's the problem."

Gladwell's explanation of notions of "active safety" versus "passive safety" left me wondering if I was actually most safe during those initial weeks after I moved to New York City, when even a rustling paper bag pushed suddenly by the wind made me jump, never mind someone walking rapidly behind me. Could I have become more complacent after my self-defense class, perhaps not unlike the roommates, lulled* into a sense of security that made me in fact more vulnerable*. "When you feel safe, you can be passive," Rapaille says, speaking of the fundamental appeal of the S.U.V. "Safe means I can sleep. I can give up control. I can relax. . . ." The actively engaged driver, who is aware of the road and

lulled: relax one's vigilance, sense of safety

vulnerable: open to attack

the looming vehicles beside it is one who is going to be more aware of his or her environment and have better response times.

Although I have no particular interest in cars, I found myself fascinated by *The New Yorker* article, which seemed a crystalline exploration of the confusing contradictions inherent* within the notion of safety. If we can't see the myriad* risks and dangers that constantly swirl around us, how do we know they're really there? Will we ever be able to gauge* what could have been if we hadn't crossed to the other side of the street. Or gone on a certain trip? Or left the house when it was quite so dark? How do we know how many invisible foes we unconsciously navigate every day of our lives? Or does some mixture of learned behavior and intuitive* response guide us from these unseen pitfalls, hence accounting for judgment, reason and experience? How do we tread every single day that narrow line between safety, real and imagined, and risk, also real and imagined, and still make our way home, each time, alive?

inherent: belonging to by nature

myriad: many, a vast number of

gauge: measure, understand

intuitive: by instinct

Works Cited

Gladwell, Malcom. "Big and Bad: How the S.U.V. Ran over Automotive Safety." *The New Yorker* (January 12, 2004): 28–33.
Murphy, Cullen. "Looking for Trouble: Get a Life—At Your Own Risk." *The Atlantic* 293.1 (January–February 2004): 193–94.

Reading for Meaning

1. What were the unfamiliar experiences Lipkin had to deal with when she first moved to New York that made her feel afraid? List them.
2. Describe Lipkin's experiences at becoming accustomed to her new environment.
3. What event turned Lipkin's sense of security into doubt? How did she react? Explain.

Reading Deeper

1. Where do you sense Lipkin came from? What in the essay gives you that feeling? Quote passages that support your ideas.
2. What effect did the Ropeik and Gray book have on Lipkin? Explain.
3. How was the self-defense course Lipkin enrolled in different from other classes?

Reading for Writing

1. Lipkin did not write this article to scare us; rather she wrote it to question our false sense of security. Think about the places you feel that

you are safest. Write a paragraph or two **describing** them, explaining why they make you feel safe.

2. In light of the recent rash of kidnappings, preparing a child or young person for a dangerous situation is wise. Write a **letter** to a young friend telling him or her how to protect himself or herself from a stranger who might be threatening or even seemingly friendly or asking for help.

WARNING SIGNS: DOES YOUR DATE HAVE VIOLENT TENDENCIES?

Doug McPherson

Dating appears to have become more complex and complicated over the years. Who calls whom for a date? Who pays for what? With the advent of the Women's Movement, more women are feeling easier about calling men for a date and paying for everything. And men are agreeing to it. However, the possibility that one might encounter danger on a date is still something that both men and women should always be aware of, but most advice articles are written for women rather than for men, making the assumption that women have more to be concerned about than men do. In the following article from the magazine Self Defense for Women *(2003), Doug McPherson gives women tips about how to recognize danger signals before problems occur.*

Prereading: Have you ever gone on a date that just didn't feel right? How did you handle it?

Prewriting: What one thing have you learned about dating in your experiences? Write a paragraph stating what you learned and what led you to learn it.

Vocabulary: Looking up and understanding the following word prior to reading should prepare you for the author's message. Other words will be defined in the margin.

adage

L earn how to recognize the danger before it hits home!

Dating can turn violent—even deadly—in seconds. The good news is there are signs you can watch for in your date's behavior to give you a heads up.

The National Domestic Violence Hotline recommends taking notice if your date has any of the following behaviors:

- Tries to embarrass you
- Attempts to control you or the date's events
- Makes decisions for you
- Acts overly jealous
- Has sudden mood swings
- Gives you a gut feeling of fear.

Mike Domitrz, who speaks on dating communication and safety and published a book earlier this year on those topics called *May I Kiss You?* (Awareness Publications, $15.95), says control is a big red flag.

"Look for anything that leads you to believe the person is trying to take control," he says. "And jealousy can be a tip off. Even on the first date, if you walk into a restaurant and another guy starts talking to you, and your date gets very jealous, that's a sign."

Domitrz also says to watch for dates who aren't flexible. "If you suggest a change in plans and the person won't hear of it, that's something to notice."

"It's also important to take part in planning the date from the start. Tell your date the kinds of things you like to do instead of letting him plan all the activities. That also lets you set a tone as an assertive person who knows what she likes," Domitrz adds.

Bring up dating history in conversation. It's OK—in fact, necessary—to do a little fact-finding. "Find out how relationships ended," he says. "If he's trashing his former girlfriends, you have to ask yourself if you want to be trashed, too."

And just because a date is well-behaved on the first date is no reason to let your guard down. Experts say some dates will "act nice" only to get what they want later.

If you do find yourself in a situation where you're uncomfortable, create space. "It's the golden rule," says Domitrz. "Get out of the situation at the earliest sign of trouble and if you have to make a scene with yelling, do it. It's much better than being assaulted."

CREATING SAFE DATES

- **Pay your half of the date.** "The old adage that a girl owes the guy something if he pays is still alive," says Domitrz. "Pay half and take care of that issue up front."

- **Date during the daytime.** "You don't find yourself in as many dangerous situations during the day," says Domitrz. "People are up, your nosy neighbor is watching and it's just a safer alternative than dating at night."
- **Go to public places.** Bowling alleys, roller-skating rinks and outdoor malls are all great date locales. Pick spots with lots of people and easy access to help should you need it.
- **Develop a good self-image.** "Self-esteem and self-confidence are key," Domitrz says. "Take stock in the value you bring as a human being." To get started, have two or three friends write letters of recommendation for you. Take those letters and write a speech about yourself in third person, then read that speech often.

Reading for Meaning

1. What are the warning signs that your date might be violent? List them.
2. What is the big "tip off" that is a warning signal according to Domitrz?
3. Why would you want to know about your date's dating history? Explain.

Reading Deeper

1. Explain what is meant by owing one's date something if he pays for the date.
2. Why do readers have to be told that it's all right to make a scene at the earliest signs of trouble? What are women generally taught? Explain.

Reading for Writing

1. Go to www.google.com and run a search for Dating Bill of Rights. You will find several Web sites that give not only the list of rights but also additional information. Review several of the sites and choose the three best sites that give the most information for someone just beginning to date. Write a **letter** to a young friend who will begin dating soon and direct him or her to the three sites you chose, explaining the benefits of each one briefly. This **exemplification letter** should sound helpful rather than preachy.
2. Today there has been a rise in online dating. Do you think there should be some general guidelines written to help both parties recognize a possibly dangerous situation before it happens? In a **process analysis** essay, give a list of suggestions to both male and female readers

about how to find a safe date online. Use the suggestions in the above article as a model.

NOT SO SAFE BACK HOME

Anna Quindlen

When most of us go to college, we do not think of the possibility that we will be assaulted by someone from our own campus. Even less do most of us think that a female cadet would be attacked and raped by her classmates. The safety of women cadets and of women who serve in the military has usually been taken for granted if they remain within the confines of their campus or their barracks. However, in February 2004, Pentagon officials went to the Air Force Academy to investigate complaints of sexual assault filed by approximately thirty-seven female cadets against other cadets. In the following article, Anna Quindlen (Newsweek, 2003) reveals the horrifying facts about how women are not only being assaulted by their own comrades, but also how those in the positions of authority are looking the other way and dismissing the issue. It makes many members of the reading public wonder who is looking out for those who are supposed to be looking out for us.

Prereading: Rape is actually a controversial topic that can be argued against strongly. How do you define rape?

Prewriting: Create a list of incidents in which a woman, in your opinion, can clearly claim she was raped.

Vocabulary: Looking up and understanding the following word prior to reading should prepare you for the author's message. Other words will be defined in the margin.

trauma

W hen the news broke that the rape of female cadets had become nearly as commonplace at the Air Force Academy as midterms or maneuvers, it came as a shock to most Americans accustomed to think-

bastion: a well-protected place

ing of the service colleges as bastions* of the very best.

But for those familiar with sexual assault in the military, and the role of women in the armed forces, the horrifying stories had an inevitable tinge of same-old same-old. And the administration reaction, of

hyperbole:
exaggeration

distress and determination to make things right, had the scent of both hyperbole* and hypocrisy.

There are surely those who think that this moment, with soldiers in the Iraqi desert and an internationally unpopular war being waged by the United States, may not be the best time to talk about the institutionalized prejudice in the nation's fighting forces.

But it is exactly the right time.

In times of peace the powers that be may conveniently forget how many women there now are on the battlefield, how hard they work and how well they perform. Military leaders may forget that if the number of women willing to enlist drops significantly, the ability of America to defend itself will drop significantly, too.

compatriots:
persons who
come from the
same country

And they may forget how terrible it is that women who must face sexual assault from the enemy as the price of war too often expect to face it from their compatriots* in peacetime. As a colonel in the Air Force whose daughter says she was attacked by a fellow cadet told *The New York Times,* "She knew she could have been captured by an enemy, raped, and pillaged* in war. She did not expect to be raped and pillaged at the United States Air Force Academy."

pillaged:
looted, robbed
during war,
especially

In fact, no soldier should expect to be assaulted by another without significant consequences. Yet that is what has happened. Those who have always been hostile to female soldiers say that this is inevitable, given the atmosphere of esprit* with which women interfere, given the machismo that is essential for trained fighting forces. This is insulting to male soldiers. The suggestion is that they are always one beer away from a sexual assault, no more able to control their violent impulses than an attack dog.

*atmosphere of
esprit:* common
spirit existing in
the members of
a group

The truth is quite different. Sexual trauma has reached epidemic proportions for women in the military—with numbers twice as high as in the civilian population, according to a Department of Defense study—because it can. The offense is not adequately investigated or punished. And the authorities send down the word by their response, and their nonresponse: sit down and shut up.

This is not only morally wrong; it will inevitably weaken the country's fighting forces. If the word is out that, as one young woman has suggested, an institution like the Academy is a place where being sexually assaulted is taken for granted, women of intelligence and ambition will look elsewhere. The Pentagon has announced that the top officials of the Air Force Academy will be replaced in an effort to change the school's culture. But it's a broader military culture that needs to change where women are concerned.

They know that there's already a khaki ceiling. The ladder to the top jobs has to include combat positions, yet women are still formally

deployments:
sending out of
troops into an
area

prohibited from most combat units. (This although the lines between deployments* is so thin as to be semipermeable; Shoshana Johnson, now a prisoner of war, was sent to Iraq as a cook.) The group that lobbied for a change in the combat ban, the Defense Advisory Committee on Women in the Services, has been weakened by the Bush administration, swayed by conservative critics who howled about its "feminist agenda." Among the new female voices in the Pentagon is one former master sergeant who opposes women in combat because "'women enjoy being protected by men.'" She says that the skills needed for fighting are "to survive, to escape, and to evade," adding, "Clearly, women do not have those as a rule."

Actually, it sounds as if those are exactly the skills women have had to acquire to fend off sexual abuse and harassment by their colleagues. Many of them may have listened with bitterness when the president, announcing the start of this war, promised the Iraqi people they would be free from "rape rooms," given the fact that for some of them the rape rooms have been their own barracks.

As their sisters did in Desert Storm, many will return from the Middle East having served in combat despite the ban, with an official wink and a nod. Maybe it's the same wink and a nod you get after you've been pinned down and penetrated by a fellow cadet, the one that says you have to go along to get along.

hanker: want
deeply

If this is a nation that uses female soldiers to defend us but is unwilling to defend them in turn, the number of ambitious women in the service may dwindle. That will satisfy those who hanker* for old, traditional sex roles. It will also mean a fighting force that has lost its very best prospects. Who could blame them? Sacrificing your life for your country is one thing. Sacrificing your body for bureaucratic convenience and antediluvian* attitudes is something else.

antediluvian:
very old; before
the biblical
flood

Reading for Meaning

1. What is the response of military authorities when rape is reported?
2. What change has the Pentagon made at the Air Force Academy to help change the culture of the institution? How do you think this will help?
3. What skills are women supposedly lacking that are needed for fighting? Who claims this?

Reading Deeper

1. Quindlen says that there are those who claim that there has always been hostility toward female soldiers and that it is "inevitable." Respond to this comment.

2. What is the significance of Bush's comments about "rape rooms" to the Iraqis? How does this affect the women in the military?

Reading for Writing

1. Find a VHS or DVD copy of *G.I. Jane* and watch it with this article in mind. Even though it is not a movie based on the training of a female soldier at a military academy, it is about a female soldier's training for war. While some of the violence against her is part of the training, where do you think training stopped and brutality began? Write a **response** to both this article and *G.I. Jane.*

2. There are various institutions that take care of the criminal actions committed by members of their organization; the armed forces are included. What do you think about institutions that handle the criminal activity of their members rather than allow the local authorities to deal with it? Write an **argumentative** essay that tries to **convince** readers to believe that these institutions should be subject to the laws of the state or that these institutions should continue to deal with their offenders.

OPEN SEASON ON KOREANS?

Elaine H. Kim

Elaine H. Kim is a professor of Asian-American Studies at the University of California, Berkeley. Professor Kim examines Asian-American culture and participates in Asian organizations in San Francisco. She has written two books, American-Asian Literature: An Introduction to the Writings and Their Social Context *(1982) and* With Silk Wings: Asian-American Women at Work *(1983). She has also written articles for* Newsday.

Prereading: Movies are frequently guilty of creating stereotypes for different ethnic populations, and many times viewers construct their beliefs about individuals based on these biased portrayals. Professor Kim questions the public's understanding of Koreans, especially Korean shopkeepers, but she secondarily critiques the portrayal of African Americans. Her criticism is accurate and can be applied to the portrayal of other diverse populations: Mexican, Japanese, Italian, the physically challenged, gays and lesbians, and others. Notice the roles in which diverse populations are portrayed or erased entirely in movies, television programs, video games, billboard ads, and so forth.

Prewriting: Look at the title. Write a paragraph explaining what you understand by "open season."

Vocabulary: Looking up and understanding the following words prior to reading should prepare you for the author's message. Other words will be defined in the margin.

Muslims   caricatures   Fu Manchu
mayhem   Moonies   Crips

A new film *Menace II Society,* directed by Allen and Albert Hughes, describes a community decimated* by poverty and violence, where African-American youth fight for day-to-day survival amid guns, drugs, friendship and rivalry, retribution* killings, God-fearing grandparents and earnest young Muslims.

decimated: reduced drastically in numbers

As a Korean American, I was horrified by one element in this milieu*. In what one reviewer called the "riveting" opening scene of this newest "inner-city" film, an African-American youth blows out the brains of a greedy Korean merchant who has urged him to "Hurry up and buy! Pay and get out." The youth also kills the merchant's garishly* made-up wife, who had been eyeing the youths as if they were going to steal something.

retribution: punishment or an act returned in kind

milieu: environment

It seems that rude and greedy Korean merchants are movies' "bad guys" of the moment. The shopkeepers who deserve to be blown away, to no one's regret, are becoming the newest Asian stereotype. *Menace II Society* is the culmination* of the racial slurs in *Do the Right Thing* and the mayhem in *Falling Down.* Besides a few other grotesque* caricatures of ragged war orphans, horny prostitutes, fanatical* Moonies and robotic nerds, there aren't any other images of Koreans in American culture. The Korean merchant stereotype joins the ranks of other stereotypes of Asians as Fu Manchu-style sinister villains, dragon ladies, and faceless hordes, all threatening the kind of "yellow peril" takeover Korean merchants are supposedly accomplishing in today's inner cities. The difference is that unlike the other stereotypes, which are rooted in fantasy, the Korean merchant can be encountered on the corner in our own neighborhoods.

garishly: tastelessly showy

culmination: highest point

grotesque: bizarre, ugly

fanatical: excessive enthusiasm

Even if they are rude and greedy, Korean merchants don't deserve to be blown away any more than the African-American characters in *Menace II Society* deserve their violent deaths. But the fact is, these types of killings are part of daily life in South Central Los Angeles. During the past six months 16 Korean-American merchants have been shot in Southern California; seven of them are dead. Last year there were 800 gang-related homicides in L.A. County. The people who live and work in the inner city are under-protected by police, under-represented by politicians and under-served by larger-scale businesses.

Korean Americans have been inserted into the public dialogue as part of a new buzz phrase in radical politics: the "black-Korean conflict." However, they have importance only as they can illuminate (or obscure) African-American experiences or the experiences of ethnic white Americans. They have no legitimacy* as subjects in their own right.

legitimacy: full rights

Not all Korean Americans are merchants. And not all Korean-American merchants are rude and greedy, just as 99 percent of African-American customers would never shoot a Korean shopkeeper. The Koreans who lost their livelihoods in the violence in Los Angeles last year were people who spent the past decade or longer working 12 to 14 hours a day, six to seven days a week, in pursuit of brave and often humble dreams that were reduced to ashes in the space of a few hours. The merchants begging and crying or standing on rooftops with guns were not there because they cared only about their money and property; they were there because their stores were the sum total of their American lives.

Last summer, every African American I talked with in South Central knew that the media distorted images of their own community as nothing but a bunch of crack houses and drive-by shootings. At the same time, their knowledge about Korean Americans was also limited by the media, which portrayed Koreans mostly as rude and greedy grocers. Let's face it, what source of information do people of color have about one another other than what the dominant culture presents?

Thus Korean immigrants talk about how the "Mexicans" looted their stores, although most of the Latino looters were identified by the press as Central American refugees. I have rarely heard Korean immigrants use the term "Latino," let alone "Central American" or even "Chicano."

I know of a Korean grocer named "Chin Ho" who was proud that his Latino customers called him by his first name. In fact they were calling him Chino, or "Chink." Mike Davis, author of *City of Quartz,* a book about the development of Los Angeles, told me that some Crips in Las Vegas bragged to him that they had burned down a Japanese store because they understood that Japan was causing job shortages in the U.S. The "Japanese" store was actually a Korean-American shop.

The Hughes brothers, Spike Lee, or any other African-American filmmaker, are not responsible for presenting a fully contextualized picture of Korean merchant life. Korean Americans need to tell their own story. So far, these immigrants have minded their own business and worked hard, sacrificing themselves to the hope that their children will become engineers or attorneys. But what we need now are cultural histo-

inscribe: to write, engrave, or print

rians and novelists and filmmakers who can inscribe* Korean Americans in images and words full of creativity and compassion.

Reading for Expectations

1. What evidence does Kim use to support her belief that violence against Koreans and African Americans is a major issue in Southern California?
2. If you are a member of one of the ethnicities Kim uses as examples of groups that have experienced discrimination, do you agree with her descriptions? Do these descriptions help you understand the discrimination Koreans experience? Explain.

Reading for Meaning

1. Although Kim is primarily concerned with discrimination against Koreans, she mentions other ethnicities that have been stereotyped and also discriminated against. Which ethnicities are they? How does she describe them?
2. How do the media and writers appear to work against Koreans? What, then, is the purpose of Kim's last sentence in the article?
3. Kim offers three movies as examples of displays of racial problems. Are you familiar with them? How does your knowledge of these movies offer a deeper understanding of Koreans' problems?

Reading to Write

1. This **informative** essay incorporates third-person point of view and first person when Kim inserts information from her own experiences. Which examples are more effective for you as a reader? Explain.
2. Kim fills her article with negative, pessimistic examples of Korean images. How do the examples included in the concluding paragraph make this an optimistic essay?
3. There are various subtle and not so subtle ways everyone is exposed to forms of discrimination daily. For example, some advertisements do not include members of different ethnicities, racial profiling is practiced, and so forth. Look for other forms of "accepted" methods of discrimination and write a short **informative** article about them. Use **exemplification** and **description.**
4. Sometimes so-called "positive" stereotypes place undue pressure on certain ethnicities to live up to unrealistic expectations. For example, educators often see Asians as brilliant in science or math. Although many Asians are exceptionally gifted in science and math, many

excel in other areas. Think about other examples of "positive" stereotypes and how they are just as unfair as negative ones. Write an **informative** article using **exemplification** and **description.**

EVIL REDUX, OR THE RETURN OF MEANINGFUL MYSTERY

Dorothy G. Clark

*Mystery has always been a subject of interest to many individuals.
Reading Agatha Christie or Stephen King novels excites many
people's imagination, wondering who committed the act in question. However, mystery takes a different turn when it is motivated
by pure evil. Then it is no longer interesting in the sense of providing amusement. In the following article, Dorothy G. Clark, assistant professor at California State University, Northridge, who
teaches about evil in literature, discusses the history of evil and
how individuals have attempted to deal with it.*

Prereading: When you hear the word *evil,* what do you think of? Do
you associate any of the incidents society experiences as caused by
evil?

Prewriting: Board games like "Clue" or video games that children play
are frequently filled with violent acts; however, there is a definite difference between a game like "Clue" and videos like *Doom* or *Mortal
Kombat.* In a paragraph, discuss how violence is or is not associated
with *evil* in games for children.

Vocabulary: Looking up and understanding the following words prior
to reading should prepare you for the author's message. Other words
will be defined in the margin.

dynamics   rehabilitation   adversary   Enlightenment

"The world is too much with us" is a line from a famous poem by the
nineteenth-century British poet William Wordsworth that captures
how many people feel today. The burdens of getting and keeping a job,
of paying bills, of commuting to and from work, along with the usually
emotional ups and downs we all experience have been added to, especially since September 11, 2001, by something new that is also very old:
the presence of evil. Until recently many people believed that human
wrongdoing was either a result of bad environment or of faulty brain
chemistry. A child whose family dynamics or poverty made him the vic-

tim of physical and psychological abuse, or of experiences that hardened him, or a person with a brain genetically programmed in the wrong way might commit ugly crimes. But therapy, rehabilitation or medication might provide remedies by changing that person's character for the better. Evil could be fixed. We believed that we could find answers to these problems by the sheer power of thought. Science, using reason, might solve the problem of human evil.

But to quote another poet, William Butler Yeats, "All changed, changed utterly" since September 11. That terrible event and the changes it made in all of our lives has been like a tear in the fabric of our neat and seemingly controlled society. What was ordinary is no longer dependable because now we know that everyday life can be wrecked in an instant. Rational explanations and solutions seem undependable, and we have been forced to face the strange and mysterious reality of evil that science cannot easily explain. We are forced to look back into our past, to the roots of our civilization, for answers.

But what we mean by evil and how we have thought about it and treated it have not been a constant thing. Evil in our culture has its own history, its own story. For a very long time, we believed that evil was real, and unfixable, but then we stopped—it seemed to disappear from our language, and now, it has come back.

There have been several ways that our culture has understood evil. For most of Western history, evil was, and still is, understood from a religious perspective. In our culture, this religious view begins with the Judeo-Christian account of the creation of Satan. Lucifer ("Light Bearer"), the most intelligent, powerful and beautiful of the angels, spiritual beings created by God to share His heavenly home, was consumed with pride and envy against God. Lucifer led one-third of the angels in a rebellion against God, which was, of course, defeated. After the rebellion was defeated, God cast Lucifer, now know as Satan (which in Hebrew mean adversary), into Hell, a state of eternal separation from Heaven and the Good.

Jealousy, envy, revenge, and continued rebellion consume Satan. Learning about God's creation of the Garden of Eden and the first humans, Adam and Eve, Satan, as the book of Genesis in the Bible recalls, tricks Eve into eating the apple of the Tree of Knowledge (an act forbidden by God); and when Adam also eats of this fruit, the fate of humanity is sealed. Adam and Eve are expelled from the Garden of Eden, and Evil enters our lives in a variety of forms: Death, illness, suffering, and sin become intrinsic* to the human experience. We, too, became fallen creatures, and evil became part of our lives. This is the religious story.

intrinsic: belonging to the nature of a thing

But why did Lucifer originally choose to rebel? What motivated Eve to disobey God and listen to Satan? Why did God allow evil to exist?

These questions have haunted theologians (people who study religion, God, and God's relation to humanity) and philosophers for centuries. The primary answer to these questions was that God gave human beings free will, allowing us to choose between good and evil. If we didn't have free will, so this explanation goes, there wouldn't be any meaning to our acting good. As a result, some theologians call the fall of Adam and Eve the Fortunate Fall because it allowed humans to learn just how free they were and how much of their salvation depends on their own action. St. Augustine, reflecting on his own experience as a young man when he chose to steal a neighbor's pears just for the sake of doing it, decided that all humans are born with "original sin"—the sin of Adam and Eve. This means that human will has been corrupted and tends to choose the evil over the good. Even though we are still free, we still need God's help to choose what is good, because Adam's sin made us incapable of such choices. Thus many Christians have believed that human beings are essentially sinners and will choose to do evil, given the opportunity, unless they seek God's help.

cosmic: great in intensity

There is an even more ancient vision of good and evil that says that there have always been and will always be two cosmic* forces in the world—Good and Evil—and these fight for control endlessly. The name for this understanding of good and evil in the universe is Manichean. Good is the creative and loving force in the universe: God, Spirit, and light; evil is the force that brings death, destruction, chaos: Satan, matter, and darkness. Many fantasy films and literature see the world this way—as a war between the forces of good and the forces of evil: *Star Wars, The Lord of the Rings, Harry Potter.* Those people who used to believe (and many still do) that Satan is a real force in the world reflect this Manichean view. In fact, almost everyone used to believe that if someone was acting badly, it was because he or she was possessed by the evil force or by Satan himself! There are still Catholic priests who perform exorcisms, a religious rite to force a demon out of a person. But some of us today don't believe that demons can possess people, or that there is a "Dark Force" in the universe, or a "Dark Side" to everyone that they cannot help but have.

The major reason some people do not hold these beliefs is because this religious vision was challenged during the eighteenth century by the rise of science and the importance placed on Reason by Enlightenment philosophers. Satan, who had been real to religious people, was seen as a superstitious belief. It simply wasn't "reasonable" to believe in such things. But what about evil? How do you explain bad things in a word that is supposed to be reasonable and created by a reasonable God? The philosopher Leibnitz came up with an answer. He said that God was ultimately reasonable, but we simply couldn't understand His whole plan. Therefore, this world of ours was "the best of all possible worlds." Things that appeared to be evil when they occurred might look less evil if we had the "Big Picture" that God enjoys.

While this view was believable when it came to accounting for natural disasters like earthquakes or personal disasters like illness or accident, it was less convincing when used to try to explain individual acts of human evil. The great philosopher Kant was not so sure. Although he believed that we were born with an internal awareness of the good and that we had free will to choose good or bad rules in our life, ultimately, he did not believe that we could ever know why we made these choices. The foundation of our choices, he believed, was inscrutable*—a mystery!

inscrutable: not understandable

There are some people who believe . . . that we are all born good, but are hurt by our environment. These people say that those who do evil may be the victims of childhood abuse or trauma of some sort—actions that make them act unkindly towards another. Or, they may grow up in a violent environment in which they see their parents or brothers or relatives or friends act violently, and so they become violent and "evil" too. There are problems with these ideas, though. Not everybody who grows up in terrible, violent and abusive situations becomes a criminal; in fact, many people from such backgrounds become loving, contributing members of society. . . .

On the other hand, there are views of human nature that see some sort of internal force . . . that creates evil inside of us: our biochemistry, for instance, or our genes. From this point of view, we are "programmed" to act badly—predetermined—and no amount of "free will" or right choosing will stop us. So the answer is for science to figure out how to fix these things, and then we'd all be good. Maybe, however, there is something about the nature of evil that surprises us, confuses us, and overwhelms us and seems to break out of the neat categories we keep trying to create to contain it. When you think about those people who chose to run the airplanes into the Twin Towers on September 11 or the suicide bombers who kill themselves along with innocent children and old people, genetic wiring or biochemistry don't seem to be the issue. Instead, they seem to be motivated by religious or ideological* reasons. Evil is complex, and one thing 9/11 seems to have shown us is that there just aren't any easy answers: The people who attacked us said they were religious and acting according to how they believed their God wished them to act.

ideological: concerned with a set of ideas or beliefs

Evil isn't just acting badly; it is something profound that startles us and feels like an eruption—like a volcano suddenly spewing lava:

shocking, violent, deadly. Although we all seem to be able to recognize it, it is difficult to explain. A year ago, a popular TV show, *Law and Order,* aired a segment (Jan. 13, 2004) that illustrated how we as a society are struggling to understand our renewed experience of evil. This show was about a young man who brutally killed three people seemingly because they were Arabs or Muslims. . . . [Who] were trying to work to increase better communication among all religions. They were clearly Good. . . .

[The program] ends with the announcement that no trial will commence because the young man was killed in jail by Muslim friends of the [third] person he had pummeled to death—an act of vengeance and retaliation kills him and reminds us of this all too common motivation for violence.

This segment of *Law and Order* ends abruptly. We are left with a cluster of possible motives swirling around these deaths: free will, genetic programming, childhood trauma, betrayal, revenge. What we cannot know is why the young killer chose to act violently and brutally in response to his emotions and situation. We are left with what Kant identified as the inscrutable foundation for our choices. We are left with mystery.

For as long as I can remember, we have believed that through science we could be in control of the world and of ourselves, that just about any problem or difficult situation could be solved. September 11 and the return of the mystery of evil have changed everything. But in a strange, odd way, this apparent loss of control may also help us to rediscover how we as human beings—our life and our world—are mysterious and marvelous. Our new awareness of this tear in the fabric of the ordinary may just allow in a new awareness of the wonder of existence, its beauties and miracles—even if that wonder is filled at times with an awe at the terror of it all.

Reading for Meaning

1. How did many believe evil could be fixed?
2. What did the belief in Satan change to with the coming of the Enlightenment? Explain.

Reading Deeper

1. Explain the concept of the Fortunate Fall. How does that belief support or oppose your own religious or philosophical beliefs about evil?
2. How do *Star Wars, The Lord of the Rings,* and *Harry Potter* have any association with a Manichean belief? Explain.
3. How would knowing the "Big Picture" help us understand why bad things happen? What does the "Big Picture" mean?

Reading for Writing

1. Based on Clark's article, write a **definition** of evil for a three-year-old and for a thirty-year old. Keep in mind that you might need a reason for introducing *evil* to a three-year-old; therefore, you might need to consider the purpose of defining the term for someone that young.
2. Using Lipkin's article and Clark's article, write a **compare and contrast** essay about the causes of evil, how to recognize evil, and how to avoid evil. Be sure to document any material you quote or paraphrase.

RHETORICAL ANALYSIS

Doug McPherson writes a process analysis article to help women recognize characteristics in their dates that might lead to violence. He gives various steps they should take as well as specific points women should be aware of. McPherson establishes his ethos immediately by referencing the National Domestic Hotline for specific behaviors and using Mike Domitrz, an authority on dating communication and the author of *May I Kiss You,* for additional information for his article. Furthermore, he uses exemplification and specific details to support his thesis. In the left-hand margin there is information that directs you to appropriate chapters in this textbook for discussion about the underlined techniques the author used to write the essay or that comments directly about the techniques the author used.

Ch. 8, Process introduces process analysis mode immediately in underlined words

Ch. 10, Persuasion author uses compelling examples and evidence to persuade with bulleted list

Ch. 1, Reading use of bullets in a reading technique

Ch. 3, Exemplification use of exemplification in list

Warning Signs: Does Your Date Have Violent Tendencies?

<u>Learn how to recognize</u> the danger before it hits home!

Dating can turn violent—even deadly—in seconds. The good news is there are signs you can watch for in your date's behavior to give you a heads up.

The National Domestic Violence Hotline recommends taking notice if your date has any of the following behaviors:

• Tries to embarrass you
• Attempts to control you or the date's events
• Makes decisions for you
• Acts overly jealous
• Has sudden mood swings
• Gives you a gut feeling of fear.

Mike Domitrz, who speaks on dating communication and safety and published book earlier this year on those topics called *May I Kiss You?* (Awareness Publications, $15.95), says control is a big red flag.

"Look for anything that leads you to believe the person is trying to take control," he says. "And jealousy can be a tip off. Even on the first date, if you walk into a restaurant and another guy starts talking to you, and your date gets very jealous, that's a sign."

Domitrz also says to watch for dates who aren't flexible. "If you suggest a change in plans and the person won't hear of it, that's something to notice."

"It's also important to take part in planning the date from the start. "Tell your date the kinds of things you like to do instead of letting him plan all the activities. That also lets you set a tone as an assertive person who knows what she likes," Domitrz adds.

Bring up dating history in conversation. It's OK—in fact, necessary—to do a little fact-finding. "Find out how relationships ended," he says. "If he's trashing his former girlfriends, you have to ask yourself if you want to be trashed, too."

And just because a date is well-behaved on the first date is no reason to let your guard down. Experts say some dates will "act nice" only to get what they want later.

If you do find yourself in a situation where you're uncomfortable, create space. "It's the golden rule," says Domitrz. "Get out of the situation at the earliest sign of trouble and if you have to make a scene with yelling, do it. It's much better than being assaulted."

CREATING SAFE DATES

- **Pay your half of the date.** "The old adage that a girl owes the guy something if he pays is still alive," says Domitrz. "Pay half and take care of that issue up front.
- **Date during the daytime.** "You don't find yourself in as many dangerous situations during the day," says Domitrz. "People are up, your nosy neighbor is watching and it's just a safer alternative than dating at night."
- **Go to public places.** Bowling alleys, roller-skating rinks and outdoor malls are all great date locales. Pick spots with lots of people and easy access to help should you need it.

- **Develop a good self-image.** "Self-esteem and self-confidence are key," Domitrz says. "Take stock in the value you bring as a human being." To get started, have two or three friends write letters of recommendation for you. Take those letters and write a speech about yourself in third person, then read that speech often.

McPherson makes this article interesting by giving examples of the behavior he discusses: jealousy, control, and so forth. By doing so, he is able to pinpoint specific characteristics readers can look for that they might not have been aware of before. The details, the steps, and the use of exemplification make this article extremely useful for individuals who might not know what to look for in a date.

REFLECTIONS ON SAFETY AND SECURITY: HOW SAFE ARE WE?

Many of us have a sense of danger, a sense that tells us that something just isn't right in our environment. Whether it is by the bristling of hair on our arms or on the back of our neck or an inability to swallow or breathe, fear is manifested in physical as well as emotional ways. Most of us have heard stories about small, frail women moving cars to get to a child pinned inside. Adrenaline, our body's response to dangerous or exciting situations, frequently gives individuals an extra boost of energy and/or power to help them survive the moment. However, this is not always the case.

What we do to help us maintain a true, as opposed to a false, sense of security is important. We can be alert for the unknown by being aware of our surroundings, having a disaster plan for ourselves and our family, and treating ourselves and our friends kindly and lovingly. Yet always expecting or anticipating the worst can be detrimental. As most of our government officials, religious leaders, and others said after September 11th, to allow terrorism to paralyze us is to allow terrorism to win. While we cannot go around blind to danger, we also cannot live in constant fear. What we can do is be good Scouts and "Be Prepared." And we can also follow Dory's advice from *Finding Nemo:* "Keep on swimming." Where do you stand?

Reflecting to Write

Informative

Fear is a subject that can be defined in a number of ways because it comes in different degrees and for different reasons. Write a **definition** and **exemplification** essay to explain the word fear.

A major issue in the media is kidnapping, mostly the kidnapping of little girls; however, little boys are also victims of kidnappers. Write a **process analysis** paper telling children what to do if they feel threatened by someone they do not know. Direct it at an audience of boys and girls six to ten years of age. Remember that they are early readers. You might choose to write one for their parents instead. Keep in mind that in 2003, one of the kidnapped victims who never came home knew exactly what to do in case she was approached by a stranger. What else could she or any other child know/have known to prevent being kidnapped and murdered?

One of the most common themes in fairy tales is Good overcoming Evil. This is also a theme that occurs in many operas, such as *The Magic Flute,* and ballets, such as *Swan Lake.* The play *The Man of La Mancha* and many movies and novels, such as *The Lord of the Rings* or *Superman,* are also concerned with Good versus Evil. Select one fairy tale, one movie, play, or ballet, and/or one novel that you are familiar with and write an **analytical informative** essay explaining how Good and Evil collide and how one overcomes the other. Do not write a plot summary.

Many times we see and hear on radio and television news about a store owner being shot and killed during a robbery. After the incident, friends and customers are interviewed and many of them say that they don't know why the owner was killed because he or she was always willing to help those who had no money, or he or she would often give candy or gum to little children when they came in the store. A major source of concern when this happens is the fact that many times bad things happen to good people. Write an **informative** paper explaining why bad things happen to good people.

Argumentative

In American literature, the novel *Sister Carrie* by Theodore Dreiser created quite a scandal because the "bad" girl triumphs in the end. In other words, the normal belief that good acts and good people would always be rewarded and that bad acts and bad people would always be punished was challenged. In the movie industry, this belief was also challenged as movie producers believed that only the good should be rewarded in the end. Thus, when the film version of the novel *Rebecca* by Daphne Du Maurier was released, the ending was changed so that the "**protagonist**" could still be the hero of the film. Write an **argumentative** essay to **convince** readers of whether filmmakers and writers should restrict themselves and their works to showing only good being rewarded and evil being punished. Use specific **examples** to support your point. You might need to do some research for information. If you use sources, be sure to document the material.

Safety and security also extend to animals and pets. If you are able to get Animal Planet on your television, watch a few episodes of *Animal Precinct* and think about how the SPCA has to work with abused animals, whether they are house pets or horses or pit bull dogs. Write a **letter** to your representative supporting or opposing harsh sentences for individuals who commit animal abuse.

In the spring of 2003, United States officials issued warnings of possible threats to our country. We were advised to stock up on nonperishable foods, water, duct tape for our windows and doors in the event of biological warfare, batteries, battery-powered radios, and other items we might need in case the worst happened. Fortunately, nothing happened. Take a **position** on this kind of preparation for emergency. Should the media repeatedly announce these kinds of messages to the general public? What about the elderly or the infirm who cannot go out and make these kinds of preparations? What do these kinds of messages do to them? What suggestions do you have? Interview several people of various ages—young as well as elderly—about how they felt when they heard these messages. Find out how extensively they prepared for disaster. Write an **argumentative** essay about the benefit or the problems that occurred because of these warnings. Include suggestions in your conclusion.

Chapter 19

Juvenile Offenders: How We Punish

Being protected by one's parents or guardians is a state that most children are accustomed to. Sometimes, however, children become irritated at what they perceive as overprotection by their elders. This protection also extends beyond the children's front door, as society also believes in the protection of youths, even when they have committed a crime. Rather than deliver the offenders into the hands of an adult justice system, society, in the form of the juvenile justice system, continues to attempt to protect youngsters who have gotten themselves in trouble. In other words, even if these youthful offenders are not doing the right things in their lives, society will try to do the right thing for them.

Sometimes members of the judicial system may find that there are "extenuating circumstances" that led a juvenile to commit illegal acts. Peer pressure, gang involvement, lack of supervision, abuse, criminal influence by adults, truancy, low IQ, mental illness, and so forth are circumstances beyond some juveniles' control. Consequently, they behave in ways that conform to their environment. Frequently, the courts take these problems into consideration and recognize that a juvenile offender was incapable of behaving otherwise and send him or her to a center for rehabilitation rather than to an adult prison for punishment. The philosophy is that a juvenile is still developing his or her sense of identity and sense of right and wrong; therefore, through training and guidance, the individual can be rehabilitated, return to society, and become a productive citizen.

On the other hand, there are those juveniles who commit serious crimes, such as rape, murder, attempted murder, arson, and so forth. Even if the offender comes from circumstances beyond his or her control, many city and state officials have found that sending the youth through the juvenile judicial system is as effective as using a garden hose to fight a forest fire. In the end, they are not rehabilitated nor is society protected. Thus, the "get tough" movement has gained enormous support from many while receiving criticism from others.

In this chapter, you will find two opposing essays that deal with the treatment of juvenile offenders. The remaining four essays describe specific juvenile offenders and the extremely serious crimes they committed. There are those who prefer to treat these juveniles with leniency and rehabilitation, calling on the lawmakers and society to remember that the offenders are children. There are also others who want to lock them up and protect society from their criminal activities.

Even though you, as a reader, do not have all the facts and evidence and cannot judge their guilt or innocence, you will read arguments from both sides about how to treat juvenile offenders. Take some time to determine your beliefs about how to try and sentence juveniles. Will you consider the crime or the age of the juvenile when he or she committed the crime? Should you consider extenuating circumstances? Would you feel differently if you or a member of your family were a victim? This is definitely a social issue that is not going to go away. How do you believe juveniles should be dealt with?

SHOULD JUVENILE OFFENDERS BE TRIED AS ADULTS?

Laurence Steinberg

Do you remember your years in middle school and high school? Do you think you were "mature" enough at those ages to tell the difference between right and wrong or to know that there would be consequences for your actions? These are issues that politicians, psychologists, and the juvenile court system are looking at in determining where juveniles should be tried for criminal offenses they commit. In the following article from USA Today *(January, 2001), Laurence Steinberg, a developmental psychologist, looks at the differences between adults and juveniles, adult courts and juvenile courts, and punishment and rehabilitation.*

Prereading: Think about any crimes that you have heard about or read about that involve juvenile criminals. Do you think that they should be treated as adults when they are in court?

Prewriting: Consider the consequences of putting a fifteen-year-old in an adult prison. Make a list of reasons why he or she should and should not be housed with adult criminals.

Vocabulary: Looking up and understanding the following words prior to reading should prepare you for the author's message. Other words will be defined in the margin.

rehabilitation   delinquent   adjudicated   alleged   malleability

---

precludes: prevents; does not include

rehabilitative: restoring or bringing to a condition of useful and constructive activity

"Transferring juveniles into a criminal justice system that precludes* a rehabilitative* response may not be very sensible public policy."

Few issues challenge a society's ideas about the natures of human development and justice as much as serious juvenile crime. Because people neither expect children to be criminals nor expect crimes to be committed by them, the unforeseen intersection between childhood and criminality creates a dilemma that most of us find difficult to resolve. The only way out of this dilemma is either to redefine the offense as something less serious than a crime or to redefine the offender as someone who is not really a child.

For the past 100 years, American society has most often chosen the first approach. It has redefined juvenile offenses by treating most of them as delinquent acts to be adjudicated within a separate juvenile justice system that is theoretically designed to recognize the special needs and immature status of young people and emphasize rehabilitation over punishment. Two guiding beliefs about young people have prevailed*: first, that juveniles have different competencies* than adults (and therefore need to be adjudicated in a different type of venue*); and second, that they have different potential for change than adults (and therefore merit a second chance and an attempt at rehabilitation). States have recognized that conduct alone—that is, the alleged criminal act—should not by itself determine whether to invoke* the heavy hand of adult criminal justice system.

prevailed: to be most common or frequent

competencies: skills needed to function in life

venue: a place or location for an event

invoke: call upon for support

In recent years, though, there has been a dramatic shift in the way juvenile crime is viewed by policy makers and the general public, one that has led to widespread changes in policies and practices concerning the treatment of juvenile offenders. Rather than choosing to define offenses committed by youth as delinquent, society increasingly is opting to redefine them as adults and transfer them to the adult court and criminal justice system.

Most reasonable people agree that a small number of young offenders should be transferred to the adult system because they pose a genuine threat to the safety of other juveniles, the severity of their offense merits a relatively more severe punishment, or their history of repeated offending bodes* poorly for their ultimate rehabilitation. However, this does not describe the tens of thousands of young people who

bodes: indicates or warns

currently are being prosecuted in the adult system, a large proportion of whom have been charged with nonviolent crimes. When the wholesale transfer to criminal court of various categories of juvenile offenders starts to become the rule rather than the exception, this represents a fundamental challenge to the very premise that the juvenile court was founded on—that adolescents and adults are different.

There are many lenses through which one can view debates about transfer policies. As a developmental psychologist, I ask whether the distinctions we draw between people of different ages under the law are sensible in light of what we know about age differences in various aspects of intellectual, emotional or social functioning. More specifically, on the basis of what we know about development, should a boundary be drawn between juveniles and adults in criminal matters and, if so, at what age should we draw it?

Developmental psychology, broadly defined, concerns the scientific study of changes in physical, intellectual, emotional, and social development over the life cycle. Developmental psychologists are mainly interested in the study of "normative" development. My concern is whether the study of normative development indicates that there are sci-

warrant: justify

differential: making a distinction between individuals

scrutiny: close, careful study of

entific reasons to warrant* the differential* treatment of young people and adults within the legal system, especially with regard to the age period most under current political scrutiny* the years between 12 and 17.

First, this age range is an inherently transitional time. There are rapid and dramatic changes in individuals' physical, intellectual, emotional, and social capabilities. If there is a period in the life span during which one might choose to draw a line between incompetent and competent individuals, this is it.

Second, adolescence is a period of potential malleability. Experiences in the family, peer group, school, and other settings still have a chance to influence the course of development. To the extent that malleability is likely, transferring juveniles into a criminal justice system

precludes: does not include

amenability: willingness

trajectories: path

cumulative: make bigger by constantly adding

that precludes* a rehabilitative response may not be very sensible public policy. However, to the extent that adolescents' amenability* is limited, their transfer to the adult system is less worrisome.

Finally, adolescence is a formative period during which a number of developmental trajectories* become firmly established and increasingly difficult to alter. Many adolescent experiences have a tremendous cumulative* impact. Bad decisions or poorly formulated policies pertaining to juvenile offenders may have unforeseen and harmful consequences that are very hard to undo.

It is only fair to ask whether or why a developmental perspective is even relevant to contemporary discussions of trying juvenile offenders in the adult criminal system After all, current discussions about trying juveniles in adult court are typically not about the characteristics of the offender, but about the seriousness and harmfulness of the offense— factors independent of the offender's age or maturity. "Adult time for adult crime"—the mantra—of the get-tough-on-juvenile-crime lobby— says nothing about the age of the offender, except for the fact that it ought to be considered irrelevant*.

irrelevant: having no effect on

I believe that it is logically impossible to make the age of the offender irrelevant in discussions of criminal justice policy. A fair punishment for an adult is unfair when applied to a child who did not understand the consequences of his or her actions. The ways we interpret and apply laws should rightfully vary when the case at hand involves a defendant whose understanding of the law is limited by intellectual immaturity or whose judgment is impaired by emotional immaturity. Moreover, the implications and consequences of administering a long and harsh punishment are very different when the offender is young than when he or she is an adult.

implications: suggested ideas with close connections

Transferring juveniles to criminal court has three sets of implications* that need to be considered in discussions about whether they should be tried as adults. First, transfer to adult court alters the legal process by which a minor is tried. Criminal court is based on an adversarial model, while juvenile court is based, at least in theory, on a more cooperative model. This difference in the climates of juvenile vs. adult court is significant because it is unclear at what age individuals have sufficient understanding of the ramifications* of the adversarial process and the different vested* interests of prosecutors, defense attorneys, and judges. Young defendants may simply not have what it takes—by the standards established by the Constitution—to be able to defend themselves in criminal court.

ramifications: consequences

vested: strong concern in maintaining or influencing a condition, especially for selfish ends

Second, the legal standards applied in adult and juvenile courts are different. For example, competence* to stand trial is presumed among adult defendants unless they suffer from a serious mental illness or substantial mental retardation. We do not know if the presumption of competence holds for juveniles, who, even in the absence of mental retardation or mental illness, may lack sufficient competence to participate in the adjudicative process. Standards for judging culpability* may be different in juvenile and adult courts as well. In the absence of mental illness or substantial deficiency*, adults are presumed to be responsible for their own behavior. We do not know the extent to which this presumption applies to juveniles, or whether the validity of this presumption differs as a function of the juvenile's age.

competence: being able or having power to perform

culpability: responsible for blame

deficiency: lacking some necessary quality

Finally, the choice of trying a young offender in adult vs. juvenile court determines the possible outcomes of the adjudication. In adult court, the outcome of being found guilty of a serious crime is nearly always some sort of punishment. In juvenile court, the outcome of being found delinquent may be some sort of punishment, but juvenile courts typically retain the option of a rehabilitative disposition*, in and of itself or in combination with some sort of punishment. This has two significant ramifications: the stakes of the adjudication are substantially greater and, in juvenile court, offenders generally are presumed amenable unless the prosecutor demonstrates otherwise. In adult court, amenability is not presumed and must instead be shown by the defendant's counsel.

disposition:
final
arrangement

In other words, decision makers within the juvenile and criminal justice systems bring different presumptions to the table. The juvenile court operates under the presumption that offenders are immature, in three different senses of the word: Their development is incomplete; their judgment is less than mature; and their character is still developing. The adult court, in contrast, presumes that defendants are mature, competent, responsible, and unlikely to change.

Which of these presumptions best characterizes individuals between the ages of 12 and 17? Is there an approximate age where the presumptions of the criminal court become more applicable to an offender than the presumptions of the juvenile court? Although developmental psychology does not point to any one age that politicians and practitioners should use in formulating transfer policies or practices, it does point to age-related trends in certain legally relevant attributes, such as the intellectual or emotional capabilities that affect decision making in court and on the street.

It is appropriate, based on developmental research, to raise serious concerns about the transfer of individuals 12 and under to adult court, because of their limited adjudicative competence as well as the very real possibility that most children this young will not prove to be sufficiently blameworthy to warrant exposure to the harsh consequences of a criminal court adjudication. For this reason, individuals 12 and under should continue to be viewed as juveniles, regardless of the nature of their offense. This does not mean that we should let them off the hook or fail to punish them. It merely means that they should be punished and held responsible within a system designed to treat children, not fully mature adults.

At the other end of the continuum, it appears appropriate to conclude that the vast majority of individuals older than 16 are not appreciably different from adults in ways that would prohibit their fair adjudication within the criminal justice system. My view is that variability* among

variability:
changes

individuals older than 12, but younger than 16 requires that some sort of individualized assessment of an offender's competence to stand trial, blameworthiness, and likely amenability to treatment be made before reaching a transfer decision. The relevant decision makers (e.g., judges, prosecutors, and defense attorneys) should be permitted to exercise judgment about individual offenders' maturity and eligibility for transfer.

mitigating: less intense or harsh

duress: threat

It is true that a bullet wound hurts just as much when the weapon is fired by a child as when it is fired by an adult, but this argument is a red herring, since we comfortably acknowledge that there are numerous situations where mitigating* factors should be taken into account when trying a defendant, such as insanity, emotional duress*, or self-defense. Immaturity is another mitigating factor. People may differ in their opinions about the extent to which, the ways in which, and the age at which an offender's maturity should be considered in court decisions. One person might believe that a boundary should be drawn at 18, another at 15, and yet another at 13. Nevertheless, ignoring the offender's age entirely is like trying to ignore an elephant that has wandered into the courtroom. You can do it, but most people will notice that something smells foul.

Reading for Meaning

1. What reasons are given by some people for transferring juveniles to the adult prison system?
2. Define developmental psychology.
3. What is the belief of those who support a get-tough-on-juvenile-crime attitude?
4. What is the difference between juvenile and adult court? Explain.

Reading Deeper

1. The last sentence of the first paragraph includes only two options. Are there other ways out of the dilemma that Steinberg discusses in that paragraph? List what you think might be alternatives.
2. What is the difference between rehabilitation and punishment when convicting a person of a criminal offense?
3. What ages are considered "juvenile" by politicians?
4. According to Steinberg, during what part of one's life span is one competent? Incompetent? Explain why.
5. Determine what you think Steinberg's thesis is for this essay. Is it stated or implied? If it is stated, quote it. If it is implied, write an explicit **thesis statement.**

Reading for Writing

1. Do you agree with Steinberg's article? Write a **response** to it, either agreeing or disagreeing with his thesis. Be sure to support your response with specific **examples.**
2. Think about specific individuals you know who could easily be classified as delinquents. Do you believe that they are mature enough and intelligent enough to understand the consequences of their actions and whether their actions are right or wrong? Consider that the individuals Steinberg is discussing are the age of middle-school and high school students. Write an essay supporting your **position** using **examples** from situations you witnessed as a middle-school or high school student.

YOUTH CRIME HAS CHANGED—AND SO MUST THE JUVENILE JUSTICE SYSTEM

Tom Reilly

In our judicial system, there are laws that were written in the 1800s that have never been revised or removed. For example, spitting on the sidewalks was a crime in some states and still remains part of the law in others. The way we treat juvenile offenders was established long ago, but it remains the same even though society, crime, and understanding of the human mind have changed. Tom Reilly (Boston Globe, 1997) explains that the system must change to meet the needs of today's society.

Prereading: Do the clothes you wore three years ago still fit you? Are they still in style? Use this example as an analogy to consider the way the juvenile justice system operates.

Prewriting: Consider the following scenario: A sixteen-year-old juvenile shoots and kills a store owner during a robbery. Should that juvenile be tried in juvenile court or adult court? Would it make any difference in your decision of the victim were a friend or relative of yours? Write a paragraph explaining your position.

Vocabulary: Looking up and understanding the following words prior to reading should prepare you for the author's message. Other words will be defined in the margin.

ward of the state   rehabilitation   predator

O n July 1, 1899, the first juvenile court in the United States was established in Cook County, Ill. It represented a dramatic shift in the way the criminal justice system and all of American society dealt with wayward or criminally involved youth. The new court was founded on the principle of "parens patriae"—the idea that children should not be treated as criminals but as wards of the state.

encapsulated: summarized

Parens patriae encapsulated* the view that children were not fully responsible for their conduct and were capable of being rehabilitated. It gave rise to the ongoing practice of terming youthful offenders "delinquents" and not criminals. Parens patriae remains the underlying philosophy of the juvenile justice system in Massachusetts and across the country. Then and now, juvenile court was designed more to protect the child than to punish bad behavior.

Until fairly recently, the juvenile justice system served our country and our children reasonably well. Beginning in the 1970s, however, the realities of juvenile crime began to change. Juvenile crime grew more violent and more common, and the system was unprepared. In recent years those changes have accelerated at an astonishing rate, and time and again, the system has proven itself helpless under the crush.

prone: tending toward

Violent juvenile crime is increasing at double the rate of violent crime committed by adults. By the year 2005, the number of teen-agers between the ages of 14 and 17 will increase by 23 percent, and it appears likely that unless we change things now, those soon-to-be-teenagers will be the most violence prone* in history.

infractions: law violations

Our juvenile justice system is outdated, designed to address infractions* like truancy and petty theft. These were serious problems a century ago, but they bear no resemblance to the "routine" infractions of the present day: everything from rape to crimes involving guns to cold-blooded murder. In 1996, juveniles are committing brutal crimes with such numbing regularity that it takes the most shocking failures of the juvenile justice system to respond to dramatize the out-of-touch mentality underlying it.

myth: unfounded or false notion

It makes no sense to change the system simply to navigate the current wave of public anger. We must instead reform the system to steer clear of the coming storm of violent juvenile crime. Parens patriae need not be fully abandoned. There are and will always be children who make poor choices, who need our help and who can be turned around. However we cannot ignore reality. Crimes such as murder are serious; they cannot under any circumstances be excused or explained away. Here, hope for rehabilitation is a myth* and public protection must be the priority.

How can we possibly treat cold-blooded juvenile killers as "delinquents" and not as the dangerous predators their own actions prove them to be? When a person, any person, brings himself to a point where he deliberately murders another human being, there is no going back. A mere hope for rehabilitation is nothing but a gamble on other people's lives. The public has a right to expect that a killer will never, ever have the chance to kill again. Juveniles accused of murder should be tried as adults and, if convicted, sentenced as adults.

For other crimes, determining whether a juvenile can be rehabilitated is problematic under the current system, so conducting the trial first makes sense. Once a determination of guilt has been made and the court has a clear view of the nature of the crime and whether or not a juvenile is dangerous or capable of rehabilitation, then a reasonable decision can be made whether to sentence as a juvenile or as an adult.

Even apart from these steps to hold juvenile offenders responsible, other aspects of the juvenile justice system must be reformed to achieve a proper balancing between respect and sensitivity toward victims and a juvenile's due process rights. Eliminating "trial de novo" tops the list. Under de novo, a juvenile has the right to be tried first before a judge. If found guilty (or delinquent), the juvenile can simply demand a new trial before a jury, forcing victims to endure a painful ordeal not once, but twice. It's time to put an end to this unfair, wasteful system.

The juvenile justice system founded nearly a century ago was in many respects visionary, but ultimately it was a system designed to address the pressing issues of its day. That day is long past. It's time for us to craft a new vision for juvenile justice in Massachusetts, where compassion for the young and common sense about crime coexist. Our new vision should reflect our belief that the system does have a responsibility to protect a child's interest, but our system has an equally important responsibility to protect the public's safety interests.

Reading for Meaning

1. Explain the meaning of "parens patriae."
2. What happened in the 1970s with regard to juvenile crime?
3. What is the difference between the "serious" crimes of the early 1900s and the "serious" crimes of today that juveniles are committing?
4. In addition to the juvenile and society, who else does Reilly say we should consider in the matter of crime?

Reading Deeper

1. What does the increase in juvenile crime mean in the future? Think as broadly as possible about this question.
2. Is Tom Reilly arguing for the abolishment of parens patriae? Why or why not?
3. Why does Reilly say that "trial de novo" should be eliminated? Explain how the process works.

Reading for Writing

1. After reading Reilly's article, determine which side you favor: giving priority to the serious juvenile offender or giving priority to public protection by trying the juvenile in the adult system. Create a list of reasons for each position, and choose the side you can defend and believe in. Write an **argumentative** essay attempting to **convince** a reader that your belief is correct.
2. Determine one way in which you would change the way juveniles are treated and write an **argumentative** essay trying to **convince** the reader that he or she should call their legislators to change the system.

A Killing Tradition

Joan Jacobs Brumberg

In 2002, John Muhammad and Lee Boyd Malvo created fear and chaos among the residents of the Washington, DC area as well as in Alabama. When they were caught, they left thirteen victims, eleven of whom died. The crime itself was enough to catch the attention of the entire nation; however, when it was discovered that Malvo was a juvenile, a different concern arose: How should he be tried—as a juvenile or as an adult? Furthermore, if he were to be tried as an adult, would he also be old enough for execution? Joan Jacobs Brumberg looks at the death penalty from a historical perspective and applies it to Malvo in an article from Nation *(2003).*

Prereading: What do you know about the Muhammad–Malvo sniper case? Find an article and read about the 21-day ordeal.

Prewriting: Capital punishment is reserved for felons whom a jury believes are a dangerous threat to society and to the prison population. While in some countries, death occurs relatively soon after the sentence is passed, in the United States, an appeal is automatic, and other appeals might follow, allowing the individual as long as ten years in prison before being executed. Write a paragraph stating your position on capital punishment with specific attention to the execution of juveniles.

Vocabulary: Looking up and understanding the following words prior to reading should prepare you for the author's message. Other words will be defined in the margin.

jurisdiction   ideology   Jim Crow laws

LEE BOYD MALVO WILL BE TRIED IN A STATE WITH A LONG HISTORY OF EXECUTING MINORS

When John Muhammad and Lee Boyd Malvo were arrested in the Washington-area sniper case last year [2002], Attorney General John Ashcroft began to push immediately for a trial in Virginia rather than Maryland. Besides his obvious partiality for a jurisdiction that executes prisoners in great numbers, Ashcroft may have known something about American legal history—namely, that Virginia has a historic tradition of executing minors, a tradition that began in the eighteenth century.

Malvo, who was 17 at the time of the murders of which he and Muhammad are accused, is scheduled to go on trial on November 10 [2003]. Muhammad's trial began in mid-October. According to Victor Streib, a professor at Ohio Northern University Law School and author of *Death Penalty for Juveniles,* there have been thirty-four people executed for crimes committed as minors in Virginia from the colonial period to the present, nearly all of them African-American boys whose victims were white females. Steib's grim inventory of cases is based on groundbreaking research originally compiled by M. Watt Espy, a self-educated historian from Headland, Alabama, and derived from state Department of Corrections records, newspapers, county histories, proceedings of state and local courts, holdings of historical societies and other listings of executions.

Because it is so hard to win on a death-penalty appeal in Virginia, the state's sentencing to execution rate for juveniles is the highest in the country: 50 percent compared with runners-up Oklahoma (29 percent), Texas (25 percent), Missouri (25 percent), and South Carolina (14 percent). Although Texas has sentenced and executed more juveniles than any other state over the past decade—one a year, on average—Virginia's courts are uniquely efficient in moving convicted youths to the electric chair in record time. Streib argues that the Virginia Supreme Court and the Court of Appeals for the Fourth Circuit are the keys to the state's

judicial venue:
a place from
which a jury is
drawn and in
where a trial is
held

supremacy:
superiority

bedeviled:
tormented

sharecropping:
tenant farmer
who gives part
of his crops to
the landowner

peonage: the
use of laborers
bound in service
because of debt

*disenfranchise-
ment:* taking
away the right to
vote

plagued:
harassed

inequity: not
being equal

cuspidor: an
object for
spitting into

pilfering:
stealing

crockery:
ceramic dishes

carping:
complaining

"greased skids." Both are deeply conservative judicial venues*, he points out, with no interest in hearing challenges to "law and order" ideology. (No wonder the Fourth Circuit has become an important source of judicial nominees in the Bush Administration.)

But Virginia does more than execute quickly. It also has the distinction of being the last state to execute a female minor, an African-American "wash girl" named, ironically, Virginia Christian. Back in 1912, when 16-year-old Virginia confessed that she had killed her employer, Ida Belote, in response to accusations that she had stolen a locket and a skirt, the stage was set for a demonstration of white supremacy* in a region already bedeviled* by sharecropping* debt peonage*, Jim Crow laws, disenfranchisement* and lynching. Newspapers in Hampton and Richmond used the example of Virginia Christian to fan the fires of bigotry and fear among the many white families in that region (and elsewhere) who had black domestic servants in their homes. As late as 1900, domestic service was the single largest category of female employment in the United States, and an increasing number of these women were black, ranging in age from early adolescence to late in life. Some African-American domestics lived with white families; others, like Virginia Christian, slept in their own homes and came to work on a daily basis. Whether live-in or not, the relationship between white matrons and their black "girls" was almost always plagued* with inequity*, and distrust on both sides.

Although Belote probably sparked the physical assault by throwing a cuspidor* at the girl she suspected of pilfering*, the all-white jury still concluded that Virginia Christian had operated with "malicious intent." After tangling with her employer, knocking over furniture and shattering some crockery*, Virginia grabbed a broom and struck the carping* Mrs. Belote in the head. When Belote fell to the floor and kept "hollering" the desperate 16-year-old tried to silence her by stuffing a dish towel into her mouth; and when that failed to work, Virginia used the broom handle to shove the towel in more tightly. Then she fled, taking a wallet with $4 and a piece of jewelry.

In some ways it was a recognizable adolescent "impulse killing," with theft as an afterthought, but in the Commonwealth of Virginia in 1912, it became something more. Derryn Enroll Moten's University of Iowa dissertation (1997) rightly called the Christian case a "paradigm" of Southern racial bigotry, but it also involved deep, contradictory attitudes about white versus black women. The murder of Ida Belote frightened white Southerners, especially women, because it raised the

specter:
something that
haunts or
disturbs the
mind

insubordination:
refusal to obey
authority

physique:
person's body
structure

contemptible:
of low standing
in a scale of
values; arousing
disrespect

accrued:
gained over time

innovation: a
new device

aesthetic:
pleasing in
appearance

clemency:
mercy

humanitarian:
promotion of
human welfare
and social
reform

felon: person
who commits a
crime
punishable by
the death
penalty or more
than one year in
prison

impoverished:
poor
template:
pattern

specter* of violent insubordination* within the intimacy of the American home. In the white press, Virginia Christian was rarely portrayed realistically as an adolescent girl. In fact, in one report, she was identified as 28 years old, and her square, heavy physique* and dark skin were used to suggest that she was threatening and contemptible*, clearly outside the protections that accrued* naturally to white girls in "the bloom of youth." In Hampton, the local paper was quick to publish a black-bordered picture of her victim, a small, delicate white woman from a prominent local family, who was a widow and a mother of five. Thirteen-year-old Harriet Belote testified at trial that her mother, before the murder, had threatened to have Virginia arrested for stealing. And her younger sister, 8-year-old Sadie, told a hushed courtroom how she found their mother's bruised and bloody body on the kitchen floor when she came home from school.

Because of the tempers aroused by the case, moderates in the community wanted the self-confessed murdered brought to trial as quickly as possible in order to avoid a lynching. After a two-day trial in Elizabeth City County Court, Virginia Christian was sentenced to death in the electric chair, a relatively new innovation* that was praised by many because it was more aesthetic* than hanging. Less than six months later, on the day after her seventeenth birthday, Virginia Christian was killed in the South's first electric chair, despite appeals by her attorneys to the Supreme Court. Like Malvo, Virginia Christian was not a sympathetic character, even for people in her own ethnic community, because of her admitted guilt. Moreover, in 1912 the lynching of innocent untried black men understandably seemed more critical. A clemency* campaign by the newly organized NAACP and directed at Governor William Hodges Mann—the last Confederate soldier to serve as governor of the Commonwealth—failed to save Virginia Christian from Christian Virginia.

At a moment in American history when the idea was gaining acceptance that even the most vicious youngsters needed a special kind of justice—in the form of a juvenile court—the Commonwealth of Virginia resisted the emerging humanitarian* impulse that was taking hold in so many other states. Despite a 1910 Virginia law that prohibited the death penalty for first-time juvenile felons*, Christian received the ultimate punishment. Because of her race and her social position, her age did not protect her in the Old Dominion.

All of this does not bode well for Malvo, a poor, emotionally impoverished* black youngster who fits Virginia's historical template* for execution. Even though the Christian case occurred almost a century ago, the Commonwealth of Virginia has not progressed very far in its attitude toward juvenile offenders. Since 1993 only three states— Oklahoma, Virginia, and Texas—have sentenced and executed juveniles. Today, just as in 1912, Virginia lags behind as more progressive states— there are now twenty-eight—outlaw the juvenile death penalty in the push to establish a new American standard of decency appropriate to the twenty-first century. Like Virginia Christian, the "boy sniper" is not an ideal poster child for the abolition cause. Although the defense team will undoubtedly have a strong case rooted in Malvo's dysfunctional* family life and subsequent domination by a psychopathic* adult, it will be an uphill struggle to rouse sympathy for him. Lee Boyd—who calls himself "John" in imitation of his surrogate* father—is most often presented in the press as a cold-blooded, premeditating murderer rather than a damaged, immature tool in the hands of a sick adult. Malvo's "dad" trained him to be a sniper and then designed a killing vehicle in which he could drive his "son" to the fun—not to play soccer or football but to shoot at human targets. Although the decision to move Malvo's trial 200 miles south, from Fairfax County to the city of Chesapeake, was a welcome gesture toward insuring a fair trial, it's probably trivial in the face of the fear the sniper case aroused and Virginia's killing tradition.

dysfunctional: abnormal; not functioning properly

psychopathic: an emotionally disordered personality characterized by pursuit of immediate gratification in criminal acts

surrogate: substitute

Regardless of the documented horrors of any specific case, the juvenile death penalty is a "shameful practice," to use the words of Supreme Court Justices John Paul Stevens, David Souter, Ruth Bader Ginsburg, and Stephen Breyer. The United States is now the only country that continues to execute juveniles. (The Democratic Republic of the Congo did it last in 2000, Iran in 2001.) And, despite all our showy commitment to extending human rights around the world, the United States is now the only country that has failed to ratify the United Nations Convention on the Rights of the Child, which includes a provision that prohibits capital punishment for those under the age of 18. What a curious position for a country whose President proclaims himself a compassionate conservative, declaring that "no child should be left behind." And what a disturbing contradiction for an administration filled to the brim with Christian moralists, people who are supposed to demonstrate, in word as well as deed, a faith in the idea of redemption* and the human capacity for change. As a historian who has studied juvenile death-penalty cases as far back as the nineteenth century, it's clear to me that these cases tend to become political footballs, used to attract voters by demonstrating the state's ability to deliver "disinterested*" justice. Malvo is an easy target, given Virginia's record, and his execution might well serve the Bush Administration's larger strategic agenda. On November 10, [2003] when Malvo goes to trial, John Ashcroft would like us to

redemption: forgiveness

disinterested: unbiased

surveillance:
close watch

believe that retribution—along with increased surveillance*—will make us a safer, more secure people. Our Attorney General is clearly willing to use a barbaric relic of the past to promote his vision of the future.

Reading for Meaning

1. What law should have protected Virginia Christian from the death penalty in Virginia? Why didn't it?
2. How many states have outlawed the juvenile death penalty? Which states still execute juveniles?
3. What is Brumberg's stand on the juvenile death penalty? How does her conclusion allow her to use her belief to critique the Bush administration? How do you feel about the conclusion?

Reading Deeper

1. Why is the Fourth Circuit "an important source of judicial nominees in the Bush administration"?
2. Who does the title refer to?
3. Why does Brumberg use Virginia Christian's name repeatedly in the article?

Reading for Writing

1. Malvo has gone to trial in Virginia and has been sentenced. Complete some research on his trial and his sentence. Write an **argumentative** paper in which you take a side to convince the readers that the sentence was or was not proper. Use documentation for any sources you use.
2. Brumberg uses the extended example of Virginia Christian which is comparable to the subject of her essay, Lee Boyd Malvo. Using this essay as a model, write an **exemplification** essay in which you use an extended example that is similar to the topic of your paper.

SENTENCING OF TEEN GIRL FUELS DEBATE OVER YOUTHS IN PRISON

Ashley Broughton

Sometimes we forget that juvenile offenses can be and are committed by females because we hear so much about male offenders. However, a juvenile female offender could be sent to adult prison just as easily as a male for committing a serious crime. In the following article from The Salt Lake Tribune *(Oct. 14, 2003), Ashley Broughton describes the crime and punishment of a sixteen-year-old female juvenile.*

Prereading: Do you remember what you were doing when you were sixteen? Do you believe that you would have been responsible enough to be tried as an adult if you had been caught committing a serious crime?

Prewriting: Are there any crimes that a juvenile can commit that you believe are so serious that the juvenile should be tried as an adult? If so, what age would the juvenile have to be sent to adult court? Write a paragraph supporting your positions.

Vocabulary: Looking up and understanding the following words prior to reading should prepare you for the author's message. Other words will be defined in the margin.

aggravated   incarcerated   felony   predators

M elinda Rose Chasteen is too young to legally drink, buy a pack of cigarettes or vote in an election.

But she is not too young to be serving a term of five years to life in the Utah State Prison.

Chasteen, who turned 16 in June [2003], was sentenced last week [October 2003] by 2nd District Judge Ernie Jones. The Ogden teen previously pleaded guilty to attempted aggravated murder, a first-degree felony, in the Dec. 1, 2002, stabbing of a guard at the Weber Valley Juvenile Detention Center.

She is now the youngest inmate in the Utah State Prison, and the only female under 18, according to state Department of Corrections records.

She also has become part of a debate that has raged for more than a decade over placing juveniles in adult prisons.

In the early 1990s, Utah and other states enacted laws to "get tough" on juveniles as concern grew about their participation in violent crimes. Utah's Serious Youth Offender Act, which lays out the path from juvenile to adult court, was passed in 1995 during a surge of gang activity. Research has shown that nationally, the number of juveniles incarcerated in adult facilities more than doubled between 1985 and 1977.

Today, that number is declining. In 1995, about 5,300 state inmates were under 18, according to the U.S. Department of Justice's Bureau of Justice Statistics. As of midyear 2002, the most recent figures available, that had dropped to 3,055 juveniles, the bureau said—only 112 of them female.

Juveniles make up less than one-half of one percent of the population in state prisons. Some experts maintain adult prison is no place for those under 18.

"You really want to reserve it for, really, the worst of the worst," said Jeffrey Fagan, a professor of law and public health at Columbia University in New York.

Research has shown that juveniles in adult facilities are more likely to witness violence—or become victims of violence—than they might anywhere else, Fagan said. While many juvenile offenders have experienced violence before, he said, the level can be far higher in an adult prison.

In addition, late adolescence can be a critical developmental stage, Fagan said. "You and I passed that stage in mixed company," he said, but juveniles in prison do not.

"Instead, they learn about adulthood from cons," he said. "I hate to be grim about it, but it's a lie-down-with-dogs, get-up-with-fleas problem."

"It is unlikely that any juvenile will serve a true life sentence in prison. When they are released, they must battle a variety of stigmas that can block transition to a normal adult life," Fagan said. Some are internal. Some are economic, meaning it may be tough for them to get a job and adjust to a workplace.

"There's a disadvantage that attaches to them," Fagan said. "They come out, basically, with their futures mortgaged."

Chasteen and co-defendant Jessica Grundie were both 15 when they were accused of planning to kill the female guard with a knife Chasteen allegedly had smuggled inside in her shoe. They apparently had planned to escape from the facility after killing other guards, stealing clothes and cars and freeing other with their futures mortgaged, according to court documents. The guard recovered from the attack. Grundie, now also 16, is set for sentencing Dec. 10.

"Chasteen is one of only three inmates under 18 at the Utah State Prison," said Corrections spokesman Jack Ford. The others are Tyler Atwood and Matthew Prieto, both 17 and serving sentences of five years to life for convictions of first-degree felony aggravated robbery. Atwood will turn 18 later this month. Prison records show 54 other inmates entered prison under the age of 18 but have since reached adulthood.

Teens receive no special favors because of their age, Ford said. "We treat them as an adult. They're certified as an adult. They're convicted as an adult."

But while female inmates are not segregated according to their crime or their behavior, as male inmates are, "we will separate [Chasteen] from the predators," Ford said.

By the time juveniles wind up in adult prison, though, they more than likely belong there, said Michael Christensen, juvenile division chief of the Salt Lake County District Attorney's Office. "At that point in time, you've got to be able to protect society," he said.

"A variety of screening factors tends to ensure that in most cases, it is indeed the worst of the worst who are sent to the adult system," Christensen said. Some juveniles may meet the initial criteria to be certified to stand trial as an adult, but because of the nature of their crimes or the circumstances, they may stay in the juvenile system, he said.

On the other hand, there are "some kids out there that would kill you in a heartbeat," Christensen said.

Even Fagan agrees that Chasteen probably deserved to go to prison.

"This is a girl who attempted to kill somebody," he said. "That's exactly the kind of narrowing and selection principles that I think is right to use."

chemotherapy: use of chemicals to treat a disease

"This is harsh medicine. It's a bit like chemotherapy*. And you really don't want to give chemotherapy to people who don't really have cancer."

Reading for Meaning

1. Where was Chasteen when she committed the crime of attempted murder? Whom did she try to kill? Was this a spur-of-the-moment act? Explain.
2. Explain the comparison of adult prison to chemotherapy.

Reading Deeper

1. If "the number of juveniles incarcerated in adult facilities more than doubled between 1985 and 1977," what different conclusions can you arrive at about juveniles, the court system, and/or the public's willingness to punish juveniles as adults? Make a list of your conclusions.
2. What does Fagan mean when he says that when the juvenile offenders are released from prison, they come out "with their futures mortgaged"?

Reading for Writing

1. Look up the number of juveniles in your state's prison system. How many of them are male? How many are female? Also find out what

crimes they committed and how old they were when they committed the crimes. Write a **letter** to your state legislator attempting to **convince** him or her about your position on trying juvenile offenders as adults and sentencing them to adult prisons.

2. In Broughton's article, she paraphrases Jack Ford's comments: "female inmates are not segregated according to their crime or their behavior, as male inmates are." Why do you think segregation according to crime and/or behavior is necessary or unnecessary? Do you think segregation should be used or should not be used in both male and female prisons? Write a list of reasons supporting and opposing segregation of prisoners according to crime and/or behavior. Choose a **position,** and write an **argumentative** essay supporting your belief.

JUSTICE FOR KIDS

Editorial from **Rutland Herald** *and* **Barre-Montpelier Times Argus**

Many minors commit crimes. That is an undeniable fact that can be supported by looking at the criminal activity statistics in your city and state. There are many reasons being given for why juveniles rob, rape, murder, and so forth; and there are many reasons given for why they should not be treated as adults. In recent years, however, many residents of communities in which crime committed by juveniles has escalated in both frequency and degree have agreed to increase the severity of the punishment given to serious offenders. In the following editorial, the author looks at several juvenile offenders, the crimes they committed, and the sentences they received.

Prereading: Is a juvenile who shoplifts in the same category as one who commits murder or as one who drives the getaway car in a robbery murder?

Prewriting: If a juvenile assaulted your grandmother and stole her purse, what kind of punishment would you want the juvenile to be given? What if your grandmother was seriously injured in the attack? Write a paragraph explaining your position about this.

Vocabulary: Looking up and understanding the following words prior to reading should prepare you for the author's message. Other words will be defined in the margin.

alleged   rhetoric   rehabilitation   heinous

Twenty years ago [1981] two teenage boys committed a crime that
shocked Vermont, partly because of the cruelty of the boys' actions,
but also because the state had no power to hold one of the boys in custody after he was 18 years old.

It was 1981 when Louis Hamlin III and James Savage raped and
murdered Melissa Walbridge, a 12-year-old girl from Essex. A second
girl survived their attack. Hamlin was 16 at the time, and Vermont law
allowed authorities to try him as an adult. But Savage was 15, and authorities had no choice but to treat him as a juvenile.

The Hamlin–Savage case comes to mind following the arrest of
James Parker, 16, and Robert Tulloch, 17, of Chelsea for the murders of
Half and Susanne Zantop, the Dartmouth College professors slain last
month [January 2001] at their Hanover, NH, home. When Parker returned
to Vermont from Indiana, where he and Tulloch had been captured,
Parker's lawyer said he would seek to have Parker tried as a juvenile.

In 1981, Vermonters were so outraged by the Walbridge murder
that Governor Richard Snelling called a special session of the Legislature to change the juvenile justice laws. The result was that, for a list of
specific serious crimes, juveniles as young as 10 years old can now be
tried as adults. In addition, the age to which the state can retain custody
of convicted juveniles was raised from 18 to 21.

In the case of Savage, the state of Vermont was forced to release
the boy when he turned 18 years old. Savage moved away, only to be
arrested for a variety of other crimes in North Dakota. Hamlin, who
was tried as an adult for the Walbridge murder, received a sentence of
45 years.

It is hard to know what might result from Parker's petition to be
tried as a juvenile because no one knows the nature of the charges
against him. His alleged role in the Zantop murders is still unclear.

In recent years, however, the trend has grown for setting aside the
customary protections for juveniles and to try them and jail them as
adults. The rhetoric of accountability has been directed to younger and
younger offenders, and the rhetoric of rehabilitation has receded* before
the outrage caused by heinous crimes.

It would seem the harsher attitude toward juveniles has been
adopted mainly for the purposes of public safety. Those guilty of certain
serious crimes are seen to be a public danger, and locking them up for
lengthy terms is a way of reassuring the public that dangerous criminals
won't be out on the street.

It is worth remembering, however, that the original justification* for
treating juveniles differently from adults was that juveniles are, in fact, different. They are not yet fully shaped as individuals, and the circumstances

receded: faded

justification:
reason for

of their crimes often allow for rehabilitation that is real and productive, both for the offender and for society. For a whole range of offenses, the juvenile justice system is based on the notion that the mistakes of young people are often best addressed by holding them accountable while also recognizing their significant potential for getting back on track.

James Savage is not the best argument for the merciful treatment of juveniles, and provision* in the law for treating some juvenile offenders more seriously than others is reasonable. But most juvenile offenders are a far cry from James Savage. As protections for juveniles within the justice system continue to weaken, it is important to remember they are there for a good reason: We should not give up on our kids.

provision:
process of
providing for

Reading for Meaning

1. What was one effect of the Walbridge murder on juvenile justice laws? Explain.
2. What happened to the 15-year-old who killed Walbridge? Explain everything that happened to him.

Reading Deeper

1. Why have the expectations for accountability changed for juveniles over the years?
2. The author of this editorial explains that "the juvenile justice system is based on the notion that the mistakes of young people are often best addressed by holding them accountable while also recognizing their significant potential for getting back on track." If the system holds the juveniles accountable and attempts to rehabilitate, what seems to be the problem? Why do many individuals want to change the treatment of juvenile offenders to adult sentences? Explain.

Reading for Writing

1. The death penalty was once considered a deterrent for criminal activity; however, criminals have shown that it generally is not. Is the possibility of receiving an adult sentence for a crime a deterrent for juvenile offenders? Take a **position** on this and write an **argumentative** essay supporting your position.
2. James Savage is an example of someone who returned to crime after being released from a juvenile center. Investigate the recidivism rate of juvenile offenders in your state. Write an **argumentative** essay in which you take a **position** about the success or lack of success rehabilitation has on juvenile offenders in your state.

The Lionel Tate Case

Editorial from the St. Petersburg Times

Murder is always considered not only a serious crime but also a horrible event, especially to the victim's family. But when a child is the victim, society looks even more harshly on the murderer. When the criminal is another child, a juvenile, all parties suffer. In the following editorial from Florida's St. Petersburg Times *(2003), the author examines the Lionel Tate case, his sentencing, and the order for a new trial four years after the murder.*

Prereading: Even if you never heard of the Lionel Tate case, think about a six-year-old being brutally killed by a twelve-year-old. Do you think you could forgive the murderer who has served four years in prison?

Prewriting: Do you believe that individuals who are not competent to stand trial because of low IQ, mental illness, or age should be given special consideration for serious crimes they commit? Write a paragraph taking a position and defending it.

Vocabulary: Looking up and understanding the following words prior to reading should prepare you for the author's message. Other words will be defined in the margin.

competency   expedite   clemency

A 12-YEAR-OLD KILLER WHO RECEIVED A LIFE SENTENCE AT AGE 14 STANDS TO GET A SECOND CHANCE. IT'S A GOOD SIGN IN A SYSTEM THAT HAD LOST ITS SENSE OF JUVENILE JUSTICE.

They may have been teenagers or even younger, but politicians called them "super-predators" and demanded long, adult-like prison sentences. Over the last decade this trend has transformed the way the criminal justice system treats juvenile offenders, and it has not been a change for the better. Consider the case of Lionel Tate, the young man from Broward County who faced a lifetime behind bars for a crime he committed at 12 years of age.

An appeals court recently ordered a new trial for Tate, saying this time his mental competency should be a factor in determining his fate.

emulating:
imitating

Tate was 12 years old when he killed a playmate, 6-year-old Tiffany Eunick. Prosecutors characterized it as an intentional act of brutality. Tiffany died of injuries that included a detached liver and skull fracture. But Tate's attorneys said the death was an accident and had occurred while Tate was emulating* pro wrestling moves he had seen on television. In a move they would come to deeply regret, Tate's attorneys and mother refused a state plea bargain offer that would have sent the young man to a juvenile detention facility for three years for second degree

lenient: mild, not harsh

murder—a reasonably lenient* sentence. Instead, at trial, a jury convicted him of first-degree murder and Tate was sentenced to life in prison. He is believed to be the youngest American to face a life sentence.

His sentence shocked even the most rigid law-and-order advocates. Governor Jeb Bush said initially that he would consider an expedited clemency process, but he ultimately decided not to intervene*.

intervene:
interference
come between

Tate came to represent the excess occasioned when prosecutors abuse their discretion to charge juveniles as adults.

A panel of the 4th District Court of Appeals has begun to set things right, ruling that Tate should receive a new trial since there was never a pretrial hearing to determine whether he was capable of understanding the proceedings* against him. The court suggested that someone

proceedings:
official record of things said or done

his age, who had developmental problems and no prior involvement with the criminal justice system, may not have been competent to stand trial.

eminently:
highly

The ruling is eminently* sensible, recognizing that preteens and some young teenagers may not have the mental capacity to appreciate what is at stake in a criminal proceeding and may be unable to assist in their own defense.

appellate:
having the power to review another court's decision and overturn it

Unfortunately, Florida Attorney General Charlie Crist has decided to challenge the court decision setting aside Tate's conviction. Crist apparently is concerned that the appellate* court decision will have implications* for other trials involving young defendants. But a pretrial competency hearing for someone as young as Tate facing adult charges is a reasonable precaution that serves the interest of justice.

implications:
influence

Broward County prosecutors, meanwhile, have offered Tate the same plea bargain the defense turned down before trial. If the appeal by the attorney general's office doesn't derail* the deal, Tate could be facing only a few more months in prison, followed by house arrest and probation. The mother of Tate's 6-year-old victim approves the plea offer, according to her attorney.

derail: take off track

Tate should be punished, but he does not deserve to spend the rest of his life in prison for a crime he committed as a 12-year-old.

Reading for Meaning

1. What was Tate's defense for killing Tiffany Eunick?
2. What is the purpose of a pretrial hearing?
3. Did Tate and his mother and attorney have any options before he went to trial as an adult? Explain.

Reading Deeper

1. The author of this editorial assumes that everyone agrees that the prosecutors in this case "abuse[d] their discretion to charge juveniles as adults." Do you believe that the prosecutor in this case abused his discretion in charging Tate as an adult? Explain.
2. Even if a juvenile does not understand the extent of the consequences, what other resources does he or she have that should explain them to him or her?

Reading for Writing

1. Write a **response** to this editorial agreeing or disagreeing with the author's position in the last sentence.
2. Consider the purpose of a pretrial hearing. It is usually used to determine if a defendant is competent to stand trial and to aid in his or her own defense. Investigate the options that are given to a juvenile when he or she is found not competent to be tried as an adult but has committed a serious offense. Write an **informative** paper about the procedures.

RHETORICAL ANALYSIS

The following editorial begins with a description of an unquestionably serious crime committed by two juveniles. The author begins with facts, explaining what the crime was and how the court tried the males who committed the crime. Through the use of facts and opinions, the author continues to explain how the residents of the state felt about the crime and what they did. He then uses a transition to move to the opposition's side of how to deal with juvenile offenders and uses language that indicates that the thoughts and feelings of the residents had changed. Rather than beginning with the thesis, the author ends his piece with his claim/thesis. In the left-hand margin there is information that directs you to appropriate chapters in this textbook for discussion about the underlined techniques the author used to write the essay or that comments directly about the techniques the author used.

Justice for Kids

Ch. 10,
Persuasion fact

Ch. 10,
Persuasion fact

Ch. 10,
Persuasion use
of facts for the
development of
the paragraph

Ch. 7,
Comparison use
of comparison

Ch. 9, Causal
use of effect

Ch. 9, Causal
paragraph
developed
through use of
cause and effect

Ch. 9, Causal
use of cause and
effect

Ch. 10,
Persuasion use
of fact

Ch. 9, Causal
effect and cause

Ch. 10,
Persuasion
transition to
opposition

Twenty years ago [1981] two teenage boys committed a crime that shocked Vermont, partly because of the cruelty of the boys' actions, but also because the state had no power to hold one of the boys in custody after he was 18 years old.

It was 1981 when Louis Hamlin III and James Savage raped and murdered Melissa Walbridge, a 12-year-old girl from Essex. A second girl survived their attack. Hamlin was 16 at the time, and Vermont law allowed authorities to try him as an adult. But Savage was 15, and authorities had no choice but to treat him as a juvenile.

The Hamlin-Savage case comes to mind following the arrest of James Parker, 16, and Robert Tulloch, 17, of Chelsea for the murders of Half and Susanne Zantop, the Dartmouth College professors slain last month [January 2001] at their Hanover, NH, home. When Parker returned to Vermont from Indiana, where he and Tulloch had been captured, Parker's lawyer said he would seek to have Parker tried as a juvenile.

In 1981, Vermonters were so outraged by the Walbridge murder that Governor Richard Snelling called a special session of the Legislature to change the juvenile justice laws. The result was that, for a list of specific serious crimes, juveniles as young as 10 years old can now be tried as adults. In addition, the age to which the state can retain custody of convicted juveniles was raised from 18 to 21.

In the case of Savage, the state of Vermont was forced to release the boy when he turned 18 years old. Savage moved away, only to be arrested for a variety of other crimes in North Dakota. Hamlin, who was tried as an adult for the Walbridge murder, received a sentence of 45 years.

It is hard to know what might result from Parker's petition to be tried as a juvenile because no one knows the nature of the charges against him. His alleged role in the Zantop murders is still unclear.

In recent years, however, the trend has grown for setting aside the customary protections for juveniles and to try them and jail them as adults. The rhetoric of accountability has been directed to younger and younger offenders, and the rhetoric of rehabilitation has receded before the outrage caused by heinous crimes.

Ch. 10,
Persuasion
opinion

<u>It would seem the harsher attitude toward juve-</u>
<u>niles has been adopted mainly for the purposes of</u>
<u>public safety</u>. <u>Those guilty of certain serious crimes</u>
<u>are seen to be a public danger, and locking them up</u>
<u>for lengthy terms is a way of reassuring the public</u>
<u>that dangerous criminals won't be out on the street</u>.

Ch. 10,
Persuasion use
of fact for
paragraph
development

<u>It is worth remembering, however, that the orig-</u>
<u>inal justification for treating juveniles differ-</u>
<u>ently from adults was that juveniles are, in fact,</u>
<u>different</u>. They are not yet fully shaped as individ-
uals, and the circumstances of their crimes often
allow for rehabilitation that is real and productive,
both for the offender and for society. For a whole
range of offenses, the juvenile justice system is
based on the notion that the mistakes of young people
are often best addressed by holding them accountable
while also recognizing their significant potential
for getting back on track.

Ch. 10,
Persuasion use
of opinion

<u>James Savage is not the best argument for the</u>
<u>merciful treatment of juveniles</u>, and provision in
the law for treating some juvenile offenders more
seriously than others is reasonable. <u>But most juve-</u>
<u>nile offenders are a far cry from James Savage</u>. As
protections for juveniles within the justice system

Ch. 10,
Persuasion
thesis in bold

continue to weaken, it is important to remember they
are there for a good reason: **We should not give up on
our kids.**

The strategy of leaving the claim/thesis until the conclusion involves using a set of facts or a body of information that might not be
popular with readers. If the author were to announce the thesis at the beginning, the readers might not be prepared to agree with it and might
continue reading. However, by giving the information that is really in
opposition to the writer's point first, the editor can use a transition to
move into the points that favor his or her case and end on the strong
points of the argument. Here the author ends with a strong concluding
sentence: the claim/thesis. There is no place left to go in the way the argument is structured.

REFLECTIONS ON JUVENILE OFFENDERS: WHO SHOULD BE GIVEN PRIORITY, THE JUVENILE OR THE VICTIM?

From the premeditated, attempted murder of a female guard to rape and murder to the sniper killing of eleven innocent victims, juveniles have become involved in serious criminal offenses. Obviously, juvenile offenses have escalated over the years since legislation was enacted to deal with juvenile crime, from pranks, such as putting detergent in fountains, to petty theft, such as shoplifting nail polish and lipstick. The criminality of the offenses has taken a serious leap, and now groups of youngsters, who were once just groups of kids, are now frequently feared gangs whose members must go through initiation rites for acceptance and as proof of their ability and bravery. But the United States is not unique. Other nations also have to deal with out-of-control youths, and they, too, must determine how to treat them: as juveniles or as adults. And if they are certified as adults, how severe should their punishment be: life sentences? Capital punishment? This is a complex issue and one that is highly controversial.

Although legislators are the ones who create laws, we, too, can have a voice in the matter of juvenile justice. By keeping informed, writing to our representatives, investigating the way they vote on such issues, and voting for candidates who represent our individual voices, we can help shape the way juvenile justice is formed. Whether we are proponents of rehabilitation for all offenders or proponents of adult sentencing and punishment, or something in between, we can make a difference. And beyond the ballot box, there are other ways to turn youngsters around, especially those without responsible adult guidance and supervision. It is up to each of us to find a way. New York's Senator Hillary Rodham Clinton suggests that it takes a village to raise a child. What is your solution?

Reflecting to Write

Group Writing

In the legislature, laws are made in committee; therefore, create a group to complete the following assignment. Assume the role of a legislator who must come up with a new bill for handling juvenile crime. Knowing the types of crimes juveniles are now committing, you must make provisions for transferring serious offenders to adult courts for adult punishment. Take into consideration the wide range of ages that falls under the designation "juvenile." Present your bill to the class for discussion and conduct a vote on whether or not to pass it as a law.

Informative

Visit the Web site for Amnesty International and find their position on adult punishments for juvenile offenders. Visit other Web sites also, such as criminal lawyers' sites, editorials of different newspapers, child advocate sites, victim advocate sites, religious groups' sites, law school sites, and so forth looking for their positions on punishments for juvenile offenders. Write an **informative, division** and **classification** essay explaining the different positions the different groups take and the reasons for their positions.

Investigate the characteristics of juvenile detention centers in your area. If you are unable to visit one as a student doing research, interview someone from a Criminal Justice Department in your university/college, someone in county services for juveniles, someone in a family law center, or a lawyer from a legal aid group to get information about what the centers are like, what kind of rehabilitation is offered, and other general/specific information about the treatment that juveniles receive there. Write a **descriptive informative** essay discussing your findings. Be sure to document your interviews and any written information you use.

Follow the story of a particular juvenile who has committed a major crime and is being processed through either the juvenile or adult justice system. Find as much background information as you can about the crime and about the individual. Write an **informative, descriptive** paper that gives all the information that you have found both positive and negative about the case. Arrive at conclusions from the material you have used. Be sure to document all material you use.

On Monday, January 26, 2004, the Supreme Court announced that it would begin to consider not giving the death penalty to killers who committed the crime when they were younger than 18. Find newspaper and magazine articles that discuss capital punishment for juvenile offenders both in the United States and in other countries. Write an **informative** essay that presents the various sides regarding the death penalty for juveniles convicted of a crime that involves killing a victim.

Argumentation

On Monday, January 26, 2004, Lionel Tate was released from prison after serving four years of a life sentence for killing six-year-old Tiffany Eunick when he was twelve-years old. He will be under house arrest for one year, and he will have to perform 8,000 hours of community service. Find newspaper and magazine articles that support or oppose this action. Take a **position** on Tate's release, and write an **argumentative** essay attempting to convince readers that Tate's release was right or wrong.

Community Service—Learning Project

Many times when juveniles are sent to juvenile detention centers, they miss out on some of their schoolwork, and they fall behind in their studies. Find a juvenile detention center near you and volunteer to tutor one or two youths in reading, math, or whatever academic area you are good in. Visit the youth you are tutoring on a regular basis, at least once each week for several weeks or as long as your instructor tells you to do so. Be sure not to do the work for the student; rather, tutor him or her in how to complete the work. After each visit, write a **reflective journal** entry describing your visit, what you did, what you learned, and how you felt about the experience. Share comments about the visit with your class, and after the tutoring is over make a **poster** or other **visuals** for an **oral presentation,** and write an **informative personal narrative.**

Chapter 20

Environment: How We Treat Our Natural World

When the first English explorers came to the New World, they sent back reports to England that they had discovered "virgin territory." What they had discovered, in fact, was land that had been settled and lived on for centuries by Native American Indians. What made the land appear to be unspoiled were the beliefs of the Indians that that land was to be used but also cared for. The animals, fowl and fish were to be hunted but not to depletion, and the forests were to be cut but only to provide necessary and usable timber. The Indians believed that if they respected Nature, she would provide them with what they needed for survival and sustenance. Because they believed that everything and everyone is connected and whatever happens to the land, air, water, and animals, eventually happens to human beings, they were careful in their treatment of their environment.

We've come a long way from the 1600s when John Smith and others began their exploration and settlement. Modernization means that we are no longer required to hunt, fish, and plow to feed ourselves. Our local grocery store provides most of our pasteurized, organically grown, squeezed, processed, frozen, packaged, canned, and bottled necessities and extras in locations that are convenient, climate-controlled and provides speedy service. Most of the time, many people don't know or care who picked their peaches, avocados, celery, or lettuce, and, unless they're concerned with mad cow disease, they certainly don't want to know how their beef is prepared nor how pork, poultry, or fish was processed. However modernization has made our lives easier, it has also removed us from our natural world, as most of the people in the United States now live in urban rather than rural areas. Granted, many residents have fled to the suburbs, which, in many cases, now look like pockets of larger city life, except for larger yards, fewer skyscrapers, and less traffic congestion. But the suburbs don't replace bucolic rural life.

Because of almost unrestricted population growth and lack of zoning laws in many places, Nature is being gradually or quickly edged out of our cities. In the early 1900s, President Theodore Roosevelt had the foresight to preserve parklands and national forests, thereby keeping green spaces safe from commercial development. But today, new measures must be taken to protect the already protected sites from overuse by tourists; air, noise, and water pollution; arsonists; and other man-made problems. Forest rangers and others who protect the parks work hard to keep the natural "natural." After all, those trails we walk on weren't part of Nature's plan.

While there are those who work hard at keeping the planet healthy for humankind, there are those who work equally hard trying to satisfy humanity's need for gas, oil, timber, housing, steel, chemicals, transportation, paper, and other modern conveniences. None of us can deny that we are dependent on all of the above commodities, and we would be hard pressed to give up any one of them. Can Nature and modern humanity co-exist in peace? Many of the large lumber companies advertise that they believe in reforestation—planting hybrid, fast-growing seedlings where they have cleared the land. Those who support damming rivers assert that they are preventing flooding and providing power. Those who support the Alaska pipeline explain how they are providing oil for refineries for gas and oil production, thus reducing our dependency on foreign oil. What they fail to mention is that the lumber companies frequently destroy old growth forests that are irreplaceable and that the dams frequently create flooding and erosion problems down stream. And no one mentions the destruction of natural habitat for the animals, fish, and fowl in the areas.

On the other hand, we live in modern homes with modern conveniences in cities and towns that are run by people who provide us with electricity, gas, and water. Life is good. Government officials—local, state, and federal—are the ones who control or fail to control our environmental problems. Organizations such as the Sierra Club, Green Peace, the Audubon Society, and others maintain lobbies to encourage or persuade legislators to vote for environmentally friendly bills. And at the grass-roots level, there are residents who organize to try to prevent the building of landfills or smokestacks in their neighborhoods. With the help of some city officials, religious leaders, and everyday citizens, progress has been made to clean up toxic waste dumps, relocate polluting industries, and reduce the size and amount of emissions from smokestacks. Informed citizens have discovered what the Native American Indians knew centuries ago: Whatever we do to the Earth will return to hurt or help us. It's

"Columbia River Basin Wilderness"   *by Anne Perrin*

time for each of us to look literally "in our own backyards" and determine what we've done lately to help the Earth.

EARTH ETHICS AND THE WEB OF LIFE

Katherine Hall

Today, more and more people, especially students, are becoming aware of the environment and the damage that is being caused by people who are more concerned about their own comfort than about the welfare of the earth. Look around your neighborhood or around your campus. What could be done better to help the planet? Starting with one small place and cleaning it up is not quite so overwhelming as believing each of us is responsible for the entire world. In the following article, Katherine Hall, a member of the Golden Key International Honor Society and student from San Francisco State University, discusses the way we treat our environment and makes suggestions for helping to improve the state of the

"A Walk Along Lake Louise"   *by Elizabeth Kessler*

planet. Discussing the various abuses people inflict on the earth, Hall suggests ways each of us can make a difference without feeling overwhelmed at the enormity of the project of saving the earth. By taking her advice, we will not only help the earth but we will also be able to connect positively with those around us.

Prereading: How environmentally aware are you? What do you do to help improve the condition of the earth?

Prewriting: How much water do you use daily? Think about the water you drink, bathe with, wash dishes with, wash your car with, wash clothes with, give to your pets, and so forth. Write a paragraph discussing how you use water in a typical day and in a typical week and draw conclusions about how this affects the earth.

Vocabulary: Looking up and understanding the following words prior to reading should prepare you for the author's message. Other words will be defined in the margin.

hectares   Amazon rain forests   depleted   extinction   dioxins
ozone   green-house effect   holistic   sustainable development
ecosystems

This we know: the earth does not belong to man; man belongs to the earth. This we know. All things are connected like the blood which unites one family. All things are connected. Whatever befalls the earth befalls the sons of the earth. Man did not weave the web of life: he is merely a strand in it. Whatever he does to the web, he does to himself.

—Seattle, Chief of the Duwamish
Suquamish and Allied Indian Tribes

latte: espresso mixed with hot or steamed milk

In the three minutes it takes Starbucks to make your latte*, hectares of Amazon rain forests are lost forever, our clean water supply is depleted, and plants and animals are pushed into extinction. While drinking your latte, the world is covered with thousands of deadly chemicals like dioxins, which cause serious reproductive and developmental problems. These chemicals not only endanger our own bodies; they accumulate in our fat tissue and are passed directly on to our children. We are all interconnected, and destroying the earth is destroying us all.

Perhaps the reason most people spend more time thinking about their coffee than the environment is because environmental issues seem enormous and overwhelming. People don't see connection between en-

degradation: impairment or wearing down

vironmental degradation* and their daily life styles.

When most people think about the environment they think of the quintessential issues like the green-house effect, the depletion of the ozone layer and cutting down the rain forests. People do not realize these huge problems result from thousands of tiny decisions that ordinary citizens made every day, such as riding a bike instead of driving the SUV.

It is not that people don't care about their world; the problem is that people feel powerless. This defeated mentality is the root of all of our ecological problems. The solution is earth ethics.

Earth ethics combines individual consciousness with active involvement based around the principles of unity, peace and concern for the environment. Earth ethics are the foundation on which a holistic society is built.

Earth ethics means treating each other and the earth with respect and compassion, along with living in ways that are less destructive and more in line with our beliefs. By invoking earth ethics in our daily lives, we stop feeling like helpless observers and start making a difference.

With earth ethics, we take back our power along with our accountability. We do not have to be full-time activists in order to make a huge difference by being resourceful. Even making a tiny change, like getting our coffee in a thermos instead of a paper cup, can eventually make a huge difference over a lifetime.

Anyone can find creative ways to help. During my free time, I used to go shopping at the mall, but now I find ways to get involved in my community; the fulfillment I get from being active in my community is worth far more than money.

I invoke earth ethics in my daily life in a variety of different ways. For example, I try to reuse things as many times as possible, shop at thrift stores, buy organic produce, support environmentally friendly businesses, vote, actively participate in the community, recycle, buy less, appreciate nature, educate myself, focus less on me and more on we, think about what I value in life. . . .

Although it is important to reduce our consumption of material goods, we can also positively change the world just by spending money. When citizens make sustainable development a priority, corporations are given incentive to use stricter environmental standards in production along with stronger regulation. Every dollar we spend is a vote of support; we can choose to spend our money on sustainable development, or we can vote for industries that thrive on waste, pollution and plunder.

There is a great awakening taking place across the world, one which starts with ordinary citizens realizing we have a huge role to play in shaping our own existence and our world. We are killing ourselves and the earth by prioritizing capital growth above social and environmental consequences.

These short-term material gains have tremendously negative long-term consequences. We are sacrificing the earth and its splendor for instant profits. Together, we can end the "race to the bottom" mentality and start using earth ethics to improve our world and ourselves.

Earth ethics is transforming communities all over the world. For example, NIMBY stands for Not in My Back Yard, and once was the driving mentality used to bring neighbors and community members together in order to stop a dump or toxic industry from being sited in a community's "back yard."

Thanks to earth ethics, activists are beginning to realize the NIMBY tactic is only a change in the system, not a change to the system; the toxins will just end up in another person's back yard. Now many activists are starting to focus on NIABY (Not in Anyone's Back Yard) in order to find environmentally friendly alternatives to polluting industries and to keep pollution out of anyone's back yard.

Democracy has to be recreated by each generation; therefore, each of us has the ability and the obligation to get involved and to make a better world. Great movements will not start from top down; they will start with ordinary citizens invoking earth ethics and demanding justice.

We can't wait for decisions to be made from top-down. We make a difference through grass roots organizing, individual action and a "bottom-up" approach.

equilibrium: state of balance

The equilibrium* of ecosystems is profoundly delicate; when we destroy one species, we start a chain reaction which destroys us all. We are all interconnected and are all strands in the web of life. However, the web is quickly unraveling, and the time we have left to repair the damage we have caused is running out.

Together, we must create a new way of living and a more ethical life. We all have the ability to shape the future; what we need to question are our own desires and priorities. Through community service, unity, and compassion towards each other and our environment, we will create a better world and a harmonious life.

Reading for Meaning

1. Define earth ethics.
2. What reason does Hall give for people not appearing to care about the world?

Reading Deeper

1. What does Hall mean by her statement: "We are killing ourselves and the earth by prioritizing capital growth above social and environmental consequences"?

2. Who has damaged the "web of life"? Give examples of how this happened.

3. When Hall tells the readers how we can practice earth ethics, she includes "each other" in her suggestions. Why is being compassionate toward "each other" part of earth ethics?

Reading for Writing

1. The quotation that Hall used at the beginning of this article is attributed to Chief Seattle as part of a letter he wrote to President Pierce. Find a copy of this "letter" and write a historical biography of how it came to be. You can find it and other versions on the Web.

2. Keep a daily **journal** for two weeks, recording all the ways you acted in an environmentally friendly way by practicing earth ethics. Record every time you recycle, pick up trash, buy organic produce, vote for an environmentally friendly candidate, or any other act that shows you care about the world. At the end of the two weeks, write a **personal narrative** based on your journal entries that discusses your behavior modification and whether you think you will continue to act in an ecologically responsible manner.

PARALYSIS ON CLEAN AIR

The New York Times *Editor (2004)*

Air, water, and food are three essentials for the survival of human beings. Without these, mankind is in danger of illness and death. But how far can we go when the air, water, and food we need are polluted with toxic chemicals? One of the jobs of our federal government is to protect our best interests; however, the federal government must also aid industry that must regulate their pollution output. Who gets the greater support: industry or mankind? The following editorial from The New York Times *discusses the way President Bush and different senators are working with the issue of clean air quality.*

Prereading: Think of the area in which you live. Is it near chemical industries? Petroleum industries? What is the quality of the air you breathe? Can you see the air when you wake up in the morning or by mid-afternoon? Think about what you are breathing.

Prewriting: If you were a major stockholder in a chemical company and the federal government ruled that the company had installed new devices to cut down on the pollution that was being emitted into the air and water at a cost of millions of dollars, how would you react: for or against the spending of possible profits to improve the air and water quality? Write a paragraph taking a side and supporting your position.

Vocabulary: Looking up and understanding the following words prior to reading should prepare you for the author's message.

fiat   limbo

Just before Christmas [2003], a federal appeals court blocked a new Bush administration rule that would have weakened existing law governing pollution from power plants and other industrial facilities. Having opposed the rule as little more than a gift to the utilities at the expense of public health, this page had no quarrel with the decision. Even so, it served as a reminder that clean air policy is increasingly being made by administrative fiat and by the courts—a ruling one day, a reversal the next. This is not productive. The public is deprived of cleaner air; industry is deprived of the regulatory certainty it needs to make the wise investment decisions.

The time has therefore come for Congress to update the 1970 Clean Air Act, last significantly revised in 1990 by President Bush's father. The point would be to simplify the regulatory maze, while at the same time ensuring big new reductions in major pollutants, including carbon dioxide, the main global warming gas.

This is asking a lot of the present Congress, which has shown little appetite for enlightened legislation. But surely even it can see that clean air policy is hopelessly stalemated. The latest ruling, for example, saved from immediate extinction a useful provision of the Clean Air Act that the Clinton administration and state officials like Attorney General Eliot Spitzer of New York had used to sue companies that failed to install pollution control equipment when they upgraded their plants. But as a practical matter the provision is in limbo.

A parallel situation is developing with respect to mercury. In early December, the Environmental Protection Agency proposed new (and industry-friendly) rules governing mercury emissions from coal-fired power plants. This proposal, too, seems to be on shaky legal ground. Even the administration's recent and generally well-intentioned proposals to limit smog and acid rain in the Eastern United States may be open to challenge.

The court's job is to swat down bad ideas. But that does nothing to end the policy stalemate. And here is where Congress could make a difference. There are three serious proposals on power plant emissions on Capitol Hill. Each offers essentially the same regulatory framework: a market-based scheme that would set national ceilings on specific pollutants but let companies figure out how best to meet them.

Where they differ is on the ceilings. The administration's are unacceptably high; we are better off with the current law, despite its administrative complexities. A second proposal sponsored by Senator James Jeffords of Vermont is much tougher, and a third proposal by Senator Thomas Carper of Delaware is somewhere in the middle. The Jeffords and Carper proposals have the further advantage of imposing limits on global warming gases, which appeals to the more enlightened utilities because it allows them to make their investment decisions with all the major pollutants in mind.

Before the debate can really move forward, President Bush will have to drop his stubborn opposition to regulating carbon dioxide. But somewhere in this mix lies a more certain clean air strategy than the one we are living with today.

Reading for Meaning

1. What new rule did Bush plan to implement before Christmas 2003? What would this have meant for air and water?
2. How does current policy affect the public and industry?
3. Which gas contributes most damage in global warming?

Reading Deeper

1. Why do you think people want to challenge rules limiting the amount of mercury, smog, or acid rain occurring in the United States?
2. What are the points that make the Jeffords and the Carper proposal better than that of the Bush administration?

Reading for Writing

1. Determine your **position** about where you stand on limiting power plant emissions. Write a **letter** to the editor in response to this editorial expressing your position.
2. Write a **letter** to your representative in Congress attempting to **persuade** him or her how to vote when the new proposal is brought up. You might need to do a little more research on the topic to discover what points those who oppose tightening the limits on power plant

emissions hold. For example, the editorial makes it clear that President Bush opposes regulating carbon dioxide. Look for material that explains his reasons.

HOTSPOTS: PRESERVING PIECES OF A FRAGILE BIOSPHERE

E. O. Wilson

The use of land by builders, investors, home owners, civic officials, and so forth leads to the destruction of habitats for insects, animals, birds, and plants. There are those who argue that human beings must have the land for growth, and there are those who argue that human beings are using more than their share, taking away land that should remain protected for the other species on the planet. In the following article from National Geographic *(2002), E. O. Wilson explains the importance of "hotspots" and what is being done to protect them.*

Prereading: How much land do you think we as human beings need? As our population grows, what happens to the land?

Prewriting: Look at the city/town in which you live. Has there been expansion of neighborhoods resulting in the cutting down of trees to build houses? Have trees been cut down so malls can be put in? Write a paragraph considering the impact of malls and neighborhoods on the environment.

Vocabulary: Looking up and understanding the following words prior to reading should prepare you for the author's message. Other words will be defined in the margin.

biosphere   beggared   geophysical   flora and fauna biodiversity   conservation

T he biosphere that gives us life is wondrously rich. The number of organisms composing it is astronomical: One million trillion insects are believed to be alive on the planet at any one time; they in turn are beggared by the bacteria, ten billion of which may reside in a single pinch of soil. And so great is the diversity of life-forms that we still have not taken its measure. During the past two centuries biologists have discovered and given formal names to somewhat more than 1.5 million species of plants, animals, and microorganisms, yet various methods of estimation place the number of all species on Earth, known and still unknown, between 3 million and 100 million.

robust: having strong and vigorous health

relentless: unceasing

aquatic: growing or living in water

extant: currently or actually existing

juggernaut: massive, destructive force

providential: occuring as if by Providence or God.

uniformly: evenly

savannas: tropical or subtropical grassland with scattered trees

opulent: ample or plentiful

In spite of this immense complexity, perhaps because of it, the biosphere is also very fragile. Although it appears robust*, it is actually a hollow shell around the planet so thin it cannot be seen edgewise from an orbiting spacecraft. Its teeming organisms are ill equipped to withstand humanity's relentless* assault on the habitats in which they live. Our species, at more than six billion strong and heading toward nine billion by mid-century, has become a geophysical force more destructive than storms and droughts. Half the world's forests are gone. Tropical forests in particular, where most of Earth's plant and animal species live, are being clear-cut at the rate of perhaps one percent a year. In shallow waters from the West Indies to the Maldives many of Earth's coral reefs are literally fading away. Polluting . . . and the introduction of alien organisms are causing the wholesale extinction of native aquatic* species. Greenhouse warming, by edging climatic zones poleward faster than flora and fauna can emigrate, threatens the existence of entire ecosystems, including those of the Arctic and other hitherto least disturbed parts of the world.

Researchers generally agree that extant* species are now vanishing at least 100 and possibly as much as 10,000 times faster than new ones are being born. Many experts believe that at the present rate of environmental change half the world's surviving species could be gone by the end of the century.

Is there a way to divert the human juggernaut* and save at least most of the remaining natural world? A providential* arrangement in the geography of life makes it at least possible. Biodiversity is not distributed uniformly* over land and sea. A large part of it is concentrated in a relatively small number of coral reefs, forests, savannas*, and other habitats scattered on and around different continents. By preserving these special places, biologists have come to agree, it should be possible to accommodate the continuing human surge while protecting a large part of Earth's threatened fauna and flora.

Among the most precious of the special places are the hotspots, which conservation biologists define as natural environments containing exceptionally large numbers of endangered species found nowhere else. The most familiar hotspots include the Philippines, California's Mediterranean-climate coast, and Madagascar. Less well-known are Chocó-Darién-Western Ecuador, the Western Ghats of India, and the Succulent Karoo of South Africa. Just 25 of the hottest of these hotspots occupy 1.4 percent of the planet's land surface, roughly equivalent to Alaska and Texas combined, yet are the exclusive homes of 44 percent of Earth's plant species and 35 percent of its birds, mammals, reptiles, and amphibians. Increasingly, these areas, among the biologically most opulent* and fascinating places on Earth, have become the focus of global conservation efforts. Their plight is stark evidence of humankind's deadly impact on nature, and their attempted rescue a beacon of hope.

Reading for Meaning

1. Provide an estimate of the number of known and unknown species on the earth.
2. How many human beings are there estimated to be by mid-century?

Reading Deeper

1. Wilson claims that human beings are more destructive to the environment than storms and drought. What evidence does he use to support his assertion?
2. What will happen if the hotspots around the globe are destroyed? What does that mean for human beings?

Reading for Writing

1. Wilson mentions the rate at which forests are being clear-cut. This topic is one which is quite controversial between the timber producers and the environmentalists. Conduct **research** about the benefits of forests to mankind and the **arguments** timber producers give for cutting down forests. Determine which side you favor and write an **argumentative** essay using the material you find to **convince** readers about your belief. Be sure to document the material you use.
2. Find a plot of trees that is scheduled for clearing so that apartments, a strip mall, a car dealership, or a new housing development can be built. Visit the site daily, watching the way the land is cleared and how they dispose of the trees. Write a **descriptive** essay that takes into consideration what the land looked like before, during, and after it was cleared. Also include why the clearing was done and any conclusions you can draw from your experience.

Eco-Pragmatists

Monte Burke

It seems that in the environmental wars, human beings can have their forests and clear-cut them, too. In the following article, published in Forbes *magazine (Sept. 3, 2001), Monte Burke describes the compromises that the Nature Conservancy has made to protect*

*the environment yet still exploit it for timber, gas wells, and other
natural resources. While there are some who applaud the efforts,
there are others who look at the profit the Conservancy is making
and question its intentions.*

Prereading: Think about your favorite natural spot that you enjoy
going to for fun or for escape or for any reason. It might be the beach,
a national forest, the mountains, or even a lake. What would you think
if a group of environmentalists bought it with the intention of allowing
three-quarters of it to be developed while saving one-quarter of it?

Prewriting: What is your position on the issue of using land protected
for an endangered species for drilling gas and oil even though the
species will probably die out forever if the land is disturbed that drastically? Write a paragraph stating and supporting your position.

Vocabulary: Looking up and understanding the following words prior
to reading should prepare you for the author's message. Other words
will be defined in the margin.

pragmatism   Sierra Club   ecosystems   Kyoto Protocol

———————————

This fall [2001] ExxonMobil Corporation will drill gas wells on a
2,263-acre preserve in Texas City, TX. Environmentalists are up in
arms because it is one of the only two places in the world where the endangered Attwater prairie chicken is found. But guess who owns this
preserve? An environmental group.

The Nature Conservancy acquired the land as a donation from
Mobil, and has reaped $5 million from the company's wells already
there. The oil money is going to come in handy in the Conservancy's efforts to protect land from clear-cutting, strip malls, and other heavy development. The organization will use most of the Texas City royalties to
buy more habitat.

The Nature Conservancy is the environmental group that environmentalists love to hate. Allowing oil drilling on a nature preserve is just
one reason. Timber giants Weyerhaeuser, Georgia-Pacific and J. M.
Huber—traditional fat targets for greens—are logging at Nature Conservancy preserves in Arkansas, Maine, North Carolina and Virginia. The
Arlington, VA-based organization has also begun developing housing
units on a rare strip of pristine* land on the eastern coast of the U.S. If
that's not enough to offend the purists*, the Conservancy has refused to
endorse the Kyoto Protocol for cutting carbon emissions.

"I used to say that the only thing not allowed on Nature Conservancy reserves were mining and slavery, and I wasn't sure about the

pristine:
unspoiled,
unpolluted

purists: those
who go strictly
by tradition

latter," fumes Kieran Suckling of the Center for Biological Diversity. "Now I may have to withdraw the former as well."

haggle: to annoy or exhaust with arguing

Founded in 1951, the Conservancy has always been out of the anti-corporate mainstream of the environmental movement. Instead of picketing corporations, it haggles* with them. New Chief Executive Steven McCormick, 50, a Conservancy lifer who was the head of the California chapter, aims to continue the tradition. His group had $655 million in revenues* this year, which includes $83 million in land sales. In the last year alone it has also acquired land worth $400 million. Its revenue is ten times the size of the Sierra Club's. The Conservancy's 5 million acres make it one of the country's largest non-government landowners.

revenues: total income produced by a given source

easement: an interest in land owned by another that entitles its holder to a specific limited use

Almost all revenues will go right out the door in more land purchases or easements*, totaling perhaps 330,000 acres. Rather than just buying unconnected postage-stamp-size plots of land, McCormick's group is acquiring entire ecosystems, making concessions* to development along the way. "This method is likely to produce far more lasting results than trying to oppose human wants and needs," says McCormick.

concessions: rights or privileges

A couple of years ago the Conservancy paid International Paper $35 million for 185,000 acres on the St. John River in Maine to save it from other timber companies. It then contracted with J. M. Huber to log 75% of the land—responsibly, of course. That means no clear-cutting and no logging near rivers. The deal has generated $1 million a year for the Conservancy.

encroaching: moving in gradually on the rights and possessions of another

The Conservancy owns or has easements on 50,000 acres of barrier islands and salt marshes on Virginia's eastern shore. Development is encroaching* and zoning laws allow one house per acre. McCormick isn't about to build 50,000 houses. But he is erecting five houses on 250 acres, away from the water, that will sell for $330,000 each, $150,000 more than comparable four-bedroom housing in the area. He believes the houses will serve as a model for the inevitable future development of nearby acreage. Says McCormick, "If we can design thoughtful developments, we can ensure biological richness and allow appropriate human use."

deforestation: clearing of forests

On the Kyoto agreement, McCormick says the treaty puts too much emphasis on energy emissions from smokestacks and autos, while missing the role of deforestation* in carbon emissions. The Conservancy's position has made it a favorite of the Bush Administration, which recently awarded it a $1.6 million grant to study forests and carbon dioxide.

What would McCormick's group do with the Arctic National Wildlife Refuge? It doesn't have a position on drilling for oil there yet but hasn't ruled out supporting it. McCormick says its Texas experience shows that careful drilling can coexist with environmental protection.

It's easy to imagine the royalties that would flow from the Arctic's 5.8 billion barrels being spent for land protection in the lower 48. This is McCormick's model: satisfy human needs while preserving acres of wetlands and forests.

Reading for Meaning

1. The Nature Conservancy is an environmental group, so why do many environmentalists hate it?
2. How does McCormick respond to people who question his working with development corporations as he buys land?

Reading Deeper

1. Of all the different environmental groups around, why do you think the Bush administration granted the Nature Conservancy a $1.6 million grant to study forests and carbon dioxide?
2. Define "clear-cutting" of forests and explain its effects on the environment.

Reading for Writing

1. Write a **letter** to Stephen McCormick supporting or opposing his projects for the Nature Conservancy. Support your position with specific reasons. If you use any sources, be sure to note where you got them.
2. The Arctic National Wildlife Refuge as a source of oil has been a point of discussion ever since President Clinton left the White House and President Bush entered. Look up the stand each president took on the Arctic National Wildlife Refuge as a place to drill for oil. List the reasons each had to support their position. Determine your **position** on the issue and write an **argumentative** essay trying to **convince** your readers whether the Refuge should be used for drilling or not. Be sure to document your sources.

THE HEART OF THE CITY

Terrell F. Dixon

For many, the term "urban nature" seems to be an **oxymoron,** *contradictory terms used together to emphasize a point. In the midst of concrete and steel, high-rise apartment buildings and towering skyscrapers, one does not normally think of a city as a space where nature is allowed to grow freely and naturally. Sometimes parks* *are "planned" in the middle of neighborhoods, but is "planned" nature the same as "natural" nature? In the following article, Terrell Dixon, associate professor at the University of Houston's Department of English who teaches literature and the environment courses, discusses the beauty, growth and preservation of one of Houston's major green spaces, Hermann Park.*

Prereading: If you grew up in a city, you might or might not have had opportunities to visit wilderness areas. Think about vacations you have taken. Were they to visit green spaces? What do you remember about them?

Prewriting: How important is green space in city life? Do you think city officials should budget more money to add new parks or green spaces to the city? Write a paragraph expressing your thoughts about the importance or lack of importance of green space in your life.

---

olfactory: relating to the sense of smell

O n a warm, drizzly day in February, there are only a very few people here. That suits us fine. Us, today, includes my dog, Rocky, who likes these rainy days when the earth's olfactory* output goes up, distractions go down, and he can sniff away without interruption, and myself. I am just happy for the wooded solitude, something that can be scarce in a city of four million people, and I enjoy how the rain changes the colors of this familiar place, the deepening greens of the grass and leaves, the familiar tree trunks and trails growing into darker grays and browns.

durability: ability to last a long time without wearing away

We are in Hermann Park, the green heart of what is now our country's fourth largest city. It is a remarkable place, not only for its considerable beauty but also for its durability*. Hermann Park, established in 1915, has survived nearly ninety years of land sales (to the nearby Medical Center), new streets through its land (necessary then to ease access to that Medical Center), and expansion of nearby streets. The most remarkable aspect of this park, however, may be simply its existence in this city.

Houston wants to be known as a city that is good for business. It traditionally has valued growth above all else. Like many American cities, our leadership sees the city mainly as a site for commerce and so measures city success with a business yardstick. We boast about: population (two million more people are expected in the next few decades), attractiveness to corporations (many major oil companies and other businesses have their headquarters here and the city constantly looks for more), big box entertainment (three new sport stadiums have been added in the last three years—at a total cost of over one billion dollars), and shopping (the usual temples of consumption abound, ranging from stand-alone Target and Wal-Mart stores to enclosed malls like the Galleria, a huge and growing structure which first grabbed national attention when—in defiance of Houston's natural heat and humidity—it installed a huge ice skating rink as its showcase attraction). We have a powerful Greater Houston Partnership working to attract business, a Port Authority helping to keep goods flowing through our large inland port, and a Sports Authority to advocate* high-priced new stadiums for our professional teams.

advocate: to plead in favor of

Houston has this park because a prominent citizen, George Hermann, gave the city land for it, and this gift happened, in part, because the times were ripe for the creation of urban parks. It began in what was an unusual period of the development of American cities. After the rapid industrial and urban growth of the nineteenth century, the last part of that century and the first part of the twentieth century saw a national change in focus. Americans sought to bring some of the beauty of nature inside of the city limits.

The name given to his collective effort was the City Beautiful Movement, and it inspired much that is good—the early, leafy suburbs and forested city parks—in the inner rings of our city. Like other parks created then, Houston's first large city park stemmed from the belief that such urban green places were a necessary antidote* to the crowding and pollution of city life. The belief was that they would improve public health as they helped relieve the stress of city life, and further that they would create a type of common democratic space, one where rich and poor could mix on equal terms and enjoy equally the benefits of nature in the city. Hermann Park fulfills those hopes today, although it has experienced tough times along the way. Hermann Park like others around the country, flourished in the early years of the century, and then, as the post-World War II suburbanization of America accelerated, began to decline around mid-century. It was not so much that Americans chose to turn their backs on nature, but simply that the quest for contact with the natural world was redirected. Instead of the common space of the common space of the central urban park, citizens switched their focus to the individually owned, suburban backyard. Interest in and funding for urban parks decreased, and parks suffered. Key parks like Houston's Hermann, held on, but they were diminished things.

antidote: remedy

Then in the last decades of the twentieth century, another major shift began. Americans started to see that with our population increasing substantially, suburbia could not fulfill its initial promise. We could develop our suburbs, and even name them—Bright Meadow, Greatwood,

pesticides: poison to destroy pests such as insects

regimented: organized to regulate or control

Silver Canyon—after the natural landscapes destroyed by them, but it was a self-defeating proposition. Suburbs for more and always more people necessitated huge highway systems with more and more air pollution. Uniform requirements for urban lawns many suburbs relied heavily on pesticides* and reduced what was left of the natural world to a regimented* green. We now see that we were not re-creating paradise after all.

With this realization came a revival of interest in urban parks, and Houston's attention turned first to this beautiful place where Rocky and I love to walk. People imagined renewal: a beautiful green space made inviting and accessible to the now richly multicultural citizenship of Houston. Large-scale restoration began, and the park now has new trails, new lighting, better drainage, a more inviting lake complete with an island for nesting birds, a native plants area as well as a carefully trimmed golf course.

This return to a mindset that cherishes our urban parks is a very good thing, but it also is precarious. These changes came through large financial gifts from wealthy private citizens mixed with some local and federal governmental funds. The restoration has also been so successful that this single park receives four million visits annually. Our expanding city needs more parks, and we need a consistent funding commitment beyond the uneven patterns of private donations. Today, for example, the city of Houston spends just thirty-three dollars a year per person on its parks, and we have just 10.9 acres of parkland for every 1,000 residents. I have been fortunate enough to live near Hermann Park during all of my years in this city, but many Houstonians have no park space nearby.

If we are to keep pace with the needs of our citizens, we need to change this. I propose that Houston initiate a trend among American cities by creating a Nature Authority. We need such a powerful governmental body whose responsibility to secure parks and green spaces (and prevent pollution) proceeds with the same fervor now devoted to business and huge stadiums. If we manage to do that, our city will continue to prosper in other ways.

Reading for Meaning

1. Dixon describes Hermann Park as "durable." Explain what he means by this.
2. Why was the donation of the land to be used as Hermann Park considered to be done at a particularly appropriate time?

Reading Deeper

1. Dixon's main topic is green space, but paragraph 2 is devoted to describing the commercial aspects of Houston. Why do you think he did this?
2. How do green spaces act as a "type of common democratic space"?

Reading for Writing

1. Assume the leadership position of the Houston (or your own city may be substituted here) Nature Authority that Dixon proposes. After you hire your staff, what would your priorities be to create more green space in your town? How would you go about it? What kind of needs assessment would you begin with? Get together in a group and choose your "leader." Then begin planning your **procedure/process** for improving the quality of the natural spaces in your town. Write up a proposal that you and your group plan to follow and present it to the class. Each group should be in competition with the others so that only one proposal will be voted as the best for the city.
2. Go to an area in your city/town that is a "green space" and sit quietly in a secluded area. Watch the animal activity for at least thirty minutes and record it. Write a description of all the different animals that appear—birds, squirrels, and so forth—and their behavior. Include your response to the experience. Then look carefully at the different kinds of vegetation. Identify the plants that you can, including the trees and flowers. Write a **descriptive** essay about your day. Include your **response** to the experience.

RHETORICAL ANALYSIS

Much like the editorial in Chapter 19, "Justice for Kids," Terrell Dixon's article, "The Heart of the City," leaves the claim for the conclusion. Dixon easily pulls his readers into the beautiful world of Hermann Park, which he describes in a very informal manner, much like the walk he takes with Rocky—relaxed and enjoying the sensory pleasures of the park in the heart of the city. Through his easy style, he establishes a rapport with the audience immediately so that he comes across as just one of us. From the physical details he provides of city spaces, readers get a description of the economic health of Houston, both from a local and national point of view. He also moves from general ideas, like "big box entertainment," to specific examples, like "three new sport stadiums," several times. He gives readers a history lesson about his favorite green space, using chronological organization, all the while maintaining his relaxed tone and convincing his readers that he knows this information from his life in Houston. (We know better, though.) As he moves to his conclusion, Dixon incorporates causal analysis, explaining the function and necessity of green spaces. Finally, he ends with his thesis statement and evidence that is difficult to rebut because of the way he developed the essay from the beginning. In the left-hand margin there is information that directs you to appropriate chapters in this textbook for discussion about the underlined techniques the author used to write the essay or that comments directly about the techniques the author used.

The Heart of the City

Ch. 2,
Description use
of sensory and
emotional
description to
develop the
paragraph

Establishes a
rapport with
audience

Chs. 2,
Description and
10, Persuasion
physical
description,
facts, and
opinions

Chs. 3,
Exemplification
and 10,
Persuasion
physical details
to support
assertions

Ch. 4, Narrative
spatial
organization

On a <u>warm, drizzly</u> day in February, there are only a very few people here. That suits us fine. <u>Us, today, includes my dog, Rocky, who likes these rainy days when the earth's olfactory output goes up</u>, distractions go down, and he can sniff away without interruption, and myself. I am just happy for the wooded solitude, something that can be scarce in a city of four million people, and I enjoy how the rain changes the colors of this familiar place, the deepening greens of the grass and leaves, the familiar tree trunks and trails growing into darker grays and browns.

We are in Hermann Park, the <u>green heart</u> of what is now our country's <u>fourth largest city</u>. It is a remarkable place, not only for its considerable beauty but also for its durability. <u>Hermann Park, established in 1915, has survived nearly ninety years of land sales (to the nearby Medical Center), new streets through its land (necessary then to ease access to that Medical Center), and expansion of nearby streets</u>. The most remarkable aspect of this park, however, may be simply its existence in this city.

Houston wants to be known as a city that is good for business. It traditionally has valued growth above all else. Like many American cities, our leadership sees the city mainly as a site for commerce and so measures city success with a business yardstick. We boast about: population <u>(two million more people are expected in the next few decades)</u>, attractiveness to corporations <u>(many major oil compa-</u>

<table>
<tr><td>

Ch. 3,
Exemplification
use of
exemplification

Use of
oxymoron. See
head note for
this article for
definition.

Ch. 3,
Exemplification
transition back
to nature

Ch. 5,
Definition
historical
background
information
throughout
paragraph

Ch. 2,
Description
chronological
organization

Ch. 2,
Description
chronological
organization in
paragraph

Ch. 9, Causal
effect and cause

Ch. 9, Causal
effects

</td><td>

nies and other businesses have their headquarters here and the city constantly looks for more), big box entertainment (three new sport stadiums have been added in the last three years—at a total cost of over one billion dollars), and shopping (the usual *temples of consumption* abound, ranging from stand-alone Target and Wal-Mart stores to enclosed malls like the Galleria, a huge and growing structure which first grabbed national attention when—in defiance of Houston's natural heat and humidity—it installed a huge ice skating rink as its showcase attraction). We have a powerful Greater Houston Partnership working to attract business, a Port Authority helping to keep goods flowing through our large inland port, and a Sports Authority to advocate high-priced new stadiums for our professional teams.

Houston has this park because a prominent citizen, George Hermann, gave the city land for it, and this gift happened, in part, because the times were ripe for the creation of urban parks. It began in what was an unusual period of the development of American cities. After the rapid industrial and urban growth of the nineteenth century, the last part of that century and the first part of the twentieth century saw a national change in focus. Americans sought to bring some of the beauty of nature inside of the city limits.

The name given to his collective effort was the City Beautiful Movement, and it inspired much that is good—the early, leafy suburbs and forested city parks— in the inner rings of our city. Like other parks created then, Houston's first large city park stemmed from the belief that such urban green places were a necessary antidote to the crowding and pollution of city life. The belief was that they would improve public health as they helped relieve the stress of city life, and further that they would create a type of common democratic space, one where rich and poor could mix on equal terms and enjoy equally the benefits of nature in the city. Hermann Park fulfills those hopes today, although it has experienced tough times along the way. Hermann Park like others around the country, flourished in the early years of the century, and then, as the post-World War II suburbanization of America accelerated, began to decline

</td></tr>
</table>

around mid-century. It was not so much that Americans chose to turn their backs on nature, but simply that the quest for contact with the natural world was redirected. Instead of the common space of the central urban park, citizens switched their focus to the individually owned, suburban backyard. Interest in and funding for urban parks decreased, and parks suffered. Key parks like Houston's Hermann, held on, but they were diminished things.

Then in the last decades of the twentieth century, another major shift began. Americans started to see that with our population increasing substantially, suburbia could not fulfill its initial promise. We could develop our suburbs, and even name them—Bright Meadow, Greatwood, Silver Canyon—after the natural landscapes destroyed by them, but it was a self-defeating proposition. Suburbs for more and always more people necessitated huge highway systems with more and more air pollution. Uniform requirements for urban lawns in many suburbs relied heavily on pesticides and reduced what was left of the natural world to a regimented green. We now see that we were not re-creating paradise after all.

With this realization came a revival of interest in urban parks, and Houston's attention turned first to this beautiful place where Rocky and I love to walk. People imagined renewal: a beautiful green space made inviting and accessible to the now richly multicultural citizenship of Houston. Large-scale restoration began, and the park now has new trails, new lighting, better drainage, a more inviting lake complete with an island for nesting birds, a native plants area as well as a carefully trimmed golf course.

This return to mindset that cherishes our urban parks is a very good thing, but it also is precarious. These changes came through large financial gifts from wealthy private citizens mixed with some local and federal governmental funds. The restoration has also been so successful that this single park receives four million visits annually. Our expanding city needs more parks, and we need a consistent funding commitment beyond the uneven patterns of private donations. Today, for example, the city of Houston spends just thirty-three dollars a year per person on its parks, and we have just 10.9 acres

Ch. 10,
Persuasion
persuasive
conclusion

Ch. 10,
claim/thesis in
the conclusion
in bold

Ch. 10,
Persuasion
strong
conclusion

of parkland for every 1,000 residents. I have been fortunate enough to live near Hermann Park during all of my years in this city, but many Houstonians have no park space nearby.

   If we are to keep pace with the needs of our citizens, we need to change this. **I propose that Houston initiate a trend among American cities by creating a Nature Authority.** We need such a powerful governmental body whose responsibility to secure parks and green spaces (and prevent pollution) proceeds with the same fervor now devoted to business and huge stadiums. If we manage to do that, our city will continue to prosper in other ways.

Because Dixon's article is informative, casual in tone, and filled with descriptions and exemplification, at the end of the next-to-the-last paragraph, readers might miss his use of rhetorical language if they are not diligent in reading skills. When he adds the following information, "Today, for example, the city of Houston spends just thirty-three dollars a year per person on its parks, and we have just 10.9 acres of parkland for every 1,000 residents," he is using important evidence to convince the reader that he has a valuable point. But if you do the math, the numbers are impressive: Houston isn't spending enough. At thirty-three dollars per person per year, in a city of 4 million, Houston spends approximately $132 million on its parks. Dixon could easily have given readers that number; however, rhetorically, that would not have been a strategically good move for making his point that the city doesn't spend enough. Thirty-three dollars per person does not sound like much to spend on green space; however, $132 million sounds like a whole lot. If you do the math, however, you will find that they are the same, but they make a different impact. The same can be said of the use of his figures for acres per resident: "10.9 acres of parkland for every 1,000 residents." That would mean that you could put approximately 100 people on a single acre of parkland, which is a whole lot of people in a small amount of space. But if you do the math and use the 4 million figure again, you will end up with a large number of acres of parkland in Houston; this will, again, give a different perspective to the reader—one that will probably not support Dixon's point even though the figure is the same as the smaller number.

   Thus, when Dixon concludes his essay with his solution to the problems he identifies, most readers are probably ready if not eager to agree with him as he ends on quite a strong assertion that shows he is interested in Houston prospering "in other ways" too. He has written a subtle but strong argument.

REFLECTIONS ON ENVIRONMENT: WHAT PART DO WE PLAY IN SAVING OUR WORLD?

From the snowy wilderness of the Arctic National Wildlife Refuge to the urban setting of our own backyards, we will find Nature in some form. In the novel, *The House on Mango Street* by Sandra Cisneros, the narrator, Esperanza, finds comfort from talking to the four skinny trees that the city planted outside her bedroom window. In her barrio environment, with its tenement housing and postage-stamp-size yard, urban nature is almost nonexistent. But when it is present, as in the chapters "Meme Ortiz" and "The Monkey Garden," the children take full advantage of it, playing, learning, and growing up.

Nature is all around us, and, as we can see from the articles in this chapter, it is another controversial issue in society. Most of the time, most of us take nature for granted, but there are times when she needs our help—by picking up someone else's litter, recycling, lobbying for stronger laws, and voting for those who promise to protect her and making sure that city councils maintain, promote, and present urban nature for ourselves and our children. On the positive side, despite the damage human beings inflict on Nature, she will continue to regenerate.

Reflecting to Write

Community Service Learning

Even if your campus does not have an Earth Day program, start one in one of your classes. This will take work that should begin months before Earth Day. If this is the winter semester that does not have Earth Day, have a Winter Earth Day. Get groups together to take part in environmentally friendly projects. For suggestions, go to the Earth Day Web site and pick projects that are easy for your group(s) to complete. As you are working on them, write **reflective journal** entries that express your thoughts about what you have done. Report to the class what your project is and how it is proceeding. On the day designated as Earth Day, plan a day of presentations to display how your groups/the groups in your class have helped others. Present visual as well as written material.

Argumentative

A freshman at a local inner-city university was heard to say that "urban nature" is a concern for rich people because working-class people are concerned with everyday living and putting food on the table. Her comment makes the topic of nature into a class issue, specifically related to inner-city neighborhoods. Think about nature and the environment in all its forms and all its locations. Write an **argumentative** essay that agrees or disagrees with the student's comments. Use specific **examples** to support your position.

Informative

Visit an inner-city neighborhood and a neighborhood that is known as upper class. Observe the amount of green space in each. Also look at the yards or lack of yards in each neighborhood. Look at the way the residents use nature by looking for potted plants, shrubs, lawns, grottos, and so forth. Write a **comparison and contrast, informative** essay **describing** the impressions you gathered about how nature works in each neighborhood. Draw conclusions in your final paragraph.

Go to your local video rental store and find the travel section. Check out a video or DVD that features places like Alaska, the Grand Canyon, the American or Canadian Rockies, Canada, the national forests, and so forth. After you have watched the video or DVD, go to the Internet and find Web sites for the location you chose. If you are a member of AAA, go to your local AAA Travel Center and get the free booklets and brochures they have about the area you selected. Write an **informative** essay **describing** the "wilderness" area that you have researched using all the material you have for background information. If you have been to that location, include **personal experiences** and any pictures you might have taken while you were there to support your paper. Be sure to document any material you use.

Go to your local hardware store or feed store and buy some seeds for herbs, flowers, or plants that will grow easily in your environment. Follow the directions for planting and caring for them and keep a daily journal of the plants' progress. If you have a camera, you might want to take pictures of the plants in the different stages—in the seed envelope, after they've been planted, when they first sprout, and so forth. When the plants have grown successfully, use them the way they were intended to be used—for cooking, decoration, or utilitarian purposes. Using your **experiences,** your daily **journal,** and pictures you took, write a **how-to** booklet for a child explaining **step-by-step** how to grow that particular plant and the purposes the plant serves. Be sure to tell the child what tools he or she will need to complete the project.

Find a piece of wooded land that has recently been sold and will be cleared and used for business purposes. Go to the neighborhoods that are closest to the land and interview ten residents. Ask them about how they feel about the clearing of the land for business purposes. Ask them if they know or knew in advance what the property was going to be sold for. Get the residents to talk to you about their feelings. Determine a **position** and using their comments as support, write an **informative letter** to a city councilman about the clearing of land for business purposes. Let the residents know that you will be writing the letter and using their comments. Get permission from the residents to use their names. If they say that you cannot, you can use what they say, but you cannot identify them.

A commercial has recently aired on television in which an unseen speaker asks a woman, "Which do you want: your car or clean air?" This is an either-or choice (also known as a false dilemma fallacy) that makes the assumption that the woman has no other options. Respond to this environmental question in a **convincing** essay offering solutions for protecting the environment beyond the one offered— losing her car.

"To Robert Frost from Texas"   *by Elizabeth Kessler*

Glossary of Literary and Composition Terms

Abstract: An idea that is not **concrete.** It is usually explained by examples. Love, patriotism, and joy are examples of abstract ideas.

Analyze: To analyze a topic is to break it down into smaller pieces so that you may get a better look at it and understand it. There are various ways to go about this. For example, if you are told to write a paper about a novel you have read, you already know that that is too large a topic to cover in three pages. Therefore, you must look at different aspects of the novel. You might want to talk about **characterization.** Or you might like to discuss the impact of the time period on the novel if it is a work that is set in a particular historic period like the Civil War, the Roaring Twenties, and so forth. As you can see from these examples, you won't attempt to discuss the entire novel within a limited number of pages, but you can **analyze** it from a more focused point of view.

Argumentative Essay: A pattern of development used to change the way readers think, using rhetorical strategies and the oppositions' views.

Assertions: Declarative statements or claims made in support of an argumentative topic.

Brainstorm: A prewriting strategy used to generate ideas. Brainstorming may be done on a general topic, for example, pets; or it may be done on a specific topic, for example, *La Llorona.*

Brainstorm, collaborative: A prewriting strategy used to generate ideas in a group.

Character: A fictional character or persona in a story.

Characterization: The method used by an author to build a character. The character may be **round**—multidimensional—or **flat**—one-sided. The character may also be **dynamic**—different at the end of the story from the way she was at the beginning of the story—or **static**—the same way at the end of the story as she was at the beginning of the story. A character may also be developed through direct exposition or indirect exposition. With **direct exposition,** readers see the character act, hear her speak, and know her thoughts and feelings as she expresses them. With **indirect exposition,** readers discover the character's traits from other characters in the story.

Chronological Development/Order: The sequence of events in a story, arranged in the order they happen in time.

Claim: An assertion that supports an argument. The central claim of an argumentative paper is the thesis. A counterclaim is an assertion that challenges the thesis.

Cliché: A frequently or over-used phrase or clause.

Clustering (webbing or mapping): A prewriting activity used to generate ideas through free association about the central topic and through free association about the ideas generated from the central topic.

Coherence: Connections between ideas in a paragraph or essay created through transitions.

Comparison and Contrast: A pattern of development in which the writer describes the similarities or differences between two subjects.

Concluding Sentence: The final sentence of a paragraph or essay that brings closure to the passage.

Conclusion: The final paragraph(s) in a work. The conclusion usually begins with a restated thesis sentence and can be developed through the use of summary, drawing conclusions from previously stated information, or giving personal opinion. It brings closure to the essay.

Concrete: A thought or word referring to something material, for example, cat, table, or book.

Conflict: A state of opposition between two or more individuals or concepts. In literature a character may be in conflict with self, another person, society, fate, deity, or technology.

Describe/Description/Descriptive: Description is a pattern of development for an informative essay. A descriptive piece of writing communicates to readers how something looks, smells, sounds, tastes, or feels. This can be accomplished through the use of adjectives, "The young blond child walked beside her tall, brunette sister." Or it can be done through the use of other patterns of development, such as exemplification, comparison and contrast, and so forth.

Details: Forms of information, such as facts, statistics, descriptions, and so forth, used to support or develop ideas.

Division and Classification: A pattern of development that divides a broad idea into smaller parts and organizes many small parts into categories.

Domino Theory: See **Slippery Slope Fallacy.**

Draft, first, final: The complete text of a work is a draft. A draft goes through various stages, beginning with the first or rough draft and proceeding through revision until it arrives at the final version.

Evaluate: To determine the quality of a given item. Students are sometimes asked to evaluate the quality of **secondary sources** they might use in a paper. At other times they are asked to evaluate the quality of another student's paper or their own, based on given criteria or standards. They are asked to determine to what extent the work meets standards of usefulness or meets given standards.

Exemplification: A pattern of development that uses examples to expand the topic.

Exposition/Expository: A pattern of development that presents information to the reader, usually a report. This is also called explanatory writing because it explains an idea or gives information.

Fallacy: Logic that is incorrect or flawed and that can manipulate the reader by appealing to fear, emotion, prejudice, and so forth. See **Slippery Slope Fallacy.**

Figurative Language: Language used in creative writing that makes comparisons (metaphors, similes, personification), exaggerates (**hyperbole**), or uses other figures of speech to create an interesting or different approach to a topic/subject.

Free Verse: Poetry that is written without predetermined poetic criteria.

Freewriting: A prewriting activity used to generate ideas by requiring the writer to write nonstop for five to ten minutes to generate ideas about a topic.

Freewriting, focused: Focused freewriting is an exercise for generating ideas about a specific topic, whereas freewriting can start with a general topic and move to a specific topic.

Generalization: A conclusion that is arrived at without sufficient evidence (hasty generalization) or one that includes everything or every person in its assertion, allowing for no exceptions (sweeping generalization). For example: Everyone should eat three meals a day.

Hyperbole: Exaggeration.

Image: A concrete picture painted in a reader's mind through the use of figurative language.

Imagery: A collection of images in a creative work.

Inductive Reasoning: A method of reasoning and argument that moves from specific ideas to a specific conclusion. Inductive reasoning can lead only to probable conclusions.

Inference: A conclusion made from known facts.

Informative Essay: An essay that provides information to the reader. Several patterns of development can be used in writing an informative essay, such as narration, description, exemplification, process analysis, cause and effect, comparison and contrast, division classification, or definition. Rather than limit a piece to one pattern of development, authors frequently mix the patterns.

Irony: A figure of speech in which the intended meaning is the opposite of the literal meaning of the written words.

Journal: A collection of thoughts, ideas, questions, opinions, conclusions drawn, and other pieces of writing that might express emotions and private beliefs. Many writers keep personal writing in journals. Journals help the writer think through problems or to release anger, frustration, or other possibly destructive feelings in a positive, nonviolent way. Journals also provide a place for writers to express their joy or excitement as well as a place to examine questions or ideas privately that they might not feel comfortable sharing with others. The material that you collect in your journal can sometimes provide you with ideas for a larger paper or for stories that you might want to write later. Sometimes your instructor requires that you keep a journal that records your responses to reading selections made for class discussion. Doing this will help you understand the text better and allow you to jot down notes or questions about the assignment that you might not understand at the time and forget before you return to class. Most journals are written in an informal manner because they are usually private and shared only with those you choose to share them with or with an instructor as an assignment.

Journalistic Questions: A prewriting activity used to generate ideas by asking the questions who? what? when? where? why? and how? about a topic.

Letter: Correspondence, either in formal or informal format.

List/Listing: A prewriting activity that enumerates items of importance about a topic. The resulting list/series of words or phrases can be used to generate other ideas.

Memoir: This is a form of life writing that not only relates aspects of one's life but also draws a lesson or an understanding from the experience(s).

Metaphor: A figure of speech that compares two unlike subjects without using the words "like" or "as."

Mode/Pattern of Development: Methods used by writers to develop their paragraphs or essays. They may be expository, comparison and contrast, narration, and so forth.

Narration: A type of composition used to inform, instruct, entertain, or interest its readers.

Narrative: A narrative tells a story and is usually organized **chronologically;** however, it may be told in other ways.

Narrator: In fiction, a narrator is the storyteller. A story might have a first-person narrator, a third-person omniscient narrator who knows everyone's thoughts and actions, a limited omniscient narrator who knows the thoughts and feelings of only one or two other characters, and so forth. The narrator may be reliable/trustworthy or unreliable/untrustworthy. In a first-person personal narrative, the narrator is usually the author.

Objective: Impersonal way of discussing an issue; without feeling or emotion.

Outline, formal, informal: A structural view of a paper's development created in a formal manner with Roman numerals and Arabic numbers, upper- and lowercase letters, and so forth, that divide the paper into major divisions and subdivisions. An informal outline is not so detailed. Each form, however, presents the writer with the basic elements of the paper so it can be written in a systematic way. All outlines are subject to change.

Paraphrase: A restatement of an idea or passage in the writer's own words to expand or clarify an idea.

Peer Analysis: An activity in which members of a student's class read and evaluate each other's writing, based on given criteria.

Personal Narrative: Personal narratives are works that tell a story. The story may be about the author, and he or she may choose to use first-person pronouns (I, me, we, us) to indicate that he or she is telling the story about himself or herself. In that case, it becomes a first-person **narration.** Usually, but not always, a narration is told in chronological order. Sometimes a narrative relates a lesson the author learned as a result of the episode he or she experienced. Readers must be careful, however, to distinguish a short story or novel, which is fiction, from a first-person narrative. Some short stories or novels are told using first-person point of view, but that does not mean that the **protagonist** is the voice of the author.

Persuasion, Persuasive Essay: In writing, persuasion is one of the purposes of communication. A persuasive essay not only attempts to convince a reader to change his mind but also to act in a specific way, for example, not only to believe that a candidate is the best person for an office, but to vote for the candidate and actively campaign for her.

Plot: The element of fiction that describes the events of a story and their relationship to each other.

Prewriting Strategies: This is a process that many writers go through before they begin to write an essay or assignment. To do this, the writer must jot down ideas. This may be done informally, to find associations between words that are related to the topic. It may be done through brainstorming, free writing, clustering, outlining, answering journalistic questions (who? what? when? where? why? how?), or exploring more in-depth questions about the topic. Every writer does not necessarily complete prewriting strategies in this way, and some may combine several forms. Others are able to think about the topic they want to write about while they drive home from classes or relax. The prewriting strategy that you choose must suit your needs and help you arrive at a clear vision of your topic, otherwise it won't work.

Process Analysis: Sometimes known as a "how-to" essay, process gives directions for completing an activity or describes a procedure.

Protagonist: This is usually the main character of the story. He or she is the character with whom the reader usually identifies and whom the reader supports when the character is in **conflict.**

Purpose of Communication/Writing: Usually there are four purposes: to entertain, to express, to inform, and to persuade.

Reader Response Journal Entry: A journal response to an assigned reading. This may be written according to the directions of the instructor, in personal response to a writing, if you agreed or disagreed with the article and why, if you liked or disliked the article and why, if you can associate with the events in the article and how, if you can identify with any of the characters/people in the article and how, if you learned anything from the article, if you would recommend this article to a friend and why, what your response to the author might be if you had a chance to talk to him or her. Your instructor might ask you to summarize the assignment, but generally a response is preferred over a summary.

Rebut: Oppose with proof to the contrary.

Reflective: Looking back and examining one's feelings, attitudes, ideas, and so forth in light of present situations.

Refute: To show or prove that an opposing point is wrong.

Secondary Source: In literary analysis, articles or information that interpret primary source material.

Simile: A figure of speech that compares two unlike subjects using the words "like" or "as," "than," and "resembles."

Slippery Slope Fallacy or Domino Theory: The prediction that numerous, unrelated effects can occur from one cause.

Spatial Description: Describing a setting in a way that shows organization of the area, for example, top to bottom, front to back, north to south, near to far.

Stereotype: A sweeping generalization that makes assumptions about all members of a race, religion, gender, nationality, age and so forth.

Style: The language, attitude, creativity, and mood an author uses as he or she writes. Some authors may use a distinctive style, such as Hemingway, who wrote stories in a journalistic style.

Subjective: Writing which uses a personal, expressive, emotional response, as opposed to **objective,** which is impersonal, analytical, and lacking feeling.

Summary: A brief restatement of a longer work, in the writer's words.

Synonym: A word that means the same thing as another word and can sometimes be used interchangeably.

Thesis: The controlling idea of an essay, usually stated in one or two sentences. It may be implied, that is, determined by reading the essay, or stated, that is, clearly announced in the essay.

Tone: The attitude the writer has toward the subject of the written work. The tone usually depends on the purpose of communication.

Topic Sentence: The controlling idea of a paragraph, usually stated in one sentence.

Transitions: Words, phrases, or sentences that provide connections between different thoughts and ideas to ensure coherence of a work.

Unity: The organizing or controlling idea that draws the parts of the writing into a whole.

Credits

"Barbie, G.I. Joe, and Play in the 1960s" by Gary Cross. Reprinted by permission of the publisher from "The Boomer's Box of Toys: Barbie, G.I. Joe, and Play in the 1960s" in *Kids' Stuff: Toys and the Changing World of American Childhood* by Gary Cross. Copyright © 1997 by the President and Fellows of Harvard College, Harvard University Press, Cambridge, MA.

"Baby" by bell hooks. From *Bone Black* by bell hooks. Copyright © 1996 by Gloria Watkins. Reprinted by permission of Henry Holt and Company, LLC.

"Just Play? Who Knew?" originally appeared as an editorial in the *Los Angeles Times* Editorial, November 2, 2002.

"A Train Wreck Called Title IX" by George Will. Originally appeared in *Newsweek,* May 27, 2002. Copyright © 2002 George F. Will. Reprinted by permission.

"The Myths of Title IX" by Maria C. González. Copyright © 2004. Reprinted by permission of the author.

"Pete Rose: America's Antihero" by John Harty III. Reprinted by permission of the author.

"No Bloom On This Rose" by Fay Vincent. Originally appeared in *Time* magazine January 9, 2004. Copyright © 2004 TIME Inc. Reprinted by permission.

"Double Standards" by Deroy Murdock. From *National Review Online.* New York Commentator, Deroy Murdock is a contributing editor with *National Review Online* (www.nationalreview.com) and a senior fellow with The Atlas Economic Research Foundation in Fairfax, Virginia (www.atlasusa.org).

"The Beach" by Stella Thompson. Reprinted by permission of the author.

"Treading The Invisible Line" by Elline Lipkin. Reprinted by permission of the author.

"Warning Signs: Does Your Date Have Violent Tendencies?" by Doug McPherson. Copyright © 2003 *Self Defense For Women,* Winter 2003.

"Not So Safe Back Home" by Anna Quindlen. Copyright © 2003 Anna Quindlen. Reprinted by permission of International Creative Management, Inc.

"Evil Redux or the Return of Meaningful Mystery" by Dorothy G. Clark. Reprinted by permission of the author.

"Open Season on Koreans?" by Elaine H. Kim. Reprinted by permission of the author.

"Should Juvenile Offenders Be Tried As Adults?" by Laurence Steinberg. From *USA Today,* Jan. 2001, Vol. 129, Issue 2668 Copyright © 2001.

"Youth Crime Has Changed—And So Must the Juvenile Justice System" by Tom Reilly, the current Attorney General of the Commonwealth of Massachusetts. This article originally appeared in the *Boston Globe* in 1997 during his tenure as District Attorney of Middlesex County in Massachusetts.

"A Killing Tradition" by Joan Jacobs Brumberg. First appeared in *The Nation.* Copyright © 2003 by Joan Jacobs Brumberg. Reprinted by permission of Georges Borchardt, Inc.

"Sentencing of Teen Girl Fuels Debate Over Youths in Prison" by Ashely Broughton. From *The Salt Lake Tribune,* October 14, 2003. Reprinted by permission of the author.

"Justice for Kids" originally appeared as an editorial in the *Rutland Herald* and *Times Argus.* Copyright © 2001. Reprinted by permission of the *Rutland Herald.*

"The Lionel Tate Case" originally appeared as an editorial in the *St. Petersburg Times.* Copyright © 2003 *St. Petersburg Times.* Reprinted with permission.

"Earth Ethics and The Web of Life" by Katherine Hall. Copyright © 2002–2003 Golden Key International Honor Society.

"Paralysis on Clean Air" originally appeared as an editorial in *The New York Times.* Copyright © 2004 by The New York Times Co. Reprinted with permission.

"Hotspots: Preserving Pieces of a Fragile Biosphere" by E. O. Wilson. Copyright © 2002 National Geographic Society.

"Eco-Pragmatists" by Monte Burke. From *Forbes,* Sept. 3, 2001, Vol. 166, No. 5.

"The Heart of the City" by Terrell F. Dixon. Reprinted by permission of the author.

Photographs

"Lost Identity, II" by Franka Bruns. Reprinted by permission of the photographer.

"Toys" by Linda Daigle. Reprinted by permission of the photographer.

"A Walk Along Lake Louise" by Anne Perrin. Reprinted by permission of the photographer.

"Song of the Humpback Whale" from *MUTTS.* Reprinted by permission of Patrick McDonnell. King Features Syndicate.

Duct Tape Cartoon. Reprinted by permission of Mike Luckovich and Creators Syndicate, Inc.

Index